# The Psychology of Marriage

# The Psychology of Marriage

## BASIC ISSUES AND APPLICATIONS

EDITED BY
**Frank D. Fincham**
**Thomas N. Bradbury**
University of Illinois at Urbana-Champaign

Foreword by John Mordechai Gottman

**THE GUILFORD PRESS**
**New York   London**

**Library of Congress Cataloging-in-Publication Data**

The psychology of marriage: basic issues and applications / edited by
    Frank D. Fincham, Thomas N. Bradbury.
        p. cm.
    Includes bibliographical references.
    ISBN 0-89862-433-9
    1. Marital psychotherapy.   2. Marriage—Psychological aspects.
I. Fincham, Frank D.   II. Bradbury, Thomas N.
    [DNLM: 1. Marital Therapy.   2. Marriage—psychology.   WM 55
P9743]
RC488.5.P786   1990
616.89'156—dc20
DNLM/DLC
for Library of Congress                                        90-3038
                                                                  CIP

*To our wives, Susan and Cindy*

# Contributors

Julian Barling, Ph.D.   Department of Psychology, Queen's University, Kingston, Ontario, Canada

Donald H. Baucom, Ph.D.   Department of Psychology, University of North Carolina, Chapel Hill, North Carolina

Sue Ann K. Bauserman, M.S.   Department of Psychology, University of Georgia, Athens, Georgia

Steven R. H. Beach, Ph.D.   Department of Psychology, University of Georgia, Athens, Georgia

Jay Belsky, Ph.D.   Department of Human Development and Family Studies, College of Health and Human Development, The Pennsylvania State University, University Park, Pennsylvania

Thomas N. Bradbury, Ph.D.   Department of Psychology, University of Illinois at Urbana–Champaign, Champaign, Illinois; Present affiliation: UCLA Neuropsychiatric Institute, Center for Health Sciences, Los Angeles, California

Charles K. Burnett, D.P.H.   Department of Psychology, University of North Carolina, Chapel Hill, North Carolina

Frank D. Fincham, Ph.D.   Department of Psychology, University of Illinois at Urbana–Champaign, Champaign, Illinois

Ian H. Gotlib, Ph.D.   Department of Psychology, University of Western Ontario, London, Ontario, Canada; Present affiliation: Doctoral Training Facility, Department of Psychology, San Diego State University, San Diego, California

Paul Haefner, B.A.   Psychology Department, Catholic University of America, Washington, D.C.

Julia R. Heiman, Ph.D.   Department of Psychiatry and Behavioral Sciences, University of Washington Medical School, Harborview Community Mental Health Center, Seattle, Washington

Richard E. Heyman, M.S.   Oregon Marital Studies Program, Department of Psychology, University of Oregon, Eugene, Oregon

Ted L. Huston, Ph.D.   Department of Home Economics, University of Texas, Austin, Texas

Neil S. Jacobson, Ph.D.   Department of Psychology, University of Washington, Seattle, Washington

George Levinger, Ph.D.   Department of Psychology, University of Massachusetts, Amherst, Massachusetts

Scott B. McCabe, M.A.   Department of Psychology, University of Western Ontario, London, Ontario, Canada

Clifford I. Notarius, Ph.D.   Psychology Department, Catholic University of America, Washington, D.C.

K. Daniel O'Leary, Ph.D.   Department of Psychology, State University of New York at Stony Brook, Stony Brook, New York

David H. Olson, Ph.D.   Family Social Science, University of Minnesota, St. Paul, Minnesota

Elliot Robins, Ph.D.   Department of Child Development and Family Relations, School of Human Environmental Sciences, University of North Carolina, Greensboro, North Carolina; Present affiliation: School for Adult and Experiential Learning, Antioch University, Yellow Springs, Ohio

Christy K. Scott, M.A.   Department of Psychology, University of Illinois at Urbana–Champaign, Champaign, Illinois

R. Taylor Segraves, M.D., Ph.D.   Case Western Reserve University and MetroHealth Medical Center, Cleveland, Ohio

Johan Verhulst, M.D.   Department of Psychiatry and Behavioral Sciences, University of Washington, Seattle, Washington

Dina Vivian, Ph.D.   Department of Psychology, State University of New York at Stony Brook, Stony Brook, New York

Robert L. Weiss, Ph.D.   Oregon Marital Studies Program, Department of Psychology, University of Oregon, Eugene, Oregon

# Foreword

The publication of this new and exciting volume demonstrates that research into the functioning of families is at a new juncture—one that represents increased precision in the description of family processes. As the chapters in this volume demonstrate, the study of families has benefited from a merging of disciplines within psychology, particularly developmental, social, and clinical psychology. Fortunately, this merger represents an increase in our theoretical understanding of the *psychology* of families.

As Fincham and Bradbury point out, we are now asking questions about such diverse things as psychopathology and marriage (chapters by O'Leary & Vivian; Gotlib & McCabe), developmental changes in families (the research of Markman), the effects of work on families (Barling), the impact of marriage on child development (Belsky), how to change families (Segraves; Heiman & Verhulst; Beach & Bauserman), the social psychology of marriage (Levinger & Huston), social cognition in marriage (Fincham, Bradbury, & Scott), and so on. More important, an area of research that was once judged as incapable of good scientific investigation will now give up its secrets to careful research. This did not happen overnight. In fact, there is a venerable history that precedes the notable publication of this volume.

In my view, the 1960s saw very creative application of observational and other methods inspired by general systems theory to the study of families. However, this observational research failed to find consistent scientific support for a single hypothesis that had been suggested by general systems theorists. Scientifically it must be judged a failure. Instead, what emerged were a few specialized empirical results suggesting, among other things, that families with pathological members communicated less clearly.

In the 1970s, things began to change in the family field for a variety of reasons, many of which were technical improvements in research technology. The tools of the new research technology included the development of good models for observation and the assessment of interobserver reliability (work by Patterson, Reid, Johnson, Hops, Weiss, and others), the development of Chronbach's generalizability theory (which unified the notions of reliability and validity), new methods for studying emotion and other nonverbal behaviors (works by Izard, Ekman, Tomkins, Knapp, Argyle, Cook, Kendon, and others), and new statistical methods for studying the stream of behavior and inferring sequences (work by Sackett, Bakeman, and others). The improvements also owed much to the development of a new and imaginative theory of social exchange proposed by Thibaut and Kelley. From developmental psychology came such contributions as the study of child–caregiver interactions (Stern, Brazelton, Clarke-Stewart, Tronick, Main, and others), the study of sibling interactions (Dunn and others), the study of attachment (Ainsworth, Sroufe, Main, Bretherton, Lamb, Harmon, and others), the "discovery" of fathers (Parke, Lamb, and others), the study of transition to parenthood (Belsky, Cowan and Cowan, and others), and the study of the effects of divorce on children (Hetherington and others).

We were left with a new technology for doing multimethod, multisystem research, and, as this volume shows, this new technology is producing phenomenal results. As we can see from the chapter by Weiss and Heyman, for example, in the field of marital interaction replicable patterns have already been discovered that discriminate satisfied from dissatisfied marriages. These patterns were not even imagined by previous writers. For example, Lederer and Jackson's *quid pro quo* hypothesis turned out simply to be wrong. Such dimensions as negative affect and negative affect reciprocity turned out to be right. Furthermore, for the first time the strong prediction of longitudinal change became a reality. Behaviorally oriented marital therapists began developing intervention procedures that had to get more complex to produce effects. The initial use of a simplistic reciprocal contracting system did not work very well and was expanded to include such things as listening and problem-solving skills (Jacobson, Margolin, and others). To establish clinically significant results that last over time is now the challenge (Jacobson, Revenstorf). Progress was made— much of it the result of a new research technology—and things turned out differently from what had been imagined a decade previous to all this effort.

What is missing? In order for this research area to get "hot," researchers need to begin sharing common methods, measures, situations, and so on. Laboratories in different locations need to be able to communicate with one another easily. Experiments need to be designed to test specific notions about mechanisms. Graduate and postdoctoral students need to be trained in the new techniques. This volume attempts to facilitate communication between psychologists and is thus a step in the right direction.

We are now a field with some clearly established phenomena. As the chapters of this book demonstrate, these phenomena exist in areas such as marital interaction, the transition to parenthood, the extensions beyond the marital context, and the treatment of marital problems. The development of theory in the future needs to be dedicated toward *explaining* these new phenomena, an observation echoed by several contributors to this book.

I think that *The Psychology of Marriage* will be referred to often as evidence of psychology's success with a new and difficult area that previously had been the province of sociology. Psychology has added insights based on its tradition of studying process and its search for explanatory mechanisms. It is pleasing to see the publication of this useful volume.

John Mordechai Gottman, Ph.D.
*University of Washington*

# Preface

The idea for this volume arose from the need to answer a simple question: what have psychologists contributed to a scientific understanding of marriage? In our attempt to answer this question we found that pertinent material was scattered across a variety of disparate sources and often crossed subdisciplinary boundaries within psychology. Although psychologists had published numerous books on marriage, virtually all appeared to be oriented to clinical practice and/or clinical research (e.g., presentations of case studies, therapeutic techniques for alleviating family and marital distress) and we were unable to find a source that highlighted and evaluated the diverse contributions that psychologists have made to the study of marriage. In the absence of a book devoted to the psychology of marriage, we were concerned that psychologists working on related topics within different subdisciplines may be unaware of relevant developments in their area and lack a common base of knowledge, that scholars in allied disciplines (e.g., communication studies, sociology, family studies) may not have immediate access to a large body of psychological material pertinent to their own work, and that graduate students interested in marriage may be left with a fragmented and incomplete understanding of what psychologists know about the marital relationship.

The purpose of this book, therefore, is to document in a single volume the progress that has been made in psychological investigations of marriage. Specifically, we have sought to produce a book that (1) evaluates critically the contribution that psychology has made to the study of marriage, and (2) points the way forward to further advances in this domain. Consistent with our goals, we asked contributors to write chapters that would be of value to readers without much prior knowledge of the topic covered in the chapter. The book includes contributions from scholars in different subdisciplines of psychology (e.g., social, clinical, developmental, organizational), a combination that is not often found in contemporary books on marriage. However, it was not our intent to produce an exhaustive "handbook" but rather to represent major areas of inquiry. It is our hope that this book will provide readers with a clear appreciation of the knowledge that has been gained from psychological research on several aspects of the marital relationship, together with an understanding of the issues, assumptions, and controversies with which researchers and practitioners working in this area are now confronted.

The book is divided into two major sections. The first, basic issues, includes chapters on topics that constitute building blocks for the study of marriage (e.g., application of social psychological theory, research methods) as well as chapters on topics that have been the focus of psychological research. The second section of the book deals with applied concerns and includes chapters on particular marital problems, marital therapy, and the prevention of marital dysfunction.

Realizing our vision for this book has been an exciting and enriching experience. In particular, we appreciate the willingness of contributors to share our vision through the mosaic of editorial markings on their manuscripts. Finally, and most importantly, this book would not have been possible without the support and understanding of our wives, Susan and Cindy. They have taught us more about marriage than can be captured on the printed page and we dedicate this book to them.

Frank D. Fincham
Thomas N. Bradbury

# Contents

## II. APPLICATIONS

# INTRODUCTION

# Psychology and the Study of Marriage

**Frank D. Fincham**
**Thomas N. Bradbury**

The present volume attempts to highlight and evaluate the various contributions that psychologists have made to understanding marriage. Although psychology has only recently begun to address systematically theoretical, methodological, and applied issues in the study of marriage, the literature within psychology has increased dramatically over the last decade. This book is among the first to provide a concise overview of the diverse work by psychologists in the marital area.

We believe that the present collection of writings demonstrates that psychologists are now committed to the study of marriage and have a great deal to contribute to our understanding of this fundamental relationship. Several areas of psychological research on marriage have been established and show continued vitality. As psychological research on marriage reaches its adolescence, it is time to take stock. What have we learned so far? Where do we need to go from here? The contributors to this volume were asked to consider these questions and thus provide a review of research in their areas and point to avenues of inquiry that would advance our understanding of the topic addressed. The need for this book is also suggested by the observation that marital research is characterized by "several distinct traditions, distinct because researchers in each tradition have not read widely, and, therefore, scholars have tended to cite only their colleagues working in the same tradition" (Gottman, 1979, p. 2). We hope to address this problem by making available a single volume that contains several traditions of psychological research on marriage.

The purpose of this chapter is to provide a background that will allow the material presented in this book to be appreciated more fully. In the first section we outline the evolution of research on marriage, paying particular attention to the emergence of psychological research. Drawing on this historical analysis, the next section summarizes some of the characteristics of contemporary psychological research on marriage.

## HISTORICAL CONTEXT

Three stages can be identified in the emergence of scientific research on marriage and the family (Christensen, 1964). The *preresearch* stage, prior to about 1850, is characterized by little systematic thinking about the family, with most ideas reflecting "traditional beliefs, religious pronouncements, moralistic exhortations, poetic phantasies, and philosophical speculation" (Christensen, 1964, p. 6). This stage gave way to a period of *social Darwinism*, during which Darwin's theory of evolution was applied to a variety of social institutions, including marriage and the family. Because of the emphasis on gradual evolutionary change, direct study of the family was forgone in favor of anecdotal and historical records.

By the turn of the century, changing economic and social conditions called public attention to problems in families and ushered in a period of *emerging science*. The desire to understand and resolve family problems led to a reduction in value-laden assumptions about family life in favor of direct study using empirically based procedures (Jacob, 1987). Although the American Sociological Society devoted its 1908 meeting to "problems of interpersonal relations in the family" (Burr, Hill, Nye, & Reiss, 1979, p. 4), it was not until the 1920s that studies of marriage were begun. The two earliest studies in this domain were on sexual behavior; both examined its role in relationship satisfaction or success (Davis, 1929; Hamilton, 1948).

### Three Research Traditions

The central status accorded to relationship quality in marital research became even more salient in two later projects that are often credited with establishing marital research as an area of empirical inquiry. In their book *Psychological Factors in Marital Happiness*, Terman, Buttenweiser, Ferguson, Johnson, and Wilson (1938) described a study of 1,133 couples who completed a questionnaire designed to identify the determinants of marital satisfaction. Burgess and Cottrell (1939) similarly reported a questionnaire study of 526 couples in *Predicting Success or Failure in Marriage*. Both books are classic texts and report studies that were prototypes for later research on the correlates of marital quality and marital stability. By the time of their publication, the scientific study of marriage and the family was well underway, as evidenced by several developments: the devotion of the October 1937 issue of the *American Sociological Review* to the family, the emergence in 1937 of the journal *Living* (later known as *Marriage and Family Living* and more recently named *Journal of Marriage and the Family*), and the appearance of some 800 articles on the family by 1938 (Aldous & Hill, 1967; for a bibliography of early work see Thurston, 1932).[1]

Although Terman was a psychologist, most of the early research on marriage was conducted by sociologists. This *sociological tradition* of research is characterized by large-scale surveys that investigated a variety of potential correlates of marital quality, ranging from demographics (e.g., income, age, religion, race) to individual psychological variables (e.g., personality traits, perception of income, childhood socialization). This genre of research dominated the marital domain for over a generation and continues today (for a review see Barry, 1970).

Perhaps the most important finding to emerge is that variables with an interpersonal focus (e.g., descriptions of the marriage) tend to be more important in predicting marital quality than those that focus solely on the individual (e.g., personality traits; see Gottman, 1979). However, some commentators have argued that advances beyond those made by early researchers have been limited. For example, a recent review of 50 years of family research concludes: "Early on [1939], Burgess and Cottrell . . . took every individual characteristic they could think of and correlated it with marital success, producing an $R$ of about .50 and

---

[1]The emphasis placed on marital quality in this review is not meant to imply an absence of interest in other topics (e.g., mate selection, family budgets) or in the use of data obtained from sources other than questionnaires (e.g., life histories, case records). However, self-reported marital quality is the most frequently studied topic in marriage (Adams, 1988) and, as shown later, this has had a profound influence on psychological research.

an $R^2$ of .25, or 25% of the variance in the dependent variable. Not a bad start, but we have not progressed much beyond that point in 50 years" (Nye, 1988, p. 315).

Despite such sentiments, the sociological tradition of research has been valuable in its recognition of the importance of the family; sociologists have remained at the forefront in identifying and studying significant family problems (e.g., marital violence and the intergenerational transmission of alcoholism). Of particular note was the identification of several correlates of marital quality. However, the discovery of these correlates was accompanied by "little or no explanation of why the correlations exist" (Raush, Barry, Hertel, & Swain, 1974, p. 4) and by the 1960s there was considerable dissatisfaction with research in the sociological tradition, particularly its reliance on self-report.[2] In 1961 Raush et al. (1974) began to examine the overt behaviors of couples engaged in improvised marital conflicts in the laboratory. This study heralded the beginning of the second major tradition of marital research and engaged psychologists in the systematic study of marriage for the first time.[3]

Evolution of the *behavioral tradition* in research on marital quality reflects several developments. Concurrent with the reaction to the sociological tradition was the emergence of a behavioral approach to marital therapy. Behavioral marital therapy began with the application of operant conditioning principles (positive and negative reinforcement) to the treatment of marriage, a noteworthy development because of the emphasis given to the observation of overt behavior. The premium placed on such "objective" information fostered greater acceptance of research on marriage in psychology, a discipline modeled after the physical sciences. Other factors that most likely facilitated psychologists' involvement in marital research include the appearance of programmatic research on group processes in social psychology, the application of general systems theory to the study of the family,

---

[2]The failure of psychologists to appreciate fully the valuable contribution of family sociologists remains an enigma. Sociological research on marriage addresses a variety of topics that have not yet gained the attention of psychologists and even in areas of overlapping interest provides a useful complement to psychological research.

[3]Some papers on marriage appeared in the psychological literature prior to this time. However, these contributions tended to be the exception rather than the rule and an identifiable body of marital research in psychology emerged only recently. In fact, little more than a decade has passed since a comprehensive review of research on the psychology of relationships concluded that most studies involved persons who were "personally irrelevant" to each other (Huston & Levinger, 1978).

developmental psychologists' interest in reciprocal relations in the family (particularly parent–child relationships), and the increased interest of clinical psychologists and psychiatrists in the role of significant others in the initiation and maintenance of individual psychopathology (for further discussion, see Bradbury & Fincham, 1990; Jacob, 1987).

Notwithstanding the importance accorded to overt behavior, the behavioral tradition never fully relinquished reliance on self-report as the criterion variable to which behavior was related. Marital quality was assessed via this modality. Not surprisingly, social learning theory, with its emphasis on mediational constructs as explanatory variables, was soon introduced to behavioral marital therapy (e.g., Jacobson & Margolin, 1979). In fact, dissatisfaction with research in the sociological tradition did not reflect a complete rejection of the importance of subjective experience. For example, Raush et al. (1974) conceptualized their seminal study in terms of object relations schemata or "organized structures of images of the self and others" (p. 43). Rather, research focused on overt behavior and intrapersonal variables (e.g., thoughts and feelings) tended to be neglected rather than explicitly rejected.

Although the 1970s witnessed the publication of numerous studies on the overt behavior of couples (see Weiss & Heyman, Chapter 3, this volume), interest in this domain was limited primarily to clinical psychologists. Indeed, a seminal book on marital interaction was written with the hope that it would "increase the interest of psychologists in research on marriage" (Gottman, 1979, p. xiii). This hope has been realized in the last decade, as interest in close relationships has mushroomed among social scientists, including psychologists. Documentation of the factors responsible for this development is beyond the scope of this chapter. It suffices to note that psychologists' interest in close relationships has created a favorable climate for the study of marriage, and articles on this relationship have appeared with increased frequency in mainstream psychology journals.

One factor that has accompanied this change in *Zeitgeist* is a recognition of the limitations of a purely behavioral account of marriage and the emergence of a *mediational tradition* of research in the 1980s. Thus, subjective factors, such as thoughts and feelings, that might mediate behavior exchanges or serve as mediators of the relation between behavior and marital satisfaction have assumed center stage. Unlike the behavioral tradition, which arose out of dissatisfaction with earlier research, the current phase of research represents an acceptance and expansion of behavioral approach.

Our brief analysis of the evolution of marital research is necessarily limited and, like any other historical account, is constructed from a particular perspective. Nonetheless, it does serve our purpose by illustrating that psychology is a relative latecomer to the study of marriage and provides some indication of the perspectives that have dominated the psychological literature on marriage. It also serves as a useful springboard for characterizing current psychological research on marriage, a topic to which we now turn.

## CONTEMPORARY RESEARCH

In this section we highlight some of the features of psychologists' work on marriage. As in our earlier historical account, we do not attempt to offer an exhaustive analysis but one that might be useful in appreciating more fully the chapters that follow.

### Applied Concerns and Marital Quality

As our historical analysis showed, social scientists became interested in marriage and the family as a result of applied concerns. These concerns continue to influence contemporary psychological research on marriage. This is evident not only in the attention given to psychopathology and marriage (Gotlib & McCabe, Chapter 8, this volume), specific marital problems (e.g., spouse abuse, see O'Leary & Vivian, Chapter 11, this volume; sexual problems, see Heiman & Verhulst, Chapter 10, this volume), and to marital therapy (see Beach & Bauserman, Chapter 12, this volume; Segraves, Chapter 9, this volume) but also in the central role accorded to marital satisfaction in more basic research (e.g., Fincham, Bradbury, & Scott, Chapter 4, this volume). The need to understand the determinants of marital satisfaction is most likely driven by the fact that it is the final common pathway that leads to marital therapy/dissolution (Jacobson, 1985). We offer three observations about the focus on marital quality.

First, despite some 50 years of research on the topic, there is no consensus on the nature of marital quality or its measurement. Widely used measures of marital quality include a variety of different types of items (e.g., reports of behaviors, global judgments) and the interpretation of responses to such measures continues to prompt concern among some researchers (cf. Fincham & Bradbury, 1987). Psychologists have considerable expertise in constructing measurement devices; the issue of measurement in marital research, including the measurement of marital quality, is one that can still benefit considerably from such expertise.

Second, the focus on marital quality is important but may restrict unduly psychologists' contribution to understanding marriage. Some of the effort expended on researching this construct (either as an independent or dependent variable) might be more profitably applied elsewhere. Psychologists have made substantial contributions to understanding other areas of marriage (e.g., for work and marriage, see Barling, Chapter 7, this volume) and a redistribution of energy devoted to research on marital quality would enhance such contributions.

Third, a factor that might facilitate further expansion of research is the exploration of phenomena discovered in the psychological laboratory in the context of marriage. There is an increasing tendency to examine the operation of psychological principles in close relationships, a development that is long overdue in psychology (see Levinger & Huston, Chapter 1, this volume). We see considerable potential in further exploitation of this trend. In addition to addressing past omissions, it has the advantage of fostering integration of disparate writings, especially the growing literature in social psychology on close relationships and the marital literature. It is also likely to strengthen the foundation for applied research and practice.

## Methodological Advances and the Unit of Analysis

Psychologists have introduced important methodological advances to the study of marriage. The most obvious of these emerges from our historical analysis and concerns skills in the observation and coding of couple interactions. Innovations in coding behavior continue to be developed. The most recent change is the coding of specific affects (Gottman & Levenson, 1986) and the linking of content and affect codes in the Marital Interaction Coding System (Weiss & Summers, 1983). The introduction of such skills has left an indelible mark on marital research. However, these advances have also been accompanied by advances in the analysis of data obtained from couples. These innovations have the potential to affect profoundly our approach to understanding marriage and are therefore briefly discussed.

The most important implication of recently introduced data

analytic techniques concerns the unit of analysis in marital research. Given the central role of spouse reports of marital quality,
it is perhaps not surprising that the individual has most often
constituted the unit of analysis in marital research (see Robins,
Chapter 2, this volume). In this regard, psychological research on
marriage reflects its parent discipline in that "American psychology has been quintessentially a psychology of the individual organism" (Sarason, 1981, p. 827). This level of analysis is entirely
appropriate for examining issues such as sex differences in marriage (see Baucom, Notarius, Burnett, & Haefner, Chapter 5, this
volume) but it fails to capture phenomena that are emergent
properties of the relationship (e.g., the degree to which spouses
reciprocate behaviors). Nonetheless, attempts have been made to
study the couple as the unit of analysis by combining (summing or
averaging) each spouse's score on a measure to form an overall
couple score. This change in the unit of analysis is an important
advance in any attempt to understand a relationship but its realization in the above form is far from optimal (for a discussion of the
issues involved, see Baucom, 1983).

   The development of data analytic techniques that allow examination of relationship properties without introducing difficult-to-
interpret couple scores is therefore a particularly important inno-
vation. Several such techniques (e.g., lag sequential analysis, time
series analysis) have been introduced in the marital literature and
have been used to study the pattern and sequence of behavior in
marital interactions. For example, these techniques have been
used to determine whether a given spouse behavior provides information about the subsequent course of interaction and have revealed important differences in the behavior exchanges of maritally distressed and nondistressed spouses (see Weiss & Heyman,
Chapter 3, this volume).

   Although such innovations have occurred almost exclusively
in the analysis of overt behavior during short conversations, in
principle they could be applied to other variables (e.g., thoughts)
over more extended periods of time. In any event, methodological
concerns regarding the collection, coding, and analysis of data are
important features of the marital literature in psychology where
differing, but complementary, units of analysis ("individual,"
"couple") are found. There is also increasing awareness of the need
to examine broader levels of analysis (e.g., by including consideration of legal, cultural, and societal contexts) to gain a more complete understanding of marriage (see Bradbury & Fincham,
Chapter 13, this volume).

## Marriage as Process

The data-analytic advances outlined above are important not only because they involve use of the couple as the unit of analysis but also because they capture the dynamic nature of marriage. Psychologists have recognized this feature of marriage, especially as it relates to the impact of children on the marital relationship (see Belsky, Chapter 6, this volume). Nonetheless, much of the available literature provides a picture of marriage as a static phenomenon, a limitation that no doubt reflects the difficulty of investigating dynamic processes.

Dramatic changes appear to be underway in this regard. Although psychologists are not strangers to longitudinal research in the marital domain (e.g., Kelly & Conley, 1987; Markman, 1981), there has been increased momentum toward conducting such research over the last few years. Indeed, we expect that this shift in emphasis will bring some major advances in our understanding of marriage. The initial fruits of this labor are already apparent in some of the ensuing chapters.

Because longitudinal research allows examination of change in marital relationships, it provides unique information about the developmental course of marriage. For example, it can address whether couples need only apply a common set of coping strategies (e.g., communication skills) to negotiate the developmental tasks confronted at different stages of marriage or whether different developmental tasks require unique coping strategies. In view of the relative infancy of psychological research on marriage, longitudinal studies can provide crucial descriptive information on normative changes in marriage. The difficulty and, in some areas, the impossibility of manipulating variables in marital research suggests another important function of longitudinal studies. In the absence of true experiments, longitudinal studies may be critical in providing information that can be used to address causal questions. Examining the causes of various marital phenomena speaks to their explanation, possibly the most important goal in scientific inquiry and a topic to which we now turn.

## Explanation in Marital Research

The emergence of the behavioral tradition was, in part, a reaction to the absence of theory and explanation in earlier research. However, theory was slow to emerge within the behavioral tradition. This is perhaps understandable in that the emphasis on observation was accompanied by the belief that description is a prerequisite to explanation and that premature theorizing is more misleading than beneficial.

After careful documentation of behavior in marital interactions, there is a growing willingness to offer conceptual frameworks that fill the function of theory (e.g., guide research and aid its interpretation). However, comprehensive theories remain infrequent in psychological research on marriage and, in this respect, the field mirrors the discipline of psychology, where the era of grand theories has long since passed.

As noted earlier, the emergence of the mediational tradition reflects an attempt to provide a more complete understanding of close relationships. One consequence is the attempt to provide general models of interaction in close relationships (see Kelley et al., 1983) and marriage (see Bradbury & Fincham, 1989). Although it might be argued that there is insufficient descriptive data to justify such models, a strong case can be made that no research is atheoretical. Thus, advances are more likely to occur with research that is guided by explicit models or theories (even if incorrect) than by ostensibly "atheoretical" research in which assumptions remain implicit. This is particularly true in the marital literature, where one can find many implicit assumptions about marriage.

Regardless of any differences in philosophy of science, the contributions of research from both the behavioral and mediational traditions are essential for advancing explanation in psychological research on marriage. A meaningful psychology of marriage requires both the identification of reliable phenomena and the existence of explanatory frameworks to guide research. The energy currently expended in both directions augurs well for the continued vitality of psychological research on marriage.


## CONCLUSION

We have traced the evolution of marital research and highlighted some features of contemporary research in order to provide a context within which the chapters in this book can be viewed. The chapters raise many more issues than we have addressed and represent, but do not exhaust, the spectrum of psychological inquiry about marriage. As will become evident, much has been achieved and much more remains to be done. The goal of this book is to provide access to the knowledge generated by psychological research and the problems encountered in its practical implementation in the hope that it will facilitate a more complete understanding of this important relationship.

# REFERENCES

Adams, B. N. (1988). Fifty years of family research. *Journal of Marriage and the Family, 50*, 5–18.

Aldous, J., & Hill, R. (1967). *International bibliography of research in marriage and the family, 1960–1964.* Minneapolis: University of Minnesota Press.

Barry, W. A. (1970). Marriage research and conflict: An integrative review. *Psychological Bulletin, 73*, 41–54.

Baucom, D. H. (1983). Conceptual and psychometric issues in evaluating the effectiveness of behavioral marital therapy. In J. P. Vincent (Ed.), *Advances in family intervention, assessment, and theory* (vol. 3, pp. 91–118). Greenwich, CT: JAI Press.

Bradbury, T. N., & Fincham, F. D. (1989). Behavior and satisfaction in marriage: Prospective mediating processes. *Review of Personality and Social Psychology, 10*, 119–143.

Bradbury, T. N., & Fincham, F. D. (1990). Dimensions of marital and family interaction. In J. Touliatos, B. F. Perlmutter, & M. A. Straus (Eds.), *Handbook of family measurement techniques* (pp. 36–61). Newbury Park, CA: Sage.

Burgess, E. W., & Cottrell, L. S. (1939). *Predicting success or failure in marriage.* New York: Prentice-Hall.

Burr, W. R., Hill, R., Nye, F. I., & Reiss, I. L. (1979). *Contemporary theories about the family.* New York: Free Press.

Christensen, H. T. (1964). Development of the family field of study. In H. T. Christensen (Ed.), *Handbook of marriage and the family* (pp. 3–32). Chicago: Rand McNally.

Davis, K. B. (1929). *Factors in the sex life of twenty-two hundred women.* New York: Harpers.

Fincham, F. D., & Bradbury, T. N. (1987). The assessment of marital quality: A reevaluation. *Journal of Marriage and the Family, 49*, 797–809.

Gottman, J. M. (1979). *Marital interaction: Experimental investigations.* New York: Academic Press.

Gottman, J. M., & Levenson, R. W. (1986). Assessing the role of emotion in marriage. *Behavioral Assessment, 8*, 31–48.

Hamilton, G. V. (1948). *A research on marriage.* New York: Lear Publications.

Huston, T., & Levinger, G. (1978). Interpersonal attraction and relationships. *Annual Review of Psychology, 29*, 115–156.

Jacob, T. (1987). Family interaction and psychopathology: Historical overview. In T. Jacob (Ed.), *Family interaction and psychopathology* (pp. 3–22). New York: Plenum Press.

Jacobson, N. S. (1985). The role of observational measures in behavior therapy outcome research. *Behavioral Assessment, 7*, 297–308.

Jacobson, N. S., & Margolin, G. (1979). *Marital therapy: Strategies based on social learning and behavior exchange principles.* New York: Brunner/Mazel.

Kelley, H. H., Berscheid, E., Christensen, A., Harvey, J. H., Huston, T. L., Levinger, G., McClintock, E., Peplau, L. A., & Peterson, D. R. (1983). *Close relationships.* New York: W. H. Freeman.

Kelly, E. L., & Conley, J. J. (1987). Personality and compatibility: A prospective analysis of marital stability and marital satisfaction. *Journal of Personality and Social Psychology, 52,* 27-40.

Markman, H. J. (1981). Prediction of marital distress: A 5-year follow-up. *Journal of Consulting and Clinical Psychology, 49,* 760-762.

Nye, F. I. (1988). Fifty years of family research, 1937-1987. *Journal of Marriage and the Family, 50,* 305-316.

Raush, H. L., Barry, W. A., Hertel, R. K., & Swain, M. A. (1974). *Communication, conflict, and marriage.* San Francisco: Jossey-Bass.

Sarason, S. B. (1981). An asocial psychology and a misdirected clinical psychology. *American Psychologist, 36,* 827-836.

Terman, L. M., Buttenweiser, P., Ferguson, L. W., Johnson, W. B., & Wilson, D. P. (1938). *Psychological factors in marital happiness.* New York: McGraw-Hill.

Thurston, F. M. (1932). *A bibliography on family relationships.* New York: National Council on Family Education.

Weiss, R. L., & Summers, K. J. (1983). Marital Interaction Coding System-III. In E. E. Filsinger (Ed.), *Marriage and family assessment* (pp. 85-115). Beverly Hills: Sage.

# PART ONE
## BASIC ISSUES

# Introduction

This section is comprised of chapters that address general issues relevant to basic research on marriage (Chapters 1 and 2) and that evaluate specific areas of such research (Chapters 3 through 8). Levinger and Huston (Chapter 1) illustrate how work in social psychology can enrich our understanding of marriage. They return to the writings of Kurt Lewin, a founding father of social psychology, and offer a comprehensive analysis in which his ideas are used to provide a social psychological framework for understanding marriage. In so doing, Levinger and Huston provide insights on such important concepts as compatibility and love. The value of their framework is emphasized by its incorporation of activity patterns as well as specific face-to-face interactions, levels of analysis that are seldom integrated in marital research.

Robins (Chapter 2), like Levinger and Huston, reminds us that interdependence is a central feature of marriage. He offers an analysis of interdependence at the interactional and psychological levels and goes on to outline their reciprocal effects on each other. Central to this discussion is the generation of viable research strategies and measurement procedures for the investigation of interactional and psychological interdependence. Robins discusses how one can collect meaningful data on interdependence for targets of inquiry that range from discrete events in an interaction to the study of patterns manifest over the course of time.

In Chapter 3, Weiss and Heyman examine one of the most intensely researched topics in the psychological literature on marriage—overt behavior in marital interaction. Their comprehensive review of the behavioral observation literature from 1980–1989 complements earlier reviews of work done in the 1970s. However, this chapter extends well beyond prior treatments and includes consideration of data that pertain to affect, overt behavior, and cognition collected via self-report, quasiobservation, and observational methods. The discrepancies noted between concurrent correlates and predictors of marital quality lead these authors to emphasize the need for longitudinal research on marriage, one of eight desiderata offered for marital research in the next decade.

Fincham, Bradbury, and Scott (Chapter 4) evaluate a relatively recent domain of systematic inquiry, the study of cognition in marriage. They address three basic questions: Why study cognition in marriage? What aspects might be studied? How are they best studied? The first question is answered in the context of documenting the emergence of research on cognition in marriage. The second question leads to a critical review of research on marriage in which an organizational framework is offered to illustrate the coherence of what is sometimes viewed as an inchoate literature. It is argued that the final question, how to study cognition, is best addressed by examining the study of marital cognition in the broader context of cognitive science, and an attempt is made to illustrate how this perspective can enrich psychological research on cognition in marriage.

Baucom, Notarius, Burnett, and Haefner (Chapter 5) are among the first to document the empirical basis for widely assumed gender differences in marriage and to explore in detail the implications of sex-role identity for marital functioning. Their review of studies showing a difference in the marital behavior of husbands and wives complements Chapter 3 and raises the intriguing question of why these differences occur. These authors note that sex-role identity, rather than gender per se, might account for such differences. Their subsequent exploration of the implications of sex-role identity is not, however, restricted to a consideration of overt behavior. It also includes examination of marital adjustment, cognition, emotion, and the implications of sex-role identity for the marital system.

In Chapter 6, Belsky reminds us that a complete understanding of marriage must include consideration of the impact of children on marriage. His careful analysis of the evidence shows that even though the presence of young children promotes marital stability, the transition to parenthood is accompanied by a decline in marital quality. Examination of the processes that might underlie such associations reveals that there are likely to be many ways in which children influence marriage. However, Belsky also shows that three individual differences relating to children—gender, temperament, and handicap—can influence their impact on marriage.

Barling's chapter (Chapter 7) on employment highlights another important variable for understanding marriage. The extensive literature on this topic is examined in terms of the effects on marital functioning of temporal employment characteristics, the subjective meaning of employment, and unemployment and the impact of marital functioning on work. The chapter therefore covers a diverse set of issues ranging from the effect of shift work on marital role performance through wife employment as a risk factor for spouse abuse to the impact of marital problems on worker accidents and absenteeism. Barling goes on to examine whether the associations found between work and marriage reflect meaningful, rather than statistical, effects and to offer a blueprint for future research on employment and marital functioning.

Gotlib and McCabe (Chapter 8) provide one of the first single, concise sources concerning the association between psychopathology and marriage. Their examination of this association focuses on three domains of research: the relation between marital status and psychopathology, the quality of marriages and marital interactions where one spouse exhibits a clinical disorder, and the findings of marital therapy outcome research in the treatment of psychopathology. Although these authors document an association between psychopathology and marital functioning, they caution against assuming that it is causal in nature and, like other contributors to this book, highlight the need for longitudinal investigations of marriage.

# CHAPTER 1

# The Social Psychology of Marriage

George Levinger
Ted L. Huston

Marriage is customarily defined as the union between man and woman that combines both sexual and economic interdependence. The average American marriage is perceived as more intimate (Veroff, Douvan, & Kulka, 1981), more behaviorally and affectively interdependent (Rands & Levinger, 1979), more intense, and more cooperative (Wish, Deutsch, & Kaplan, 1976) than any other close relationship. Marriage differs, however, from other social ties in the strength of the barriers that surround the relationship. Such barriers result initially from the partners' commitment to care for one another; later they become part of the stable context that affects spouses' ongoing interaction.

This chapter sets forth a broadly conceived social psychological framework for examining the marital dyad. Beginning with Kurt Lewin's conception of the forces that affect people's life-space and their activity fields, we develop a conception of how the psychological world (life-space) of spouses affects their behavior and show how the behavior of each spouse alters the partner's life-space. The structure of the relationship, the stable behavioral patterns that emerge with time, results from the spouses' experience in acting and reacting to each other's actions and communications. Either directly or indirectly, each partner's life-space is affected continuously by the other's behavior.

Our analysis moves between the molar activity patterns that provide the broad outlines of a marriage relationship and the relatively molecular events that are part of marital interaction. These two levels of analysis are often treated separately, with sociologically oriented social psychologists focusing on activity patterns and individually oriented social psychologists centering their study on the microevents that occur during face-to-face interaction. To illustrate these contrasting levels of analysis, we spotlight the marital lifestyle of a hypothetical couple—Paul and Gail Shaw.

A major goal is to suggest how communication patterns create marital lifestyles (as reflected in spousal activity patterns) and how the preferences of the spouses provide a basis for communication, which is often stimulated by one spouse's activities thwarting the goals of the other. The psychological identities of the spouses, as well as the context in which they live, are reflected in both molar activity patterns and interactional microprocesses. Marital harmony and conflict are grounded in the meshing of partners' goals and preferences; they can be inferred by watching specific interactions (at the micro level) and from information about general activity patterns (at the molar level). To predict how people will respond subjectively to events, social psychologists look for information about people's goals; compatible marriages are those where spouses have mutually facilitative goals and play complementary roles in their achievement.

## PHENOMENA OF SOCIAL PSYCHOLOGICAL CONCERN

Sociologists, and more recently clinical psychologists and social psychologists, have attempted to study marriage from a variety of perspectives. Sociologists have tended to emphasize the macro level; they have concerned themselves with types of marriage—such as "the institutional versus the companionate" (Burgess & Locke, 1945) or "the parallel versus the interactional" marriage (Bernard, 1964)—marital adjustment (Locke, 1951), or sex differences in marital power (Blood & Wolfe, 1960). Clinical psychologists have been more concerned with interpersonal processes, employing either systematic observation of marital behavior (e.g., Gottman, 1979; Raush, Barry, Hertel, & Swain, 1974) or clinical case-by-case description. Social psychologists have looked at marriage mainly as a locus for applying concepts relevant to understanding the range of ongoing relationships, such as causal attribution (e.g., Thompson & Kelley, 1981), task versus social role division (e.g., Bales & Slater, 1955; Levinger, 1964), social power (e.g., Raven, Centers, & Rodrigues, 1975), or conflict and social exchange (e.g., Braiker & Kelley, 1979).

With few exceptions, social psychologists have been more interested in underlying psychological and interpersonal phenomena of marriage than in marriage as a social institution. The most important marriage-relevant phenomena, though, can be grouped under the following three rubrics: (1) buildup of a close relationship; (2) marriage maintenance and interaction; and (3) distress, decline, and breakup.

## Relationship Buildup

Social psychologists have done much research on interpersonal attraction and the antecedents of developing a close relationship (see Berscheid, 1985a; Huston & Levinger, 1978). If mutual attraction is sufficient to encourage interaction, theories of social exchange suggest that the partners assess both their absolute and their comparative levels of benefit and cost to decide on whether and how long to continue the relationship (see Huston & Burgess, 1979; Levinger, 1979). Later during this process, partners may reexamine their mutual suitability (e.g., Hill, Rubin, & Peplau, 1976; Huston, Surra, Fitzgerald, & Cate, 1981; Levinger, Senn, & Jorgensen, 1970), when issues of relational investment (Rusbult, 1983) or commitment (e.g., Johnson, in press) may become relevant.

## Marriage Maintenance

Marriage may be maintained by external barriers or structures—the province mainly of sociologists and economists—and by the provision of intrinsic satisfactions (see Levinger, 1965). Like other social relationships, marriages can be considered with regard to two dimensions—solidarity and status.

Regarding solidarity, a couple's satisfaction is enhanced by dealing well with issues of self-disclosure, trust, and conflict. Open disclosure of one's feelings, especially positive feelings (Levinger & Senn, 1967), and the responsive acceptance of the other's disclosures are important ingredients of building and maintaining intimacy (e.g., Altman & Taylor, 1973; Reis & Shaver, 1988). Beyond that, the demonstration of a willingness to sacrifice one's self-interest for the partner's benefit is crucial for the maintenance of trust (Holmes & Rempel, 1989). How conflict is resolved also influences the viability of a marriage; as discussed later in this chapter, confronting differences—though sometimes costly in the short run—tends in the long run to bolster a pair's intimacy (e.g., Gottman & Krokoff, 1989; Peterson, 1983).

Regarding status, the equitable distribution of power and task performance are also central for marital satisfaction (e.g., Huston, 1983). Early social psychological analyses of marital resources and task performance (Herbst, 1952; Wolfe, 1959) have had an important impact on later sociological treatments of the marital power balance (e.g., Blood & Wolfe, 1960; Safilios-Rothschild, 1976).

## Deterioration and Breakup

Psychologists have tended to focus on marital distress, whereas sociologists have focused mainly on divorce and separation. Social psychological analyses of marriage deterioration have focused on issues of economic and psychological stress, perceived inequity, unfavorable comparisons with the rewards and costs to be obtained in alternative relationships, and the loss of mutual trust (e.g., Berscheid & Campbell, 1981; Holmes & Rempel, 1989; Levinger, 1983).

Although far more systematic research has been directed at the beginnings and endings of close relationships than on their middle stages, this chapter concentrates on ongoing marriage relationships after they are formed and before there is much thought of separation. To do so, it adopts a viewpoint that helps integrate both the micro- and macroanalytic properties of pair interaction and interdependence.

## MARRIAGE AND THE LIFE-SPACE

In one of his first writings on interpersonal relations, Kurt Lewin (1940/1948) analyzed "the background of conflict in marriage." He wrote that the marital group is characterized by the spouses' high interdependence, with each partner affecting "central regions" of the other's psychological world. Furthermore, marital relationships compete with spouses' commitments to other groups, such as family, friendship networks, occupational groups, and the wider community.

Lewin's paper was probably the first formal treatment of marriage as a social psychological phenomenon. His analysis showed that conflicts can arise from a variety of sources, including the diversity of the spouses' roles and memberships, their different, sometimes contradictory goals, and the discrepant meanings spouses attach to events and circumstances in their marriage. Lewin viewed pair interdependence as arising out of a combination of (1) the partners' personal needs and long-standing dispositions, (2) the spouses' social and physical environments, and (3) both transient and enduring forces within the marriage itself. Subsequent social psychological treatments of marriage and other long-term relationships (e.g., Kelley et al., 1983) have been influenced by Lewin's views on causality, but his ideas concerning the life-space have rarely been applied to marriage. We thus examine Lewin's conceptualization of the life-space before connecting it to the behavioral organization of marriage.

Life-space refers to "the totality of psychobiological factors which produce effects in a person's life at any given moment" (Leeper, 1943, p. 210). It locates a person, P, at any given moment, in a psychological field divided into "regions" referring to P's "present or contemplated activities" (Leeper, 1943, p. 214). Lewin's idea of life-space conveys that much of human action is based on an actor's current psychological world, that this current world incorporates past experience, that the actor's movements are largely regulated by his or her views of their consequences, and that the actor's psychological world changes through feedback from the environment. Lewin used the life-space concept to examine a husband's and wife's subjective states in connection with their individual and joint activities.

## Valences and Barriers

At any given moment, P sees some activities as attractive (positive goal regions) and others as unattractive or repulsive (negative goal regions). Valent regions exert "driving forces" either toward or away from the region and thus guide a person's behavior. In contrast, forces against entering or leaving a region are considered "restraining forces" or barriers. Theoretically, P's behavior is driven by attractions and repulsions; barriers affect behavior only if the actor contemplates leaving one region for another (Levinger, 1965).

### An Illustrative Case

Imagine a husband who is sitting in his living room before dinner and has just finished reading the newspaper. His life-space can be divided into various regions identified with activities he might perform in the immediate future (e.g., washing the dishes, working in his workshop, reading a book). Each region has either a positive or a negative valence; the husband's action will depend on the relative valences of these regions. Moreover, a person's life-space typically changes with action: the husband might begin to read a book, with this activity setting in motion changes in the valences of other regions. When after half an hour he thinks about his wife coming home from her work, he might feel an increasing pull toward doing the dishes that litter the kitchen sink.

Valences associated with particular regions are linked both to past and to possible future circumstances. The husband's valence for doing the dishes is more positive this evening than last, for instance, because he recalls his wife complaining about the unfairness of his always leaving the dishes for her to do, and he is more aware that straightening the kitchen will improve their relationship. Soon, therefore, he may stop reading and start working in the kitchen.

The husband's actions are also affected by restraining forces. Until he had relaxed from his day's work, he felt unwilling to move out of his comfortable chair to do housework (barriers between regions). His awareness of how strongly his wife feels about his doing more of the housework, coupled with his commitment to maintaining her marital satisfaction, led him to contemplate seriously no alternative other than those that would please his wife, or at least not displease her.

This example illustrates how an actor's psychological world is connected to his or her activities. Changes in activity patterns reflect changes in the valences (and barriers) associated with regions in the life-space.

## Valences and Their Determinants

Valence has been used as a broad, umbrella-like term of varying specificity and stability. Thus, valences can be short-term and centered on a specific line of action (e.g., washing the dishes during the next 15 minutes) or long-term and very general (e.g., as when a married person's love affects the valence of a host of activities that might bear on the spouse's well-being). Behavior is, of course, determined by multiple psychological forces that combine to determine the valences of particular lines of action. Whether a husband will wash dishes, for example, may depend on his positive orientation toward marriage or housekeeping responsibilities in general; on his momentary mood; on his current desire to please his wife; on his felt competence (or lack thereof) in the activity, especially if he finds failure frustrating; and on a host of other stable and unstable factors. Personal, situational, and interactional factors all contribute to a given action (or lack of action).

Some goals or activity regions are universally sought (e.g., eating and drinking at appropriate intervals), but even such regions become neutral or even negative after a need is satisfied. Other activities (e.g., physical exercise or intimate personal disclosure) are valued positively by some and abhorred by others.

Building an enduring relationship depends both on the partners' previous values or dispositions and on their development of new interpersonal dispositions (Kelley, 1979). Living together requires the performance of maintenance tasks (e.g., housekeeping, food preparation, and financial decision-making), communication, and the pursuit of social activities (e.g., relations with kin and friends, as well as private recreations). The extent to which activities are valued by each spouse, both generally and at any particular time, has important effects on the marriage. The valences husbands and wives attach to particular activities create psychological conditions conducive to harmony or conflict. Particular patterns of valences within a marriage may encourage or discourage the joint pursuit of activities and, over time, create a highly interdependent relationship or one of lesser interdependence. The degree to which spouses live together harmoniously rather than in conflict reflects the extent to which lines of action chosen by each spouse either enhance or limit the chances of goal achievement of their partner. Harmony can also be achieved at one spouse's expense, as when a spouse abandons goals that conflict with those of the partner.

## Individual Differences in Valences

The term "valence" usefully abstracts the common relevance of a diverse set of stable and changing psychological conditions to the ways people act and react to events, both real and potential. Values, needs, and personality dispositions denote relatively stable qualities that distinguish people regarding the consequences they seek to make happen (or try to avoid). To the extent that values, needs, and personality dispositions have ramifications for how people behave and respond to others, they are reflected in valences associated with particular lines of action and contexts. The more impact an attribute has on the valences, and the more diverse the actions and contexts affected, the more significant is the attribute as a predictor of actions and reactions.

A person with a particular set of values generally seeks to create an environment that reflects those values. If such values are central, many aspects of the person's life space will be affected. A husband with traditional sex-role attitudes, for example, may avoid performing certain tasks around the house (e.g., cleaning, laundry), and he may criticize his wife if she fails to do these jobs. An individual who has particularly strong affiliative needs will seek out settings populated by affable, friendly people. Similarly, a person who has strong needs to control will seek familiar settings and compliant people as partners. As obvious as these points may seem, the failure to explore empirically the connections between people's social and psychological attributes, their psychological fields (recurring themes in their life-space), and the extent to which they act toward a particular person in a specific fashion or react to interpersonal events in one way rather than another, has flawed research on the psychological roots of close relationships. The study of compatibility testing in courtship and marriage, for example, has had limited success because few attempts have been made to link individual-difference variables to partners' inclinations to create lifestyles and interpersonal patterns (see Huston et al., 1981; Levinger & Rands, 1985). Many of the general attributes that have been examined have limited effects on people's inclinations to be drawn toward one region rather than another, or to behave one way rather than another in connection with a particular other person. For example, similarity in religious background, particularly for people who are weakly committed to a religion, may not affect either partner's valences enough to influence their reactions. Moreover, attitudes that are currently directed toward the partner (e.g., strong feelings of love) may overwhelm, or at least mute, all but the strongest general psychological dispositions.

## Love and Valences

Love brightens regions of a person's life-space that contain the spouse. When a husband's love for his wife is activated, the valences associated with various lines of action that bear on her are colored by his love. The love-primed husband may imagine settings that involve his wife as imbued with positive affect and picture himself as happier, more relaxed, sexually charged, or secure in such settings. Such a husband would seek out his wife's company unless countervalent motives are also activated or unless barriers in the field prevent him from doing so. Once in his wife's presence, the husband's love (if it remains activated) is reflected in the valences he associates with various ways of acting or reacting to her. Lovers are disposed to express affection, give each other emotional and moral support, show an interest in each other's activities, give gifts and perform chores for one another, tolerate each other's demands, and to be happier, more secure, and more relaxed when near each other (Swensen, 1972). Love also has a darker side, a side that might be activated either when the object of one's love fails to reciprocate the lover's strong feelings or when the loved one blocks important goals (Berscheid, 1988).

Love as attraction is a multifaceted construct, an umbrella under which at least three distinct types or components of love can be distinguished (see Kelley, 1983; Sternberg & Barnes, 1988), which have different origins and implicate distinctive lines of action. *Romantic, passionate, or erotic love* is fueled by mystery, illusion, novelty, and perhaps by sexual frustration. It generates an intense absorption in the loved one, an absorption that produces a powerful drive to be together, a drive that colors wide areas of the life-space, creating a glow in those areas that include the partner and making other regions opaque by comparison (Berscheid, 1988; Berscheid & Walster, 1978). *Companionate or pragmatic love*, sometimes labeled friendship or intimacy (Kelley, 1983), creates a desire to seek out the loved one as a companion. This love arises from a history of working as a well-functioning unit. The loved one is central to the life-space of the companionate lover when the lover wants to play, work out a personal problem, or reminisce about past events. *Altruistic love* emphasizes the welfare of another, leading to actions that promote the other's happiness (Kelley, 1983). Salient valences in the altruistic lover's life-space reflect the desire to enhance the life of the loved one.

Most conceptions of love emphasize either its *hot* (i.e., passionate, erotic) aspects or its *warm* (i.e., intimate, companionate, altruistic) facets. In general, the process of building a close relationship entails partners becoming increasingly attracted to each other; in some couples warmth and intimacy develop first, in others passion and infatuation. One or both of these components is usually perceived as necessary for creating a commitment to an enduring relationship.

In marriage, the partners' initial desire for closeness and interdependence is reinforced by moral and structural supports (Johnson, in press). Wanting or needing the partner and the relationship are bolstered by a sense of obligation. That is, personal commitment, which stems mainly from positive valences, is supplemented by moral and structural commitments (or barriers). The wedding vows and the support of the two partners' family and friendship network are intended to confirm the durability of the attraction. We now turn, therefore, to the long-term structural supports and constraints within which marriages function over the long run.

## BARRIER FORCES AND MARITAL COMMITMENT

Lewin's second important concept is that of "barriers," regions in the life-space that offer resistance to "locomotion." Like valences, barriers can be stable or unstable and general or specific to a particular time and situation. Most social psychological writings about marriage, however, have focused on stable and general barriers. Some barrier regions are mainly internal to a relationship (e.g., the problems associated with coordinating the partners' desires). Other barriers are mainly external, serving as boundaries that prevent certain activities from taking place outside the relationship. For example, the marriage contract and divorce laws restrain the partners from engaging in actions that might terminate the marriage. Any aspect of a relationship can be a source of barrier forces if it leads a member to anticipate high legal, social, financial, or emotional costs of pursuing a line of behavior (see Levinger, 1965, 1976).

The advantage of strong barriers against leaving a marriage is that, under conditions of valence instability, they prevent partners from readily terminating their relationship. Even highly satisfying marriages are likely to have their ups and downs. Barriers reduce the temptation to dissolve a relationship during down periods rather than tolerate the difficulties and work to overcome them. The disadvantage of strong barriers is that partners may come to take their bond for granted or rely primarily on restraining forces to maintain it, thus undermining its intrinsic attractiveness (Rosenblatt, 1977). A second disadvantage of strong barriers is that they hold together people who may be better off independent.

Berscheid and Campbell (1981) have discussed the effects on American marriages of reduced economic, legal, religious, and social barriers, as well as of barriers attributable to children. The more open the environment, the more likely spouses will be to consider alternative possibilities. With today's decreasing economic dependence of wives on husbands, the lessening of legal obstacles or of church opposition, and the decreasing stigma of divorce for either ex-spouses or their children, marriage partners now face fewer obstacles to ending their marriage if either should become sufficiently dissatisfied to look for an alternative.

The reduced barriers against ending marriages also have had important *indirect* effects. Berscheid and Campbell (1981) suggest that as more marriages end, more people are added to the pool of alternative partners for spouses in existing marriages, thereby increasing the probability that some of these available people will appear more attractive than the current partner. Thus, the burden of remaining in a marriage will fall increasingly on its intrinsic value (on "the sweetness of its contents," Berscheid & Campbell, 1981, p. 222).

The point is that *both* valences and constraints are important components of a satisfying and stable marriage. Accordingly, Sternberg (1986) has emphasized the complementarity among the "intimacy" and the "commitment" components of a balanced love relationship, and others (e.g., Johnson, in press) have underscored the contribution of both "personal" and "structural" factors for keeping people in a relationship.

## MARRIAGE AND THE BEHAVIORAL FIELD[1]

Valences and barriers represent the subjective side of human action. Actors are presumed to act either because they are drawn toward some activity more than to others or because barriers impede them from carrying out activities they might otherwise pursue (Lewin, 1940/1948). Lewin did not assume that all lines of action an outsider might believe relevant to an actor's situation are represented in the actor's life-space. Moreover, a person's life-space at a particular moment may suggest a line of action so clearly that other possibilities are not given conscious consideration. The line taken in such situations will seem, both to the actor and to others, as almost driven or subconsciously motivated.

[1]This section draws heavily on material from Huston (1989).

## Illustration: A Day in the Life of Gail and Paul Shaw

A person's activity can be thought of as a stream of movement punctuated into discrete coherent units with beginnings, endings, and transition points. Consider Gail Shaw's morning, as illustrated in Figure 1.1 (adapted from Huston, 1989). Gail, a wife in a somewhat conventional marriage, is the mother of two teen-agers, a girl of 17 and a boy of 16. Gail wakes up at 6:30 a.m. and, during the next 30 minutes, makes coffee, gets the morning paper, awakens Paul (her husband), and makes breakfast for the family (while Paul drinks his coffee and reads the paper); she then gets her two teen-agers out of bed. These individual "activities," when considered over time, form a pattern. Figure 1.1 shows Gail's activities through the day and evening, as well as those of her husband, daughter, and son. The figure includes only activities that are descriptive of family life. The shaded boxes enclose activities done together by two or more members of the nuclear family. The clear boxes show blocks of time in which the family members carry out activities away from home, sometimes in the company of others.

This portrait of a day in the life of the Shaws, incomplete as it is, provides clues concerning many aspects of their marriage. The activities within the Shaw family seem well coordinated, and family life seems to have a formal air about it. Gail orchestrates the morning activities, with each person playing what seems like a well-rehearsed role. It is easy to imagine the teenagers being inexorably drawn to the breakfast area once they get out of bed, particularly if the mother's pattern is predictable and her expectations are clear. Paul reads the morning paper while Gail prepares breakfast; Paul goes to work outside the home, and Gail takes care of most of the household work; when the teen-agers return home from school, the daughter, rather than the son, puts laundry away and helps the mother prepare the dinner. As we progress through the day, we get the sense that shared understandings, many of which reflect traditional ideas about marital and family roles, are being played out. We do not know, of course, whether this particular day is representative or whether our ideas concerning the psychological and sociocultural roots of these patterns are correct. We have no independent information about what goes on in the various family members' heads as they move about during the day, nor have we connected such cognitive mapping to family members' more general attitudes and social backgrounds.

People do particular kinds of activities again and again, and these activities are often pursued in particular social contexts. The phrase "behavioral field" was coined by Herbst (1952) to identify the scope of activities in the day-to-day life of a particular person. Herbst argued that the activities that make up the day-to-day life of families can be grouped into "regions" or "areas." Our summary of the Shaws' day attempts to capture the contours of their family life by viewing their specific behaviors as representative of types of activities and notes how family members pursue activities with friends, extended family, schoolmates, and co-workers. The valence associated with engaging in a particular activity may have more to do with the person's feelings about others than with the intrinsic value of the activity itself (see earlier discussion of valences and love). Thus Huston (1989) found that a husband's love for his wife predicted how much a couple pursued leisure together rather than apart. Snyder and Simpson (1984) have found that some people tend to choose activities in order to be with people they like, whereas others mainly choose people in order to pursue activities they enjoy.

Dividing activities into subgroups is useful analytically for the same reasons it is useful to assemble questionnaire items into scales. Patterns of activities, when grouped and aggregated over time, provide a basis for describing a couple's individual and group fields. Most family-related activities can be placed into three major categories, based on whether the activity is primarily *instrumental, recreational,* or *conversational.* Preparing breakfast, doing the dishes, making the bed, taking the trash out, doing the laundry, and ironing clothes are instrumental activities that Herbst (1952) classified into a region he called "household activities." Watching television, visiting friends or relatives, and going on a picnic are leisure pursuits.[2] Each of these major regions can be subdivided further into "subregions." Atkinson and Huston (1984), for instance, divided household activities into clusters according to whether they are performed normatively by husbands, by wives, or by both spouses.

## Characterizing Spouses' Individual and Group Behavioral Fields

Figure 1.1 provides a glimpse of the Shaws' lifestyle. But just as it is dangerous to generalize about the marriage as a whole from patterns observed during a single interaction episode, it is equally risky

[2]The "work" and "play" clusters are distinguishable phenomenologically in terms of whether the valence associated with the activity is primarily based on a feeling of obligation or of enjoyment. Millar and Tesser (1989) have shown that work activity is sustained by progress toward task completion; play continues only as long as it is enjoyable.

# LOG OF ACTIVITIES

| Time | Mother (Gail) | Father (Paul) | Daughter | Son |
|------|---------------|---------------|----------|-----|
| **6:30 AM** | Wakes Up<br>Makes Coffee<br>Gets Newspaper<br>Awakens Husband<br>Makes Breakfast | | | |
| **6:45** | " " | Gets Coffee<br>Reads Paper<br>" " | | |
| **7:00** | Awakens Kids | | | |
| | **EATS BREAKFAST** | **EATS BREAKFAST** | **EATS BREAKFAST** | **EATS BREAKFAST** |
| | Reads Paper<br>Does Dishes<br>Dresses | Dresses<br>Leaves for Work | Dresses<br>" | Dresses<br>Reads |
| | | | **DRIVES TO SCHOOL** | **RIDES TO SCHOOL** |
| **7:45** | Makes Bed | | | |
| **8:00** | Straightens House | | | |
| **10:00** | Drives to Mother's House<br>COFFEE WITH MOTHER<br>ERRANDS WITH MOTHER | AT WORK | AT SCHOOL | AT SCHOOL |
| **11:45** | LUNCH AT RESTAURANT WITH MOTHER<br>GROCERY SHOPPING WITH MOTHER<br>DROPS MOTHER OFF | | | |
| **2:00 PM** | Watches TV | | **DRIVES HOME**<br>Puts Laundry Away<br>Watches TV | **RIDES HOME**<br>Changes Clothes<br>Shoots Baskets<br>Reads Sports Magazine<br>" " " "<br>" " " "<br>" " " " |
| **2:30** | Does Laundry | | | |
| **4:00** | Iron Clothes | | | |
| **4:15** | Sorts Laundry | | | |
| **4:30** | | Drives Home | | |
| **5:00** | Phones Friend | Greets Family<br>Has Drink | | |
| | **PREPARES DINNER** | | **PREPARES DINNER** | |

M O R N I N G

D A Y T I M E

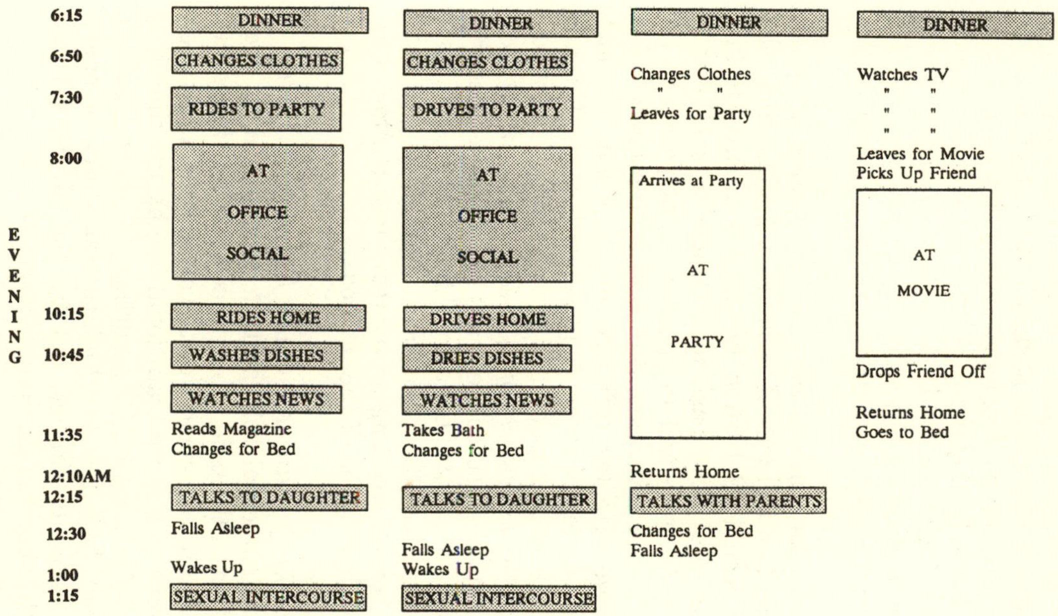

Figure content — timeline chart, "A day in the life of the Shaw family."

|  | | | | |
|---|---|---|---|---|
| 6:15 | DINNER | DINNER | DINNER | DINNER |
| 6:50 | CHANGES CLOTHES | CHANGES CLOTHES | Changes Clothes | Watches TV<br>"<br>"<br>" |
| 7:30 | RIDES TO PARTY | DRIVES TO PARTY | Leaves for Party | Leaves for Movie<br>Picks Up Friend |
| 8:00 | AT<br>OFFICE<br>SOCIAL | AT<br>OFFICE<br>SOCIAL | Arrives at Party<br>AT<br>PARTY | AT<br>MOVIE |
| E V E N I N G — 10:15 | RIDES HOME | DRIVES HOME | Returns Home | Drops Friend Off |
| 10:45 | WASHES DISHES | DRIES DISHES | TALKS WITH PARENTS | Returns Home<br>Goes to Bed |
| | WATCHES NEWS | WATCHES NEWS | Changes for Bed<br>Falls Asleep | |
| 11:35 | Reads Magazine<br>Changes for Bed | Takes Bath<br>Changes for Bed | | |
| 12:10AM | TALKS TO DAUGHTER | TALKS TO DAUGHTER | | |
| 12:15 | Falls Asleep | Falls Asleep | | |
| 12:30 | | Wakes Up | | |
| 1:00 | Wakes Up | | | |
| 1:15 | SEXUAL INTERCOURSE | SEXUAL INTERCOURSE | | |

FIGURE 1.1. A day in the life of the Shaw family.

to draw conclusions about the spouses' individual and overlapping behavioral fields from what happens during a single day. Gail may rarely visit with her mother, and this may be one of the few times Paul and Gail have attended an office party together. To portray a marriage or family group reliably, it is necessary to sample their activities over a representative time period. The ideal length of the sampling period depends on the frequency with which the events of interest occur and on the level of detail sought (see Robins, Chapter 2, this volume). Activities that are frequent and consistent across days and weeks can be summarized reliably with just a few days of sampling, whereas infrequent events may require extensive sampling.

Huston and his colleagues devised a daily phone interview schedule to describe key features of spouses' individual and joint behavioral fields (Huston, 1989; Huston, Robins, Atkinson, & McHale, 1987). The procedure provides a basis for characterizing (1) *instrumental role patterns* (as reflected in spouses' participation in the paid labor force and their involvement in household-related work), (2) marital *companionship* (as reflected in the event to which spouses engage in activities together, converse with each other, and the affective tone of their time together), and (3) spouses' individual and joint *involvement with members of their social network*, particularly friends and kin. The procedure was used to gather descriptions of a large sample of couples' behavioral fields at three points in time—as newlyweds, after they had been married a year, and shortly after their second wedding anniversary (see Huston et al., 1987, for a detailed description of the method).

### Illustration: Describing Paul and Gail's Behavioral Fields

Paul and Gail's instrumental role pattern, as indexed by their relative participation in the paid labor force and their individual and joint involvement in household work, evolved from a relatively untraditional pattern to a more traditional one by the time they had been married for 2 years. The vertices of the triangle in Figure 1.2 represent the extent to which responsibility for household work was primarily carried out by the husband (right corner), the wife (left corner), or done together (the apex).[3]

---

[3]This characterization is based on actual data taken from a couple who seemed to be moving toward a pattern much like that of Paul and Gail Shaw. This couple was chosen not only because it is easy to imagine Paul and Gail's earlier marital lifestyle going through similar transitions but also because the available data allow us to consider hypotheses concerning how valences and barriers are reflected in marital patterns.

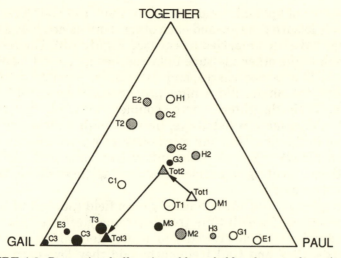

**FIGURE 1.2.** Proportional allocation of household tasks over three time points. The arrows connecting the totals across the three times show the shift in the proportional involvement of Paul and Gail in the household work. The more frequently performed tasks were increasingly performed by Gail rather than Paul. (The larger the symbol, the more frequently the task was performed.) Key: C, child care; E, errands; G, grocery shopping; H, handyman, repairs; M, meal preparation; O, other, miscellaneous; T, tidy house, clean; Tot, total; 1,2,3, wave of data collection.

The pattern shows how changes in Gail's work roles interrelate with changes in the allocation of household work between the spouses (Paul works full time throughout all three waves of data collection). As a newlywed, Gail works part time while she is a student finishing her undergraduate degree. The balance of household work is tilted toward Paul, who carries out half again as many tasks as Gail. The pattern changes somewhat over the first year. Gail has joined Paul as a full-time employee, and the division of tasks is closer to equal, although Gail now performs a slightly higher percentage of the housework than Paul. A large increase has occurred in the proportion of the housework done by the spouses together (role sharing). It is worth noting that Paul and Gail perform fewer household tasks each year (only about 60% as many 2 years into marriage as when they were newlyweds). By their second wedding anniversary, Gail is no longer employed outside the home, having left the labor force 3 months earlier, just before their daughter was born. Gail now carries out nearly three-quarters of the household work on her own; the couple rarely does any of this work together.

In terms of spousal *companionship*, Paul and Gail have centered their leisure time around each other, both as newlyweds and after they have been married a year (see Figure 1.3). The centrality of each to the other's leisure field reaches its apex 1 year into marriage. This period corresponds, it will be recalled, with the time when the Shaws did a high proportion of household work together. Their daughter's birth, coupled with the changes in marital role patterns noted above, brought with it a considerable reduction in the time Gail and Paul pursued leisure together as a couple; it almost seems as if the infant has come physically between them, creating a barrier that resists their doing things together as a pair.

The *affective tone* of the Shaws' group field (pursuit of activities together) shifts with time from extremely affectionate (even by the standards of newlyweds) to moderately affectionate. As newlyweds, Paul and Gail frequently said they love each other, and they engaged in sex an average of more than once a day. Two years later, Paul's expressed affection toward Gail changed to where he was affectionate about half as often as when they were newlyweds; Paul's expression of negativity, or displeasure, toward Gail about doubled over the same time period. The frequency of sexual intercourse remained high over the first year, but it declined considerably with parenthood.

We can now turn to the Shaws' involvement with members of their *social network*. Are Gail and Paul more connected with kin or with friends? Judging from their leisure patterns (see Figure 1.3), the Shaws spend more than twice as much time with kin than friends. During the first 2 years of marriage, Paul individually and the spouses as a pair were considerably more often involved with kin than with friends. Gail rarely pursued leisure outside her marriage until after she became a mother, and then she averaged more than an hour and a half a day with kin and friends, with the time balanced somewhat toward kin. Paul's own leisure time receded considerably with time. Indeed, once the Shaws became parents, Paul's leisure away from the nuclear family withered away to almost nothing.

## Interpretation

We have considerable additional information about Gail and Paul with which to interpret their behavioral patterns and to speculate about why they changed over the course of the first 2 years of their marriage (see Huston, 1989). Gail and Paul entered marriage much in love with each other, Paul having somewhat less tradi-

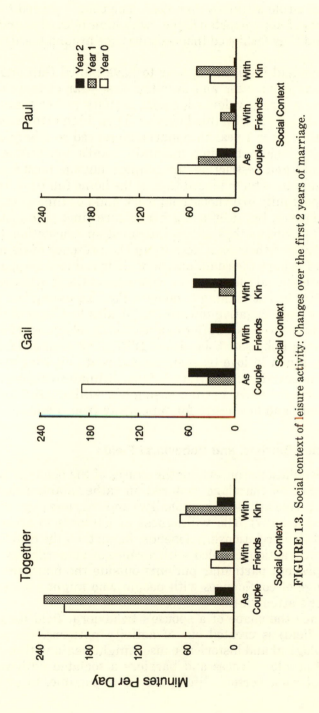

FIGURE 1.3. Social context of leisure activity: Changes over the first 2 years of marriage.

tional sex-role attitudes than Gail. The couple shared two leisure interests of key importance (i.e., watching television and socializing), and they fashioned their leisure time around these two activities.

Love and eroticism appear to have pulled Gail and Paul together as newlyweds and over the first year of their marriage, creating a strong valence for joint activity rather than activities pursued alone or with third parties. Their high involvement in the paid labor force 1 year into marriage served as a barrier around the relationship, helping maintain Paul's involvement in the household and restricting the couple's outside leisure activities. The daughter's birth placed Gail in the home full time, increasing her opportunity to do household work and her time to visit friends and relatives, but decreasing her leisure time with just her husband. The Shaws thus settled into a rather conventional lifestyle, with much of their joint activity in the presence of their child or others. Perhaps the combination of their reduced companionship, their traditional roles, and the centering of Gail's attention around the infant had something to do with Paul becoming less affectionate and more negative toward Gail. Gail's low level of negativity may have served as a buffer against the development of a negative spiral (see Robinson & Jacobson, 1987). The spouses, nonetheless, remain much in love by their second wedding anniversary. But Paul's negativity, if continued, may ultimately reduce Gail's attraction to the marriage, increasing her willingness to reciprocate negativity and her desire for time away from Paul.

### Valences, Barriers, and Behavioral Fields

Our speculations concerning the causes of the behavioral patterns in the Shaws' marriage centered on rather stable valences (e.g., love, sex-role attitudes, personality) and barriers (e.g., work roles, birth of a baby). The willingness of partners to erect barriers around their relationship depends, in part, on the development of strong attraction, coupled with a sense of vulnerability. Barriers often prevent particular pursuits outside the marriage (e.g., the exchange of confidences with people who might compete for the partner's attention).

Since the shape of a spouse's behavioral field (or a couple's group field) is created out of activity patterns, the search for psychological and historical causes might begin with a consideration of stable valences and barriers associated with various regions of each person's life space. It is possible, in principle, to follow a particular couple over time, gathering information about valences, barriers, and the spouses' individual and overlapping behavioral fields. Thus we might discover that changes in valences associated with regions of the life-space, and the placement or removal of barriers, alter spouses' individual and overlapping behavioral fields. Cross-sectional analyses could examine how variations in the characteristics of the spouses (e.g., their sex-role attitudes or their love toward each other) and the circumstances surrounding the relationship (e.g., work roles, parenthood) bear on the structure of their individual and joint behavioral field. Such a strategy would not examine valences and barriers directly, but it would focus on how personality, values, and role commitments come to be reflected in behavioral fields. The success of such research hinges on whether it focuses properly on qualities that pertain to the valences and barriers associated with the relevant behavioral field.

## Illustration: Gender-Related Dispositions and Behavioral Fields

Normative rules for male and female social roles, and for men's "masculinity" and women's "femininity," presumably lie beneath the surface of "traditional" marital behavior patterns (Peplau, 1983). The connection between the psychological attributes of marriage partners and their marital behavior patterns, however, has rarely been investigated empirically.

Huston's (1989) study of newlyweds, the PAIR project, examined how spouses' patriarchal attitudes and the extent to which they ascribe stereotypically "masculine" or "feminine" qualities to themselves come to be reflected in the development of traditional marital activity patterns. People who describe themselves as stereotypically masculine (instrumental) do not tend to disavow also being stereotypically feminine (expressive), and vice versa. Moreover, neither "masculinity" nor "femininity" correlates with sex-role attitudes (Spence & Helmreich, 1978).

The right-hand side of Table 1.1 summarizes how newlyweds' sex-role attitudes (patriarchal to egalitarian) and their self-descriptions as "masculine" or "feminine" bear on marital activity fields (Atkinson & Huston, 1984; Huston, 1989). Gender-related attitudes and identities exert a strong influence on marital patterns. For instance, spouses with patriarchal values, who ascribe to themselves stereotypically appropriate qualities (and deny those qualities identified with the other gender) tend to establish a traditional marital pattern. The more patriarchal the spouses'

**TABLE 1.1.** Gender Constructs and Marital Behavior Patterns

| Attribute | Gender-related construct | Illustrations | Association of attributes with behavior patterns |
|---|---|---|---|
| **Values** | | | |
| Sex-role attitudes | Patriarchal vs. egalitarian | "The decisions about what is best for a community should be left in the hands of men" | The more spouses' attitudes tend toward egalitarianism, the less unequal the distribution of household labor and the less household work is divided along traditional lines; moreover, egalitarian spouses perform household tasks less frequently. The less patriarchal the husbands, the more central their wives are to leisure time usage; the more wives subscribe to patriarchal values, the more leisure time they spend with kin. |
| **Personality** | | | |
| Expressive | Stereotypically feminine | Emotional, gentle, helpful, warm | The higher husbands and wives are in expressivity, the more central they are to each other's leisure; husbands high in expressivity carry out a higher proportion of household work; the higher husbands and wives are in expressivity, the more affectionate they are with each other; wives who are highly expressive are less negative toward their husbands; wives spend less time pursuing leisure with friends if they and/or their husbands are expressive. |
| Instrumental | Stereotypically masculine | Independent, makes decisions easily, stands up well under pressure | Husbands high in instrumentality spend less leisure time with their wives and more with friends. |

*Note.* The personality measures and sex-role attitudes scale used were developed by Spence and Helmreich (1978); the information concerning behavior patterns is based on phone interview data drawn from the first wave of Huston's longitudinal study of newlyweds.

sex-role attitudes, the less household work crosses traditional gender boundaries. Sex-role attitudes are also evident in the propensity of husbands to make their wives central to their leisure pursuits and in wives' tendency to spend leisure time with kin. Spouses low in expressivity (in traditional femininity) tend to keep their feelings to themselves. Husbands high in instrumentality (traditional masculinity) tend to pursue leisure more frequently with friends and less often with their wives.

The diversity of gender-related attitudes and identities has produced a variety of marital patterns, reducing the prominence of the traditional pattern. This was recently shown by our analysis of PAIR Project data (Johnson, Huston, Levinger, & Gaines, 1989), in which four distinct marital patterns were identified after 2 years of marriage: (1) a traditionally sex-typed "parallel" pattern in which the husband was the main breadwinner, the wife in charge at home, and their recreation fairly separate; (2) a "symmetrical" pattern in which the spouses were nearly equally involved in work outside the home and in leisure activities with kin and friends, household task performance was minimally sex-typed, but spouses did few leisure activities together; (3) a "differentiated–companionate" pattern, intermediate between the parallel and symmetrical marriages in instrumental-role differentiation, but with more leisure-time companionship than either of the first two groups; and (4) a "role-reversed" pattern, usually the wife's temporary or permanent greater employability or the husband's physical disability. The first two configurations were the most common.

Any particular marriage may, over the course of time, move from one to another such pattern. For example, Paul and Gail Shaw changed from a relatively symmetrical pattern before the birth of their children to a differentiated-companionate pattern.

## MICROBEHAVIORAL PROCESSES IN MARRIAGE

Molar activities are made up of microbehavioral events. Any of the social activities carried out by a married couple can be put under a microscope and examined in detail. Such microscopic analyses of single episodes have been a primary focus of research on marriage by clinical psychologists interested in comparing communication in distressed couples with that in happily married pairs (see Weiss & Heyman, Chapter 3, this volume).

Figure 1.4 (adapted from Huston, 1983) takes us to the early evening of the Shaws' day portrayed in Figure 1.1. Paul and Gail are now in their middle years. Paul, at 41, is now an upwardly mobile sales manager in a large company. Gail, 39, has not worked outside the home since the birth of their first child but, with Paul's encouragement, has recently started to think about a new career.

Paul and Gail are in their bedroom getting ready to go to a party at Paul's office. Gail thinks mainly about wearing something cheerful and comfortable; the bright yellow sundress with its open back seems appropriate to her on this warm, late-summer evening. When Paul sees Gail take her yellow dress out of the closet, however, he thinks back to the last party when she wore it, where he heard admiring comments and also some muffled whistles. Gail's easy manner and good looks are attractive to men, and she enjoys their attention. He decides to dissuade her from wearing the sundress.

Gail first cannot understand Paul's objections. Then she begins to suspect he wants to keep her on a tight rein and in the background. This idea upsets her. At the same time, she believes that now is not the time to make a scene, and so she does what he asks. Gail notes that Paul appears to take her compliance for granted; he does not even acknowledge it with a thank you. This adds to her "put-upon" feeling, but she does not reveal how she feels, at least not for the moment.

Paul's success in getting Gail to change dresses transforms his uncomfortable feelings to a pleasant sense of self-assurance; at the same time, Gail's state changes from relaxation to mild distress. Paul has dominated Gail, but his success also has created ill feelings. If we assume that this scene continues patterns that began early in the Shaws' marriage, we would expect that Gail has developed some negative feelings toward Paul and that she sometimes avoids him. Several studies suggest that a history of negative interaction creates marital dissatisfaction that, in turn, creates a tendency for spouses to reduce leisure time together (e.g., Huston, 1989; also see Weiss & Heyman, Chapter 3, this volume).

## Behavior and Meaning

The behavior enacted in this episode is "meaningful" in that it reflects Paul's and Gail's assumptions, beliefs, and attitudes about each other and, moreover, produces cognitive and affective consequences. Behavioral coding schemes inevitably describe "behavior" in terms of actual or presumed consequences. Paul's assertion, "You really should wear your blue outfit," for example, can be

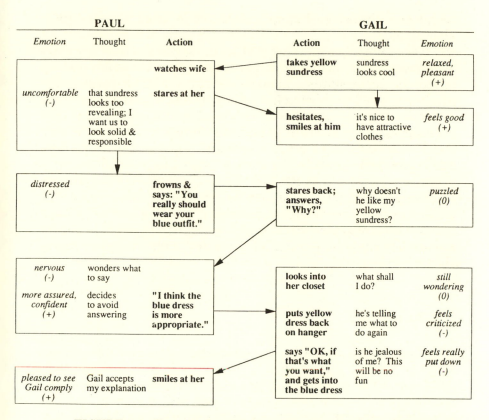

**FIGURE 1.4.** Illustration of an interchange between Paul and Gail.

seen as reflecting his own prerogatives. These prerogatives, in turn, may be anchored in paternalistic values reinforced by his role as the breadwinner. Gail's returning the yellow dress to the hanger in favor of the blue dress might be coded as "compliance," but the negative affect generated during the episode points to a noncompliant attitude.

Scholars studying cognitive–affective processes that accompany interaction have focused primarily on the connections among attribution, emotion, and marital satisfaction (see Baucom, Epstein, Sayers, & Sher, 1989; Bradbury & Fincham, 1990) rather than on the linkage between the motivational systems of the actors and what happens when they interact. The interaction between Gail and Paul, for example, provides clues about their relative *status* and *solidarity* (actual and desired), two dimensions of universal significance to human relationships (e.g., Carson, 1965; Leary, 1957).

It is commonly suggested that status-seeking actions are complemented by status-giving responses and that a couple's *complementarity* on the status dimension creates a feeling of relational equilibrium and well-being (e.g., Carson, 1965). At the same time, it is also reasonable to believe that *equality* is of great importance "in cooperative relations in which the fostering . . . of enjoyable social relations is a primary emphasis" (Deutsch, 1975, p. 146). The interaction shown in Figure 1.4 illustrates a complementary behavioral pattern, with Paul's "directive" assented to by Gail, but it also suggests that Gail does not feel good about the exchange. To understand the exchange, it is necessary to delve deeper into the compatibility of actors' motives and goals than is usually done by researchers studying microlevel processes in marriage (Shaver & Hazan, 1985).

## COMPATIBILITY

Although marital compatibility is displayed in specific interactions in the present, it is grounded in the spouses' individual and joint pasts and is realized in the future of their relationship. From the standpoint of Lewin's field theory, a compatible couple is one in which both partners' valences and barriers serve to build and maintain their relationship, where both the individual and the joint pulls and pushes are congruent with a couple's total well-being.

Compatibility is *the capacity to exist together in harmony.* Two partners are "compatible" if they have shown evidence of this capacity through their harmonious behavior in a variety of circumstances and when they feel comfortably attuned to each other (Berscheid, 1985b; Levinger & Rands, 1985). Overt compatibility can be defined as "the ratio of facilitating to interfering events between Person and Other" (Levinger & Rands, 1985, p. 311). Either partner's actions, or lack thereof, may either facilitate, interfere with, or have no effect at all on the other's goal achievement. Pairs with high facilitation/interference ratios generally promote one another's aims, whereas those with low ratios often fail to do so. Nevertheless, overt appearances of harmony can mask covert feelings of strain or suffering.

Several things should be noted. First, compatibility is multifaceted, not unidimensional. A couple may be highly facilitative in some areas of their life (e.g., in their recreational behavior) and not in other areas (e.g., in their housework or in disciplining their children). Furthermore, what helps one partner may hinder the other. For example, a husband who gives his wife overly detailed driving instructions for delivering a package to a friend's home may ensure that she gets there, but may make her feel belittled and patronized.

Second, the areas of incompatibility in a marriage can vary widely in importance and in ease of resolution. As Braiker and Kelley (1979) have suggested, conflicts can vary from the very specific to the very general. Specific "behavioral" differences may be easiest to discuss or resolve, whereas "normative" and "personality" differences are more difficult to deal with. For example, two partners may differ behaviorally about how they make a bed or fold sheets, rather simple topics for adjustment. At the normative level, they may differ in their standards about how much or what kind of housework the husband and wife should do, or about what each considers "clean" or "neat"; such differences take longer to identify and are harder to resolve. At the personality level, two spouses may differ in tempo (e.g., one quick and spontaneous, the other slow and cautious), in feelings of security and insecurity, or in the need for sociability; such dispositional sources of conflict are especially difficult to deal with.

Third, compatibility is not necessarily "good" in itself. Although incompatibility can be a source of stress, it does not therefore follow that spouses should typically sacrifice their own goals in order to further those of their partner. Berscheid (1985b, p. 158) has suggested that relationships can be *both* "compatible" and "unhealthy" (e.g., relationships between drug addicts who help maintain each other's chemical dependencies). A pair may get along well in the short run, but one or both individual members may be traveling toward disaster. All close relationships have some degree of tension between a pair's total welfare and each partner's individual well-being, an opposition between mutuality and individuation. Maximizing a couple's mutuality may submerge one or both spouses' personal well-being.

Finally, there is no necessary correlation between a pair's compatibility and its closeness. Pairs who have little interdependence often appear highly compatible as long as neither partner places important demands on the relationship, and as long as neither explores the range of their unresolved problems. But as their interaction increases in frequency, intensity, and diversity, partners inevitably encounter unanticipated areas of friction.

Often partners develop a relationship without sampling many areas of incompatibility. If they commit themselves to the relationship after limited experience, they are likely later to find unresolved conflicts that, at best, require their attention and, at worst, continue to remain unresolvable. For example, a woman may be attracted to a man after she discovers he strongly favors the Equal Rights Amendment and sex equity in the workplace, and she may assume that these sentiments will generalize to their entire relationship. After they start living together, however, she discovers that his concern with equality does not extend to certain important areas of their relationship (e.g., housework).

The concept of compatibility has many facets. The compatibility of any given relationship may be a riddle wrapped in an enigma, to be unpackaged only after years of testing and broad experience.

## Determinants of Marital Compatibility

What leads two spouses to be compatible with one another? We may attribute their harmony mainly to personal or to environmental qualities—a meshing of the partners' own prior *personal qualities*, traceable to dispositional similarities or complementarities that already existed at their first meeting or to an *environment* that provides support rather than disruption of their interconnections. They can also be attributed to their development of a viable mutual *relationship*, with a history of open discussion and successful joint problem solving.

### Personal Determinants

Compatibility used to be conceived in terms of combinations of fixed personal characteristics, or of basic needs and dispositions, as in need complementarity (e.g., Winch, 1958) and similarity theories (e.g., Byrne, 1969) of relationships. But such theories were poor predictors of actual relational development in long-term relationships (see Levinger & Rands, 1985). For one thing, they failed to consider a couple's macrocontext and to specify linkages between partners' personal qualities and their specific interactional connections. They also failed to specify the domains where complementarity or similarity is most conducive to harmony and mutual satisfaction. For example, the fit between a passive–receptive and an active–dominant spouse would be *psychologically* compatible, but if the first spouse is male and the second is female, it may create problems in their relationship with kin or colleagues; that is, it may be incompatible with their social environment (Kerckhoff, 1974).

Beyond that, these theories have failed to consider temporal changes in people's dispositions, in their environments, or in the demands of their relationship. For example, the traditional role division a couple assumed in a 1960s environment can become unsatisfying for the same wife or husband in the 1980s. Or a couple's religious differences, which both spouses tolerated early in their marriage may become a source of distress when their children become old enough for religious education. Thus, in trying to predict pair harmony, approaches to compatibility that emphasize personal dispositions have generally failed to account for more than a small portion of the variance (e.g., Kerckhoff, 1974; Levinger, 1983).

It is possible, of course, that some personality types will be congenial partners regardless of whom they might be paired with, whereas others will cause difficulty for any potential mate (Kelly & Conley, 1987). Some people are *characteristically* generous, friendly, and accepting (e.g., Epstein & Feist, 1988) and thus generally easier to get along with than people who are miserly, reclusive, and insecure. But despite recent personological findings on the importance of a *secure* "attachment style" for maintaining satisfying love relationships (e.g., Shaver, Hazan, & Bradshaw, 1988), there is no solid evidence showing that certain clearly definable personality types have more harmonious marriages than certain other types.

## Environmental Determinants

Psychological analyses of marital compatibility rarely acknowledge the crucial importance of a couple's environment for either bolstering or diminishing marital harmony. It is probably less clear that the environment facilitates harmony than that it can severely *disrupt* it. Either the distal environment (e.g., bad economic or housing conditions, social values of faithlessness, or pressures for high social and geographic mobility) or a couple's proximal environment (e.g., antagonistic relatives, loss of a job, a commuter marriage, or the disruption of supportive family networks) can interfere markedly with the relationship.

In contrast, an environment that supports both individuals and their marriage relationship would include the following features. First, it would contain an accessible network of family and friends who are helpful in thinking through relationship problems and supportive of the marriage. Second, the spouses' occupations would be mutually facilitative, or at least noninterfering. Having one spouse be the (externally oriented) breadwinner and the other the (internally oriented) homemaker was the traditional solution, but today's dual-career spouses find new structural solutions for complementing each other's efforts and availability. Along with that, the couple's economic resources would exceed its economic demands, ensuring that their relationship is not overwhelmed by financial pressures.

### Relational Determinants

Knowledge of only the partners' personalities and their external environment is insufficient for predicting how harmoniously they will live together. It is also necessary to know how their association has transformed their joint life-space, that is, the internal environment of the relationship. In what ways has their psychological relationship changed as a consequence of their interaction patterns? How well do they coordinate their mutual actions, thoughts, and feelings?

The marital activity fields discussed earlier are also instances of relational constructions. Here one can ask two complementary questions relating to how harmoniously the couple functions as a unit. How well does the pattern satisfy the partners' own individual goals? How well do the partners coordinate their activities to minimize interference? The answers to both questions are important for predicting the long-term fate of a marriage.

### Illustration: Compatibility in the Shaws' Marriage

Let us return to the Shaws. When they first knew each other, Paul and Gail were highly satisfied, and they manifested considerable harmony. They enjoyed similar movies and both liked hanging out with the same crowd of friends. They loved talking with each other, and, in general, they had similarly sociable, "laid-back" personalities.

Furthermore, after Paul and Gail announced their engagement, their environment was supportive. Their families and nearest friends were glad to see Paul and Gail marry. Paul and Gail also had few problems in developing compatible work and family roles at the beginning of their marriage; both accepted the conventional idea that Gail should work until they had children, after which Paul would have responsibility for providing economically, and she would be responsible for their home and most of the child care. Over the years the Shaws' economic situation became increasingly comfortable, and they are now able to pay for vacations and other extras without worrying about overspending their budget.

The couple has been compatible in various areas of their relationship. Despite their relatively conventional division of labor, Paul has long taken responsibility for chores such as grocery shopping or straightening the kitchen. He has also taken an interest in the children and has been responsive to Gail's friends and relatives. Gail, on the other hand, has been a success as a wife and mother and an enjoyable companion. Despite these areas of compatibility, though, their mutual support recently has been limited to mainly the sphere of satisfactory role performance and less to the sharing of feelings and of leisure time.

Gail has come to believe that something has been missing emotionally. She has tried to put it aside until recently, but she has become increasingly dissatisfied with the quality of their communication. (Paul is still largely unaware of her dissatisfaction.) Gail feels that, since their children were small, Paul has often treated her more as his *image* of a good wife and helpmate than as a unique person in her own right. Paul, for his part, has encouraged Gail to get a job outside the home, anticipating that she would want a career of her own once the children have been raised. Gail has recently decided to seek work outside the home, even though she enjoys being the hub of day-to-day family life. The marriage has therefore reached an important transition point, one that will require psychological and behavioral adaptation for both Paul and Gail.

## Styles of Dealing with Incompatibility

Some couples experience many occasions of disharmony, others encounter few. Pairs in which the partners' goals differ greatly find cooperation more costly than those in which their goals and interests are mutually promotive. But even the most harmonious pair faces situations, or even whole areas in their relationship, in which the spouses' interests differ. A couple's style for dealing with conflicts has implications for the future of the relationship; thus compatibility is tied to a pair's problem-solving style.

Some sources of conflict, especially those that derive from two stable personalities or an unyielding environment, are nearly immutable. They are likely to inspire tolerance or evasion. More active forms of dealing with differences include contentiousness (pushing one's own interests), compromise (settling for halfway solutions), or vigorous attempts at collaboration to find the best joint benefit.

Pruitt and Rubin (1985) have proposed a "dual concern model," which suggests that response to a conflict is driven by some combination of concerns for one's own and for the other's outcomes. The model suggests that low assertiveness reflects low concern with one's own outcomes and results either in *avoiding* or in *yielding* behavior, depending on one's concern with the *other's* outcomes. High assertiveness, on the other hand, indicates high concern with own outcomes and can be displayed by either *contending*, win-at-all-costs conduct or by *collaborative* attempts at joint problem resolution, depending once again on one's concern with the other's interests. *Compromise* (sometimes erroneously equated with joint problem solving) falls somewhere between avoidance and collaboration, or between yielding to a partner and pushing only one's own interests (see Thomas, 1976).

### Consequences of Differing Styles of Conflict Resolution

Avoiding the discussion of a difference may result in its persistence. Some differences (e.g., in styles of setting a table or of scrubbing pots) can be ignored with little harm; such trivial problems often cost more to confront than to overlook. On the other hand, habitual conflict avoidance is likely to produce unresolved tensions. Furthermore, it is often hard to know what is a minor and what is a major difference, so that a history of avoidance may leave partners unprepared for dealing with truly important issues.

Yielding to the other may be a useful style when a person is unsure, wants to show reasonableness, wants to build up credits for later getting his or her own way on more important issues, or wishes at all costs to preserve harmony. On the other hand, if yielding becomes chronic, respect is apt to be lost and the opportunity for future influence reduced (Pruitt, 1981; Thomas, 1976). In other words, used in moderation, giving in to the other can preserve harmony and elicit reciprocity. Used to excess, yielding can lead a person to be treated as a doormat and promote the other's contending style.

Contending is, of course, the opposite of yielding. It is assertive and uncooperative, oriented toward winning one's own outcomes regardless of the other's outcomes, and aiming for control over the situation. It may be suitable in emergencies, when decisive action must be taken quickly, or when one wants to demonstrate strength. On the other hand, it can lead to two kinds of undesirable consequences, the escalation of the conflict or the suppression of opposing points of view.

Compromising is more assertive than avoidance or yielding, and more cooperative than avoidance or contention, but it is an intermediate strategy. Compromising means splitting the difference, meeting the other halfway. It is often an expedient tactic, but it is rarely creative and often fails to do justice to both parties' underlying interests.

Collaborating to resolve a problem jointly is the principal way to go beyond a zero-sum conception of an interpersonal conflict. It entails searching for the issues that each partner cares most about and finding an integrative solution that appeals to both. The aim is to integrate one's own objectives with those of the other, to arrive at a settlement that is better than merely splitting the difference (Pruitt, 1981). The advantages of integrative problem solving are its creativeness and the high mutual acceptability of its results. Its disadvantages are the time it takes and the possibility that no alternative can be found that clearly benefits both partners more than a simple compromise.

The five styles here enumerated are strategic choices rather than directly observable behaviors. In contrast to the behavior-observational focus of clinical researchers who study marital conflict in controlled settings (see Weiss & Heyman, Chapter 3, this volume), the dual-concern model attends as much to spouses' underlying positions as to their overt actions. In other words, it focuses on each partner's underlying goals or wants (or valences) and tries then to connect those goals to their actions.


## TRANSFORMATIONS

Borden and Levinger (1990) have identified three broad categories of interpersonal adaptation to differences in close relationships on a continuum from (1) situational conformity through (2) relationship-oriented accommodation, and (3) relationship-transcendent dispositional change. These three categories parallel Kelman's (1958) three basic processes of social influence: compliance, identification, and internalization.

Situational conformity parallels the "yielding" style of resolving conflicts. It means going along with another pragmatically, but without changing one's own behavioral preferences. For example, a husband puts away his clothes neatly in order to please his wife but for no other reason. Here public compliance occurs without private change, as when we agree to do things despite our wishes to the contrary. Such adaptations are highly dependent on the other's presence. If the other person should leave, our actions or attitudes revert to their former condition.

Relationship-oriented accommodation is longer lasting and reflects significant adaptations in one's feelings or preferences to match those of one's partner. The more we care for our partner, the greater our tendency to transform our valences. Kelley (1979) has called this a "transformation of motivation." For example, the above husband would begin to enjoy folding his clothes before putting them away, because he knows his wife values neatness and his actions show his love for her. If the relationship deteriorates, however, the impetus for this form of adaptation weakens or disappears. In other words, like Kelman's process of identification, change that results from motivational transformations depends on the continuing significance of the relationship.

Dispositional changes are the third form of adaptation. They require much more time to develop, but they become independent of the continued existence of the relationship. The above-mentioned husband would enjoy neatness for its own sake; it would become his personal preference regardless of his feelings for his wife.

All three processes reduce the occasion for conflict in a marriage by altering the valences or barriers that exist in one or both spouses' life-space. Situational conformity entails only short-term changes in a person's valences to take into account current demands. Motivational transformation implies a more continuing alteration in one's goals or values, but the stability of that change depends on the durability of a caring relationship. Dispositional transformations signify long-term stable changes in one's valences, leading to a long-term convergence in the individual spouses' goals, interests, or behavior patterns.[4] On theoretical grounds, we believe that both motivational and dispositional transformations operate in long-term intimate relationships so as to reduce the emergence of conflicts. However, it is exceedingly difficult to demonstrate such conflict-preemptive transformations *empirically*; to do so, one would need to conduct lengthy longitudi-

---

[4]The fact that Kelly's (1955) longitudinal study of marriages failed to find evidence of such convergence, in *personality traits*, does not weaken our hypothesis. Far sharper measures over a far wider range of *changeable* attributes, especially in personal preferences and personal styles, are needed to test the hypothesis adequately.

nal studies of long-term relationships—beginning before intimacy develops and covering a multitude of valent topics—and to collect repeated measures of each partner's styles and preferences.

Positive motivational and dispositional transformations imply a history of caring for one's partner, a concern about the other's outcomes. Such motivational transformations can benefit a marriage by directly demonstrating one's concern, showing flexibility and willingness to embrace the spouse's wants. Convergent dispositional transformations, in contrast, are hypothesized to bring partners together, gradually and imperceptibly over a period of months or years, through a change in their underlying valences and styles.

## CONCLUSION

This chapter has focused on the social psychology of marriage by building on Kurt Lewin's (1940/1948) early social psychological analysis. Our own examination has highlighted both personal and structural factors that influence marriages, and it has focused both on specific time-bound interactions and on broader, more enduring patterns. Following Lewin, we have tried to strike a balance between individual and relational concerns, between the life-spaces of individual spouses and the joint spaces of the couple as a whole.

From our perspective, the central characteristic of the marriage relationship is its interdependence, as suggested by Lewin 50 years ago. In American marriages, this interdependence is not only sexual and economic but also emotional and communicational. It is built and maintained through the partners' mutual attraction and goal-directed behavior (as guided by their valences) and reinforced by the social and family structures (barriers) associated with their mutual commitment.

We have built on Lewin's concept of the behavioral field to show how it operates in actual marriages as they develop over time. Spotlighting one illustrative couple, both early and later in their marital history, we have scrutinized their interaction and their activity patterns, looking at their division of work, their pursuit of leisure, and their emotional interplay.

We should emphasize that there is no single "best" way of viewing a marital relationship. Psychologists will generally focus on the behavioral specifics of observable interaction and will often ignore the wider sociocultural context. Sociologists, in contrast, are likely to emphasize the external context and pay less heed to behavioral interactions. As social psychologists, we have focused on both sets of variables and have privided some details for pursuing a field-theoretic point of view. On the one hand, we have emphasized the importance of studying interactive sequences, as has often been done by behavioral researchers with a clinical psychology orientation. On the other hand, our field-theoretic viewpoint draws attention to more molar behavioral fields, or activity patterns, and to the needs and goals that guide each partner's actions, foci that are often neglected by behavioral researchers. All such activity occurs, of course, within the larger field consisting of other family members, kin, and the society at large. The psychological understanding of marriage will be enriched from attention to the interplay among all those elements.

# ACKNOWLEDGMENT

We thank Gilbert Geis for his helpful comments on an earlier version of this chapter.

# REFERENCES

Altman, I., & Taylor, D. A. (1973). *Social penetration: The development of interpersonal relationships*. New York: Holt, Rinehart & Winston.

Atkinson, J., & Huston, T. L. (1984). Sex role orientation and division of labor early in marriage. *Journal of Personality and Social Psychology, 41*, 330–345.

Bales, R. F., & Slater, P. E. (1955). Role differentiation in small decision-making groups. In T. Parsons & R. F. Bales (Eds.), *Family, socialization, and interaction process* (pp. 259–306). New York: Free Press.

Baucom, D. H., Epstein, N., Sayers, S., & Sher, T. M. (1989). The role of cognitions in marital relationships: Dysfunctional, methodological, and conceptual issues. *Journal of Consulting and Clinical Psychology, 57*, 31–38.

Bernard, J. (1964). The adjustments of married mates. In H. T. Christensen (Ed.), *Handbook of marriage and the family* (pp. 675–739). Chicago: Rand-McNally.

Berscheid, E. (1985a). Interpersonal attraction. In G. Lindzey & E. Aronson (Eds.), *Handbook of social psychology* (vol. 2, pp. 413–484, 3rd ed.). New York: Random House.

Berscheid, E. (1985b). Compatibility, interdependence, and emotion. In W. Ickes (Ed.), *Compatible and incompatible relationships* (pp. 143–162). New York: Springer-Verlag.

Berscheid, E. (1988). Some comments on love's anatomy: Or, whatever happened to old-fashioned lust? In R. J. Sternberg & M. L. Barnes (Eds.), *The psychology of love* (pp. 359–374). New Haven: Yale University Press.

Berscheid, E., & Campbell, B. (1981). The changing longevity of close relationships: A commentary and forecast. In M. J. Lerner & S. C. Lerner (Eds.), *The justice motive in social behavior*. New York: Plenum.

Berscheid, E., & Walster, E. (1978). *Interpersonal attraction* (2nd ed.). Reading, MA: Addison-Wesley.

Blood, R. O., & Wolfe, D. M. (1960). *Husbands and wives: The dynamics of married living*. New York: Free Press.

Borden, V. H. L., & Levinger, G. (1990). Interpersonal transformations in intimate relationships. In W. H. Jones & D. Perlman (Eds.), *Advances in personal relationships* (vol. 2). London: J. Kingsley Publishers.

Bradbury, T., & Fincham, F. (1990). Attributions in marriage: Review and critique. *Psychological Bulletin, 107*, 3–33.

Braiker, H. B., & Kelley, H. H. (1979). Conflict in the development of close relationships. In R. L. Burgess & T. L. Huston (Eds.), *Social exchange in developing relationships* (pp. 135–168). New York: Academic Press.

Burgess, E. W., & Locke, H. J. (1945). *The family: From institution to companionship*. New York: American.

Byrne, D. (1969). Attitudes and attraction. In L. Berkowitz (Ed.), *Advances in experimental social psychology* (vol. 4, pp. 35–89). New York: Academic Press.

Carson, R. C. (1965). *Interaction concepts of personality*. Chicago: Aldine.

Deutsch, M. (1975). Equity, equality, and need: What determines which value will be used as the basis of distributive justice? *Journal of Social Issues, 31*(3), 137–149.

Epstein, S., & Feist, G. J. (1988). Relation between self-acceptance and other-acceptance and its moderation by identification. *Journal of Personality and Social Psychology, 54*, 309–315.

Gottman, J. M. (1979). *Marital interaction: Experimental investigations*. New York: Academic Press.

Gottman, J. M., & Krokoff, L. J. (1989). Marital interaction and satisfaction: A longitudinal view. *Journal of Consulting and Clinical Psychology, 57*, 47–52.

Herbst, P. G. (1952). The measurement of family relationships. *Human Relations, 5*, 3–35.

Hill, C. T., Rubin, Z., & Peplau, L. A. (1976). Breakups before marriage: The end of 103 affairs. *Journal of Social Issues, 32*(1), 147–167.

Holmes, J. G., & Rempel, J. K. (1989). Trust in close relationships. *Review of Personality and Social Psychology, 10*, 187–220.

Huston, T. L. (1983). Power. In H. H. Kelley, E. Berscheid, A. Christensen, J. H. Harvey, T. L. Huston, G. Levinger, E. McClintock, L. A.Peplau, & D. R. Peterson, *Close relationships* (pp. 169–219). New York: W. H. Freeman.

Huston, T. L. (1989). *When the honeymoon's over: Strain and adaptation in marriage*. Unpublished manuscript.

Huston, T. L., & Burgess, R. L. (1979). Social exchange in developing relationships: An overview. In R. Burgess & T. Huston (Eds.), *Social exchange in developing relationships* (pp. 3–28). New York: Academic Press.

Huston, T. L., & Levinger, G. (1978). Interpersonal attraction and relationships. *Annual Review of Psychology, 29*, 115–156.

Huston, T. L., Robins, E., Atkinson, J., & McHale, S. (1987). Surveying the landscape of marital behavior: A behavioral self-report approach to studying marriage. In S. Oskamp (Ed.), *Family processes and problems: Social psychological aspects* (pp. 45–72). Beverly Hills: Sage.

Huston, T. L., Surra, C., Fitzgerald, N., & Cate, R. (1981). From courtship to marriage: Mate selection as an interpersonal process. In S. Duck & R. Gilmour (Eds.), *Personal relationships (vol. 2): Developing personal relationships* (pp. 53-88). London: Academic Press.

Johnson, M. P. (in press). Commitment to personal relationships. In W. H. Jones & D. Perlman (Eds.), *Advances in personal relationships* (vol. 3). Greenwich, CT: JAI Press.

Johnson, M. P., Huston, T. L., Levinger, G., & Gaines, S. O. (1989). *Patterns of married life*. Unpublished manuscript.

Kelley, H. H. (1979). *Personal relationships: Their structures and processes*. Hillsdale, NJ: Erlbaum.

Kelley, H. H. (1983). Love and commitment. In H. H. Kelley, E. Berscheid, A. Christensen, J. H. Harvey, T. L. Huston, G. Levinger, E. McClintock, L. A. Peplau, & D. R. Peterson, *Close relationships* (pp. 265-314). New York: W. H. Freeman.

Kelley, H. H., Berscheid, E., Christensen, A. Harvey, J. H., Huston, T. L., Levinger, G., McClintock, E., Peplau, L. A., & Peterson, D. R. (1983). *Close relationships*. New York: W. H. Freeman.

Kelly, E. L. (1955). Consistency of the adult personality. *American Psychologist, 10*, 654-681.

Kelly, E. L., & Conley, J. J. (1987). Personality and compatibility: A prospective analysis of marital stability and marital satisfaction. *Journal of Personality and Social Psychology, 52*, 27-40.

Kelman, H. C. (1958). Compliance, identification, and internalization: Three processes of attitude change. *Journal of Conflict Resolution, 2*, 51-60.

Kerckhoff, A. C. (1974). The social context of interpersonal attraction. In T. L. Huston (Ed.), *Foundations of interpersonal attraction* (pp. 61-78). New York: Academic Press.

Leary, T. (1957). *Interpersonal diagnosis of personality*. New York: Ronald Press.

Leeper, R. W. (1943). *Lewin's topological and vector psychology: A digest and a critique*. Eugene: University of Oregon.

Levinger, G. (1964). Note on need complementarity in marriage. *Psychological Bulletin, 61*, 153-157.

Levinger, G. (1965). Marital cohesiveness and dissolution: An integrative review. *Journal of Marriage and the Family, 27*, 19-28.

Levinger, G. (1976). A social psychological perspective on marital dissolution. *Journal of Social Issues, 32*(1), 21-47.

Levinger, G. (1979). A social exchange view on the dissolution of pair relationships. In R. L. Burgess & T. L. Huston (Eds.), *Social exchange in developing relationships* (pp. 169-193). New York: Academic Press.

Levinger, G. (1983). Development and change. In H. H. Kelley, E. Berscheid, A. Christensen, J. H. Harvey, T. L. Huston, G. Levinger, E. McClintock, L. A. Peplau, & D. R. Peterson, *Close relationships* (pp. 315-359). New York: W. H. Freeman.

Levinger, G., & Rands, M. (1985). Compatibility in marriage and other relationships. In W. Ickes (Ed.), *Compatible and incompatible relationships* (pp. 309-332). New York: Springer-Verlag.

Levinger, G., & Senn, D. J. (1967). Disclosure of feelings in marriage. *Merrill-Palmer Quarterly, 13*, 237-249.

Levinger, G., Senn, D. J., & Jorgensen, B. W. (1970). Progress toward permanence in courtship: A test of the Kerckhoff-Davis hypotheses. *Sociometry, 33*, 427-443.

Lewin, K. (1948). The background of conflict in marriage. In G. Lewin (Ed.), *Resolving social conflicts* (pp. 84-102). New York: Harper. (Originally published 1940)

Locke, H. J. (1951). *Predicting adjustment in marriage: A comparison of a divorced and a happily married group.* New York: Holt.

Millar, M. G., & Tesser, A. (1989). The effects of affective-cognitive consistency and thought on the attitude-behavior relation. *Journal of Experimental Social Psychology, 25,* 189-202.

Peplau, L. A. (1983). Roles and gender. In H. H. Kelley, E. Berscheid, A. Christensen, J. H. Harvey, T. L. Huston, G. Levinger, E. McClintock, L. A. Peplau, & D. R. Peterson, *Close relationships* (pp. 220-264). New York: W. H. Freeman.

Peterson, D. R. (1983). Conflict. In H. H. Kelley, E. Berscheid, A. Christensen, J. H. Harvey, T. L. Huston, G. Levinger, E. McClintock, L. A. Peplau, & D. R. Peterson, *Close relationships* (pp. 360-396). New York: W. H. Freeman.

Pruitt, D. G. (1981). *Negotiation behavior.* New York: Academic Press.

Pruitt, D. G., & Rubin, J. Z. (1985). *Social conflict: Escalation, stalemate, and settlement.* New York: Random House.

Rands, M., & Levinger, G. (1979). Implicit theories of relationship: An intergenerational study. *Journal of Personality and Social Psychology, 37,* 645-661.

Raush, H. L., Barry, W. A., Hertel, R. K., & Swain, M. A. (1974). *Communication, conflict, and marriage.* San Francisco: Jossey-Bass.

Raven, B. H., Centers, R., & Rodrigues, A. (1975). The bases of conjugal power. In R. E. Cromwell & D. H. Olson (Eds.), *Power in families* (pp. 216-240). New York: Wiley.

Reis, H. T., & Shaver, P. (1988). Intimacy as an interpersonal process. In S. Duck (Ed.), *Handbook of personal relationships* (pp. 367-389). New York: Wiley.

Robinson, E. A., & Jacobson, N. S. (1987). Social learning theory and family psychopathology: A Kantian model of behaviorism. In T. Jacob (Ed.), *Family interaction and psychopathology: Theories, methods, and findings* (pp. 117-162). New York: Plenum.

Rosenblatt, P. C. (1977). Needed research on commitment in marriage. In G. Levinger & H. L. Raush (Eds.), *Close relationships: Perspectives on the meaning of intimacy* (pp. 73-86). Amherst: University of Massachusetts Press.

Rusbult, C. E. (1983). A longitudinal test of the investment model: The development (and deterioration) of satisfaction and commitment in heterosexual involvement. *Journal of Personality and Social Psychology, 45,* 101-117.

Safilios-Rothschild, C. (1976). A macro- and micro-examination of family power and love: An exchange model. *Journal of Marriage and the Family, 38,* 355-362.

Shaver, P., & Hazan, C. (1985). Incompatibility, loneliness, and "limerence." In W. Ickes (Ed.), *Compatible and incompatible relationships* (pp. 163-184). New York: Springer-Verlag.

Shaver, P., Hazan, C., & Bradshaw, D. (1988). Love as attachment: The integration of three behavioral systems. In R. J. Sternberg & M. L. Barnes (Eds.), *The psychology of love* (pp. 68-99). New Haven: Yale University Press.

Snyder, M., & Simpson, J. A. (1984). Self-monitoring and dating relationships. *Journal of Personality and Social Psychology, 47,* 1281-1291.

Spence, J. T., & Helmreich, R. L. (1978). *Masculinity and femininity: Their psycho-*

*logical dimensions, correlates and antecedents.* Austin: University of Texas Press.

Sternberg, R. J. (1986). A triangular theory of love. *Psychological Review, 93,* 119–135.

Sternberg, R. J., & Barnes, M. L. (Eds.). (1988). *The psychology of love.* New Haven: Yale University Press.

Swensen, C. H. (1972). The behavior of love. In H. A. Otto (Ed.), *Love today: A new exploration* (pp. 86–99). New York: Association Press.

Thomas, K. (1976). Conflict and conflict management. In M. D. Dunnette (Ed.), *Handbook of industrial and organizational psychology* (pp. 889–935). Chicago: Rand McNally.

Thompson, S. C., & Kelley, H. H. (1981). Judgments of responsibility for activities in close relationships. *Journal of Personality and Social Psychology, 41,* 469–477.

Veroff, J., Douvan, E., & Kulka, R. A. (1981). *The inner American: A self-portrait from 1957 to 1976.* New York: Basic Books.

Winch, R. F. (1958). *Mate selection: A study of complementary needs.* New York: Harper.

Wish, M., Deutsch, M., & Kaplan, S. J. (1976). Perceived dimensions of interpersonal relations. *Journal of Personality and Social Psychology, 33,* 409–420.

Wolfe, D. M. (1959). Power and authority in the family. In D. Cartwright (Ed.), *Studies in social power* (pp. 99–117). Ann Arbor, MI: Institute for Social Research.

CHAPTER 2

# The Study of Interdependence in Marriage

## Elliot Robins

Valid and reliable descriptive data are essential if we are to build a science of relationships in general and of marriage in particular. In their overview of research methods in the study of close relationships, Harvey, Christensen, and McClintock (1983) argued forcefully for the critical importance of accurate descriptive data: "In order to answer questions about *why* people do what they do in close relationships, we must first have sufficient information about *what* they do in those relationships" (p. 467). Insofar as the goal of accurate description cannot be achieved without a unified conceptual approach to both theory and measurement (Herbst, 1965), the measurement of interdependence in marriage ought to flow from a sound theoretical analysis of the nature of that interdependence. Therefore, such an analysis is the first step in marital research.

Interdependence is the central construct in the study of close relationships. In this chapter, I focus on the nature of the data that can be obtained about the two *levels* of interdependence: (1) marital interaction and (2) the cognitions and attitudes of marriage partners about each other and about their relationship. I discuss each of these levels of interdependence, the interactional and the psychological, and describe in general terms the methods available for obtaining data about each level. In doing so, I argue that the nature of the data desired by the researcher ought to influence heavily the methodological approach used, within the limits of practicality. Finally, I examine the reciprocal effects of interactional and psychological interdependence in marriage and some of the research implications of these reciprocal effects.

In recent years there has been a burgeoning interest in the study of close relationships (Duck & Perlman, 1985). Theoretical works on close relationships (e.g., Hinde, 1979; Kelley, 1979; Kelley et al., 1983; Levinger & Raush, 1977; Scanzoni, Polonko, Teachman, & Thompson, 1989) have stressed the similarities to be found across various relationships rather than emphasizing differences among, say, marriages, friendships, and parent–child dyads. Indeed, some observers have been so impressed by this unifying tendency that they have viewed it as a paradigm shift (Scanzoni et al., 1989). The present chapter falls within this new paradigm, for most of what is said about research methods in studying marriage applies as well to other personal relationships. The approach taken here is primarily conceptual and theoretical; discussions of specific methodological approaches for particular variables are available elsewhere. Also omitted are issues of research design and the use of specific designs to infer causal connections between variables. These are general considerations in social science research, and sophisticated treatments of design issues are readily available. Instead, the emphasis is placed on the researcher's careful specification of the aspects of the marital relationship about which information is needed and on the subsequent identification of the most useful methods for gathering such information.

## TWO LEVELS OF INTERDEPENDENCE

In marriage, as in other groups, there is mutual influence—the actions of each partner have effects on the other. More specifically, two types of momentary events occur during dyadic interaction. *Interpersonal events* are the observable behaviors of each partner. *Subjective events*, not directly observable, are the moment-to-moment thoughts and emotions of each partner that arise during interaction (Huston & Robins, 1982). In addition to these momentary occurrences, participants in ongoing relationships draw many conclusions about the partner and the relationship. These cognitive–evaluative judgments or *subjective conditions* "are the relatively stable attitudes, attributions, and beliefs about either the partner or the relationship that arise, at least in part, out of interaction" (Huston & Robins, 1982, p. 903). Subjective conditions are focused on the partner and on the relationship with the partner, and they are therefore a subset of the multitude of attitudes, beliefs, and psychological dispositions that each partner holds.

It is thus possible to speak of two levels of interdependence, the interactional level and the psychological level (cf. Hinde, 1979; Kelley, 1979). At the interactional level, each partner's actions (interpersonal events) affect the subsequent actions and covert responses (subjective events) of the other. At the psychological level, mutual influence is apparent in each partner's having developed somewhat stable attitudes and beliefs about the relationship and the partner (subjective conditions). As discussed in greater detail below, the two levels of interdependence are causally interrelated in an ongoing, cyclical manner.

Differing approaches are needed to measure these two levels of interdependence. In the past, many researchers have taken methods used in measuring subjective conditions and attempted to apply these methods to the study of interaction patterns. For example, respondents have frequently been asked to make global judgments about such interaction variables as frequency of conflict or time spent together, just as they might be asked to report on beliefs they hold. Indeed, a common justification for this procedure has been the argument that only the respondents' beliefs about their behavior are of importance, not the behavior itself. Although, for example, asking respondents to provide attributions for the spouse's behavior may be the method of choice, asking them to summarize the extent of their time together may be a relatively ineffective method of assessing their companionship. This important problem is examined in depth later in the chapter.

## INTERACTIONAL INTERDEPENDENCE

Recognition of the several levels at which interaction can be analyzed is fundamental to the study of interactional interdependence in marriage. Four such levels are diagrammed in Figure 2.1.

First, at the microinteractional level the researcher is interested in the overt actions of the partners as well as their moment-to-moment cognitions and affective responses. As interest shifts beyond the individual overt and covert behaviors of each partner, a second level is reached. Here, the researcher may investigate sequences of events or episodes of interaction. These sequences and episodes may be of varying length and content but are confined to one occasion. At the third level, that of relationship pat-

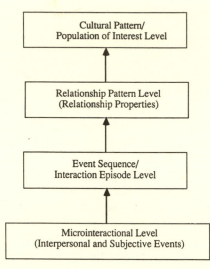

FIGURE 2.1. Levels of analysis of interactional interdependence.

terns, the researcher examines consistencies and recurrences of events, event sequences, and episodes within each relationship being studied. The most inclusive level is that of cultural patterns of interaction or, as is the case in many lines of research, patterns found in a specific population of interest to the researcher. At this level, the researcher generalizes across many relationships in an attempt to characterize the interaction patterns found in a specific population or a particular culture, or to ascertain the causes and consequences of such patterns. With the aid of the following example, events, event sequences, episodes, and relationship patterns will be discussed in greater detail.

### Tennis, Anyone?

The setting is a mixed-doubles tennis match. Two married couples are playing, with the husband of Couple 1 paired with the wife of Couple 2, and vice versa. For simplicity, only the statements of Husband 1 and Wife 1 are presented. The ball is in play and hit to Wife 1 at the net. She hits it back, and it is not returned.

H 1: The ball is out!
W 1: What? You're kidding, that ball was in the middle of the alley. Are you sure you were looking?

H 1: No it wasn't. It was out by at least a foot. I saw it!

W 1: (*Angrily*) Well, you're blind then, because I saw it with my own two eyes. I couldn't have missed it, it was so clear. (*Calmer now*) Look at where the print was left.

H 1: (*Shakes his head "no," refuses to look*)

W 1: (*Again yelling*) I know it was in!

About 3 minutes later. Wife 1 has maintained an angry expression.

H 1: Hey, I really think the ball was out. There's just no reason to get so upset over a game.

W 1: Look, I know the ball was in. I saw it, and I don't want to discuss it. If you keep on talking about it, I'm going to leave.

About 10 minutes later. Wife 1's team has been steadily losing. She has apparently been deliberately missing shots by hitting balls out of play and into the net. She has hit a few balls extremely hard directly at her husband and at Wife 2 even after the point has ended. Her team then loses another point.

W 1: I am sick and tired of this. (*Smashes ball at the fence*)

H 1: (*Reasonable tone*) Look. I think the ball was out; you think the ball was in. You can't change someone else's opinion. Let's just forget it. It was only one point, not Wimbledon.

W 1: (*Quietly*) I know it was in.

A few more points are played.

W 1: Dammit! (*Hurls her racket against the fence and walks off the court*)

## Microinteraction, Event Sequences, and Interaction Episodes

This example is probably best described as an *interaction episode*. This term is employed here to characterize a relatively extended interaction sequence that is classifiable to the participants and to observers who share or understand the cultural background of the participants. Episodes have a beginning, a middle, and an end. When scripted, an episode resembles a little story, not necessarily as affect-laden as the example. Participants and researchers alike might characterize the example as a "conflict" or a "fight," or even as a "tennis match." Other episodes might be a shared household task, a conversation about work, or eating a meal together. In short, episodes are marked by "thematic coherence" (McClintock, 1983, p. 85), which arises from shared cultural understandings of participants and observers.

The episode presented above is composed of several *event sequences* or brief series of actions in which the overt behavior of each partner may influence the overt behavior and subjective responses of the other. Sequences are somewhat dependent on their interactional context for their meaning. For example, the sequence

H: The ball is out!
W: What? You're kidding . . .

taken in isolation is not readily interpretable beyond noting that the husband has made a statement with which the wife apparently disagrees. The causes and consequences of this clash and the persistence of the spouses in asserting their respective positions cannot be ascertained from the single sequence.

At an even more microinteractional level, a researcher can examine individual behavior units or subjective responses of each partner without regard to their place in a sequence. Such events no longer have any immediate interactional context, although they can still be characterized, for example, as a statement or a question or as demonstrating positive, negative, or neutral affect.

It is possible to be very precise about the varieties of microinteractional units and event sequences if both interpersonal and subjective events are considered and the number of elements in the sequence is not arbitrarily constrained. Huston and Robins (1982), for example, identified eight different types of units, ranging from the individual behavior units of one partner to pairings of event sequences. It is necessary for each researcher to specify the events or sequence of events that will be examined.

### Relationship Patterns (Relationship Properties)

By themselves, isolated events, sequences, or episodes are rarely of interest to researchers. Exceptions to this principle do occur, because a single event or episode may have a substantial impact on the future development of the relationship, as when the spouses reach a decision to have a child or when one hits the other or when one announces an intent to separate. But for the most part, the researcher's interest is in the patterned recurrence of interactional events, sequences, and episodes.[1] The goal is to identify the patterns or regularities that occur in each relationship, often so that consistent patterns across many relationships of a particular type (e.g., distressed versus nondistressed; new parents versus couples without children) can be discovered. In the present work, the term *relationship properties* is used to refer to identifiable regularities in interactional interdependence. These interactional consistencies include patterns both of interpersonal events and subjective events, recurrent sequences of such events or combinations of them, and recurrent interaction episodes.

In considering the tennis match, several questions involving relationship properties come readily to mind: Does this couple frequently disagree? Do they often do so publicly? When they disagree, is it typically the case that the wife acts in an angry manner and the husband remains calm? Are their overt behaviors typically congruent or incongruent with their internal emotional states? Are the sequences during conflict marked by repeated disagreements and summarizing of one's own position rather than by validation of the partner's statements, attempts to summarize the partner, and proposals of solutions? What kinds of episodes typically follow a conflict for this couple? Questions such as these may require gathering data on many instances of interaction, presumably over an extended period of time, in order to obtain reliable data on relationship patterns. The less consistent the partners are in their interaction, the larger is the sample of events that would be required for a reliable estimate of a relationship property (cf. Epstein, 1980).

Because of the vital importance of the relationship property construct in research on marriage, it is discussed in detail here. I believe that insufficient theoretical and empirical attention has been given to this construct and its limitations. A relationship property is perhaps best understood as a generalization about interaction over time rather than as a directly observable entity. What people "typically" or "usually" do is an abstraction built by aggregating single events or sequences of behavior that are recognized as particular instances by the participants and/or defined as particular instances by a researcher. The proper method of aggre-

---

[1]Many researchers are also interested in patterns of what might be called relationship-relevant events, those that have, or could have, an effect on the relationship but take place away from the partner. For example, a wife's playing tennis with a friend decreases her availability to her husband. Peplau (1983) has used the term "indirect interdependence" to refer to the influence of such solitary or extradyadic social events on the primary relationship.

gating these instances into "relationship properties" thus becomes a conceptual issue as well as one of measurement. There is no agreed-on time period that delimits a relationship property, and there is usually no more than an assumption that an unknown degree of interactional consistency is present. Indeed, it is probably reasonable to assume that some aspects of interactional interdependence will be enacted with great consistency, whereas others may show only minimal patterning.

Figure 2.2 shows the marital dyad under the microscope, using gradually decreasing magnification. Each "C" stands for the occurrence of a conflict episode. In Figure 2.2a, we observe a couple (let us suppose them to be unreactive to an observer's presence) in their home between 11 a.m. and 12 noon on Saturday, January 8. There were no episodes of conflict noted. What would this 1 hour of observation reveal about patterns of conflict in this relationship? The answer may be very little, because the period of observation was insufficient. Yet even this conclusion depends on our theory about the extent to which dyads are consistent in their interaction. Let us now extend our visit to the rest of the day, from 11 a.m. to 11 p.m. As shown in Figure 2.2b, one episode of conflict is observed, between 5:15 and 5:30 p.m. Are we now satisfied as to the frequency of occurrence of conflict episodes? We might question whether we have observed "a typical day." Perhaps the couple interacted more than usual, or less; perhaps one or both are especially irritable or under stress or unusually relaxed. Returning the next day for an additional 12 hours, we observe one brief quarrel at 8:30 p.m. Intuitively we may now feel that we have devoted sufficient time to observation. As Figure 2.2c shows, we have coded one, and only one, conflict episode on each of 2 successive days. We have 24 hours of observational data on this couple, and we might feel that we have offered a sufficient sacrifice to the gods of reliability.

Suppose, however, that we are not yet convinced that we have a representative sample of behavior; after all, the degree of sampling error is unknown. We then implement our second strategy: the completely valid behavioral self-report diary. For the week of January 10 to 16, the couple reports three conflicts (Figure 2.2d); this rate per day of 0.43 conflict episodes is considerably lower than the rate of 2.0 (two conflicts in 24 hours) obtained by observing the couple for 12 hours per day on January 8 and 9. How much better off are we at this point? Our theories about the stability of interpersonal behavior are now strongly affecting our views of the need for further data. Insofar as we are convinced that dyads will

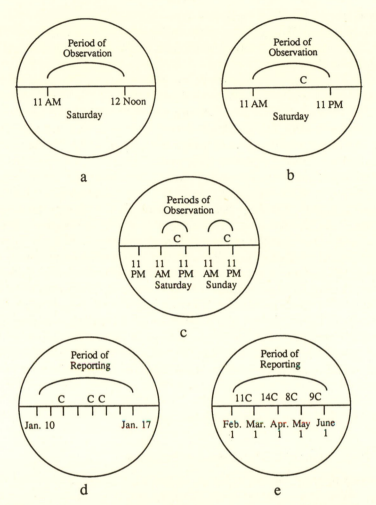

FIGURE 2.2. Observation of the marital dyad over time. Note. The letter C stands for the occurrence of a conflict episode.

show high levels of consistency in their behavior from one interaction to the next, from hour to hour, from day to day, we may be convinced that a full week's data are ample for reliably estimating a relationship property. To the extent that we view interaction as less traitlike, we may still be wondering what longer-term data might reveal. To explore this issue we now persuade the couple to keep their conflict diary over a 4-month period, from February 1 to May 31. Figure 2.2e shows the results of this procedure. In

February, 11 conflict episodes are reported; in March, 14; in April, 8; and in May, 9. The daily means for each month are 0.39, 0.45, 0.27, and 0.29, respectively; the daily mean for the entire period is 0.35.

These hypothetical results bring out several interesting issues. First, there is daily and monthly variability in the occurrence of conflict. Second, the factors causing this variability are unknown. The partners may have spent varying amounts of time together, may have been more or less stressed, or may have had to deal with more or less emotionally involving issues. Third, it is clear that the notion of relationship property assumes consistency in the relationship. From a quantitative perspective, the relationship property concept assumes that there is a mean value for the phenomenon, and it treats variability around that mean as measurement error. Fourth, the relationship property concept excludes change during the period of measurement. To use the concept, the data must be aggregated to form a summary index of central tendency; possible change during the observation period is ignored. This simplification of the dyadic relationship by disregarding development or change might even be viewed as the fundamental assumption underlying the relationship property concept. For most research purposes, this assumption is probably necessary. But it is important to be aware of it, for without this recognition, relationships tend to be viewed in excessively static terms. This tendency to assume long-term consistency is evident in the following discussion of approaches to the measurement of relationship properties.

## The Measurement of Relationship Patterns

As noted earlier, researchers are generally interested in individual occurrences of interpersonal and subjective events, event sequences, and interaction episodes only as a means to the end of identifying relationship patterns. The major issue, therefore, in the measurement of relationship properties in any particular study is whether to gather data directly at the level of the relationship property or at the level of the individual occurrence. In a world of perfect measurement, this issue would reduce itself to the question of whether the researcher or the respondent would perform the task of aggregating events, sequences, or episodes into relationship properties. In actuality, however, many sources of unreliability and threats to construct validity are potentially operative in any method of measurement chosen, given the circumstances of a particular study (Huston & Robins, 1982). Choosing a method of measurement often involves a compromise between optimal procedures and practical constraints.

## Aggregate Level of Measurement

To illustrate the various approaches to measurement of relationship patterns, consider the measurement of companionship in leisure activities. Let us imagine that the researcher is interested in the proportion of leisure activity that is shared with the partner, as opposed to that engaged in alone or with others. A common strategy in this domain is to ask one or both partners to generalize about their interaction patterns. In effect, this strategy is a request by the researcher for an estimate of a relationship property. This can be done in a variety of ways with respect to the measurement of leisure companionship. At the most inclusive level, the following single item might be asked of one partner:

> Do you and your mate engage in outside interests together?
>    a. All of them
>    b. Most of them
>    c. Some of them
>    d. Very few of them
>    e. None of them

This question is taken from one of the most frequently used instruments in marital research, Spanier's (1976) Dyadic Adjustment Scale. Although this item was not intended to be used alone, it is nevertheless a question about a relationship property and serves to illustrate the problems inherent in measuring properties at this level. A respondent who wishes to provide an accurate answer to this question faces formidable difficulties. First, the question is phrased in the present tense, with no specified time frame. The respondent must therefore impose an arbitrary time frame around the question (e.g., past month, past year, entire duration of the relationship). There is little reason to suppose that all respondents will impose similar time frames on the question. (It has already been noted that any time frame will be completely arbitrary, but arbitrary consistency ought to produce more valid results than random inconsistency.) Second, the phrase "outside interests" is vague. Each respondent may define this phrase somewhat differently, as it is far from clear which leisure or other activities would or would not count as "outside" ones.

Even more complex are the tasks of recall and computation that are required for an accurate response (Harvey et al., 1983;

Huston & Robins, 1982; Huston, Robins, Atkinson, & McHale, 1987). Having, let us say, imposed a 6-month time frame and having decided to include all leisure activities done outside the home, the respondent (e.g., the husband) must then attempt to recall each leisure activity done individually by each spouse and jointly by both. Having done this, the respondent is in a position to calculate two proportions: the proportion of his own leisure activities done jointly (activities done together divided by the sum of activities done together and activities done by the husband alone or with others) as well as the proportion of his wife's leisure activities done jointly. Having obtained these two figures, the respondent must then divine what the researcher means by "most," "some," and "very few." He now has two proportions to combine somehow into one idiosyncratically defined response category.

To the extent that the foregoing description of the respondent's problem-solving behavior seems implausible or ludicrous, the faith of the researcher in the respondent's motivation and abilities seems equally fantastic. Even if the respondent were to attempt to answer the question in the manner indicated, he may be unable to retrieve many of the relevant episodes from memory, perhaps because their impact or significance may affect their availability in memory (Nisbett & Ross, 1980). If perfect recall were possible, the respondent might err in the calculation of the proportions necessary to answer the question. In reality, it seems unlikely that a respondent will be motivated to apply such precise methods of solution to such an ambiguous problem. Instead, the respondent may approach the question much differently than the researcher may have intended. In the best case, he may search his memory for several recent instances of leisure activities, note how many of these involved spousal companionship, and fit this rough estimate to one of the response categories. More realistically, he may give a socially desirable response, attempt to please the investigator, or substitute the report of a presumed cultural norm (Shweder & D'Andrade, 1980), all of which would probably result in a high level of shared leisure being reported.

The particular global question under discussion thus includes several sources of unreliability: ambiguities of the time frame, the term "outside interests," and the response categories and (in the event the respondent attempts to answer the question as asked) the possibility of errors in mental arithmetic. The question also results in several threats to construct validity (Cook & Campbell, 1979), that is, there are several sources of systematic bias that may arise in its use. These include biases reflecting the respondent's reactivity, the selective recall of events more readily available in memory, and "task substitution" (Huston & Robins, 1982), in which the respondent rejects the task and does something else (e.g., reports a cultural norm).

Researchers have often framed their questions more precisely in an attempt to minimize the problems discussed above. For example, a more complex and sophisticated approach to measurement of leisure companionship at the aggregate level was reported by Holman and Jacquart (1988). Respondents were presented with a list of 76 leisure activities. The time frame of interest was specifically stated as the previous 12 months. Respondents were first asked to indicate the number of times they had engaged in each activity, with nine response categories available: never, about once a year, about twice a year, about three to six times a year, about 7 to 11 times a year, about 12 to 36 times a year (or one to three times a month), about once or twice a week, about three to five times a week, one or more times a day. Having provided the estimate of the quantity of participation in each activity, respondents were then asked to indicate the "degree of interaction with spouse" for each activity. Four response categories were available: without spouse, with spouse with little or no interaction, with spouse with moderate interaction, and with spouse with a great deal of interaction. Interaction was defined for the respondents as "the amount of communication that occurred during the activity." From these data the researchers calculated the overall total for each of the four categories of shared or separate leisure.

This method reduces the sources of unreliability and threats to validity. The time frame is unambiguous (although there is no guarantee that respondents will adhere to it). Response categories for frequency of occurrence are clear, although several are rather broad. The problems of recall of episodes in general as well as selective bias in recall have not been eliminated, but the long list of activities ought to improve recall of the less important or less frequent ones. The focus on specific activities should also decrease the respondent's tendency to answer in a socially desirable or stereotyped fashion.

The researchers' solution to measuring the extent of companionship for each activity is interesting in the light of the relationship property concept. The researchers' assumption is in essence what Gottman (1982) calls *deterministic*: the behavior will be enacted similarly on each occasion. Thus, each of the 76 activities is characterized as either not done with the spouse at all or involving low, moderate, or high levels of interaction with the spouse. Aside from the ambiguity inherent in the latter three categories, it is likely that the level of interaction might vary from one occasion to the next because of situational factors or individual mood states (e.g., varied responses to a television show when watching together; feeling more or less communicative when dining out together); that is, a *probabilistic* assumption may be more appropriate. In the absence of instruction, each respondent must decide on a procedure for assigning varied companionship experiences within each type of leisure activity to a single response category. Will the respondent compute the mean or identify the mode? Will the respondent follow the same procedure for all 76 activities? The computational requirements for Holman and Jacquart's measure now seem quite demanding; the facilitation of recall by using a long list of activities seems to be offset by the difficult task of estimating the degree of interaction typical of each.

The above examples serve to illustrate the variety of ways that researchers have attempted to measure leisure companionship in marriage at the aggregate level. Parallel illustrations of aggregate-level measurement could be found for other relationship properties such as decision making, conflict, and shared household tasks. Although such methods are efficient, requiring only pencil and paper and a few minutes of each respondent's time, they are plagued with a variety of problems of reliability and validity. In examining event-, sequence-, and episode-level approaches to the measurement of relationship properties, we will see that different problems of reliability and validity emerge.

### Event, Sequence, and Episode Level of Measurement

In contrast to seeking direct estimates of relationship properties from respondents, the researcher may choose to collect data at the level of the individual occurrences of each event, sequence, or episode. At the end of the data collection period, the researcher aggregates the data to create an estimate of the relationship property. A variety of procedures have been developed to gather event-level data. These include direct observation of ongoing behavior, the use of videotaping or filming as a substitute for this, and either concurrent or short-term retrospective event-by-event reporting or recording by relationship participants.

The nature of the data sought will constrain the choices available to the researcher. For example, accurately categorizing very brief interaction sequences will be most readily accomplished by direct observation or videotaping. (For detailed discussions of the

various approaches to the observation and coding of marital interaction and analysis of the resulting data, see Gilbert & Christensen, 1985; Gottman, 1987; Markman & Notarius, 1987.) Measurement of subjective events requires some ingenuity. One
approach involves immediate reporting by participants, such as
indicating the intended impact of messages sent and the impact of
those received (Gottman, Notarius, Markman, Bank, & Yoppi,
1976). Another approach uses replay of a videotaped interaction to
the respondent to aid the respondent's recall of the thought processes and emotional states that occurred during the interaction.
A third possibility involves the random interruption of respondents (e.g., using pagers) and asking them to record their current
subjective states (e.g., Larson & Csikszentmihalyi, 1983).

Measurement of episodes such as leisure activities may be
accomplished in a variety of ways. Although direct observation of
behavior is an option, researchers tend to avoid using it in circumstances in which days or weeks of observation would be necessary
to obtain a large sample of episodes. Instead, gathering data at the
level of the individual episode has often been accomplished
through a variety of behavioral self-report procedures. These are
most commonly either variations on a diary procedure or the
securing of episode-level verbal reports from respondents. Two
examples are presented to illustrate the various strengths and
liabilities of episode-level recording or reporting.

In a time budget study of 60 married couples, Shaw (1985,
1986) used a diary procedure to gather data on leisure time use.
Wives and husbands separately filled out a time budget diary for
each of 2 days, a weekday deemed by the couple to be a "typical
work day" and a weekend day deemed to be a "typical nonwork
day." As soon as possible following completion of the diary, each
respondent was interviewed and asked to categorize each activity
(episode) as one of four possibilities: "leisure," "work," "a mixture
of work and leisure," or "neither work nor leisure." Because the
specific activities were listed, however, researcher-imposed categories of activity such as recreation time could also be compiled
apart from respondents' subjective categorizations.[2]

Although Shaw did not use her data to construct relationship
properties such as each spouse's proportion of total leisure that is
shared with the partner, this treatment of the data is certainly
possible. Spouses' reports can be compared to see which activities

---

[2]The issue of insider versus outsider perspectives on relationships has been
discussed at length by Olson (1977).

have been done together and which separately. The major problem with the diary approach as used ordinarily is the limited sample of behavior obtained; this issue was discussed in detail earlier in the consideration of conflict episodes. Shaw has taken steps to secure data for days that respondents believe are "typical," having them nominate these days beforehand and having them confirm this afterwards. Nevertheless, "typical" does not mean "invariant," and respondents may allow a great deal of leeway in what they regard as a day like any other. If respondents can be persuaded to cooperate, diaries kept for a greater number of days should increase the accuracy of the estimate of the relationship property for whatever time frame is chosen.

Other problems of reliability and validity also arise in the use of diaries. There is no way for the researcher to be certain that respondents are completing the diary according to instructions. Instead of recording each event immediately after it occurs, respondents may record only at intervals, consulting their memories or their spouses to reconstruct the sequence of activities. Routine or seemingly trivial episodes may be omitted, and some forgetting may occur. In addition, some "editing" in the service of social desirability may be expected. Respondents may be unwilling to report behaviors regarded as excesssively personal (e.g., sex, grooming) or socially disapproved (e.g., taking drugs, gambling), especially when it is so easy to conceal these in a diary by stretching the time allotted to preceding and following events.

An alternative to the diary approach was developed by Huston and his colleagues (Huston et al., 1987) in a longitudinal study of the marital adaptation of newlyweds. A telephone interview procedure was employed in order to gather event-level and episode-level data on several activity domains of the marital relationship: household tasks, leisure activities, positive and negative interaction events, conflict episodes, and conversations. The telephone procedure was employed at each of the three phases of the project, spaced 1 year apart. Each phase also included an individual face-to-face interview with each partner, focusing primarily on the subjective aspects of the relationship. At the conclusion of the face-to-face interview, a series of nine telephone calls was tentatively scheduled. A calendar indicating the date and time of each call was given to the couple, and a copy was kept by the researchers. The telephone procedure was complex and detailed, with careful attention to issues of sampling, facilitation of recall, and confidentiality between spouses. The researchers describe the procedure as follows:

The telephone interviews encompassed nine calls spaced over a 2- to 3-week period. Couples were called on each of the five weekdays and on two Saturdays and two Sundays, with the calls being placed about every second day. Calls were usually made between 5 and 11 p.m., when both spouses were home. Each partner was spoken with individually; the spouse not being interviewed was asked to allow the partner to respond in private. Moreover, the procedure made it difficult for an eavesdropping partner to make sense of his or her spouse's answers because many of the responses were given as a simple "yes" or "no" or as a number indicating time and frequency. Each spouse was asked to report on various events that had occurred during the 24-hour period ending at 5 p.m. on the day of the call. Any calls missed by the respondents were later rescheduled. (Huston et al., 1987, p. 53)

For leisure activities, respondents were asked about the occurrence of 30 activities, such as working on a hobby, going to a party, or entertaining friends. Each couple had been given a list of these activities during the face-to-face interview, and the respondent consulted the list during the telephone interview. For each activity, respondents reported each instance of its occurrence during the 24-hour period covered by that day's phone call. For each instance, the following data were obtained: the duration of the activity and the identity of the other participants, if any (e.g., spouse, friends). Thus, each partner reported on his or her leisure activities undertaken with and without the spouse. Aggregation of the episode-level data into relationship property estimates was done by the researchers.

This labor-intensive method of gathering episode-level data presents an interesting contrast to the diary method. A diary, when filled out according to instructions, is a greater intrusion into the flow of interaction than the telephone recall approach. A diary also demands a higher level of involvement throughout the measurement period. Demands of the telephone procedure are high only while respondents are on the phone, when they must attempt to recall details of their daily behavior. On the other hand, the telephone method undoubtedly loses some episodes that are not recalled or that respondents do not want to report, and it is probably subject to less accuracy with respect to the duration of episodes than would be the case when recording is done immediately. The relatively brief time span between occurrence and reporting in the telephone procedure is an attempt to maximize the accuracy of recall, as is supplying the respondents with a list of the activities about which they are asked. As in the diary method and in event-level approaches generally, the demand on respondents for mental arithmetic in order to aggregate the data is eliminated. Finally, the telephone procedure described here sampled a relatively large number of days, allowing a more reliable estimate of relationship properties. But theoretical problems of the temporal boundaries of a relationship property and the consistency of occurrence of the events of interest remain unsolved. Indeed, 9 days of data may provide a very stable estimate of certain relationship patterns (e.g., household tasks the wife does alone), whereas it provides a relatively unreliable estimate of other patterns (e.g., amount of time the partners spend in conversation with each other).

In a world of infinite resources and nonreactive respondents, direct observation and concurrent recording of behavior (coupled with concurrent reporting by respondents of subjective events) would generally be the method of choice for the measurement of interactional interdependence. Because of practical limitations, researchers have often turned to aggregate-level measures of relationship properties. Such measures are not all alike; their careful construction can increase their validity and reliability. The strongest methodological advantages, however, appear to reside in carefully collected event-level and episode-level data. Although direct observation of behavior is not always feasible, other event-level approaches offer exciting possibilities for gathering more precise and more valid data on relationship patterns.

## PSYCHOLOGICAL INTERDEPENDENCE

In all but the briefest, most stereotyped, or most highly role-regulated interactions, the participants are likely to develop ideas and draw conclusions about each other and the relationship. In marriage, each spouse will have developed a rich store of cognitions—often affectively laden ones—about such issues as the partner's characteristics, motivations, and goals, attitudes toward the partner, what to expect in future interaction with the partner, relationship rules or norms, and the quality of the relationship or of various aspects of it. Many scholars have argued that understanding the nature of the partners' psychological interdependence is essential to interpreting their interaction (e.g., Bradbury & Fincham, 1990; Braiker & Kelley, 1979; Hinde, 1979; Kelley et al., 1983).

This multiplicity of cognitive–evaluative judgments focusing on the partner and the relationship are, as mentioned earlier, referred to here as "subjective conditions." Scholars have generally regarded these as relatively stable attitudes and beliefs, as dispositions to respond in a certain manner. Subjective conditions are viewed as being "in place" and ready for activation at the relevant moments of interaction. Although numerous investigations have been carried out in which long-term change in subjective conditions has been examined (e.g., marital satisfaction, love), measurement operations have almost always assumed short-term invariance in subjective conditions. As a result, an excessive amount of error often is included in values obtained for subjective conditions in studies in which subjective conditions are assumed to be stable traits.

A good example of the foregoing is the measurement of marital satisfaction. An illustrative study is that of Mitchell, Newell, and Schumm (1983), who examined the internal consistency reliability and test–retest reliability of the three-item Kansas Marital Satisfaction Scale in a sample of 106 young employed married mothers. Internal consistency was extremely high (Cronbach's alpha = .96) whereas test–retest reliability over a 10-week period was substantially lower ($r = .71$). The high internal consistency indicates that there is very little measurement error attributable to the sampling of items from the hypothetical domain of all possible marital satisfaction items (Nunnally, 1978). Therefore, the lower figure for test–retest reliability indicates that respondents' marital satisfaction tends to be somewhat unstable, even over a 10-week period. Two factors may contribute to this finding. First, some respondents may have actually experienced change in their level of marital satisfaction during the 10 weeks. A second possibility is that there exists a degree of state variability in marital satisfaction—that a person's contentment with the spouse is somewhat responsive in the short term to his or her own mood or to interactions with the partner or with others.

The research of Wills, Weiss, and Patterson (1974) strongly supports this second possibility. Seven couples participated in a study of the effects of pleasant and unpleasant interactions with the spouse, as well as the effects of outside experiences, on daily marital satisfaction. Respondents kept checklists of pleasurable and displeasurable instrumental and affectional spouse behaviors for three periods—morning, afternoon, and evening—for each of 14 consecutive days. They also rated the affective quality of experiences outside the marital dyad, and their satisfaction with the marriage, for these same time periods. Daily aggregates of the affective interaction variables were computed and used to predict the daily average marital satisfaction. The authors unfortunately did not report the extent of fluctuation in marital satisfaction, but clearly there was variability, and this variability was to a considerable extent predictable from each person's daily experiences. For husbands, over 21% of the variance in daily average marital satisfaction was predictable from their affective experiences; for wives, over 34% of the variance was accounted for. This study therefore not only demonstrates state variability in marital satisfaction, but clearly indicates that the interactional experiences of the spouses are important contributors to this fluctuation in satisfaction.

The foregoing discussion implies that subjective conditions may best be conceptualized as having both a relatively stable, traitlike component and a statelike component that may vary from day to day or even from moment to moment depending on the respondent's mood, situation, or recent experiences (Huston & Robins, 1982). It is plausible that the various subjective conditions will show different patterns of state variation; some judgments or evaluations may show minimal tendency to fluctuate, whereas others may show a great deal of variability around a stable mean. Figure 2.3 illustrates some of these possibilities. In each case, the solid line indicates the actual level of the subjective condition over a 14-day period, and the dotted line represents the mean of these daily values. *A* shows a subjective condition for which there is minimal state variability (e.g., a judgment about the extent to which the spouse is intelligent). *B* shows a subjective condition that is rather sensitive to daily experience (e.g., marital satisfaction). *C* represents a usually invariant subjective condition, but one that may be susceptible to extreme short-term fluctuation if certain unusual events occur (e.g., trust, which might be negatively affected by the partner's actions while intoxicated at a party). Of course, a type *B* subjective condition could also show the kinds of changes evident in *C*.

## The Measurement of Psychological Interdependence

It is clear from the preceding discussion that the measurement of psychological interdependence presents a sampling problem entirely analogous to that involved in the measurement of interactional interdependence. To the extent that a subjective condition shows little state variability, a single occasion of measurement may capture it with great precision if a valid and internally consistent measure is used. Subjective conditions that vary even moderately over the short term present a much greater measure-

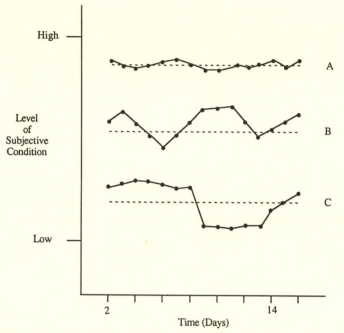

**FIGURE 2.3.** Traitlike and statelike components of subjective conditions. Solid circles, daily values; dotted line, mean values.

ment problem. The typical researcher, although interested in the traitlike component or average level of the subjective condition, measures it on only one occasion. Any variability arising from the statelike component is thereby allowed to become part of the random error of measurement, thus attenuating the association between subjective conditions and other variables. As is the case with relationship properties, a more accurate estimate of the mean value of the subjective condition can be obtained by employing repeated within-person measurement, preferably on several occasions. Such a procedure would not only yield increased accuracy, but it would also allow the investigation of the extent, causes, and consequences of statelike variability in subjective conditions.

Related to the issue of temporal fluctuation is the problem of assessing whether lasting change has occurred in a subjective condition. Again the problem is analogous to that found in the assessment of relationship properties. Any line of demarcation will be arbitrary. In certain longitudinal investigations, important events occur that provide a theoretical basis for expecting change, for example, a wedding ceremony, the birth of the first child, the last child's leaving home, or the retirement of a spouse. In studies of this type, the life event provides a natural dividing point; but the occurrence of such an event does not mean that either subjective conditions or relationship properties will necessarily change suddenly. Gradual but stable long-term changes in subjective conditions may result from the cumulative impact of small changes in interaction patterns rather than sudden changes in subjective conditions arising from the effect of one or a few events or episodes.

The best source of information about a person's subjective conditions is the person himself or herself. Spouses often attribute attitudes and beliefs to each other, and these judgments may be of interest in themselves, but spouses are relatively fallible sources of information about each other's subjective conditions. (See Huston & Robins, 1982, for a discussion of alternative methods of measuring subjective conditions.) In asking the respondent to report his or her subjective conditions, researchers have often relied on a single question or global rating. A single-item scale implicitly assumes a very narrowly defined construct of interest. Because any single item always underrepresents the target construct and contains irrelevancies (Cook & Campbell, 1979), it will yield a score that includes both random error and systematic bias. These problems are reduced by using instruments that include at least several items measuring a single construct. Further advances in our knowledge of marriage require the development of internally consistent and valid multi-item instruments to measure subjective conditions, instruments that can match in reliability and validity the increasingly sophisticated approaches to the measurement of interactional interdependence.

## RECIPROCAL EFFECTS OF INTERACTIONAL AND PSYCHOLOGICAL INTERDEPENDENCE

A major objective in the study of marriage is to capture the ongoing, subtle, and complex interplay of the interactional and psychological levels of interdependence. As Hinde states, "To understand relationships fully, . . . it is necessary to come to terms not only with their behavioral but also with their affective/cognitive aspects, and to do so whilst recognizing that they are inextricably interwoven" (1979, p. 15). The essence of the argument in this chapter has been that in order to accomplish this ambitious goal, sound approaches are necessary in the measurement of interactional and psychological interdependence. Implicit in the discussion has been the importance of assessing stability and change over time in relationships. Time assumes importance not only in examining interaction sequences but also in conceptualizing relationship properties and subjective conditions and in studying their reciprocal effects.

It is likely that mainstream research on marriage will continue to emphasize the traitlike components of relationship properties and subjective conditions. An important goal of marital research is the clarification of the reciprocal effects of the various aspects of interactional and psychological interdependence in both maintaining stability and inducing change in marital relationships. A comprehensive model of interdependence in marital relationships (based on Kelley et al., 1983, and, to some extent, on Huston & Robins, 1982) is presented in Figure 2.4.

Figure 2.4 draws attention to several important features of marital relationships worthy of extensive research, and these aspects have many implications for measurement. Foremost is the focus on both partners in the relationship. It has become increasingly difficult to defend marital research in which only one partner is studied, except in those investigations in which the interest is purely in the subjective conditions of wives or of husbands. The study of marital interdependence requires data on both spouses. This is only partly because each spouse may regard the relationship differently from the other, as Bernard (1972) noted in a discussion of "his" and "her" marriage. Just as importantly, various aspects of each partner's psychological interdependence, as well as other psychological dispositions each holds, will affect their interaction. Therefore, in order to understand the forces affecting interaction patterns, the subjective conditions and other dispositions of both partners must be known.

A second important feature of Figure 2.4 is the representation of reciprocal influences or feedback loops and the resulting system forces promoting both stability and change. Events and conditions arising in the social and physical environment of the married couple can affect not only each spouse's subjective views of the partner but also those beliefs and dispositions that are not specifically oriented to the marital relationship yet that may have an influence on their interaction patterns (e.g., gender role preferences, self-esteem). In addition, environmental conditions can affect interaction directly. Once in place, these changes in inter-

Spouse "A"

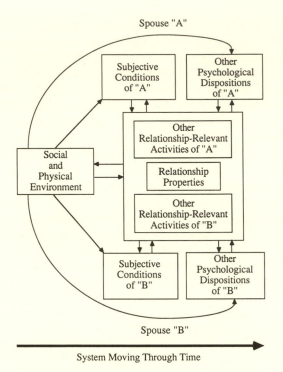

Social and Physical Environment

Subjective Conditions of "A"

Other Psychological Dispositions of "A"

Other Relationship-Relevant Activities of "A"

Relationship Properties

Other Relationship-Relevant Activities of "B"

Subjective Conditions of "B"

Other Psychological Dispositions of "B"

Spouse "B"

System Moving Through Time

**FIGURE 2.4.** Interdependence in marriage.

actional interdependence may in turn lead to changes in the subjective conditions of each partner or in other psychological dispositions, which then contribute to further change in the interaction. Alternatively, environmental forces may promote stability in the relationship by limiting the possibility of changes in interaction or by reinforcing the existing subjective conditions of each partner. In reality, a multiplicity of causal conditions are operative, some of which promote stability in dyadic interdependence and others of which promote change. Marriages must be conceptualized as open systems in order to understand both change and stability over time (Hinde, 1979; Kelley et al., 1983).

A third implication of Figure 2.4 concerns the pace of change over time. In any particular marriage, changes in the various aspects of interdependence may occur quickly, slowly, or not at all. Periods of rapid change may be followed by years of great stability, and some couples, at least in retrospect, report no changes at all that they regard as significant (Marks, 1986). Across marriages, certain relationship properties may change more quickly than others, and some subjective conditions may be more inherently stable than others. Also, it can be expected that lags will occur between changes in one part of the system and changes in other parts. For example, Markman (1981) found that the extent to which couples rated their interaction as positive during a structured laboratory exercise did not predict their satisfaction with the relationship at the time but did predict satisfaction on two occasions several years later. Kelly, Huston, and Cate (1985) found that conflict during the engagement period, although unrelated to feelings of love at that time, was negatively associated with wives' love for the partner and with both spouses' marital satisfaction 2 years after marriage. It is clear that longitudinal research designs are needed in order to disentangle the complex reciprocal causal influences affecting marital interdependence.


## CONCLUSION

A central theme of this chapter is the need to understand interdependence in relationships. The sound measurement of marital relationships depends on a clear differentiation between interactional and psychological interdependence. Researchers have often used methods more appropriate to measuring psychological interdependence, such as questionnaire items asking for global assessments, in order to measure interactional interdependence. A more accurate and detailed understanding of interactional interdependence results when researchers gather data at the level of the event, event sequence, or interaction episode, rather than directly at the level of the relationship property.

A more difficult theoretical problem confronts us in dealing with variability in interdependence. Most research on marriage has focused on central tendencies in relationship properties and subjective conditions and has ignored variability. This focus on traits rather than states may result from implicit theories that overemphasize consistency in relationships (cf. McGrath, 1988), or it may be a result of the practical impediments to taking multiple repeated measures on individuals and couples. In either case, the consequence is the same—variability in interdependence tends to be eliminated from our thinking or viewed as measurement error rather than being seen as an important feature of relationships. Duck and Sants (1983) argue persuasively that intimate relationships are less structured and more variable than our models of them have often suggested. It behooves us, therefore, to address this short-term fluidity in our research rather than confining our interest to short-term stability and long-term change.

Our theories of relationships have a profound effect on our approaches to their measurement. We must be certain that our theoretical assumptions are not built into our measurement strategies and instruments in such a way as to preclude disconfirmation of these theories. A careful consideration of the theoretical underpinnings of the measurement of marital interdependence will aid us greatly in providing the descriptive information needed to further our understanding of close relationships.

# REFERENCES

Bernard, J. (1972). *The future of marriage.* New York: World.

Bradbury, T. N., & Fincham, F. D. (1990). Attributions in marriage: Review and critique. *Psychological Bulletin, 107,* 3-33.

Braiker, H. B., & Kelley, H. H. (1979). Conflict in the development of close relationships. In R. L. Burgess & T. L. Huston (Eds.), *Social exchange in developing relationships* (pp. 135-168). New York: Academic Press.

Cook, T. D., & Campbell, D. T. (1979). *Quasi-experimentation: Design and analysis issues for field settings.* Chicago: Rand McNally.

Duck, S., & Perlman, D. (1985). The thousand islands of personal relationships: A prescriptive analysis for future explorations. In S. Duck & D. Perlman (Eds.), *Understanding personal relationships: An interdisciplinary approach* (pp. 1-15). London: Sage.

Duck, S., & Sants, H. (1983). On the origin of the specious: Are personal relationships really interpersonal states? *Journal of Social and Clinical Psychology, 1,* 27-41.

Epstein, S. (1980). The stability of behavior: II. Implications for psychological research. *American Psychologist, 35,* 790-806.

Gilbert, R., & Christensen, A. (1985). Observational assessment of marital and family interaction: Methodological considerations. In L. L'Abate (Ed.), *The handbook of family psychology and therapy* (vol. 2, pp. 961-988). Homewood, IL: Dorsey.

Gottman, J. M. (1982). Temporal form: Toward a new language for describing relationships. *Journal of Marriage and the Family, 44,* 943-962.

Gottman, J. M. (1987). The sequential analysis of family interaction. In T. Jacob (Ed.), *Family interaction and psychopathology: Theories, methods, and findings* (pp. 453-478). New York: Plenum.

Gottman, J. M., Notarius, C., Markman, H., Bank, S., & Yoppi, B. (1976). Behavior exchange theory and marital decision making. *Journal of Personality and Social Psychology, 34,* 14-23.

Harvey, J. H., Christensen, A., & McClintock, E. (1983). Research methods. In H. H. Kelley, E. Berscheid, A. Christensen, J. H. Harvey, T. L. Huston, G. Levinger, E. McClintock, L. A. Peplau, & D. R. Peterson, *Close relationships* (pp. 449-485). New York: W. H. Freeman.

Herbst, P. G. (1965). Problems of theory and method in the integration of the behavioral sciences. *Human Relations, 18,* 351-359.

Hinde, R. A. (1979). *Towards understanding relationships.* London: Academic Press.

Holman, T. B., & Jacquart, M. (1988). Leisure-activity patterns and marital satisfaction: A further test. *Journal of Marriage and the Family, 50,* 69-77.

Huston, T. L., & Robins, E. (1982). Conceptual and methodological issues in studying close relationships. *Journal of Marriage and the Family, 44,* 901-925.

Huston, T. L., Robins, E., Atkinson, J., & McHale, S. M. (1987). Surveying the landscape of marital behavior: A behavioral self-report approach to studying marriage. In S. Oskamp (Ed.), *Family processes and problems: Social psychological aspects (Applied Social Psychology Annual 7)* (pp. 45-72). Newbury Park, CA: Sage.

Kelley, H. H. (1979). *Personal relationships: Their structure and processes.* Hillsdale, NJ: Erlbaum.

Kelley, H. H., Berscheid, E., Christensen, A., Harvey, J. H., Huston, T. L., Levinger, G., McClintock, E., Peplau, L. A., & Peterson, D. R. (1983). *Close relationships.* New York: W. H. Freeman.

Kelly, C., Huston, T. L., & Cate, R. M. (1985). Premarital relationship correlates of the erosion of satisfaction in marriage. *Journal of Social and Personal Relationships, 2,* 167-178.

Larson, R., & Csikszentmihalyi, M. (1983). The experience sampling method. In H. T. Reis (Ed.), *Naturalistic approaches to studying social interaction* (pp. 41-56). San Francisco: Jossey-Bass.

Levinger, G., & Raush, H. L. (Eds.). (1977). *Close relationships: Perspectives on the meaning of intimacy.* Amherst, MA: University of Massachusetts Press.

Markman, H. J. (1981). Prediction of marital distress: A five-year follow-up. *Journal of Consulting and Clinical Psychology, 49,* 760-762.

Markman, H. J., & Notarius, C. I. (1987). Coding marital and family interaction: Current status. In T. Jacob (Ed.), *Family interaction and psychopathology: Theories, methods, and findings* (pp. 329-390). New York: Plenum.

Marks, S. R. (1986). *Three corners: Exploring marriage and the self.* Lexington, MA: D. C. Heath.

McClintock, E. (1983). Interaction. In H. H. Kelley, E. Berscheid, A. Christensen, J. H. Harvey, T. L. Huston, G. Levinger, E. McClintock, L. A. Peplau, & D. R. Peterson, *Close relationships* (pp. 68-109). New York: W. H. Freeman.

McGrath, J. E. (1988). Introduction: The place of time in social psychology. In J. E. McGrath (Ed.), *The social psychology of time: New perspectives* (pp. 7-17). Newbury Park, CA: Sage.

Mitchell, S. E., Newell, G. K., & Schumm, W. R. (1983). Test-retest reliability of the Kansas Marital Satisfaction Scale. *Psychological Reports, 53,* 545-546.

Nisbett, R., & Ross, L. (1980). *Human inference: Strategies and shortcomings of social judgment.* Englewood Cliffs, NJ: Prentice-Hall.

Nunnally, J. C. (1978). *Psychometric theory* (2nd ed.). New York: McGraw-Hill.

Olson, D. H. (1977). Insiders' and outsiders' views of relationships: Research strategies. In G. Levinger & H. L. Raush (Eds.), *Close relationships: Perspectives on the meaning of intimacy* (pp. 115-135). Amherst, MA: University of Massachusetts Press.

Peplau, L. A. (1983). Roles and gender. In H. H. Kelley, E. Berscheid, A. Christensen, J. H. Harvey, T. L. Huston, G. Levinger, E. McClintock, L. A. Peplau, & D. R. Peterson, *Close relationships* (pp. 220-264). New York: W. H. Freeman.

Scanzoni, J., Polonko, K., Teachman, J., & Thompson, L. (1989). *The sexual bond: Rethinking families and close relationships.* Newbury Park, CA: Sage.

Shaw, S. M. (1985). Gender and leisure: Inequality in the distribution of leisure time. *Journal of Leisure Research, 17,* 266–282.

Shaw, S. M. (1986). Leisure, recreation, or free time? Measuring time usage. *Journal of Leisure Research, 18,* 177–189.

Shweder, R. A., & D'Andrade, R. G. (1980). The systematic distortion hypothesis. In R. A. Shweder (Ed.), *Fallible judgment in behavioral research* (pp. 38–58). San Francisco: Jossey-Bass.

Spanier, G. B. (1976). Measuring dyadic adjustment: New scales for assessing the quality of marriage and similar dyads. *Journal of Marriage and the Family, 38,* 15–28.

Wills, T. A., Weiss, R. L., & Patterson, G. R. (1974). A behavioral analysis of the determinants of marital satisfaction. *Journal of Consulting and Clinical Psychology, 42,* 802–811.

# CHAPTER 3

# Observation of Marital Interaction

**Robert L. Weiss**
**Richard E. Heyman**

What makes a happy marriage happy? What do spouses in unsatisfying marriages do that makes their marriages conflict-prone? For the better part of this century, marital researchers from various disciplines have struggled to answer such questions. This chapter focuses on what we as marital researchers have learned over the last 20 years by observing couples and having spouses observe each other.

Despite the implied behavioral focus of "observation," comprehensive assessment of marital behaviors in the '80s includes data from affective, behavioral, and cognitive channels. Furthermore, behavioral analyses of marital interaction not only include these three areas of assessment but also tap them in three different ways: (1) self-report, (2) quasiobservational (spouses separately recording each others behaviors), and (3) behavioral "coding" of interaction samples, using systems that either record discrete behaviors or give global ratings of constructs.

Although the three modalities attempt to measure the same construct—marital behaviors—they do so in unique ways. Self-report methods inquire about interaction style or some other global view of marital interaction. Quasiobservational methods, on the other hand, are a cross between self-report and behavioral observation in that spouses use a checklist to record pleasing and displeasing behaviors that occurred during the day (e.g., Weiss & Perry, 1983). Instead of rating global concepts, spouses in essence replace outside observers in the recording of behavioral events.

Behavioral coding, in contrast, employs *outsiders* to record behaviors. These observers learn a set of behavioral definitions, that guide them as they watch the interactions. Discrete or "microbehavioral" systems break down the behaviors observed into a sequence of behavioral codes, which can then be analyzed using sophisticated statistical techniques. Global or "molar" systems train coders to watch the entire interaction and then rate the spouses on certain dimensions, such as supportiveness, withdrawal, or positivity. Recently, a hybrid system has been developed that has coders make "global" ratings for every "discrete" unit (i.e., each sentence) during the interaction (Roberts & Krokoff, 1990).

Integrating observational findings is sometimes difficult because different approaches to coding can result in very different pictures of marital interaction depending on the "richness" or "surplus" meaning of the codes used (Weiss, 1989). The greater the degree of inference required of the coder in making an observation, the less likely it is that acceptable interobserver agreement will be reached. Thus, at times, the most interesting theoretical concepts may not be represented in studies using observational coding. Higher-level concepts are sometimes synthesized from more rudimentary, more easily definable behavioral acts, with varying success. We feel compelled to forewarn the reader that the study of marital interaction may not always capture one's favorite theoretical constructs—to be sure, it may even seem quite barren at times! We do hope, however, that by surveying what we have found and identifying the most promising paths for future exploration, we will incite and excite you to add further creativity to the empirical study of marital interaction.

The study of marital interaction is predicated on a number of assumptions. The first is that one can discern order or patterning in the interaction behaviors of spouses. Patterning means redundancy, that is, certain sequences of husband–wife interactions are repeated temporally and therefore are predictable in some sense. Evidence of such patterning allows us to build a body of information about interactions. Second, it is assumed that patterning observed in the interactions of maritally distressed couples will differ from that of maritally satisfied couples. That is, marital distress is expressed in interaction behaviors and not just self-report. Third is the equally important assumption that samples of marital interactions taken at time 1 predict marital variables at time 2. Such longitudinal investigations are most important for understanding the development of marital adjustment and are to be preferred to data from cross-sectional studies. Finally, we must assume that samples of marital interaction represent typical patterns of interaction and that it is safe to extrapolate from limited (e.g., often laboratory) observations to more naturalistic interactions. These are a few of the major assumptions one makes in studying marital interaction.

This chapter reviews literature on the behavioral studies of marital interactions by focusing on the three modes of generating relevant data: self-report, quasiobservation, and observational coding. Our intent is to provide a representative sample of published studies rather than to chronicle every available study. We have also limited our coverage to representative studies that update major reviews in this area. The reader will find a bias in favor of reporting findings rather than a meticulous appraisal of research methodology. Finally, we shall look into our crystal ball and forecast what theoretical developments may await us.

## SELF-REPORT AND QUASIOBSERVATIONAL APPROACHES TO MARITAL INTERACTION

For all their insistence on behavioral rigor, one finds self-report a strange—yet acceptable—bedfellow among adherents to behavioral study of marital interaction. The relative cost-effectiveness of self-report over behavioral observation has made it an attractive option even among the faithful (cf. Jacobson, 1985).

Quasiobservational methods for measuring spouse interaction, putatively more behavioral than self-report, actually refer to a continuum ranging from self-report to true spouse observation. When does self-report become spouse observation? All things being equal, the continuum reflects the degree of temporal delay between the occurrence of a criterion event and the reporting of the event. Most self-report deals with varying degrees of recollection (e.g., the use of daily diaries), not with observation of immediate relationship behaviors. If spouses are asked to report on immediate events, much as an observer might, their reporting, technically, would be known as "tracking." However many occasions of spouses tracking one another actually involve delays between the supposed occurrence of the event and the formal coding of its occurrence. It is the degree of this temporal delay that is of concern. The longer the delay the more the observational mode becomes self-reported retrospections (diaries), not tracking.

Related to the question of when self-report becomes quasiobservation is the issue of the molarity of the events being reported on. As used here molarity refers not only to the size of the unit of observation but also to the number and complexity of inferences necessary for observers to agree that a specific event has occurred. As more and more context is needed to "understand" the events, the greater the likelihood that self-report and not quasiobservation is involved.

The limitations of retrospective methods are all too familiar (cf. Huston, Robins, Atkinson, & McHale, 1987; Robins, Chapter 2, this volume). In addition to these limitations we must assume (1) that spouses are capable of accurately recalling and expressing verbally events in their past interactions, events that are no doubt affectively valenced, and (2) that there would be agreement between spouses' and outside observers' tracking of the same events. Clearly if spouses are to function as substitute observers, they must provide the same information that outsider observers provide. Short of this, the data are samples of spouse interpretation (idiosyncratic perceptions), which may be useful as a sample of cognitions about interactions but not as samples of interaction behaviors *per se*. With these considerations before us, we turn to findings reported from self-report and quasiobservational studies of marital interaction.

### Self-Report of Marital Interaction

Margolin (1987) has reviewed the literature on participant observation as a method of marital assessment, thus making it possible for us to narrow our discussion of the various self-report methods. We have selected data from two different sources, Peterson and Rapinchuk (1989) and Christensen (1988), as most relevant to our consideration of self-reporting on marital interaction. Both approaches are similar in conception in that they attempt to capture either critical (conflict/disagreement) incidents or interaction cycles within marital interactions, which in turn are used to describe more global styles of interaction. The Peterson approach, for example, uses descriptions of critical incidents, generated by the spouses themselves, as data for categorizing transactions (e.g., defining eight interaction cycles called "mutual enjoyment, aggression/injury, mutual affection," etc.). The method requires a considerable degree of inference. An interaction record might deal with the circumstances of sexual approach by one partner and the subsequent rejection by the other.

Christensen implied the interaction record by having raters classify the contexts within which interactions occurred as well as general interaction patterns illustrated for each context. Thus, coders classified contexts (e.g., household tasks) and interaction patterns (e.g., mutual enjoyment). A self-report inventory was developed that asked couples to choose from various alternatives for each of three stages: leading up to, during, and after the conflict. The various interaction options included avoidance, demanding, withdrawing, blaming, and negotiating, among others. Partners rate whether these patterns fit their own relationship style.

Taken together there were few surprises in the findings reported for these approaches. Negative cycles have been found to characterize maritally distressed couples, whereas positive cycles characterize nondistressed couples. In outcomes judged to be constructive, affection was reciprocated (by either spouse) 63% of the time, but only 27% of the time in outcomes judged to be destructive. Finally, statistically significant correlations were found between self-reported marital satisfaction (the Dyadic Adjustment Scale; DAS) and positive ($r = .79$) and negative styles ($r = -.55$); once again the pattern, independent of which spouse was initiating or responding, was associated with marital satisfaction.

Recently, Heyman, Weiss, and Eddy (1990a) developed a self-report measure of withdrawal in intimate relationships that combines features of self-report and quasiobservation by having couples make *global* estimates of the frequency of *specific* conflict behaviors (e.g., "When my partner and I argue, I storm out of the room in anger"). They found that these ratings provided significant interspouse agreement on each other's conflict behaviors (e.g., agreement on withdrawal: $r = .41$, $p < .0005$). In addition, ratings of partner's withdrawal were related to marital satisfaction (DAS) and self-reports of partner abuse. Of particular note is the finding that both self-report of withdrawal and report on partner's withdrawal correlated significantly with outsider coding of videotaped sample interactions (respectively, $r = .33$ and .39, $p < .01$). Although the magnitude of these correlations is small, they do establish a connection between self-report and coded public behaviors.

Anticipating our later discussion of findings from behavioral observational studies, we may note at this point that self-reports of marital interactions provide evidence of patterned negative affect reciprocity. However, as with correlations among all self-report measures, the contribution of method variance may be considerable. The gain in cost-effectiveness (over behavioral observation) must be tempered by this fact. We must establish that couples are not merely reporting a generalized positive or negative sentiment—happiness or unhappiness with a partner can be expressed in as many tests as one chooses to administer!

### Quasiobservation: The Spouse Observation Checklist

In the late 1960s a group of investigators at Oregon applied various methods for tracking partner behaviors relevant to spouse interactions, first by using variations on *in vivo* tracking and subsequently by use of checklists (cf. Weiss & Perry, 1983). For example, spouses tracked ongoing affectional behaviors during certain periods of each day. This technology evolved rapidly into what is now known as the Spouse Observation Checklist (SOC); earlier versions had been referred to (immodestly) as the "universal checklist of pleases and displeases" (cf. Weiss, Hops, & Patterson, 1973). A "please" or "displease" (P or D) was a specific identifiable behavior ("spouse kissed me") the frequency of which each spouse recorded separately. Initially the events were preassigned to either the P or D category. Subsequently the items were presented without regard to valence, and subjects recorded them as Ps or Ds. Customized listings were prepared for individual couples using their baseline endorsements of events that seemed to be germane to their interactions; at that time the approximately 500 items had been entered on IBM cards, and a customized sort was made as needed for each therapy case.

The seminal study in this area was reported by Wills, Weiss, and Patterson (1974), using the original listing of Ps and Ds. The object of the study was to determine how much variance in daily marital satisfaction was accounted for by behaviors relevant to marital interaction (i.e., pleases and displeases); the study sought to determine patterns of reciprocity between spouses for either P or D events. Couples were first trained to make and record daily observations of their interactions and then provided data for 14 consecutive days using categories of affectional, instrumental, and other (nonmarital, i.e., work-related) Ps and Ds. (Frequencies of affectional Ps and Ds were tracked *in vivo* using individual "golf counters"; the frequencies of all other behaviors were recorded on special forms divided into three daily time blocks.) Data were collected by phone twice a day from each couple. In order to gauge whether individual spouses were recording accurately, one of the phone calls on day 12 instructed husbands to double their typical rate of affectional Ps, and a specific target number was provided to each husband. Husbands were also instructed not to inform their wives of this procedural change.

The major findings of this study were that (1) approximately 25% of the variance of daily marital satisfaction ratings (DSR) was accounted for by the maritally relevant Ps and Ds; (2) affectional and instrumental Ds decreased DSR more than affectional and instrumental Ps increased DSR; (3) the priming of husbands was generally successful in that wives' affectional Ps increased significantly on the critical days, although their instrumental pleases increased significantly also on these days; and (4) as a measure of within-couple daily reciprocity, the average correlation between husband and wife daily frequencies of displeasurable events was .59 ($p = .01$), but only .29 (ns) for pleasurable events.

In their assessment-focused review, Weiss and Perry (1983) listed 17 studies that had been reported subsequent to the original Wills et al. (1974) SOC study. Many of these studies highlighted important methodological concerns related to those identified in the introduction to this section, including issues of spouse agreement. Some have focused on issues of validity, such as differences in exchange rates for Ps and Ds between maritally distressed and nondistressed groups, whereas others have addressed conceptual issues. Thus, Weiss (1978) and Jacobson, Follette, and McDonald (1982) suggested that maritally distressed couples would be more immediately responsive to both positive and negative exchanges.

A number of studies have reported difficulty in obtaining spouse agreement on SOC events (mean agreement = 50%), and there is some indication that magnitude of agreement is related to marital distress (cf. Elwood & Jacobson, 1988). In view of these observations, it is important to determine whether the SOC is best viewed as a quasiobservation measure or merely as another self-report of cognition.

Elwood and Jacobson (1988) assessed the extent to which the SOC qualifies as an observational measure by suggesting that spouses as observers—just as any other behavioral observers—require training before we can expect them to make reliable (show interrater agreement) observations. In their study they solicited couples from the community and randomly designated one spouse as the recorder of events received (the usual SOC recording mode) and the other as the self-monitor of events. (Thus, the recorder's item "spouse complimented me" had a corresponding self-monitor item that read "I complimented spouse.") The extent of training was varied over three groups of couples. One group was explicitly trained to resolve their disagreements (e.g., by exchanging SOC records daily and discussing what each said they provided against what the other person recorded as having received). Another group was merely made aware that reliability would be checked by the experimenters, but nothing was said about exchanging lists. The control group kept SOC and self-monitoring records with no intention of reliability checking.

As expected, relative to the awareness and control groups, the training group showed significantly greater mean percentage agreement for the second week of training and again at posttest baseline (mean agreement = 61%). However, on a subsequent unannounced agreement check, the training group dropped in their mean agreement to 34%, which was very similar to mean agreement attained at that time by the other two groups. No relationship between agreement and marital satisfaction was found; the authors note that the magnitude of such a relationship in previous studies was quite small. (Results using kappa, which controls for chance agreement, were essentially the same.) No data were reported on the association between SOC and daily satisfaction rating.

Huston et al. (1987) employed SOC technology as part of a longitudinal investigation designed to describe the behavioral structure of marriage relationships. These authors were interested in describing marriages at the event level rather than at the level of perceptions of the marriage. All couples showed large declines in mean frequencies of affectional behaviors. Since there were no corresponding changes in reported negative behaviors, the authors concluded that decreased positivity rather than increased negativity characterizes the shift away from the honeymoon period.

Margolin (1981) reported a fairly typical pattern of positive to negative events as a function of marital distress and the length of the relationship. There was an overall decrease in the ratio of frequency of pleases to displease over the four childbearing stages (groups) for both happily and unhappily married groups (e.g., from 22:1 to 4:1 for happily married and from 5:1 to 3:1 for the unhappily married groups). Her unhappily married couples, relative to the happily marrieds, showed significantly greater evidence of negative reciprocity on a day-to-day basis.

As indicated above, 25% of the variance in daily relationship satisfaction can be accounted for with quasiobservation of behavioral events. Broderick and O'Leary (1986) investigated the relative importance of affect, attitude, and SOC data in studying the relationship between behavioral events and marital satisfaction. Self-report measures of positive feelings toward spouse, commitment, and exchange orientation were included together with 7 days of SOC data. Not surprisingly they found a very high correlation between "positive feelings" and the DAS (both self-report measures), accounting for approximately 74% of the satisfaction variance, and generally lower correlations between the SOC data and satisfaction, accounting for 6% to 17% of the variance. The attitude and SOC measures generally explained very little *unique* variance in satisfaction when positive feelings were included in a multiple regression analysis; when positive feelings were omitted from the analysis both attitude and SOC mesaures accounted uniquely for small amounts of satisfaction variance.

## The Epistemological Road Ahead

One fascinating question, awaiting further study, is how couples utilize behavioral data to form cognitions about their relationship. Do the behavioral data help to define affective responses? How, as participants in close relationships, do we gain relationship knowledge? The various modes of self-report and quasiobservational studies attempt to deal with this larger issue. But the difficulty in achieving spouse agreement (without prior training) suggests that "events" are largely in the eyes of the beholder. The problems with participant observation are legion, and asking couples either to record from memory or to track their own behaviors provides a bouillabaisse of data—a mix of affect, behavior, hope, and some reality. So long as we stay within method (e.g., verbal report), correlations among measures are reasonable: couples can report on what they do and how these acts relate to satisfaction. Crossing methods, a more stringent observational test, provides some evidence for convergence among what spouses know and what we see them doing.

Although frequencies of behaviors are important, they obviously do not tell the entire story. People do not track behavior as trained observers. They use categories that economically summarize experience, perhaps in a mindless way. Consequently, questions remain as to the interface between cognitions and behaviors, and all the more so as we become more interested in the role of attributions in marital behaviors. We might also argue that the presence of strong affects prevents agreement between insiders' and outsiders' observations. If self-report and quasiobservational approaches are to add substantially to our knowledge, we must consider their relationship to actual behaviors. The remainder of this chapter focuses on the observations trained observers make of interactions.

## BEHAVIORAL OBSERVATION OF COUPLES: 1980–1989

To borrow an image from Salvador Minuchin (1984), collecting the marital observation literature is like building a marital kaleidoscope. Look at the interesting, colorful finding there! Oh, but wait, turn to the next study, and everything looks different—but isn't the new one just as interesting as the first! Although there are substantive concordances in the literature, viewing couples through the eyes of hundreds of researchers and almost as many methodologies is apt to produce kaleidoscopic vertigo. In such a brief chapter we cannot even hope to bring the past decade of couples research into sharp focus. Our goal is to provide a selective review of what we as observers have learned about marriage in the last 10 years and what seem to be the most promising areas for further exploration.

Because two comprehensive reviews of the observational literature from the 1970s already exist (Gottman, 1979; Schaap, 1984), we reviewed every study involving the observation of couples that was published between January 1980 and June 1989. We concentrate on those that we feel made the most significant contributions to the observational study of marriage. We also briefly report the findings of the bulk of the remaining studies.

Although marital observation grew out of the ethological and behavioral traditions, the last 10 years have seen promising studies of affect, behavior, cognition, and clinical disorders within an observational framework. The findings in each area are discussed briefly, followed by a comprehensive discussion and recommendations for future research. We should note, however, that affect, behavior, and cognition are overlapping constructs, and thus classifying studies that blend two or three of the constructs is done somewhat arbitrarily.

### Affect

#### Measurement of Affect
Because affect is at the heart of marriage, it is not surprising that affective variables have provided the most consistent findings in

the marital observation literature. However, the majority of the affective data in the field were collected with behavioral observational coding systems. Affect findings generated by these systems are more appropriately classified as behavioral/affective and are discussed in subsequent subsections. In order to give a historical context for the observation of affect in marriages, we briefly discuss the different ways such systems incorporate affect.

The Marital Interaction Coding System (MICS; Weiss & Summers, 1983), one of the first and the most widely used coding systems, has nonverbal affect codes, affect/behavior codes, and behavior codes. The affective tone of the interaction is preserved by the MICS (and a recent update of the MICS by Heyman, Weiss, & Eddy, 1990b, gives affect and affect/behavior codes priority over behavior codes if they occur simultaneously), but because the MICS uses some affective/behavioral blends, it does not entirely isolate affect from behaviors.

The Couples Interaction Scoring System (CISS; Gottman, 1979) was derived partially from the MICS but codes behavior and affect separately—content is coded from a transcript of the interaction, whereas affect is coded from the videotape. The CISS affect ratings—along with the talk-table procedure, which has couples rate the speaker intent and listener impact of every statement during a problem-solving discussion—were the most direct measures of affect developed during the 1970s (i.e., they attempted to separate affect from content).

Affect research in the 1980s employed far more sophisticated measures of emotion. The series of studies by Robert Levenson and John Gottman (e.g., Gottman, 1990; Levenson & Gottman, 1983, 1985) not only provided astounding findings but also introduced methodological breakthroughs in the measurement of affect in marriages.

The first study (Levenson & Gottman, 1983) introduced to the marital field the idea of measuring physiological markers of affect (heart rate, skin conductance, circulatory constrictions, and general body movement) both during the interaction itself and during a video replay of the interaction. During the video replay, spouses provided continuous ratings of their affect on a rating dial with positive–negative poles. The video recall procedure was valid (i.e., spouse's physiological patterns while watching the video significantly replicated those experienced during the original interaction, Gottman & Levenson, 1985) and represented a much less intrusive method of obtaining self-report than the talk-table.

## Affect Results

Levenson and Gottman (1983) found that "physiological linkage" (i.e., how closely spouses' physiological responses matched one another during the interactions) accounted for an extraordinary 59% of the variance in marital satisfaction. When we consider that behavioral measures using trained observers are able to account for no more than 30% of the variance in marital satisfaction (Gottman & Levenson, 1986), this finding is indeed impressive.

In addition, the couples' self-reports of affect explained a significant percentage of variance in satisfaction (16%), over and above that of physiological linkage (Levenson & Gottman, 1983). Thus, self-reported affect adds nonredundant information to physiological measures of affect obtained during conflict.

The rating dial findings (Levenson & Gottman, 1983) revealed several differences between distressed and nondistressed couples. Distressed wives rated more negative affect than did nondistressed wives during the events-of-the-day (low conflict) discussion and less positive affect during the high-conflict problem discussion. Sequential analysis revealed that distressed wives were more likely to immediately (simultaneously) reciprocate their husband's negative affect and were more likely to reciprocate positivity during and immediately following their husband's positive affect.

Thus, in addition to being "locked together" physiologically, distressed wives seem to be responding to their husbands' affect in a similar locked-in manner. These findings extend results from several studies in the 1970s (e.g., Gottman, 1979), but the fact that physiological linkage, self-report of affect, and physiological variables accounted for 80% of concurrent satisfaction clearly demonstrates the predictive value of direct physiological measures of affect.

In terms of prediction, how well do these variables predict *future* satisfaction? Interestingly, physiological linkage was *not* related to satisfaction 3 years later (Levenson & Gottman, 1985). Simple measures of physiological arousal, however, predicted satisfaction inconceivably well: husbands' heart rate during the problem interaction accounted for 85% of the deterioration in satisfaction. Skin conductance for both husbands and wives also predicted deterioration remarkably well.

Self-reported affect was predictive only of the wives' satisfaction 3 years later. During the events-of-the-day discussion, deterioration was related to less positivity by the husband, more positivity by the wife, and less reciprocation of the wife's negative affect by the husband. The problem discussion results showed that less negative affect by the husband and more negative reciprocity by the wife resulted in marital deterioration. Furthermore, self-report of affect is related only to the *wife*'s future satisfaction, which Gottman (1990) believes implicates the wife as the "emotional barometer" of the relationship (i.e., her reaction to conflict discussions is critical to future satisfaction). However, considering the strong association between husband's physiological responses and later satisfaction, it is possible that certain husbands are less likely to *report* swings in affect, thus limiting the predictive power of their self-reports.

Levenson and Gottman's (1985) findings also point toward husband withdrawal as the key factor in decreased marital satisfaction—during the low-conflict interaction, deteriorating marriages were marked by an uninvolved husband and a wife who tried to draw him out. During the high-conflict tasks, deteriorating marriages were characterized by low experienced conflict by the husband and high locked-in qualities to the wives' negative affect exchange.

Given that physiological measures can almost perfectly predict deterioration of relationships, can observers and/or couples *see* affective cues that relate to these measures of deterioration? Critics (e.g., Weiss & Heyman, 1990) have pointed out that the clinical utility of physiological findings is extremely limited if neither couples nor therapists can distinguish such cues.

Gottman (1990) recently presented further findings from the Levenson and Gottman studies that indicate that observers can indeed see such affect indicators. For the husband's heart rate, these cues were (in declining order of importance) husband's self-report of affective tone, coder's ratings of a husband sadness–wife anger sequence, and coded base rates of husband sadness, husband whining, and wife sadness. For husband skin conductance, the variables were wife whining–husband anger, wife's affective self-report, husband sadness–wife anger, wife sadness–husband anger, wife whining, and husband whining–wife anger. For wife's skin conductance, significant variables were husband whining, husband sadness, and wife whining–husband anger (Gottman, 1990).

In sum, it appears that depressive behaviors (sadness and whining) and coercive sequences (depressive behavior followed by anger) are associated with long-term deterioration of the marriage. We should note that anger *per se* was not significantly related to deterioration (Gottman, 1990), only anger following an aversive behavior by the partner (i.e., coercion, see Patterson,

1982). The implications of these studies, both from a theory-generating and a theory-testing point of view, will be discussed in the final subsection. Finally, although these studies were well conducted, they have not been replicated yet, either by independent labs or by Levenson and Gottman. Considering the small sample (30 couples for the initial study and 19 couples for the follow-up) comprising volunteer couples from Indiana, further work needs to be conducted using this paradigm before we can safely rely on Levenson and Gottman's findings.

## Behavior: Cross-Sectional Studies

How does the behavior of happy couples differ from that of unhappy couples? This question has occupied the observational literature for the past 20 years. Etiological questions were eschewed by social learning theorists, who believed the key to understanding and treating dysfunctional relationships was in the here and now. Like the general systems theorists' notion of *equifinality* (many "causes" could result in the same outcome, rendering cause–effect epistemology of normal science useless), behavioral marital researchers felt that behaviors that *maintained*, not the ones that "caused," the distress had the greatest clinical utility.

The literature of the 1970s showed clear differences between distressed and nondistressed couples. For example, distressed couples, compared to nondistressed couples, were more negative in problem-solving interactions, made personal attacks, used coercion, engaged in negative and positive reciprocity cycles, and employed fewer problem-solving behaviors and positive listener behaviors (Schaap, 1984).

### Distressed versus Nondistressed Couples: Base Rates

Results from the 1980s were consistent with prior findings. Satisfied couples use more assent (Margolin & Wampold, 1981; Revenstorf, Hahlweg, Schindler, & Vogel, 1984; Schaap, 1984), approval/caring (Birchler, Clopton, & Adams, 1984; Cousins & Vincent, 1983; Schaap, 1984), empathy (Birchler et al., 1984), agreement (Fichten & Wright, 1983; Margolin & Wampold, 1981; Revenstorf et al., 1984; Schaap, 1984), humor (Fichten & Wright, 1983; Revenstorf et al., 1984; Schaap, 1984), smile/laugh (Margolin & Wampold, 1981; Revenstorf et al., 1984; Schaap, 1984), positive physical touch (Margolin & Wampold, 1981; Revenstorf et al., 1984), problem description (Birchler et al., 1984; Margolin & Wampold, 1981), problem solutions (Birchler et al., 1984; Floyd,

O'Farrell, & Goldberg, 1987; Margolin, Burman, & John, 1989; Margolin & Wampold, 1981; Schaap, 1984), involvement (Margolin et al., 1989), positive verbal (Birchler et al., 1984; Hooley & Hahlweg, 1989; O'Farrell & Birchler, 1987; Schaap & Jansen-Nawas, 1987) and positive nonverbal behaviors (Birchler et al., 1984; Schaap & Jansen-Nawas, 1987; Margolin et al., 1989), negative verbal behaviors (Birchler et al., 1984), and normative movements (Revenstorf et al., 1984).

Satisfied couples use more confirming, feeling description, and instrumental questioning behaviors (Ting-Toomey, 1983). They make more specific *behavioral* complaints (as opposed to personality complaints), are more likely to agree when their partners complain about them, are more likely to couple complaints with positive affective cues (Alberts, 1988), and are more responsive (Koren, Carlton, & Shaw, 1980) and accepting (Hooley & Hahlweg, 1989).

Dissatisfied couples emit a higher level of global negativity (Cousins & Vincent, 1983; Notarius, Benson, & Sloane, 1989) and various negative behaviors: criticism (Hooley & Hahlweg, 1989; Fichten & Wright, 1983; Koren et al., 1980; Revenstorf et al., 1984; Schaap, 1984), hostility and displeasure (Roberts & Krokoff, 1990), put-down (Revenstorf et al., 1984; Schaap, 1984), excuse (Schaap, 1984), deny responsibility (Revenstorf et al., 1984; Schaap, 1984), no response (Revenstorf et al., 1984), not tracking (Revenstorf et al., 1984), and negative nonverbal behavior (Hooley & Hahlweg, 1989). They also complain more (Revenstorf et al., 1984), make more *personal* characteristic complaints, and pair complaints with negative affect (Alberts, 1988).

The literature is contradictory for eye contact (Revenstorf et al., 1984, and Schaap & Jansen-Nawas, 1987, found satisfied couples use more, whereas Schaap, 1984, found they were more likely to not track), interruption and command (Margolin & Wampold, 1981, found satisfied couples use more, whereas Schaap, 1984, and O'Farrell & Birchler, 1987, found dissatisfied couples use more), and disagreement (Fichten & Wright, 1983, found satisfied couples use more, whereas Schaap, 1984, and Hooley & Hahlweg, 1989, found dissatisfied couples use more).

## Distressed versus Nondistressed Couples: Sequential Patterns

In addition to emitting different *levels* of positive and negative behaviors, distressed and nondistressed couples are distinguishable by the pattern or structure of their behavior exchanges. Dissatisfied relationships are marked by confront → confront, confront → defend, complain → defend, and defend → complain sequences (Ting-Toomey, 1983). They are more likely to respond to complaints with countercomplaints (Alberts, 1988). Both distressed and nondistressed couples exhibit positive reciprocity; however, distressed couples were the only ones who immediately recriprocated negative behaviors (Hooley & Hahlweg, 1989; Margolin & Wampold, 1981).

Schaap (1984) found that in satisfied marriages wife's positive affect was reciprocated by the husband, and both partners reciprocated negative affect. Distressed couples showed the opposite pattern for positive reciprocity: husband positives were reciprocated by the wife. Furthermore, distressed couples displayed a wife aversive → husband acquiesce pattern—negative behavior by the wife resulted in less negative behavior by the husband.

Roberts and Krokoff (1990) also found asymmetric patterns of withdrawal. Satisfied couples displayed patterns of wife withdrawal → husband withdrawal and husband negative affect → wife negative affect. In dissatisfied marriages two patterns were found: wife displeasure → husband displeasure and husband withdrawal → wife hostility. These researchers found that whereas affective tone accounted for 50% of the variance between satisfied and dissatisfied groups, husband withdrawal evoking wife hostility accounted for an additional 20%.

### Gender Differences: Base Rates
Wives display more smile/laugh (Jacob & Krahn, 1988; Margolin & Wampold, 1981), humor (Jacob & Krahn, 1988), complain (Fichten & Wright, 1983; Margolin & Wampold, 1981), criticize (Fichten & Wright, 1983; Jacob & Krahn, 1988; Margolin & Wampold, 1981), disagree (Fichten & Wright, 1983; Jacob & Krahn, 1988), and positive nonverbal (O'Farrell & Birchler, 1987) behaviors. Negative wife behavior is correlated to the steps she has taken toward divorce (Floyd et al., 1987). Husbands use more excuses (Margolin & Wampold, 1981), negative nonverbal behavior (O'Farrell & Birchler, 1987), no-eye-contact (Margolin & Wampold, 1981), and agreement (Fichten & Wright, 1983). Fichten and Wright (1983) also found that distressed wives and happy husbands tended to deny responsibility more (see Baucom, Notarius, Burnett, & Haefner, Chapter 5, this volume).

### Behavior: Longitudinal Studies

As mentioned above, marital researchers have, for the most part, concentrated on the here and now, believing that current behaviors maintain the differences between happy and unhappy couples. Several studies from the 1980s, however, indicate that this trust in the "power of the present" was misplaced. In fact, we are so firmly convinced that advancement in this field is fundamentally dependent on longitudinal findings that we considered eliminating the prior section on cross-sectional findings as irrelevant and potentially misleading. Although we do not advocate ignoring completely the cross-sectional findings, we find it imperative to point out that longitudinal studies (e.g., Levenson and Gottman's studies on affect), indicate that correlates of concurrent satisfaction are often either irrelevant to or have opposite associations with future satisfaction.

## Concurrent and Long-Term Satisfaction: Base Rates

The first studies to demonstrate this pattern are Markman's (1979, 1981) studies employing the talk-table to obtain spouse's own ratings of the impact of their partner's behavior. Impact ratings were not related to concurrent satisfaction or to satisfaction 1 year later, but they were significant predictors of satisfaction $2\frac{1}{2}$ ($r = .67$) and 5 years ($r = .59$) later.

Markman (1982) also uncovered preliminary evidence for a counterintuitive pattern: husband's behavioral "deficits" (i.e., interrupt, mind-read, disagree, and summarize self) were not significantly associated with satisfaction concurrently but were moderately correlated ($r = .46$) with satisfaction 1 year later. Although Markman did not control for initial levels of satisfaction, his finding is especially interesting in retrospect, because it is similar to those found in Gottman and Krokoff (1989), which we believe to be a landmark paper.

Gottman and Krokoff found that husband's negative behavior (collapsing MICS codes) was moderately negatively correlated with both husband's and wife's concurrent satisfaction but was strongly correlated with *increases* in marital satisfaction measured 3 years later. Analyses of specific content areas yielded similar results: positive verbalization by the wife was associated with concurrent satisfaction for both partners but was associated with deterioration over time for both partners. In contrast, husband conflict engagement was associated with concurrent dissatisfaction but longitudinal increases in satisfaction for both partners. Wife conflict engagement, although related to both partners' concurrent satisfaction, was related to improvement in the wife's satisfaction only. Conversely, husband's disagreement accompanied by neutral affect was negatively related to concurrent satisfaction but a good predictive sign for the husband only. The same wife behavior was related to long-term improvement for both partners.

Some behaviors were not significant predictors of concurrent satisfaction but were significant predictive of future outcomes: compliance by the wife resulted in long-term declines for both partners; husband withdrawal resulted in husband's, but not wife's, declines; and husband mind-read with neutral affect was linked to increases for both partners. Affective states (coded with Gottman's new specific affect coding system, SPAFF) fitting this pattern are wife fear (predictive of deterioration for the wife), wife sadness (deterioration for both partners), and husband whining (deterioration for husband).

Many behaviors were related to concurrent satisfaction but not to either partner's future outcomes: husband global positivity, wife global negativity, husband defensiveness, wife stubbornness, wife withdrawal. Husband contempt and wife anger, as coded by the SPAFF, also fit this pattern.

Overall, this study demonstrated that (1) different behaviors predict concurrent and longitudinal satisfaction; (2) some behaviors, such as the husband's negativity, conflict engagement, and disagreement, are associated with relationship difficulties in the short run but with improvement in the long run; (3) wife's positivity, on the other hand, is adaptive in the short run but maladaptive in the long run; (4) husband's withdrawal and whining and wife's sadness and fear, which have little impact at the time, are predictive of negative change. Replication of this study is especially important because of the increased probability of chance findings when over 50 tests are conducted at the $p < .05$ level of significance. (Even with this overly liberal criterion, Gottman and Krokoff discussed nonsignificant trends in the abstract and discussion as if they were significant.)

## Concurrent and Long-Term Satisfaction: Sequential Patterns

Filsinger and Thoma (1988) found that negative reciprocity during a problem discussion predicted relationship dissolution 1½ years later. Positive reciprocity predicted dissolution at 1½, 2½, and 5 year follow-ups. In addition, 80% of the couples with high levels of female interruptions of the male dissolved over the 5-year period. These longitudinal results lend support to the previously mentioned SOC and observational findings that maritally distressed couples are more stimulus bound, that is, more likely to respond in a tit-for-tat manner.

## Cognition

A number of studies have provided data supporting the hypothesis that cognitions play a mediating role in marital behavior (see also Fincham, Bradbury, & Scott, Chapter 4, this volume). One commonly used paradigm is the use of a talk-table or communication box, which forces spouses to take turns giving and receiving communications. They pause between turns to rate the intent and impact of the statement on a five-point positivity/negativity scale. Typically, coders also rate the statements on the same scale. Talk-table ratings are an affective/cognitive measure—we have already mentioned findings that seem more closely aligned with affect research and now present studies that used the procedure to test cognitive hypotheses.

This paradigm has been used in several studies to test the "sentiment-override" hypothesis (Weiss, 1980), which states that spouse's behaviors frequently have more to do with global feelings of affection/disaffection than with the actual valence of the stimulus. Floyd and Markman (1983), studying community couples, found that impact ratings were not correlated with the valence of the message as coded by observers. Impact ratings, however, were correlated to observer's ratings of the message the spouse was *sending.* Floyd (1988) replicated this study with premarital couples and found that the sentiment-override pattern held for males only; females decoded accurately. Yet Notarius et al. (1989) found that distressed wives tended to rate partner's neutral behaviors as negative and also were more likely to respond negatively, indicating that *distressed* females may use sentiment override. Thus, length of relationship and satisfaction may influence whether females decode correctly, whereas all males may typically employ sentiment override.

Self-reports of causal attribution for relationship events have been shown to be related to base rates and sequences of behavior. The number of negative behavioral acts for both husbands and wives during an observed interaction correlates with the perceived degree to which the spouse caused the problem and how much responsibility he or she bears for the problem. The rate of positive behaviors is related to these cognitions for the wife only (Fincham & Bradbury, in press).

The probability that the husband will reciprocate positive wife behaviors decreases if he believes she is the cause of the problem and that her actions are intentional, selfishly motivated, and blameworthy. The husband will reciprocate negative behaviors if he believes his wife's contributions to the problem are intentional. Correspondingly, the wife's engagement in positive reciprocity decreases if she believes her husband's motivations are selfish and his acts intentional. She will reciprocate his negative behaviors if she believes the problem resides in him or is stable, selfishly motivated, and blameworthy (Bradbury & Fincham, 1988).

## Clinical Disorders and Marriage

Marital interaction has been studied within three clinical areas of interest, namely, depression, alcoholic marriages, and spouse abuse. We briefly review findings from these areas to illustrate how interaction research with clinical groups can advance our understanding of marriage (see also Gotlib & McCabe, Chapter 8, and O'Leary & Vivian, Chapter 11, this volume).

### Depression

Base rate analyses of observational coding of couples with a depressed partner indicate that depressed wives have increased levels of dysphoric affect and verbalizations (Hautzinger, Linden, & Hoffman, 1982; Ruscher & Gotlib, 1988), lower positive affect and statements (Hops et al., 1987; Ruscher & Gotlib, 1988), make negative self-related and positive partner-related verbalizations (Linden, Hautzinger, & Hoffmann, 1983), and have lower intended and perceived positiveness and higher negativity (Kowalik & Gotlib, 1987) during problem discussions.

Several studies have used sequential analyses to examine the interaction patterns of depressed/distressed, depressed/nondistressed, and nondepressed/nondistressed couples. Biglan and his colleagues (Biglan et al., 1985; Hops et al., 1987) used coercion theory (Patterson, 1982) to predict that depressed behavior by wives would be aversive and thus reduce the probability that their husbands or children would respond aggressively. They indeed found that, in the depressed/distressed group only, depressed behavior by the wife resulted in a reduction in the probability that the husband (Biglan et al., 1985) and children (Hops et al., 1987) would respond aggressively. Although both coercive (husband or children aggressive) and supportive (husband facilitation) behaviors reduced the probability of the wife's depressive behavior, husbands of depressed wives showed high levels of aggressive behavior and low levels of facilitation.

Nelson (1988), however, found a seemingly divergent pattern. Husbands in the nondepressed/distressed group (a group not included in the Biglan et al., 1985, and Hops et al., 1987, studies) were significantly less likely to respond to depressed behaviors with aggressive behaviors than were husbands in depressed/distressed or nondepressed/distressed marriages. Nelson (1988) speculated that the differences between his results and those of the Biglan group may be caused by husbands of depressed wives habituating to the depressed behavior of their wives, making them less coerced by the depressed behavior. He found that wives in the depressed/distressed group emitted significantly more depressed behaviors than wives in the other groups, most likely because these behaviors no longer provided the suppression they once did. He proposed that the results from his study and the Biglan et al. study would be compatible if the husbands in the Biglan et al. study had been exposed to the coercive behaviors for less time than the husbands in his own study.

However, further examination of the results of Nelson (1988) in Beach and Nelson (1990) explain more fully the discrepancy with Biglan et al. (1985). Greater suppression of aggressive behavior by depressive behaviors was associated with shorter duration of discord within both depressed groups (depressed/distressed and nondepressed/distressed). Also, the nondepressed/discordant couples reported marital discord of shorter duration than their depressed counterparts, which accounted for the group differences in depressive suppression of aggressive behavior.

Thus, for couples whose marriages have been discordant for a brief time, a depressive behavior will suppress aggressive responses by the partner. However, as discord continues over time, this relationship weakens, probably because the husband habituates to this behavior—it no longer stops his aggressive response.

## Alcohol

Three well-controlled studies compared the interactions of alcoholic couples and control couples. Couples with an alcoholic partner were less positive (Jacob & Krahn, 1988; Jacob, Ritchey, Cvitkovic, & Blane, 1981; O'Farrell & Birchler, 1987), more negative (Jacob et al., 1981), and interrupted more (O'Farrell & Birchler, 1987) than nondistressed couples. These findings do not seem to be unique to alcoholic couples, however, because these base rates did not distinguish them from depressed (Jacob &

Krahn, 1988) or distressed (O'Farrell & Birchler, 1987) couples. O'Farrell and Birchler (1987) found preliminary support for the hypothesis that alcoholic couples have higher levels of negativity (e.g., criticism, disagree, put down) than depressed or nondistressed couples when drinking but not when sober. O'Farrell and Birchler (1987) found a pattern unique for alcoholic husbands: they accepted responsibility more than their wives did. Alcoholic husbands also denied responsibility more than nondistressed husbands.

## Spouse Abuse

Recently, Margolin and her colleagues (Margolin, John, & Gleberman, 1988; Margolin et al., 1989) and Smith and O'Leary (1987) used affective coding systems to study the problem discussions of physically abusive couples. Margolin et al. (1989) had couples reenact marital conflicts in their homes. They reported that physically abusive couples displayed more overt hostility than other conflictual couples. Abusive couples maintained this hostility (along with increasing patronizing statements) during the last third of the conflict, whereas other conflictual couples decreased these behaviors. Correspondingly, the other conflictual groups increased, and the abusive couples decreased, their problem-solving behaviors during the final third. Physically abusive husbands differed from husbands in other conflict groups in observers' ratings of overall defensiveness and in increasing levels of uninvolvement and despair and decreasing warmth as the conflict discussion unfolded.

Margolin et al. (1988) found that physically abusive husbands displayed more negative behaviors and negative voice tone than husbands in other types of conflictual marriages. In addition, wives in physically abusive relationships differed from wives in the other conflict group by their higher escalation of negative affect during the middle segments of the discussion. On a postinteraction questionnaire, abusive men reported more sadness, fear, anger, physiological arousal, and feeling attacked than the other husbands. Similarly, Smith and O'Leary (1987) found that the expression of negative affect during an audiotaped premarital problem discussion was a strong longitudinal predictor of spousal aggression, though *observer*-rated arousal was not. Vivian and O'Leary (1987) also used audiotaped discussions, and found that physically aggressive couples displayed significantly more criticism, negative affect, and negative affect reciprocity than nonabusive/distressed couples. Both groups showed reciprocity of positive affect and of negative and positive content.

Vivian, Smith, Sandeen, and O'Leary (1987) again used audiotaped discussions. They found that aggressive couples agreed less, and wives of abusive husbands criticized more, than nonaggressive couples. Sequential analysis revealed that whereas abused wives reciprocated the husbands' negative *content* more than did nonabused wives, abusive husbands were more likely to reciprocate negative *affect* than nonaabusive husbands. Vivian's group found no differences in the base rates of overall positivity or negativity. They concluded that aggressive discordant couples are only moderately different in their approach to problem solving than nonaggressive/discordant couples.

## CONCLUSIONS AND RECOMMENDATIONS: THE DIRECTIONS FOR THE 1990s

After examining the considerable volume of information about marital interactions, we thought we had a marital kaleidoscope: the pieces, interesting and beautiful in isolation, seemed nonetheless to form a confusing, obfuscating filter for our observational understanding of couples. Having now sorted through the fragments, we believe that the pieces really form a jigsaw puzzle, as so many of the parts fit together nicely.

We feel that the 1980s studies' largest contributions are the following:

1. *Longitudinal study is crucial.* Concurrent patterns that relate to satisfaction are different from, and often opposite from, long-term patterns. Factors most important in the long run seem to be physiological arousal; depressive behaviors; coercive responses to depressive behaviors; husband's conflict engagement, willingness to behave negatively, and lack of withdrawal; wife's lack of positiveness during high-conflict discussions; and perceived impact of partner's behavior, perhaps because sentiment override results in behavior being driven by impact rather than by the actual qualities of the partner's message.

Future research should explore why concurrent and longitudinal findings diverge. For example, physiological linkage by itself may not be predictive of future deterioration, but high-linkage/high-arousal groups may be particularly prone to deterioration (a possibility never discussed in Gottman and Levenson's papers). Research exploring the differences between concurrent and future predictors is in its infancy, but we are firmly convinced that future breakthroughs depend on it.

2. *Coercion theory explains most important negative patterns.* Coercive processes involve behaviors with the following characteristics: "(1) they are aversive; (2) they are used contingently; (3) they produce a reliable impact upon the victim; (4) the reaction of the victim has both a short-term and a long-term impact upon the aggressor" (Patterson, 1982, p. 13). Coercive patterns linked with dissatisfaction by 1980s research include depressive behavior → angry response, negative behavior → negative response, wife aversive → husband acquiesce, and husband withdraw → wife anger.

3. *Depression must be taken into account by marital researchers.* Coercion also seems to be implicated in the interactions of couples with a depressed partner. Because marital distress has been shown to precede depression in longitudinal studies (e.g., Beach, Arias, & O'Leary, 1988; Lin, Dean, & Ensel, 1986; Monroe, Bromet, Cornell, & Steiner, 1986), it seems highly likely that the development of depression in distressed marriages is the result of the same coercive processes that are associated with the deterioration of the marriage. Further research must be conducted to identify marital factors (i.e., affect, behavior, and/or cognitions and sequences) that are longitudinally linked to distress and depression while controlling for alternative explanations.

Furthermore, because there is a high concordance of distress and depression, researchers must recognize that "distressed" groups will contain significant levels of depression and "depressed" groups will contain significant levels of distress. Any researcher who wishes to study one phenomenon in the absence of the other must select the groups carefully and also recognize that such homogeneous groups are not reflective of the overall population.

4. *Physiological measures of affect should be used.* Physiological measures appear to provide a highly predictive affective pipeline. If the Levenson and Gottman findings hold true, researchers should conduct large-scale longitudinal studies that attempt to discover what observable behavioral and affective patterns are related to the affective measures that predict marital deterioration.

Furthermore, Gottman and Levenson (1986) have constructed a physiological extension of coercion theory: the escape-conditioning model. They proposed that not only are coercive behaviors reinforcing in a behavioral sense (reducing the probability of an aversive response by the spouse) but also certain aversive sequences reduce diffuse physiological arousal (an aversive condition) for both partners and are thus physiologically reinforcing. Gottman and Levenson (1986) proposed that escape conditioning could lead to the structured, stereotyped behavioral sequences of distressed couples.

Once again, longitudinal study is crucial to the testing of the escape-conditioning model. However, a complete testing of the hypothesis would require taking physiological and behavioral measurements at later points in time (not merely the usual collection of self-reports of satisfaction) to see if couple-characteristic escape moments do indeed lead to higher levels of reinforced sequences and lower levels of satisfaction in the future. In addition, if one is interested in the development and implications of escape-conditioned aversive sequences, the population of choice to study would be newly married couples, who presumably are only beginning to develop such sequences.

5. *Improved recruitment procedures should replace samples of convenience.* Krokoff (1987) detailed a three-stage recruitment process that produced a sample much closer to the actual demographic make-up of the population of the United States. Krokoff conducted a telephone survey of marital satisfaction, identified a pool of interested couples, mailed a letter explaining the purpose of the study, and held informational home meetings. The resulting sample matched the population more closely than typical observation study samples on age, marital length, blue collar/white collar status, education, and number of children (i.e., they were older, had been married longer, were more likely to be blue collar, were less educated, and had fewer young children living at home). Because withdrawal, especially by the husband, seems to be an important factor in marital distress (Gottman, 1990), this procedure appears to be especially important, as it serves to recruit couples less likely to be communication-oriented than those typically recruited. Krokoff (in press) has found, however, that even with the improved recruitment procedures, those couples who chose not to participate were more likely to contain a withdrawn husband.

6. *Withdrawal will emerge as a critical factor in distress.* As noted above, various findings converge on the importance of withdrawal in the development of marital distress. Gottman's complicated, impressive new theory (Gottman, 1990) proposes that with-

drawal, which he calls "pattern X," results in the continuation of diffuse physiological arousal generated from marital friction and, over time, the deterioration of the marriage. Research in the 1990s should test this model in conjunction with the escape-conditioning hypothesis, which will necessitate the collection of physiological measures.

7. *Sequential analyses should be used.* With the refinement of lag-sequential analyses in the 1980s (e.g., Allison & Liker, 1982; Wampold & Margolin, 1982), researchers have become much more willing to extend their investigations beyond mere base rate analysis. As indicated above, *sequences* of behavior appear to be just as important, if not more important, than base rates. We also suggest that researchers employ the transformed kappa statistic (Wampold, 1989), which is superior to the statistics currently in use (Wampold & Kim, 1989).

8. *Social psychoneuroimmunology.* Levenson and Gottman (1983, 1985) demonstrated that physiological linkage and arousal are related to distress and deterioration. Epidemiological studies have demonstrated the negative health, psychopathological, and mortality effects of distress and separation/divorce (see Bloom, Asher, & White, 1978). Furthermore, recent studies by Kiecolt-Glaser and colleagues (Kiecolt-Glaser et al., 1987, 1988) have isolated certain immunologic deficiencies in distressed and separated/divorced spouses. These converging results strongly imply that marital interaction influences immunology through direct physiological means. We believe that a promising area of research in the 1990s will be the identification of behavioral/affective sequences that have direct immunodeficient actions.

# ACKNOWLEDGMENT

The authors wish to thank Amy Davis for her help in the many stages of preparing this chapter.

# REFERENCES

Alberts, J. K. (1988). An analysis of couples' conversational complaints. *Communication Monographs, 55,* 184–197.

Allison, P. D., & Liker, J. K. (1982). Analyzing sequential categorical data on dyadic interaction: Comment on Gottman. *Psychological Bulletin, 91,* 393–403.

Beach, S. R. H., & Nelson, G. M. (1990). Pursuing research on major psychopathology from a contextual perspective: The example of depression and marital discord. In G. Brody & I. E. Sigel (Eds.), *Family research* (vol. 2, pp. 227–259). Hillsdale, NJ: Erlbaum.

Beach, S. R. H., Arias, I., & O'Leary, K. D. (1988, August). *Life events, marital discord, and depressive symptomatology.* Paper presented at the 96th Annual Convention of the American Psychological Association, Atlanta.

Biglan, A., Hops, H., Sherman, L., Friedman, L. S., Arthur, J., & Osteen, V. (1985). Problem-solving interactions of depressed women and their husbands. *Behavior Therapy, 16,* 431–451.

Birchler, G. R., Clopton, P. L., & Adams, N. L. (1984). Marital conflict resolution: Factors influencing concordance between partners and trained coders. *American Journal of Family Therapy, 12,* 15–28.

Bloom, B. L., Asher, S. J., & White, S. W. (1978). Marital disruption as a stressor: A review and analysis. *Psychological Bulletin, 85,* 867–894.

Bradbury, T. N., & Fincham, F. D. (1988, November). *The impact of attributions in marriage: Attributions and behavior exchange in marital interactions.* Paper presented at the Convention of the Association for Advancement of Behavior Therapy, New York.

Broderick, J. E., & O'Leary, K. D. (1986). Contributions of affect, attitudes, and behavior to marital satisfaction. *Journal of Consulting and Clinical Psychology, 54,* 514–517.

Christensen, A. (1988). Dysfunctional interaction patterns in couples. In P. Noller & M. A. Fitzpatrick (Eds.), *Perspectives on marital interaction* (pp. 31–52). Philadelphia: Multilingual Matters Ltd.

Cousins, P. C., & Vincent, J. P. (1983). Supportive and aversive behavior following spousal complaints. *Journal of Marriage and the Family, 45,* 679–682.

Elwood, R. W., & Jacobson, N. S. (1988). The effects of observational training on spouse agreement about events in their relationship. *Behaviour Research and Therapy, 26,* 159–167.

Fichten, C. S., & Wright, J. (1983). Problem-solving skills in happy and distressed couples: Effects of videotape and verbal feedback. *Journal of Clinical Psychology, 39,* 340–352.

Filsinger, E. E., & Thoma, S. J. (1988). Behavioral antecedents of relationship stability and adjustment: A five-year longitudinal study. *Journal of Marriage and the Family, 50,* 785–795.

Fincham, F. D., & Bradbury, T. N. (in press). Cognition in marriage: A program of research on attributions. In D. Perlman & W. Jones (Eds.), *Advances in personal relationships* (vol. 2). London: J. Kingsley Publishers.

Floyd, F. J. (1988). Couples' cognitive/affective reactions to communication behaviors. *Journal of Marriage and the Family, 50,* 523–532.

Floyd, F. J., & Markman, H. J. (1983). Observational biases in spouse observation: Toward a cognitive/behavioral model of marriage. *Journal of Consulting and Clinical Psychology, 51,* 450–457.

Floyd, F. J., O'Farrell, T. J., & Goldberg, M. (1987). Comparison of marital observation measures: The Marital Interaction Coding System and the Communication Skills Test. *Journal of Consulting and Clinical Psychology, 55,* 423–429.

Gottman, J. M. (1979). *Marital interaction: Empirical investigations.* New York: Academic Press.

Gottman, J. M. (1990). How marriages change. In G. R. Patterson (Ed.), *Depression and aggression in family interaction* (pp. 75–101). Hillsdale, NJ: Erlbaum.

Gottman, J. M., & Krokoff, L. J. (1989). Marital interaction and marital satisfaction: A longitudinal view. *Journal of Consulting and Clinical Psychology, 57,* 47–52.

Gottman, J. M., & Levenson, R. W. (1985). A valid procedure for obtaining self-report of affect in marital interaction. *Journal of Consulting and Clinical Psychology, 53,* 151–160.

Gottman, J. M., & Levenson, R. W. (1986). Assessing the role of emotion in marriage. *Behavioral Assessment, 8,* 31–48.

Hautzinger, M., Linden, M., & Hoffman, N. (1982). Distressed couples with and without a depressed partner: An analysis of their verbal interaction. *Journal of Behavior Therapy and Experimental Psychiatry, 13,* 307–314.

Heyman, R. E., Weiss, R. L., & Eddy, J. M. (1990a). *Self-report and observational measures of withdrawal in marital interactions.* Manuscript submitted for publication.

Heyman, R. E., Weiss, R. L., & Eddy, J. M. (1990b). *Marital Interaction Coding System—IV.* Unpublished manuscript, University of Oregon, Eugene.

Hooley, J. M., & Hahlweg, K. (1989). Marital satisfaction and marital communication in German and English couples. *Behavioral Assessment, 11,* 119–133.

Hops, H., Biglan, A., Sherman, L., Arthur, J., Friedman, L. S., & Osteen, V. (1987). Home observations of family interactions of depressed women. *Journal of Consulting and Clinical Psychology, 55,* 341–346.

Huston, T. L., Robins, E., Atkinson, J., & McHale, S. M. (1987). Surveying the landscape of marital behavior: A behavioral self-report approach to studying marriage. *Applied Social Psychology Annual, 7,* 45–72.

Jacob, T., & Krahn, G. L. (1988). Marital interactions of alcoholic couples: Comparison with depressed and nondistressed couples. *Journal of Consulting and Clinical Psychology, 56,* 73–79.

Jacob, T., Ritchey, D., Cvitkovic, J. F., & Blane, H. T. (1981). Communication styles of alcoholic and nonalcoholic families when drinking and not drinking. *Journal of Studies on Alcohol, 39,* 1231–1251.

Jacobson, N. S. (1985). The role of observational measures in behavioral therapy outcome research. *Behavioral Assessment, 7,* 297–308.

Jacobson, N. S., Follette, W. C., & McDonald, D. W. (1982). Reactivity to positive and negative behavior in distressed and nondistressed marital couples. *Journal of Consulting and Clinical Psychology, 50,* 706–714.

Kiecolt-Glaser, J. K., Fisher, L. D., Ogrocki, P., Stout, J. C., Speicher, C. E., & Glaser, R. (1987). Marital quality, marital disruption, and immune function. *Psychosomatic Medicine, 49,* 13–34.

Kiecolt-Glaser, J. K., Kennedy, S., Malkoff, S., Fisher, L., Speicher, C. E., & Glaser, R. (1988). Marital discord and immunity in males. *Psychosomatic Medicine, 50,* 213–229.

Koren, P., Carlton, K., & Shaw, D. (1980). Marital conflict: Relations among behaviors, outcomes, and distress. *Journal of Consulting and Clinical Psychology, 48,* 460–468.

Kowalik, D. L., & Gotlib, I. H. (1987). Depression and marital interaction: Concordance between intent and perception of communication. *Journal of Abnormal Psychology, 96,* 127–134.

Krokoff, L. J. (1987). The correlates of negative affect in marriage. *Journal of Family Issues, 8,* 111–135.

Krokoff, L. J. (in press). The relationship between the husband's emotional involvement and participation in research on marital relationships. *Journal of Family Issues.*

Levenson, R. W., & Gottman, J. M. (1983). Marital interaction: Physiological linkage and affective exchange. *Journal of Personality and Social Psychology, 45*, 587–597.

Levenson, R. W., & Gottman, J. M. (1985). Physiological and affective predictors of change in relationship satisfaction. *Journal of Personality and Social Psychology, 49*, 85–94.

Lin, N., Dean, A., & Ensel, W. (1986). *Social support, life events, and depression.* New York: Academic Press.

Linden, M., Hautzinger, M., & Hoffmann, N. (1983). Discriminant analysis of depressive interactions. *Behavior Modification, 7*, 403–422.

Margolin, G. (1981). Behavior exchange in happy and unhappy marriages: A family life cycle perspective. *Behavioral Assessment, 12*, 329–343.

Margolin, G. (1987). Participant observation procedures in marital and family assessment. In T. Jacob (Ed.), *Family interaction and psychopathology: Theories, methods, and findings* (pp. 391–426). New York: Plenum.

Margolin, G., Burman, B., & John, R. S. (1989). Home observations of marital couples reenacting naturalistic conflicts. *Behavioral Assessment, 11*, 101–118.

Margolin, G., John, R. S., & Gleberman, L. (1988). Affective responses to conflictual discussion in violent and nonviolent couples. *Journal of Consulting and Clinical Psychology, 56*, 24–33.

Margolin, G., & Wampold, B. E. (1981). Sequential analysis of conflict and accord in distressed and nondistressed marital partners. *Journal of Consulting and Clinical Psychology, 49*, 554–567.

Markman, H. J. (1979). The application of a behavioral model of marriage in predicting relationship satisfaction of couples planning marriage. *Journal of Consulting and Clinical Psychology, 45*, 743–749.

Markman, H. J. (1981). The prediction of marital distress: A five year follow-up. *Journal of Consulting and Clinical Psychology, 49*, 760–762.

Markman, H. J. (1982, November). *The longitudinal study of communication and psychopathology in premarital dyads.* Paper presented at the Annual Meeting of the Association for Advancement of Behavior Therapy, Los Angeles.

Minuchin, S. (1984). *Family kaleidoscope.* Cambridge, MA: Harvard University Press.

Monroe, S. M., Bromet, E. J., Cornell, M. M., & Steiner, S. C. (1986). Social support, life events, and depressive symptoms: A one-year prospective study. *Journal of Consulting and Clinical Psychology, 54*, 424–431.

Nelson, G. M. (1988, November). *Communication interactions of married couples with and without a depressed wife.* Paper presented at the Annual Meeting of the Association for Advancement of Behavior Therapy, New York.

Notarius, C. I., Benson, P. R., & Sloane, D. (1989). Exploring the interface between perception and behavior: An analysis of marital interaction in distressed and nondistressed couples. *Behavioral Assessment, 11*, 39–64.

O'Farrell, T. J., & Birchler, G. R. (1987). Marital relationships of alcoholic, conflicted, and nonconflicted couples. *Journal of Marital and Family Therapy, 13*, 259–274.

Patterson, G. R. (1982). *Coercive family process.* Eugene, OR: Castalia.

Peterson, D. R., & Rapinchuck, J. G. (1989). *Patterns of affect in destructive and constructive marital conflicts.* Unpublished manuscript, Rutgers University, New Brunswick, NJ.

Revenstorf, D., Hahlweg, K., Schindler, L., & Vogel, B. (1984). Interaction analysis of marital conflict. In K. Hahlweg & N. S. Jacobson (Eds.), *Marital interaction: Analysis and modification* (pp. 159–181). New York: Guilford Press.

Roberts, L. J., & Krokoff, L. J. (1990). A time-series analysis of withdrawal, hostility, and displeasure in satisfied and dissatisfied marriages. *Journal of Marriage and the Family, 52,* 95–105.

Ruscher, S. M., & Gotlib, I. H. (1988). Marital interaction patterns of couples with and without a depressed partner. *Behavior Therapy, 19,* 455–470.

Schaap, C. (1984). A comparison of the interaction of distressed and nondistressed married couples in a laboratory situation: Literature survey, methodological issues, and an empirical investigation. In K. Hahlweg & N. S. Jacobson (Eds.), *Marital interaction: Analysis and modification* (pp. 133–158). New York: Guilford Press.

Schaap, C., & Jansen-Nawas, C. (1987). Marital interaction, affect and conflict resolution. *Sexual and Marital Therapy, 2,* 35–51.

Smith, D. A., & O'Leary, K. D. (1987, July). *Affective components of problem-solving communication and their relationships with interspousal aggression.* Paper presented at the Third National Family Violence Research Conference, Durham, NH.

Ting-Toomey, S. (1983). An analysis of verbal communication patterns in high and low marital adjustment groups. *Human Communication Research, 9,* 306–319.

Vivian, D., & O'Leary, K. D. (1987, July). *Communication patterns in physically aggressive engaged couples.* Paper presented at the Third National Family Violence Research Conference, Durham, NH.

Vivian, D., Smith, D. A., Sandeen, E. E., & O'Leary, D. K. (1987, November). *Problem-solving skills and emotional styles of physically aggressive maritally discordant spouses.* Paper presented at the 21st Annual Convention of the Association for Advancement of Behavior Therapy, Boston.

Wampold, B. E. (1989). Kappa as a measure of pattern in sequential data. *Quality and Quantity, 23,* 171–187.

Wampold, B. E., & Kim, K. H. (1989). Sequential analysis applied to counseling process and outcome: A case study revisited. *Journal of Counseling Psychology, 36,* 357–364.

Wampold, B. E., & Margolin, G. (1982). Nonparametric strategies to test independence of behavioral states in sequential data. *Psychological Bulletin, 92,* 755–765.

Weiss, R. L. (1978). The conceptualization of marriage from a behavioral perspective. In T. J. Paolino & B. S. McCrady (Eds.), *Marriage and marital therapy: Psychoanalytic, behavioral and systems theory perspectives* (pp. 165–239). New York: Brunner/Mazel.

Weiss, R. L. (1980). Strategic behavioral marital therapy: Toward a model for assessment and intervention. In J. P. Vincent (Ed.), *Advances in family intervention, assessment and theory* (vol. 1, pp. 229–271). Greenwich, CT: JAI Press.

Weiss, R. L. (1989). The circle of voyeurs: Observing the observers of marital and family interactions. *Behavioral Assessment, 11,* 135–148.

Weiss, R. L., & Heyman, R. E. (1990). Marital distress. In A. S. Bellack, M. Hersen, & A. E. Kazdin (Eds.), *International handbook of behavior modification and therapy* (2nd ed., pp. 475–501). New York: Plenum.

Weiss, R. L., Hops, H., & Patterson, G. R. (1973). A framework for conceptualizing marital conflict: A technology for altering it, some data for evaluating it. In L. D. Handy & E. L. Mash (Eds.), *Behavior change: Methodology concepts and practice* (pp. 309–342). Champaign, IL: Research Press.

Weiss, R. L., & Perry, B. A. (1983). The Spouse Observation Checklist: Developments and clinical applications. In E. E. Filsinger (Ed.), *Marriage and family assessment: A sourcebook for family therapy* (pp. 65-84). Beverly Hills: Sage.

Weiss, R. L., & Summers, K. J. (1983). Marital Interaction Coding System-III. In E. E. Filsinger (Ed.), *A sourcebook of marriage and family assessment* (pp. 85-115). Beverly Hills: Sage.

Wills, T. A., Weiss, R. L., & Patterson, G. R. (1974). A behavioral analysis of the determinants of marital satisfaction. *Journal of Consulting and Clinical Psychology, 47,* 802-811.

CHAPTER 4

# Cognition in Marriage

Frank D. Fincham
Thomas N. Bradbury
Christy K. Scott

Although recent years have witnessed an explosion of research on cognition in marriage, there has been little attempt to address several basic questions. Why study cognition in marriage? What aspects of cognition might be studied? How does one most fruitfully study them? The need to address such questions is emphasized by the observation that research on cognition in intimate relationships "has not resulted in a cohesive literature" (Sillars, 1985, p. 278) and currently shows "little coherent direction of movement" (Baucom, Epstein, Sayers, & Sher, 1989, p. 31). Our goals, therefore, are to organize and review existing research and to offer a research agenda that addresses systematically basic issues relating to cognition in marriage. To accomplish these goals we pay particular attention to the tacit principles underlying existing research and draw connections to nonmarital areas of investigation in psychology and to cognitive science more generally. Before turning to these tasks, we provide a brief historical account of research on cognition in intimate relationships so that the current status of the field might be more fully appreciated.

## THE EMERGENCE OF RESEARCH
## ON COGNITION IN MARRIAGE

In this section we seek to show that the systematic study of cognition in marriage is of recent origin, emerged in response to clinical concerns, and provides one answer to the question, "Why study cognition in marriage?" We conclude the section by providing a more complete answer to this fundamental question.

The science of family studies was motivated by the need to understand and alleviate problems in families, and it is therefore not surprising that the marital literature has focused largely on marital quality. The earliest studies typically examined the association between marital quality and a variety of demographic, individual difference, and family variables. Although some of these large-scale surveys included phenomenological variables, most were atheoretical (Barry, 1970), and no identifiable literature emerged on cognition in marriage.

In the 1970s, a second research tradition emerged that explicitly eschewed self-report and focused on the observation of marital behavior in distressed and nondistressed couples. Despite the discovery of a behavioral profile associated with marital distress (see Weiss & Heyman, Chapter 3, this volume) the discrepancy between spouses' reports of behavior and between spouses' and trained observers' reports of behavior highlighted the need to investigate spouses' interpretations and evaluations of partner behavior.

Recognizing the solid, albeit incomplete, foundation provided by behavioral research, investigators began in the 1980s to study cognitive and emotional factors that might enrich our understanding of marital interaction. Such factors were presumed to influence behavior exchanges and therefore emerged as a critical element in understanding the association between observed behavior and satisfaction. This development also reflects the ascendance of cognitive-behavior modification, and much of the interest in the study of covert factors in marriage lay in its potential to increase the efficacy of marital therapy. However, the emergence of research on cognitive and emotional factors in marriage also arose in the context of several broader changes within psychology. These changes are acknowledged rarely by marital researchers, yet they are critical to providing a comprehensive account of cognition in marriage. Four changes are therefore briefly outlined.

Perhaps the most obvious development was the reemergence of a subspecialty representing the interface of social and clinical psychology (see Hill & Weary, 1983). Indeed, the mark of social psychology on the study of marital cognition is indelible because most of the research in the latter domain has focused on causal attributions or explanations, a topic that dominated social psychology for over two decades. Equally important, though less obvious in its impact on marital cognition research, is the recent emergence of a science of close relationships (see Duck, 1988). This multidisciplinary endeavor provided respectability to basic research on relationships in psychology, a topic that most research psychologists had hitherto avoided. Although the research generated by these two developments and by clinically oriented marital researchers could be mutually beneficial, the cross-fertilization that occurs between these areas remains far from optimal.[1]

A third development is the burgeoning research on affect within psychology. Of particular relevance here is a growing interest in the interplay between cognition and affect, a topic that has received virtually no attention from marital researchers (see Bradbury & Fincham, 1987a, 1989a, for exceptions). Finally, the emergence of cognitive science elevated the study of cognition to center stage in psychology. However, as we show later in the chapter, the information-processing metaphor integral to cognitive science has been ignored in marital research.

It is our view that a comprehensive research agenda for investigating marital cognition will emerge only when connections are drawn to these broader developments. The review and research prospectus offered in the next two sections of the chapter therefore attempts to make such connections. Before turning to these tasks, we consider briefly the fundamental question, "Why study cognition in marriage?"

One reason for studying marital cognition is provided by the evolution of research on marital quality: understanding cognition appears to be critical for understanding variance in marital quality. But is it? After all, Levenson and Gottman (1983, 1985) have shown that affect, especially physiological indices of affect, accounts for most of the variance in concurrent (80%) and future (up

---

[1]Several factors may account for the paucity of cross-fertilization. First, a staggering number of professional affiliations, organizations, and publications vie for psychologists' attention. Second, the multidisciplinary and multisubdisciplinary nature of the close relationship and social–clinical research, respectively, require greater effort to identify and appreciate fully relevant research in these areas. Third, the foci of research differ: close relationship researchers are not primarily interested in relationship quality but in a variety of variables that may enhance our understanding of relationships, whereas social–clinical research is often motivated by the application of social psychological theory rather than by clinical problems. Consequently, a fourth factor that militates against cross-fertilization between the fields is the different populations studied. The study of dating couples tends to dominate research in the literature on personal relationships, and neither this field nor the social–clinical literature focuses specifically on relationship dysfunction.

to 85%) marital quality (see Bradbury & Fincham, 1987b; Weiss & Heyman, Chapter 3, this volume). Although the value of such work is indisputable, it sheds little light on the cognitive components of emotion, particularly cognitive antecedents of emotional experience. The importance of understanding such antecedents is evidenced by Levenson and Gottman's (1985) explanation for their finding that physiological activity before interaction predicted changes in marital satisfaction 3 years later. They argue that the physiological indices of affect reflect *expectations* about the interaction that stem from the couple's learning history. This account necessarily assumes such processes as encoding and representation of the experimental situation, retrieval of relevant information from memory, and so on. Thus, even though the authors tend to couch their explanation in terms of "behavior" and "affect," it is decidedly cognitive. In sum, the significance of emotion in marriage is, *ipso facto*, a reason for studying cognition in marriage whether or not cognition accounts for unique variance in marital quality. Consequently, it behooves marital researchers to note that "the absence of a viable account of the emotions compatible with a general theory of cognition renders existing theories of both inadequate" (Ortony, Clore, & Collins, 1988, p. 5).

Even if one admits to the importance of cognition, it is still legitimate to ask why it needs to be studied specifically in the context of marriage. In view of the vast literature on cognition, and particularly the recent explosion of research on cognition in social psychology, it would seem reasonable to assume that much is already known about cognition in relationships. However, the use of such knowledge for understanding marriage is fraught with difficulty. For example, cognitive psychologists have found that the cognitive processes manifest in a given situation depend on the person's familiarity with the knowledge domain investigated, the task content within a domain, the physical, psychological, and emotional context in which the task is presented, and the purpose of performing the task (e.g., Claxton, 1988). In view of such findings, extrapolation from even the most socially oriented studies of cognition is unwise, because these studies typically examine judgments about hypothetical others under conditions that seldom incorporate features of everyday life (e.g., interaction with the other person; see Ostrom, 1984). Thus, the study of cognition in marriage has the potential not only to increase our understanding of intimate relationships but also to advance the study of social cognition.

## REVIEW AND CRITIQUE

In this section we evaluate what is known about cognition in marriage and suggest that most research can be organized in terms of two major topics, beliefs and attributions. Because reviews of this domain already exist (Arias & Beach, 1987; Baucom & Epstein, 1990; Bradbury & Fincham, 1990; Fincham & Bradbury, in press-a; Fletcher & Fincham, in press; Thompson & Snyder, 1986), our analysis focuses on prototypic studies and attempts to identify the underlying themes or principles that motivate this research. We argue that considerable progress has been made in the study of marital cognition but that the domain of inquiry has been unnecessarily restricted in scope. This conclusion leads naturally to the question, "What further aspects of cognition might be studied?," an issue that we address following our review of existing research.

### Beliefs

A vast number of studies can be seen to provide information on beliefs. For example, many studies designed to investigate marital events are relevant here because answers to the general questions used (e.g., absence of a time frame, no reference to a specific event, and so on; see Robins, Chapter 2, this volume) are likely to reflect beliefs about the spouse or relationship rather than the retrieval of specific memories (see Ericsson & Simon, 1980). In addition, studies that investigate beliefs specifically encompass a wide variety of referents (e.g., the self, partner's personality). We limit our analysis to studies on beliefs pertaining to relationships and, owing to the poor quality of early studies, focus on those that have emerged subsequent to the behavioral tradition (for reviews of early work see Barry, 1970; Tharp, 1963).

Most recent work on relationship beliefs focuses on the *content* of spouses' beliefs. The idea underlying this research is that some relationship beliefs are likely to be dysfunctional and will lead to relationship distress. Thus, changing such beliefs could be an important vehicle for alleviating marital distress. Most emphasis has been placed on unrealistic relationship beliefs and on beliefs regarding efficacy in resolving marital conflicts.[2] Each is considered in turn.

[2]Several other topics relevant to understanding cognition in close relationships have been subject to study (see Bradbury & Fincham, in press), including trust (Holmes & Rempel, 1989), commitment (Kelley, 1983), intimacy (Reis & Shaver, 1988), and mental models underlying attachment styles (Shaver, Hazan, &

Epstein and his colleagues (e.g., Epstein & Eidelson, 1981; Eidelson & Epstein, 1982) reasoned that whereas irrational beliefs held by individuals about themselves (see Ellis & Grieger, 1977) are relevant to relationship dysfunction, unrealistic beliefs specific to relationships would provide even more information about marital distress (see also Newman & Langer, 1988, for similar ideas regarding "interpersonal premises"). Accordingly, they constructed the Relationship Belief Inventory (RBI), a measure of unrealistic relationship beliefs based on the irrational beliefs emphasized in rational emotive therapy and on clinical experience (e.g., that disagreement is destructive, partners cannot change). They showed that relationship beliefs combined with irrational beliefs about the self were better than beliefs about the self alone in predicting expectations of therapy outcome, preference for maintaining rather than terminating the relationship, and marital satisfaction (Eidelson & Epstein, 1982).

Further research using the RBI has shown that (1) its inverse relation to marital satisfaction is highly reliable (e.g., Epstein, Pretzer, & Fleming, 1987; Fincham & Bradbury, 1989a); (2) some beliefs correlate with interactants' ratings of communications following a videotaped review of an interaction (Gaelick, Bodenhausen, & Wyer, 1985); and (3) it is related in the expected manner to a number of correlates of marital distress (e.g., reports of communication behaviors, Epstein et al., 1987; marital attributions, Fincham & Bradbury, 1987a). Most research on unrealistic relationship beliefs has involved uncritical use of the RBI, and problems with this instrument have only recently been recognized (e.g., heterogeneity of items that hinders interpretation, see Baucom & Epstein, 1990; Emmelkamp et al., 1988).

In contrast, a common assessment instrument has not yet emerged in research on efficacy. Interest in this construct stems instead from the intuitively compelling belief that efficacy expectations are likely to be "a central determinant of successful . . . coping" (Doherty, 1981, p. 43). That is, spouses who believe that they cannot execute the behaviors necessary for resolving conflict are likely to act helpless in conflict situations, whereas spouses with high efficacy expectations are likely to engage in problem-solving behavior. Although efficacy expectations have been emphasized by therapists (e.g., Weiss, 1984) and have been incorpo-

---

Bradshaw, 1988). Because the nature of these constructs remains uncertain, and because they often tend to be operationalized in a manner specifically designed for the study of dating relationships, we do not include them in our review.

rated into cognitive models of marital conflict (Doherty, 1981; Fincham & Bradbury, 1987b; Fincham, Bradbury, & Grych, 1990), data relating to efficacy expectations in marriage are only beginning to emerge.

Efficacy has been found to relate positively to marital satisfaction (Bradbury, 1989; Fincham & Bradbury, 1989b; Notarius & Vanzetti, 1983; Weiss, 1984) and to correlate with the spouses' ratings of the helpfulness of partner behaviors during a videotaped replay of a marital interaction (Weiss, 1984), with wives' quality of approaches to problem solving as rated by trained observers (Bradbury, 1989), with rates of positive behavior during marital interaction (Weiss, 1984), with observers' rating of spouses' satisfaction with problem-solving discussions (Weiss, 1984), with spouses' reports of helpless behavior (Fincham & Bradbury, 1987b), and with other correlates of marital satisfaction (e.g., attributions, Fincham & Bradbury, 1989a). In addition, efficacy predicted satisfaction 12 months later with initial levels of satisfaction statistically controlled (Bradbury, 1989; Fincham & Bradbury, 1989b). Unfortunately, the foregoing findings pertain to several quite different operationalizations of efficacy and the problems encountered in applying this construct to relationships (e.g., spouse versus couple efficacy, the role of motivation) have received little attention.

A further body of knowledge about relationship beliefs emerges from a potpourri of studies loosely connected by their relevance for understanding the *structure* or organization of beliefs. Two different principles motivate these studies. One principle relates to the structure of *inter*spouse beliefs and specifies that the correspondence or similarity between spouses' beliefs is more important for marital satisfaction than the beliefs themselves. Until recently, data supporting a relationship between satisfaction and actual (e.g., Corsini, 1956) and perceived (e.g., Murstein & Beck, 1972) similarity were limited to personality traits. However, Arias and O'Leary (1985) have extended this research and shown that happily married couples, as compared to distressed couples, perceived greater similarity between themselves and their spouses in the definition of several concepts considered to be important ingredients of a good marriage (e.g., love, commitment, communication).

The second principle reflected in this research pertains to the *intra*spouse level of analysis. A dominant theme here is that "couples who have more complex cognitive structures for understanding their relationships would be more adaptable . . . in their interactions" (Neimeyer, 1984, p. 259). Raush, Barry, Hertel, and

Swain (1974), who conducted one of the first observational studies of marriage, emphasized the importance of flexible "object relations schemata." However, the empirical investigation of cognitive structure occurred much later with the emergence of a broader interest in close relationships, and only a few studies focus on the marital dyad. For example, Tyndall and Lichtenberg (1985) found that a measure of cognitive complexity, intolerance of ambiguity, predicted reports of interaction style. In contrast, Fincham and Bradbury (1989a) found no relationship between an attribution-specific measure of cognitive complexity and marital satisfaction. Because cognitive complexity is related to a person's degree of knowledge and interest in a given area (Fletcher, Danilovics, Fernandez, Peterson, & Reeder, 1986), research on cognitive complexity in other relationships cannot be generalized to marriage. Research on marriage also needs to include measures of complexity that are specific to this relationship.

Finally, there is a body of research that is relevant to both inter- and intrapersonal levels of analysis. Fitzpatrick (1988) has developed a topology of marriage based on assessment of spouses along the dimensions of ideology (conventional versus unconventional), interdependence (high versus low), and conflict (high versus low). Using empirical criteria, she characterizes spouses as traditional (conventional ideology, high interdependence, and high conflict), separate (conventional ideology, low interdependence, and low conflict), and independent (unconventional ideology, high interdependence, and high conflict). By comparing the perspectives of husbands and wives, four couple types (traditionals, separates, independents, and mixed) are identified. In an impressive program of research, Fitzpatrick shows that the types are related to a variety of factors in marriage (e.g., sex-role orientation, satisfaction, numerous interactional behaviors, linguistic codes). Most important in the present context is the claim that the marital types are psychologically real and can be viewed as marital schemata or knowledge structures. That is, they characterize individuals and serve to direct attention and influence the encoding, retrieval, and processing of information. This claim is made *post hoc* but has the potential to advance significantly research on cognition in marriage should it be empirically validated.

## Attributions

The bulk of the research on cognition in marriage has focused on attributions or explanations that spouses make for marital events.

This reflects recognition of the importance of attributions for treatment (e.g., Jacobson & Margolin, 1979), the earlier-mentioned prominence of attribution research in social psychology, and the fact that many couples presenting for marital therapy often feel helpless about resolving their problems. This last observation led researchers to draw on the attributional reformulation of learned helplessness (Abramson, Seligman, & Teasdale, 1978) and this affected subsequent research profoundly. It determined not only the types of attributions investigated (causal attributions) but also the manner in which they were investigated (spouses rated the causes of marital events along various causal dimensions). Thus, in initial studies distressed and nondistressed spouses were asked to identify the cause of a marital event (usually a partner behavior) and indicate the extent to which the cause was located in the partner (causal locus), remained constant over time (causal stability), and affected many areas of the marriage (causal globality).

Following recognition that issues of responsibility and blame are central to marriage (Fincham, 1983), particularly for distressed couples, an attempt was made to expand the attributions studied. Whereas causal attributions concern who or what produced an event, responsibility entails an assessment of who is accountable for the event once its cause is known (see Bradbury & Fincham, 1990; Shaver, 1985). Spouses were therefore also asked to rate responsibility criteria such as partner motivation, intent, and blameworthiness. The initial theme in this research was to show that causal and responsibility attributions were related to marital satisfaction. The results of the 23 studies addressing this issue are summarized in Table 4.1 (for a detailed review see Bradbury & Fincham, 1990).

As predicted, compared to nondistressed spouses, distressed spouses are more likely to see the cause of negative marital events as stable, global, and located in the partner, and to see the partner's behavior as intentional, selfishly motivated, and blameworthy. The converse pattern is found for positive events. That is, relative to their nondistressed counterparts, distressed spouses make attributions that are likely to maximize the impact of negative behavior and minimize the impact of positive behavior. These findings are robust and occur in at least half of the studies conducted; no data have been reported to support attributions opposite to those outlined above.

A second theme in attribution research was to establish that the attribution–satisfaction association was not simply an artifact.

**TABLE 4.1.** Support for Attribution Dimensions Measured for Positive and for Negative Marital Events

| Attribution dimension | Number of studies | Support n | Support % | No support n | No support % |
|---|---|---|---|---|---|
| Positive events | | | | | |
| Locus | 12 | 7 | 59% | 5 | 42% |
| *Unstable* vs. stable | 9 | 6 | 66% | 3 | 33% |
| *Specific* vs. global | 9 | 9 | 100% | 0 | 0% |
| Intent | 4 | 3 | 75% | 1 | 25% |
| *Selfish* vs. unselfish motivation | 2 | 2 | 100% | 0 | 0% |
| *Blameworthy* vs. praiseworthy | 2 | 2 | 100% | 0 | 0% |
| Negative events | | | | | |
| Locus | 13 | 9 | 69% | 4 | 31% |
| Unstable vs. *stable* | 11 | 7 | 63% | 4 | 36% |
| Specific vs. *global* | 10 | 10 | 100% | 0 | 0% |
| *Blameworthy* vs. praiseworthy | 8 | 5 | 63% | 3 | 38% |
| Intent | 6 | 4 | 67% | 2 | 33% |
| *Selfish* vs. unselfish motivation | 3 | 3 | 100% | 0 | 0% |

*Note.* Support was assigned to a study if the results were entirely consistent with the hypothesis under consideration or if they were consistent for either sex, for any of the groups studied, or for any operational definition of the dimension used. Where possible, the endpoint of the attribution dimension that is hypothesized to be associated with marital dissatisfaction is shown in italics. This table summarizes the findings reviewed by Bradbury and Fincham (1990; see also Fincham & Bradbury in press-a).

This theme was manifest in several different ways. Initially, the reactive method used to measure attributions raised the question of whether unsolicited attributions occurred in marriage. Holtzworth-Munroe and Jacobson (1985) found that attributions coded from open-ended responses to partner behavior were not only related to marital satisfaction but also to spouses' ratings of the causes on underlying causal dimensions. In a similar vein, the hypothetical partner behaviors used in several studies to ensure standard stimuli raised the possibility that different findings would be obtained when spouses judged real behaviors. Fincham and Beach (1988) showed that although attribution ratings of hypothetical behaviors were more extreme than those of real behaviors, the same pattern of differences distinguished distressed from nondistressed spouses.

A further manifestation of concern about the validity of the attribution–satisfaction association centered on whether the association represented a marital phenomenon *per se*. That is, attributions and marital satisfaction could be associated because both constructs covary with depression (see Gotlib & McCabe, Chapter 8, this volume; Robins, 1988). Fincham, Beach, and Bradbury (1989) conducted two studies to investigate this possibility. In the first, depression was assessed via self-report in a sample of community wives, whereas in the second, wives were diagnosed as clinically depressed following a structured diagnostic interview. Responsibility attributions made for hypothetical partner behaviors accounted for variance in marital satisfaction with levels of depression held statistically constant, and attributions of depressed and nondepressed wives who were maritally distressed did not differ. However, both groups differed in the usual manner from happily married wives. In sum, no evidence has been reported to suggest that the attribution–satisfaction association is an artifact.

A third theme in attribution research involves identifying the parameters that influence attributions in marriage. For example, it is now apparent that unsolicited attributions are more likely to occur for negative than positive partner behavior (Camper, Jacobson, Holtzworth-Munroe, & Schmaling, 1988; Holtzworth-Munroe & Jacobson, 1985), a finding that also obtains for attributions communicated spontaneously in marital conversations (Holtzworth-Munroe & Jacobson, 1988). In a related vein, there is some evidence that the impact of an attribution for partner behavior may vary as a function of the attribution a spouse makes for his or her own behavior. Several studies show that distressed spouses make more benign attributions for their own behavior than for partner behavior (e.g., Fichten, 1984; Fincham & Beach, 1988; Kyle & Falbo, 1985; Lavin, 1987), whereas nondistressed spouses either make more benign attributions for partner behavior than own behavior (Fincham, Beach, & Baucom, 1987) or are even-handed in their attributions for self and partner behavior (Fincham & Beach, 1988; Lavin, 1987).

In view of the encouraging data reviewed thus far, it is perhaps not surprising that a fourth theme focuses on the potential causal relationship between attributions and satisfaction. Much of the interest in attributions stemmed from the implicit assumption in clinical writings that attributions might initiate or maintain relationship distress (e.g., Bagarozzi & Giddings, 1983), yet data on this causal hypothesis were slow to emerge. However, three longitudinal studies provide some evidence consistent with a causal relationship between attributions and satisfaction. Fletcher, Fincham, Cramer, and Heron (1987) found that attributing the maintenance of a romantic relationship equally to oneself and one's partner was related to greater happiness with the relationship 2 months later. In a second study, Fincham and Bradbury (1987b) assessed marriages at two points separated by a 12-month interval and found that initial causal and responsibility attributions predicted wives', but not husbands', later marital satisfaction. This relationship did not simply reflect a general association between cognitive variables and satisfaction over time because unrealistic relationship beliefs did not predict later satisfaction. Bradbury (1989) also found that attributions predicted marital satisfaction over a 12-month period, but only for husbands and not wives.

Although the reason for the sex difference is unclear, two further findings aid the interpretation of these three studies. First, the effects of initial happiness/satisfaction were removed from the longitudinal associations reported, a procedure that is not always followed in longitudinal research on marriage.[3] Second, attempts to predict later attributions from earlier happiness/satisfaction were unsuccessful in all cases. Although promising, these findings should be regarded as tentative and need to be supplemented by other sources of data because longitudinal studies yield only correlations and hence cannot establish causal relations. Experiments in this area are practically and ethically infeasible, but therapy outcome research could provide information on the causal relationship between attributions and satisfaction. Unfortunately, the existing outcome studies that relate to this question yield inconsistent results (see Bradbury & Fincham, 1990), and none has yet examined the critical question of whether changes in attribution are correlated with changes in satisfaction.

A final theme relates to the fundamental assumption that attributions influence behavior. Despite the widespread acceptance of this assumption, attempts to investigate it are rare. Fincham and Bradbury (1988) showed that causal attributions (seeing the cause of a marital difficulty as stable, global, and located in the partner) and responsibility attributions (viewing partner behavior contributing to the difficulty as intentional, selfish, and blameworthy) correlated positively with negative behaviors for both husbands and wives and negatively with wives' positive be-

---

[3]Interpretational ambiguity arises when initial satisfaction is not controlled in longitudinal associations. That is, any association between a variable measured at time 1 and later satisfaction could simply result from variance that the variable shares with initial satisfaction.

haviors during discussions in which the couples attempted to resolve the difficulty. Moreover, a husband is less likely to reciprocate his wife's positive behaviors to the extent that he sees her as the cause of the problem and views her behavior that contributes to the problem as intentional, selfishly motivated, and blameworthy. A husband is also more likely to reciprocate negative wife behaviors to the extent that he sees her contribution to the problem as intentional. On the other hand, a wife is more likely to engage in negative reciprocity if she views the cause of the problem as stable, locates it in her husband, and sees his behavior as selfishly motivated and blameworthy and to engage in positive reciprocity if she believes her husband's acts are selfishly motivated and intentional (Bradbury & Fincham, 1988a).

Bradbury (1989) also found that attributions were related to specific affects exhibited in a problem-solving discussion. An index of causal attributions (summed ratings of partner locus, causal stability, and globality) correlated positively with husbands' whining and wives' anger and negatively with wives' sadness. A similar index for responsibility attributions (summed ratings for intent, selfishness, and blameworthiness) correlated negatively with wives' interest and positively with wives' anger and contempt. The associations reported between attributions and behavior are not the result of shared variance with marital satisfaction because this variable was partialed out of the correlations in both studies. Thus, there is some evidence that attributions are related to base rates of behavior, sequences of behavior, and expressions of emotion.

With an association between attributions and behavior established, Fincham and Bradbury (1988) manipulated attributions for a negative partner behavior in the laboratory to investigate the impact on subsequent behavior toward the partner. They found that the behavior of distressed spouses was affected by the manipulation: spouses who located the cause of the negative behavior in their partner were more negative toward their partner in a subsequent discussion than those who attributed the negative behavior to the circumstances. However, they also exhibited more positive behavior toward the partner. To account for this unexpected finding, it was argued that an internal attribution for the negative partner behavior led to greater arousal in distressed spouses and the valence of the behavior resulting from this arousal was influenced by the constraints of the laboratory situation (i.e., public behavior recorded on videotape), thereby leading spouses to present themselves in a balanced way to the experimenters. In any event, there is preliminary evidence consistent with the view that attributions influence behavior.

The five themes identified do not exhaust the issues investigated in attribution research. For example, attention has been devoted to measurement issues (e.g., relating to causal dimensions, Fincham, 1985b; Bradbury & Fincham, 1989b; spontaneous attributions, Bradbury & Fincham, 1988b; Holtzworth-Munroe & Jacobson, 1988; Stratton et al., 1986), responsibility for contribution to marital activities (e.g., Fincham & Bradbury, 1989c), attributions for turning points in the relationship (Lloyd & Cate, 1985; Surra, Arizzi, & Asmussen, 1988), attributional style (Baucom, Sayers, & Duhe, 1989), individual difference variables (e.g., Bradbury & Fincham, 1988c; Fincham & Bradbury, 1989a), and the role of attributions in jealousy (Buunk, 1984), relationship termination (e.g., Fletcher, 1983; Harvey, Weber, Galvin, Huszti, & Garnick, 1986), sexual dysfunction (Fichten, Spector, & Libman, 1988), and marital violence (see Holtzworth-Munroe, 1988). However, the five themes outlined do serve to organize most of the work done in this domain and suggest that research exhibits more coherent direction of movement than might first appear. However, the coherence underlying this literature emerges only when the assumptions reflected in this research are made explicit, a characteristic that is often absent from papers on marital cognition.

## Critique

Unlike previous reviewers, we believe that considerable progress has been made in research on cognition in marriage. However, this literature is fast approaching a crossroad in that it is no longer sufficient simply to continue in the same manner along the paths outlined earlier. For example, expanding the study of unrealistic beliefs beyond the Relationship Belief Inventory or studying attributional style or pattern would be useful, but such advances by themselves would provide a limited understanding of cognition in marriage. There is a need to advance to a new phase of research on beliefs and attributions and to consider anew the subject of study in marital cognition research. In the remainder of this section, we outline briefly how to enrich existing lines of research and identify new avenues of inquiry.

A fundamental omission in the existing literature is research on the relationship between cognitions that occur during interaction, "on-line" cognitions, and interactional behavior. Instead, it has been assumed, rather than demonstrated, that general beliefs or attributions affect on-line cognitions which, in turn, influence behavior. Ultimately, a microanalysis of cognition and behavior is needed. For example, a spouse could be asked to indicate the perceived intent of each partner communication in an interaction, and the relationship between this attribution and the spouse's response to the communication could be examined.

The abovementioned assumption, that cognitions influence behavior, reflects the seeds of an integrative framework relating cognition, behavior, and satisfaction. That is, it is assumed implicitly that the influence of cognition on satisfaction is mediated by behavior. There is a need for the articulation of integrative frameworks relating cognition, behavior, and satisfaction and for research guided by such theoretical analysis (for one such framework see Fincham & Bradbury, in press-a). In a related vein, the absence of research and theory that integrates affect and cognition in marriage renders our understanding of this relationship incomplete.

In addition to advancing current research foci, there is a clear need to expand the scope of cognitions studied in marriage. Baucom, Epstein, et al. (1989) have taken a noteworthy step in this direction and argued that five categories of cognition are important for understanding marriage, namely, assumptions, standards, selective attention, attributions, and expectancies.[4] However, simply expanding the cognitive *contents* studied in marriage is insufficient because any understanding of marital cognition based solely on content rests on a dubious assumption, namely, that the study of phenomenal experience is sufficient to understand cognition. We see this assumption as questionable because people do not have access to the vast majority of cognitive processes that underlie conscious thoughts even though they may become aware of some of the products or outcomes of these processes (Neisser, 1967). Greater attention therefore

[4]Although selective attention is defined as a cognitive process, the discussion of Baucom, Epstein, et al. (1989) focuses on judgments about behavior (cognitive content) and does not address process *per se.* Similarly, even though they are construed as knowledge structures or schemata, the description of these categories focuses on cognitive content, and hence the implications of principles governing their representation and organization, interaction with cognitive processing, and so on remain to be elaborated.

needs to be paid to the nonconscious construction of phenomenal experience.

Although the study of cognitive *structure* in marriage represents a step in the right direction, our review shows that research on this topic is quite limited. Most studies are stimulated by a longstanding research tradition on cognitive complexity, and rarely has the study of cognitive structure been related to developments in cognitive psychology or cognitive science where the representation of knowledge is a central concern (Hunt, 1989).

Drawing a connection to cognitive science provides an additional advantage in that it highlights the single most important omission in research on cognition in marriage, the study of cognitive *processes*. There appears to be little unanimity about what exactly constitutes cognitive science, but most cognitive scientists agree that it deals with the representation of knowledge and the processes or operations that transform it (Sharkey, 1986). Thus, cognitive science provides another perspective on what might best constitute the subject of study in marital cognition research. In the next section we explore the implications of cognitive processes for understanding cognition in marriage.

## TOWARD A MORE COMPLETE UNDERSTANDING OF COGNITION IN MARRIAGE

In this section we argue that the information-processing approach (IPA) in cognitive science has the potential to advance the study of marital cognition. We illustrate how the IPA might enrich our understanding of cognition that occurs between interactions and during interactions in marriage. However, the realization of this potential in future research will require alternatives to the questionnaire method that now dominates investigations of marital cognition. Our treatment of this topic therefore addresses the final basic question posed at the outset of this chapter: "How does one study cognition?"

The IPA replaced stimulus–response psychology in the 1950s and, despite its dominance in contemporary psychology, is not easily defined. It does not represent a specific theory but is "at best a way of talking about . . . phenomena" (Mandler, 1985, p. 90) and "a methodology for theorizing" (Anderson & Bower, 1973, p. 136). Researchers who use the IPA share a common set of intellectual commitments and attitudes that shape their choice of theoretical perspectives, research problems, and methodology.[5] As noted earlier, one of the commitments is a desire to understand cognitive processes, a task that necessarily requires consideration of cognitive structures, processes, products, and their interrelations. Despite the emphasis on cognitive processes in this section, we therefore discuss cognitive products and structure where relevant.

Perhaps the most obvious means of exploring the IPA in marriage is to use general "stages" of processing (e.g., encoding, representation, storage, retrieval) to structure the discussion. Although consistent with many applications of the IPA, such an approach is unlikely to optimize the contribution of marital research to social cognition because it does not start with the phenomena of interest. Instead we follow an important precedent from the study of memory, one of the oldest and the most widely studied topics in cognitive psychology. According to Morris (1988, p. 91), research on memory had "little relevance to the way memory is used in everyday life" until Neisser (1978) asked a simple question, "What do we use the past *for*?" This question led to a "natural history" of memory phenomena and to the incorporation of ecologically relevant variables into the study of memory.

Following this precedent, we believe that a reevaluation of marital cognition research is facilitated by considering how cognition is used in marriage. Although several uses at various levels of specificity can be generated, we argue that a central function of cognition in marriage is to understand past and present relationship events and to predict and guide future relationship behaviors. This perspective points to the potential influence of goals, needs, and affect on cognition and questions the prevailing view in marital cognition research of spouses as totally rational and conscious. It suggests also that a cognitive account of marriage must include cognition that occurs between marital interactions and cannot be limited to cognition that occurs during interaction (see Bradbury

---

[5]Owing to space limitations, our description is necessarily limited and is therefore subject to the danger of oversimplification. Lest it appear otherwise, we do not want to deny the diversity among cognitive scientists in emphases and even evaluation criteria. For example, the artificial intelligence community tends to reject the experimental criterion of cognitive psychology (data generation for hypothesis testing) in favor of sufficiency, a demonstration that a particular information-processing system can handle the problems solved by humans. The reader is referred to alternative sources for a more complete description of the IPA (Hunt, 1989; Lachman, Lachman, & Butterfield, 1979) and its application to clinical psychology (Fincham & Bradbury, in press-b; Ingram, 1986).

& Fincham, 1989a). Our discussion below therefore reflects this distinction.

Cognitions that occur between interactions necessarily involve constructions of previously experienced events (memory), and these constructions are most likely to reflect the deliberate attempts at recall that dominate the study of memory in psychology. For example, when trying to understand the cause of a recent argument, a spouse may attempt to recall similar arguments and determine whether the causes of these arguments aid in understanding the cause of the present one. In fact, determining the implication of the cause of the present argument for the future (judging the stability of the cause) rests on recall of the causes of past arguments and/or knowledge about the general properties of the cause in question. It is therefore important to understand factors that might affect the retrieval of relationship-relevant material from memory.

The realization that the organization or structure of stored material made recall possible had a profound influence on the study of memory in cognitive psychology (Mandler, 1985). As a consequence, a central concept in the contemporary study of memory is relatedness; that is, the stronger the relations among elements of a stored structure, the greater its integration, the more easily it is retrieved as a unit, and the more likely that elements of the structure will activate the whole. Thus, a spouse whose representation of the partner is highly integrated, as compared to minimally integrated, is likely to recall more information about the partner when processing a negative partner behavior. Assuming that the integrated structure is not dominated by negative elements, the behavior is therefore less likely to be interpreted in negative terms. In contrast, a less integrated structure could result in only a few related, negative elements of the structure being accessed, which would, in turn, affect the processing of the behavior. In sum, the organization of memories carries implications for what is recalled and is therefore either subject to processing or brought to bear on the processing of new information.

A second factor that influences recall is affect. Although affect has traditionally been neglected in cognitive psychology, a spate of recent research has documented the influence of mood on memory (see Blaney, 1986; Ucros, 1989). This assumes particular importance in marriage, especially in view of the central role of affect in this relationship and the association between depression and marital distress (see Gotlib & McCabe, Chapter 8, this volume). For example, the finding that current mood causes selective retrieval of affectively congruent material implies that negative material is more easily retrieved by distressed than nondistressed spouses and is therefore more likely to influence cognitive processing (for a series of propositions and corollaries concerning affect and cognition in marriage, see Bradbury & Fincham, 1987a).

Mood-congruent recall has far-reaching implications. It can result in the spouse basing his or her judgments about the partner or the marriage on a biased data base. Moreover, the judgment may affect later cognitions long after the mood passes. This is because what is stored in memory is the event to which the spouse is exposed (e.g., partner failed to kiss spouse goodbye) as well as an abstracted summary, judgment, or inference about the event (e.g., partner was uncaring). When further judgments are made, the abstracted representation, rather than the original event, is often recalled (Wyer, Srull, & Gordon, 1984). In fact, with the passage of time, the spouse might be able to recall that the partner was uncaring but not be able to recall the behavior on which this judgment was initially based. Such processes are likely to be particularly important for enduring mood states (e.g., depression), which make chronically accessible mood-congruent information.

The significance of retrieval processes for understanding marital cognition is emphasized further by the fact that people often terminate information searches as soon as they have sufficient information to make a judgment with an acceptable degree of confidence. This means that information most *accessible* in memory or most salient at the time of the judgment is likely to influence the judgment. As Bruner (1957) notes, the accessibility of constructs is determined, in part, by the person's current expectancies, goals, needs, and recent experiences. This again points to the importance of understanding the functions of cognition in marriage and the need to understand the conditions under which spouses think about the marital events. At the very least, we need to translate the general beliefs studied in marriage into expectancies and to incorporate the study of goals and needs in marital cognition research. Although cognitive psychologists have tended to overlook such variables, they are gaining the attention of social psychologists interested in cognition (see Cantor & Malley, in press; Read & Miller, 1989).

In contrast, the impact of recent experience has been carefully documented. Information made salient in one context may affect subsequent processing of unrelated material in a different context, a phenomenon known as priming. Thus, for example, a spouse who thinks about a past marital interaction soon after reading a scathing review of a movie might be primed to process the marital event in terms of negative concepts. Such priming effects have been demonstrated for judgments about hypothetical others and for nonsocial stimuli, but the extent to which they occur for strongly held views of a familiar other remains an empirical question.

Thus far we have emphasized deliberate recall and processing of marital events that occur between interactions. However, it is important to acknowledge that recall of marital events often is not effortful. That is, marital events may come to mind and be processed in the absence of deliberate recall. The parameters governing such recall are unknown, and the relative absence of research on nondeliberate memories is a "mystery in the sociology of our science" (Mandler, 1985, p. 94). This chapter is not the place to address this deficit (nor do we profess the expertise to do so). It suffices to note that a complete account of cognition in marriage requires an understanding of noneffortful recall. Instead, we turn to consider cognition that occurs in the context of ongoing marital interaction or what we have labeled "on-line" processing.

As any marital therapist can testify, behavior in marital interactions is often overlearned, unfolds at an astonishing speed, and appears to proceed without much thought. This does not deny the importance of cognitive antecedents to behavior, it simply suggests that the kind of deliberate and effortful cognitions studied thus far by marital researchers are unlikely to dominate interaction sequences. At the risk of belaboring the point, it behooves us to remember that the cognitive domain should not be equated with conscious thought, a confusion that has seriously hampered exploration of the interplay between cognition and emotion (see Branscombe, 1988).

In view of these observations, it is important to make explicit a fundamental distinction underlying our earlier discussion of cognitive processes, namely, controlled versus automatic processing (Shiffrin & Schneider, 1977). Briefly stated, controlled processing is initiated deliberately, whereas automatic processing is triggered by stimuli and operates outside of awareness. Table 4.2 summarizes the properties associated with these two forms of processing. We argue that most processing during marital interaction is likely to be automatic. That is, spouses will experience the results of the processing as phenomenally immediate, will not see the products of these processes as constructions or interpretations, and are therefore very unlikely to question the validity of their judgments. Stated differently, automatic processing in inter-

**TABLE 4.2.** Properties of Automatic and Controlled Processing

| Automatic | Controlled |
| --- | --- |
| No capacity demand | Limited by capacity of attention and short-term memory |
| Fast | Slow |
| Effortless | Effortful |
| No awareness | Involves awareness |
| Involuntary | Voluntary |
| Not verbalizable | Often verbalizable |
| Ballistic | Controllable |
| Requires extensive training to develop Considerable practice needed for change | Can be adopted quickly More easily changed with new information |
| Does not lead directly to new learning | Leads directly to new learning |
| Performance improves with practice | Rapid development of asymptotic performance |
| Context-free | Context-sensitive |

actions is likely to affect the very perception of interactional behavior, and spouses are as likely to doubt the validity of such perceptions as they are to doubt their perceptions of the inanimate world (e.g., that the sky is blue). Finally, it is important to note that lawful relations between events can be recorded via automatic processing, and this form of processing therefore permits rudimentary causal perception and the prediction of future events.

The introduction of automatic processing to the study of marital cognition follows more closely the stimulus for researching this domain than any issue investigated to date. Recall that the discrepancy in the coding (perception) of spouse behaviors (between spouses and between spouses and trained coders) stimulated research on cognition in marriage. However, marital cognition research has not focused on the immediate perception of behavior but on the cognitions available via controlled processing. But controlled or conscious processing capacity is limited by a number of variables, including attention. As a result, judgments made under cognitions of uncertainty or in complex situations such as marital interactions are likely to be influenced by existing knowledge that gives rise to expectations and by simple cognitive heuristics or rules.

As a consequence, many spouse reports of reasons for behavior, what led them to interpret a partner behavior in a particular manner, and so on, are likely to be *a posteriori* constructions that draw on the limited amounted of information available in consciousness. This does not imply that spouse reports are never valid, only that they are valid under a limited set of conditions (see Ericsson & Simon, 1980). It seems unlikely then that an understanding of the discrepancies between spouses or between spouses and observers will emerge by asking people what led them to code (perceive) the behavior in a particular manner. How then does one study cognitive processes? Before addressing this question, we illustrate briefly the operation of automatic processing in marital interaction.

The automatic processes described in our discussion of cognition between interactions can also be applied to on-line cognition. For example, the accessibility of constructs influences the encoding of a partner behavior and may be primed by recent experience. Thus, a telephone call from a demanding mother immediately prior to a partner's polite request for help with a chore might be processed in terms of the construct "demanding" and therefore be experienced as aversive. Mood may similarly affect construct accessibility and the encoding of partner behavior. Of particular relevance in marriage is the fact that some constructs can be used so frequently and consistently (e.g., because of an enduring mood state, a behavioral style that evokes a consistent response from others) that they become chronically accessible. That is, they are used to interpret behaviors even though they are not activated by environmental events or controlled thought processes. The importance of affectively valenced, chronically accessible constructs in marriage is emphasized by the phenomenon of "sentiment override." Weiss (1980) uses this term to signify that spouses' responses to partner behavior are determined largely by their general sentiment toward the partner rather than by anything about the behavior itself. The notion of construct accessibility provides a more complete account of this phenomenon and is intended to facilitate the limited research conducted on sentiment override.

Such effects can be seen as part of the informational role of automatic processing. That is, automatic processing can alter ongoing controlled processing by attracting attention to a specific stimulus (i.e., entering it into short-term or working memory). According to Shiffrin and Schneider (1977), all incoming stimuli are subject to automatic processing, but only some are selected for controlled processing. Although spouses may be able to provide valid self-reports of some controlled processes (i.e., reports dealing with information currently in short-term memory; see Ericsson & Simon, 1980), such reports may tell us little about the phenomenon investigated. For example, what may distinguish distressed and nondistressed spouses is not how they consciously process partner behavior but what aspects of partner behavior gain attention and are made available for controlled processing. The different rates of positive and negative behavior recorded by distressed and nondistressed spouses may reflect such differences and have indeed been interpreted in terms of selective attention (e.g., Baucom, Epstein, Sayers, & Sher, 1989). Nonetheless, no data have emerged on automatic processes in marriage. This most likely reflects the need for alternate methodologies to self-report of cognitions. We therefore consider briefly how to study marital cognition in the remainder of this section.

Perhaps the single most important contribution of cognitive psychology to the study of marriage lies at the level of methodology. One of the most pervasive methodologies used by cognitive psychologists is mental chronometry. The idea that the time to access and process information could reveal information about cognition has been prevalent since Donders developed the concept over 125 years ago, and elaborate uses of response time can be found in contemporary cognitive psychology. (For an introduction to mental chronometry see Pachella, 1974.) Such uses, combined with the technological skills often needed to use response time, can make the implementation of this methodology appear formidable, especially to the marital researcher accustomed to the use of questionnaires. We therefore illustrate how the simple uses of response time can advance marital research.

Consider again the concept of sentiment override. It is believed that the general sentiment experienced toward the partner affects not only responses to partner behavior but also responses to questions about the partner or the marriage. Our analysis of this phenomenon in terms of construct accessibility suggests numerous possible studies. For example, if distressed spouses access negative constructs more easily than nondistressed spouses, they should be able to recall more negative than positive material about the marriage (e.g., partner characteristics or behaviors) in equivalent time periods. Conversely, nondistressed spouses should report more material in the time period devoted to positive recall. Such a study could be conducted with a stopwatch.

A more technologically demanding study is one that measures time taken to process stimuli and to respond to them. For example, spouses could be asked to indicate whether a set of trait adjectives applies to their partner. Distressed spouses should take less time to read (process) negative trait adjectives than positive trait adjectives (assuming adjectives are equated for frequency, degree of likability, etc.), a pattern that should be replicated for deciding on the applicability of the adjectives. Again, the converse pattern of responses should be found for nondistressed spouses. Needless to say, one might also expect group differences in the number of negative and positive traits attributed to the spouse (cognitive content), the level of analysis to which current research is restricted.

Moving to an even shorter time frame, one could present valenced stimuli subliminally (using a very brief exposure time and masking the stimulus once presented to avoid awareness of semantic content) and examine its impact on later processing of marital material. It might be expected that it would be easier to activate automatically negative categories that influence subsequent processing in distressed spouses than nondistressed spouses. Nondistressed spouses, on the other hand, may be influenced more by positive stimuli. Interpretation of such a study would require the inclusion of control groups that were not exposed to the subliminal material.

Such analyses may appear to be far removed from the concerns of clinically motivated researchers. However, response time can also be used in clinical settings. For example, we have utilized the speed with which a spouse recalls positive versus negative characteristics of the partner during a clinical interview as a rough index of the accessibility of affectively congruent knowledge structures relating to the partner. In any event, it is important to remember that response times, like physiological measures, are simply indices of hypothesized internal processes. The pattern of response times may be consistent with the processes hypothesized, but they do not speak directly to the existence of such processes.

There are numerous other methodologies for "getting inside the head" (see Taylor & Fiske, 1981). For example, clustering and sequencing of recalled material can reveal much about the structure of representations. This can be illustrated by returning to our example of the clinical interview in which the spouse is asked to recall positive and negative partner behaviors. It is possible to examine the behaviors reported by the spouse for sequence, clustering, and quantity to gain information about the nature of the spouse's representation of his or her partner. Consider a wife who describes her husband's day-to-day behavior by listing five actions that she sees as selfish and then mentions appreciatively two chores he regularly completes. The order of the behaviors (negative before positive), clustering of "selfish" behavior, and the relative number of negative events suggest that she has a representation of her husband that is primarily negative and in which the trait "selfishness" is used to organize husband behavior. (For further examples of how cognitive methodologies might be translated into clinical assessment, see Kihlstrom & Nasby 1981.)

Although these brief illustrations do not exhaust the methods used in cognitive psychology that could advance the study of marital cognition, we believe that their use is likely to yield handsome dividends. For example, we anticipate that measures of cognitive process, like physiological indices of affect, are likely to account for substantially larger portions of variance in marital satisfaction than self-report measures. In any event, the incorporation of more diverse methods of studying marital cognition is a prerequisite for expanding this domain of inquiry.

## CONCLUSION

Our goals in this chapter were to review and organize existing research on cognition in marriage and to outline possible avenues for future research. From our review, we conclude that when the assumptions motivating research on marital cognition are made explicit, the literature shows far greater coherence than previously assumed. However, it also shows that research conducted to date is quite limited. First, few studies address some of the most fundamental assumptions regarding cognition in marriage (e.g., that beliefs and attributions influence behavior), a factor that may reflect the early stage of inquiry in this field. Second, research has focused narrowly on cognitive content and, within this area, on beliefs and attributions. Consequently, there is a clear need to expand the study of cognition in marriage. Recognition of this need leads to basic questions about the subject of inquiry in marital cognition research, how to proceed with such inquiry, and so on.

Mindful of such questions, we have suggested that significant advances will occur in future research when greater attention is paid to cognitive structure and when cognitive processes are incorporated into the study of marital cognition. To this end, we drew connections with cognitive psychology and cognitive science. Such advances will also be facilitated by further integration of marital research and related domains of inquiry, especially the recently emerged field of close relationships.

To date, clinical concerns have motivated most of the research on marital cognition, and the attempt to explain variance in marital quality dominates research. This has served us well in establishing a body of research on cognition in marriage. However, the expansion needed in this field includes a willingness to embrace the study of multiple facets of cognition in marriage regardless of their immediate clinical relevance. The combined efforts of clinical and basic researchers are therefore required for a complete understanding of cognition in marriage and for the emergence of integrative research that will advance our understanding of marriage and of cognition.

# REFERENCES

Abramson, L. Y., Seligman, M. E. P., & Teasdale, J. (1978). Learned helplessness in humans: Critique and reformulation. *Journal of Abnormal Psychology, 87*, 49–74.

Anderson, J. R., & Bower, G. H. (1973). *Human associative memory*. Washington, DC: Erlbaum.

Arias, I., & Beach, S. R. H. (1987). The assessment of social cognition in the context of marriage. In K. D. O'Leary (Ed.), *Assessment of marital discord* (pp. 109–137). Hillsdale, NJ: Erlbaum.

Arias, I., & O'Leary, K. D. (1985). Semantic and perceptual discrepancies in discordant and nondiscordant marriages. *Cognitive Therapy and Research, 9*, 51–60.

Bagarozzi, D. A., & Giddings, C. W. (1983). The role of cognitive constructs and attributional processes in family therapy: Integrating intrapersonal, interpersonal, and systems dynamics. In L. R. Goldberg & M. L. Aronson (Eds.), *Group and family therapy* (pp. 207–219). New York: Brunner/Mazel.

Barry, W. A. (1970). Marriage research and conflict: An integrative review. *Psychological Bulletin, 73*, 41–54.

Baucom, D. H., & Epstein, N. (1990). *Cognitive-behavioral marital therapy*. New York: Brunner Mazel.

Baucom, D. H., Epstein, N., Sayers, S., & Sher, T. G. (1989). The role of cognition in marital relationships: Definitional, methodological, and conceptual issues. *Journal of Consulting and Clinical Psychology, 57*, 31–38.

Baucom, D. H., Sayers, S. L., & Duhe, A. (1989). Attributional style and attributional patterns among married couples. *Journal of Personality and Social Psychology, 56*, 596–607.

Blaney, P. H. (1986). Affect and memory: A review. *Psychological Bulletin, 99*, 229–246.

Bradbury, T. N. (1989). *Cognition, emotion, and interaction in distressed and nondistressed couples.* Ph.D. dissertation, University of Illinois.

Bradbury, T. N., & Fincham, F. D. (1987a). Affect and cognition in close relationships: Towards an integrative model. *Cognition and Emotion, 1*, 59–87.

Bradbury, T. N., & Fincham, F. D. (1987b). The assessment of affect in marriage. In K. D. O'Leary (Ed.), *Assessment of marital discord* (pp. 59–108). Hillsdale, NJ: Erlbaum.

Bradbury, T. N., & Fincham, F. D. (1988a, November). *The impact of attributions in marriage: Attributions and behavior exchange in marital interactions.* Paper presented at the Twenty-Second Annual Convention of the Association for Advancement of Behavior Therapy, New York.

Bradbury, T. N., & Fincham, F. D. (1988b). Assessing spontaneous attributions in marital interaction: Methodological and conceptual considerations. *Journal of Social and Clinical Psychology, 7*, 122–130.

Bradbury, T., & Fincham, F. (1988c). Individual differences factors in close relationships: A contextual model of marriage as an integrative framework. *Journal of Personality and Social Psychology, 54*, 713–721.

Bradbury, T. N., & Fincham, F. D. (1989a). Behavior and satisfaction in marriage: Prospective mediating processes. *Review of Personality and Social Psychology, 10*, 119–143.

Bradbury, T. N., & Fincham, F. D. (1989b, November). *An instrument for assessing attributions in marriage: Rationale and initial validation.* Paper presented at the Twenty-Third Annual Convention of the Association for Advancement of Behavior Therapy, Washington, DC.

Bradbury, T. N., & Fincham, F. D. (1990). Attributions in marriage: Review and critique. *Psychological Bulletin, 107*, 3–33.

Bradbury, T. N., & Fincham, F. D. (in press). The psychology of close relationships: Clinical and social perspectives. In C. R. Snyder & D. Forsyth (Eds.), *Handbook of social and clinical psychology.* New York: Pergamon Press.

Branscombe, N. R. (1988). Conscious and unconscious processing of affective and cognitive information. In K. Fiedler & J. Forgas (Eds.), *Affect, cognition and social behavior* (pp. 3–24). Toronto: Hogrefe.

Bruner, J. S. (1957). On perceptual readiness. *Psychological Review, 64*, 123–152.

Buunk, B. (1984). Jealousy as related to attributions for the partner's behavior. *Social Psychology Quarterly, 47*, 107–112.

Camper, P. M., Jacobson, N. S., Holtzworth-Munroe, A., & Schmaling, K. B. (1988). Causal attributions for interactional behaviors in married couples. *Cognitive Therapy and Research, 12*, 195–209.

Cantor, N., & Malley, J. (in press). Motivation and individual differences in close relationships. In G. Fletcher & F. Fincham (Eds.), *Cognition in close relationships.* Hillsdale, NJ: Erlbaum.

Claxton, G. (1988). How do you tell a good cognitive theory when you see one? In G. Claxton (Ed.), *Growth points in cognition* (pp. 1–31). London: Routledge.

Corsini, R. J. (1956). Multiple predictors of marital happiness. *Marriage and Family Living, 18*, 240–242.

Doherty, W. J. (1981). Cognitive processes in intimate conflict: II. Efficacy and learned helplessness. *American Journal of Family Therapy, 9*, 35–44.

Duck, S. (1988). Introduction. In S. Duck (Ed.), *Handbook of personal relationships* (pp. xiii–xvii). New York: Wiley.

Eidelson, R. J., & Epstein, N. (1982). Cognition and relationship maladjustment: Development of a measure of dysfunctional relationship beliefs. *Journal of Consulting and Clinical Psychology, 50*, 715-720.

Ellis, A., & Grieger, R. (1977). *Rational–emotive therapy: A handbook of theory and practice.* New York: Springer Publ. Co.

Emmelkamp, P. M. G., van Linden van den Heuvel, C., Ruphan, M., Sanderman, R., Scholing, A., & Stroink, F. (1988). Cognitive and behavioral interventions: A comparative evaluation with clinically distressed couples. *Journal of Family Psychology, 4*, 365-377.

Epstein, N., & Eidelson, R. J. (1981). Unrealistic beliefs of clinical couples: Their relationship to expectations, goals, and satisfaction. *American Journal of Family Therapy, 9*, 13-22.

Epstein, N., Pretzer, J. L., & Fleming, B. (1987). The role of cognitive appraisal in self-reports of marital communication. *Behavior Therapy, 18*, 51-69.

Ericsson, K. A., & Simon, H. (1980). Verbal reports as data. *Psychological Reports, 87*, 215-251.

Fichten, C. S. (1984). See it from my point of view: Videotape and attributions in happy and distressed couples. *Journal of Social and Clinical Psychology, 2*, 125-142.

Fichten, C. S., Spector, I., & Libman, E. (1988). Client attributions for sexual dysfunction. *Journal of Sex and Marital Therapy, 14*, 208-224.

Fincham, F. D. (1983). Clinical applications of attribution theory: Problems and prospects. In M. Hewstone (Ed.), *Attribution theory: Social and functional extensions* (pp. 187-203). Oxford: Blackwell.

Fincham, F. D. (1985a). Attributions in close relationships. In J. H. Harvey & G. Weary (Eds.), *Attribution: Basic issues and applications* (pp. 203-234). New York: Academic Press.

Fincham, F. D. (1985b). Attribution processes in distressed and nondistressed couples: 2. Responsibility for marital problems. *Journal of Abnormal Psychology, 94*, 183-190.

Fincham, F. D., & Beach, S. R. (1988). Attribution processes in distressed and nondistressed couples: 5. Real versus hypothetical events. *Cognitive Therapy and Research, 12*, 183-190.

Fincham, F. D., Beach, S. R., & Baucom, D. H. (1987). Attribution processes in distressed and nondistressed couples: 4. Self–partner attribution differences. *Journal of Personality and Social Psychology, 52*, 739-748.

Fincham, F. D., Beach, S. R., & Bradbury, T. N. (1989). Marital distress, depression, and attributions: Is the marital distress-attribution association an artifact of depression? *Journal of Consulting and Clinical Psychology, 57*, 768-771.

Fincham, F. D., & Bradbury, T. N. (1987a). The impact of attributions in marriage: A longitudinal analysis. *Journal of Personality and Social Psychology, 53*, 510-517.

Fincham, F. D., & Bradbury, T. N. (1987b). Cognitive processes in close relationships: An attribution-efficacy model. *Journal of Personality and Social Psychology, 53*, 1106-1118.

Fincham, F. D., & Bradbury, T. N. (1988). The impact of attributions in marriage: An experimental analysis. *Journal of Social and Clinical Psychology, 7*, 147-162.

Fincham, F. D., & Bradbury, T. N. (1989a). The impact of attributions in marriage: An individual difference analysis. *Journal of Social and Personal Relationships, 6*, 69-85.

Fincham, F. D., & Bradbury, T. N. (1989b, November). *Cognition and marital dysfunction: The role of efficacy expectations.* Paper presented at the Twenty-Third Annual Convention of the Association for Advancement of Behavior Therapy, Washington, DC.

Fincham, F. D., & Bradbury, T. (1989c). Attribution of responsibility in close relationships: Egocentric bias or partner-centric bias? *Journal of Marriage and the Family, 51,* 27–35.

Fincham, F. D., & Bradbury, T. N. (in press-a). Cognition in marriage: A program of research on attributions. In D. Perlman & W. Jones (Eds.), *Advances in personal relationships* (vol. 2). London: J. Kingsley Publishers.

Fincham, F. D., & Bradbury, T. N. (in press-b). Social cognition: Implications for behavioral assessment and behavior therapy. In P. Martin (Ed.), *Handbook of behavior theory and psychological science.* New York: Pergamon Press.

Fincham, F. D., Bradbury, T. N., & Grych, J. H. (1990). Conflict in close relationships: The role of intrapersonal phenomena. In S. Graham & V. S. Folkes (Eds.), *Attribution theory: Application to achievement, mental health and interpersonal conflict* (pp. 161–184). Hillsdale, NJ: Erlbaum.

Fitzpatrick, M. A. (1988). *Between husband and wife: Communication in marriage.* Beverly Hills: Sage.

Fletcher, G. J. O. (1983). The analysis of verbal explanations for marital separation: Implications for attribution theory. *Journal of Applied Social Psychology, 13,* 245–258.

Fletcher, G. J. O., Danilovics, P., Fernandez, G., Peterson, D., & Reeder, G. D. (1986). Attributional complexity: An individual differences measure. *Journal of Personality and Social Psychology, 51,* 875–884.

Fletcher, G. J. O., & Fincham, F. D. (in press). Attribution processes in close relationships. In G. Fletcher & F. D. Fincham (Eds.), *Cognition in close relationships.* Hillsdale, NJ: Erlbaum.

Fletcher, G. J. O., Fincham, F. D., Cramer, L., & Heron, N. (1987). The role of attributions in the development of dating relationships. *Journal of Personality and Social Psychology, 53,* 510–517.

Gaelick, L., Bodenhausen, G. V., & Wyer, R. S. (1985). Emotional communication in close relationships. *Journal of Personality and Social Psychology, 49,* 1246–1265.

Harvey, J. H., Weber, A. L., Galvin, K. S., Huszti, H. C., & Garnick, N. N. (1986). Attribution in the termination of close relationships: A special focus on the account. In R. Gilmour & S. Duck (Eds.), *The emerging field of personal relationships* (pp. 189–201). Hillsdale, NJ: Erlbaum.

Hill, M. G., & Weary, G. (1983). Perspectives on the *Journal of Abnormal and Social Psychology*: How it began and how it was transformed. *Journal of Social and Clinical Psychology, 1,* 4–14.

Holmes, J. G., & Rempel, J. K. (1989). Trust in close relationships. *Review of Personality and Social Psychology, 10,* 187–220.

Holtzworth-Munroe, A., & Jacobson, N. S. (1985). Causal attributions of married couples: When do they search for causes? What do they conclude when they do? *Journal of Personality and Social Psychology, 48,* 1398–1412.

Holtzworth-Munroe, A., & Jacobson, N. S. (1988). Toward a methodology for coding spontaneous causal attributions: Preliminary results with married couples. *Journal of Social and Clinical Psychology, 7,* 101–112.

Hunt, E. (1989). Cognitive science: Definition, status, and questions. *Annual Review of Psychology, 40,* 603–629.

Ingram, R. E. (Ed.). (1986). *Information processing approaches in clinical psychology.* New York: Academic Press.

Jacobson, N. S., & Margolin, G. (1979). *Marital therapy: Strategies based on social learning and behavior exchange principles.* New York: Brunner/Mazel.

Kelley, H. H. (1983). Love and commitment. In H. H. Kelley, E. Berscheid, A. Christensen, J. H. Harvey, T. L. Huston, G. Levinger, E. McClintock, L. A. Peplau, & D. R. Peterson, *Close relationships* (pp. 265–314). New York: W. H. Freeman.

Kihlstrom, J. F., & Nasby, W. (1981). Cognitive tasks in clinical assessment: An exercise in applied psychology. In P. C. Kendall & S. D. Hollon (Eds.), *Assessment strategies for cognitive-behavioral interventions* (pp. 287–317). New York: Academic Press.

Kyle, S. O., & Falbo, T. (1985). Relationships between marital stress and attributional preferences for own and spouse behavior. *Journal of Social and Clinical Psychology, 3,* 339–351.

Lachman, R., Lachman, J. L., & Butterfield, E. C. (1979). *Cognitive psychology and information processing: An introduction.* Hillsdale, NJ: Erlbaum.

Lavin, T. J. (1987). Divergence and convergence in the causal attributions of married couples. *Journal of Marriage and the Family, 49,* 71–80.

Levenson, R. W., & Gottman, J. M. (1983). Marital interaction: Physiological linkage and affective exchange. *Journal of Personality and Social Psychology, 45,* 587–597.

Levenson, R. W., & Gottman, J. M. (1985). Physiological and affective predictors of change in relationship satisfaction. *Journal of Personality and Social Psychology, 49,* 85–94.

Lloyd, S. A., & Cate, R. M. (1985). Attributions associated with significant turning points in premarital relationship development and dissolution. *Journal of Social and Personal Relationships, 2,* 419–436.

Mandler, G. (1985). *Cognitive psychology: An essay in cognitive science.* Hilldale, NJ: Erlbaum.

Morris, P. (1988). Memory research: Past mistakes and future prospects. In G. Claxton (Ed.), *Growth points in cognition* (pp. 91–110). London: Routledge.

Murstein, B. I., & Beck, G. D. (1972). Person perception, marriage adjustment, and social desirability. *Journal of Consulting and Clinical Psychology, 39,* 296–303.

Neimeyer, G. J. (1984). Cognitive complexity and marital satisfaction. *Journal of Social and Clinical Psychology, 2,* 258–263.

Neisser, U. (1967). *Cognitive psychology.* Englewood Cliffs, NJ: Prentice-Hall.

Neisser, U. (1978). Memory: What are the important questions? In M. M. Gruneberg, P. E. Morris, & R. N. Sykes (Eds.), *Practical aspects of memory* (vol. 3, pp. 3–24). London: Academic Press.

Newman, H. M., & Langer, E. J. (1981). Post-divorce adaptation and the attribution of responsibility. *Sex Roles, 7,* 223–232.

Newman, H. M., & Langer, E. J. (1988). Investigating the development and courses of intimate relationships. In L. Y. Abramson (Ed.), *Social cognition and clinical psychology: A synthesis* (pp. 148–173). New York: Guilford Press.

Notarius, C. I., & Vanzetti, N. A. (1983). The Marital Agendas Protocol. In E. E. Filsinger (Ed.), *Marriage and family assessment* (pp. 209–227). Beverly Hills: Sage.

Ortony, A., Clore, G. L., & Collins, A. (1988). *The cognitive structure of emotions.* Cambridge: Cambridge University Press.

Ostrom, T. M. (1984). The sovereignty of social cognition. In R. S. Wyer & T. K. Srull (Eds.), *Handbook of social cognition* (vol. 1, pp. 1-38). Hillsdale, NJ: Erlbaum.

Pachella, R. G. (1974). The interpretation of reaction time in information-processing research. In B. H. Kantowitz (Ed.), *Human information processing: Tutorials in performance and cognition* (pp. 41-82). Hillsdale, NJ: Erlbaum.

Raush, H. L., Barry, W. A., Hertel, R. K., & Swain, M. A. (1974). *Communication, conflict, and marriage.* San Francisco: Jossey-Bass.

Read, S. J., & Miller, L. C. (1989). Inter-personalism: Towards a goal-based theory of persons in relationships. In L. Pervin (Ed.), *Goal concepts in personality and social psychology* (pp. 413-472). Hillsdale, NJ: Erlbaum.

Reis, H. T., & Shaver, P. (1988). Intimacy as an interpersonal process. In S. Duck (Ed.), *Handbook of personal relationships* (pp. 367-390). New York: Wiley.

Robins, C. (1988). Attributions and depression: Why is the literature so inconsistent? *Journal of Personality and Social Psychology, 54,* 880-889.

Sharkey, N. E. (1986). Introduction. In N. E. Sharkey (Ed.), *Advances in cognitive science* (vol. 1, pp. 13-21). New York: Halsted Press.

Shaver, K. G. (1985). *The attribution of blame: Causality, responsibility, and blameworthiness.* New York: Springer-Verlag.

Shaver, P., Hazan, C., & Bradshaw, D. (1988). Love as attachment. In R. J. Sternberg & M. L. Barnes (Eds.), *The psychology of love* (pp. 68-99). New Haven: Yale University Press.

Shiffrin, R. M., & Schneider, W. (1977). Controlled and automatic human information processing: II Perceptual learning, automatic attending, and a general theory. *Psychological Review, 84,* 127-190.

Sillars, A. L. (1985). Interpersonal perception in relationships. In W. Ickes (Ed.), *Compatible and incompatible relationships* (pp. 277-305). New York: Springer-Verlag.

Stratton, P., Heard, D., Hanks, H. G. I., Munton, A. G., Brewin, C. R., & Davidson, C. (1986). Coding causal beliefs in natural discourse. *British Journal of Social Psychology, 25,* 299-313.

Surra, C. A., Arizzi, P., & Asmussen, L. A. (1988). The association between reasons for commitment and the development and outcome of marital relationships. *Journal of Social and Personal Relationships, 5,* 47-63.

Taylor, S. E., & Fiske, S. T. (1981). Getting inside the head: Methodologies for process analysis. In J. H. Harvey, W. Ickes, & R. F. Kidd (Eds.), *New directions in attribution research* (vol. 3, pp. 459-506). Hillsdale, NJ: Erlbaum.

Tharp, R. G. (1963). Psychological patterning in marriage. *Psychological Bulletin, 60,* 97-117.

Thompson, J. S., & Snyder, D. K. (1986). Attribution theory in intimate relationships: A methodological review. *American Journal of Family Therapy, 14,* 123-138.

Tyndall, L. W., & Lichtenberg, J. W. (1985). Spouses' cognitive styles and marital interaction patterns. *Journal of Marriage and the Family, 11,* 193-202.

Ucros, C. G. (1989). Mood state-dependent memory: A meta-analysis. *Cognition and Emotion, 3,* 139-169.

Weiss, R. L. (1980). Strategic behavioral marital therapy: Toward a model for assessment and intervention. In J. P. Vincent (Ed.), *Advances in family intervention, assessment and theory* (vol. 1, pp. 229-271). Greenwich, CT: JAI Press.

Weiss, R. L. (1984). Cognitive and strategic interventions in behavioral marital therapy. In K. Hahlweg & N. S. Jacobson (Eds.), *Marital interaction: Analysis and modification* (pp. 337–355). New York: Guilford Press.

Wyer, R. S., Srull, T. K., & Gordon, S. E. (1984). The effects of predicting a person's behavior on subsequent trait judgments. *Journal of Experimental Social Psychology, 20,* 29–46.

# CHAPTER 5

# Gender Differences and Sex-Role Identity in Marriage

**Donald H. Baucom**
**Clifford I. Notarius**
**Charles K. Burnett**
**Paul Haefner**

Characteristic patterns often emerge to define the roles of husbands and wives, especially when couples become distressed. Marital therapists frequently encounter distressed wives who complain of relationship discord but report being unable to convince their husbands to enter therapy. Interviews with husbands and wives also reveal gender-related patterns. For example, from wives we hear, "I can't stand that he's so damned unemotional and expects me to be the same. He lives in his head all the time, and he acts like anything that's emotional isn't worth dealing with" (Rubin, 1983, p. 73). Their husbands respond, "When she comes after me like that, yapping like that, she might as well be hitting me with a bat. . . . No matter what I say it's no good. I try to keep my cool and be logical, but nothing works" (Rubin, 1976, pp. 115–116).

Understanding the nature of differences between husbands and wives in marriage and the origin of these differences requires careful study of happy and unhappy couples over time. There is a need to study the full range of marital satisfaction in order to determine whether observed differences result from sex differences, marital distress, or some interaction between the two. In addition, cross-sectional comparisons of distressed and nondistressed couples may yield a different picture of husbands and wives than that which emerges from longitudinal study of relationships. Consequently, longitudinal investigations may reveal quite different information as a function of the stage of relationship that is studied. For example, variables that predict marital adjustment in the early years of marriage may not predict adjustment in later years.

An important challenge for researchers is to identify the proper domain of relational and/or individual variables to study. The current chapter addresses this challenge by examining how communication behaviors and sex-role identity can further our understanding of gender differences in marriage. In the first section, we document gender differences in the behavioral correlates and the behavioral predictors of marital distress. The second section explores the utility of sex-role identity for understanding various aspects of marriage including marital behavior.

## GENDER DIFFERENCES IN MARITAL BEHAVIOR

Our analysis of gender differences in the marital behavior of distressed and nondistressed couples focuses on communication. The rationale for emphasizing communication behaviors is twofold. First, spouses recognize communication as among the most important aspects of their relationship. For example, Geiss and O'Leary (1981) report that communication problems are the most frequent presenting complaints among couples requesting marital therapy. Second, detailed interactional analyses of problem-solving discussions in distressed and nondistressed relationships have accounted for upward of 80% of the variance in the classification of couples as distressed or nondistressed (Gottman, 1979; Gottman, Markman, & Notarius, 1977; see Weiss & Heyman, Chapter 3, this volume).

We provide a selected review of research on the interactional behaviors of husbands and wives in distressed and nondistressed relationships. We do not review studies that placed spouses in analogue situations (e.g., Gottman & Porterfield, 1981; Noller, 1980). In order to avoid confounding gender differences with relationship satisfaction, we survey only those studies that focused on marital behavior and included marital satisfaction as a factor in the design. The results of these studies are organized along two dimensions, situational context (low versus high conflict) and temporal relationship to marital satisfaction (correlates versus predictors of distress). It is important to acknowledge and to account for both contextual and temporal influences because men and

women may respond to stressor situations in quite different ways
(Stoney, Davis, & Mathews, 1987), and, as noted earlier, correlates
of distress at a particular point in time may not predict later
satisfaction. Table 5.1 summarizes the findings of our review.

Each of the four main cells of the table paints a portrait of the
behaviors of husbands and wives in happy and unhappy relationships. It is important to emphasize that the behaviors of husbands
and wives are mutually interdependent, and thus it is difficult to
determine if any particular spouse behavior is the cause of the
partner's response or is a reaction to the partner's preceding behavior or disposition. Recognition of this fact leads us toward
systemic interpretations of the data and away from holding an
individual responsible for a given outcome. Nevertheless, it may
turn out that hubands or wives are indeed more responsible for
certain outcomes, and we look forward to future research to clarify this issue.

## Communication Behaviors of Husbands and Wives in Distressed Relationships

According to social learning theory, distressed spouses will exchange too few positive behaviors and too many negative behaviors (e.g., Jacobson & Margolin, 1979). As a correlate of declining
positive sentiment toward the relationship and the spouse,
partners engage in a number of negativistic cognitions to explain
their relationship difficulties (see Fincham, Bradbury, & Scott,
Chapter 4, this volume). Experiencing a surfeit of negative events
and a paucity of positive interactions, and armed with cognitions
detrimental to the relationship, maritally distressed individuals
experience a wide range of negative emotions, particularly anger,
anxiety, and depression. Thus, the behaviors, cognitions, and emotions of the couple become interwoven to constitute the phenomenon of marital distress.

Cross-sectional studies of husbands and wives in distressed
and nondistressed relationships bear testimony to this analysis.
The results of several such studies that focus on interactional
behavior are summarized on the left-hand side of Table 5.1. It can
be seen that spouses in distressed relationships display more disagreement, are more critical of their partners, and appear more
contemptuous of each other than spouses in a happy marriage.

Although several similarities in the behavior of distressed
husbands and wives are apparent from the table, important differences also emerge. Discord seems to affect husbands and wives

differently. In the problem-solving (high-conflict) situations studied, the behavior of distressed wives appears to be more negative than that of distressed husbands (and more negative than nondistressed wives and nondistressed husbands as well). In a recent study, observers coded 63% of the distressed wives' speaker turns as negative, compared to 46% of the distressed husbands (Notarius, Benson, Sloane, Vanzetti, & Hornyak, 1989). A more precise description of the negativity displayed by distressed wives is provided by Gottman and Krokoff (1989). They found that distressed wives displayed more noncompliance, put-downs, commands, and complaints. These differences in frequencies, although informative, do not tell us about the patterning or the structure of communication that characterizes husbands and wives.

Sequential analyses applied to codes describing a stream of behavior reveal how one partner's behavior is linked systematically to interactional antecedents. Several studies have assessed the sequential dependencies characterizing husbands and wives in distressed and nondistressed relationships. Gottman et al. (1977) investigated a spouse's capacity to "edit" out a negative reply to a message that appeared to elicit a negative impact. This construct was defined as the probability that a speaker would display negative affect immediately after displaying negative affect while listening to her partner. For distressed husbands and wives, and for nondistressed husbands, there was a strong likelihood of becoming a negative speaker if, while listening, negative affect was displayed. However, nondistressed wives were much less likely to become negative speakers after being negative listeners. Thus, nondistressed wives decrease the likelihood of long chains of negative exchange with their partners that are so characteristic of distressed marital interaction (Gottman, 1979; Margolin & Wampold, 1981; Hahlweg, Reisner et al., 1984; Schaap, 1982).

Editing was defined in a different manner by Notarius et al. (1989), and a different pattern of results emerged. They viewed editing as the likelihood that a speaker's behavior would be positive (as seen by an observer) immediately after receiving a negative behavior (as seen by an observer) that she viewed as negative. Under this definition of editing, the role of distressed wives was most notable. Although all spouses were very likely to become negative speakers after receiving a negative message as subjectively negative, nondistressed husbands and wives and distressed husbands were about equally likely to disrupt a negative exchange cycle by offering a positive response (approximately 15% of the

**TABLE** 5.1. Behaviors That Discriminate between Husbands and Wives in Distressed and Nondistressed Relationships: Cross-Sectional and Longitudinal Findings

| Correlates of distress | Predictors of distress |
| --- | --- |

*Results for husbands*

| | |
| --- | --- |
| In low-conflict situations<br>  Husbands become negative speakers<br>  after being negative listeners<br>  (GMN) | In low-conflict situations<br>  Husbands feel less positive<br><br>  Husbands less likely to feel positive<br>  after wives feel positive (LG2)<br><br>  Males more likely to reciprocate<br>  females' positive behavior (FT) |
| In high-conflict situations<br>  Husbands disagree more and are<br>  more critical of wives<br><br>  Husbands show more contempt (GK)<br><br>  Husbands less likely to feel positive<br>  after wives feel positive (LG) | In high-conflict situations<br>  Husbands feel less negative (LG2)<br><br>  Males more likely to reciprocate<br>  females' negative behavior (JML)<br><br>  Husbands display less disagree-<br>  ments and criticism (GK) |

*Results for wives*

| | |
| --- | --- |
| In low-conflict situations<br>  Wives feel more negative affect (LG) | In low-conflict situations<br>  Wives feel more positive (LG2)<br><br>  Females more likely to reciprocate<br>  males' positive behavior<br><br>  Females interrupt (FT) |
| In high-conflict situations<br>  Wives become negative speakers<br>  after being negative listeners<br>  (GMN)<br><br>  Wives more likely to receive a nega-<br>  tive, neutral, or positive message<br>  from partner as negative<br><br>  Wives are unlikely to respond posi-<br>  tively after receiving a negative<br>  message from partners as negative<br>  (NBS)<br><br>  Wives feel less positive affect<br><br>  Wives more likely to feel negative<br>  after husbands feel negative<br><br>  Wives more likely to feel positive<br>  after husbands feel positive (LG)<br><br>  Wives disagree more and are more<br>  critical of husbands | In high-conflict situations<br>  Wives more likely to feel negative<br>  after husbands feel negative (LG2)<br><br>  Females more likely to reciprocate<br>  males' positive behavior (JML)<br><br>  Wives agree more and are more ap-<br>  proving of husbands<br><br>  Wives show more sadness (GK) |

**TABLE 5.1.** (continued)

| Correlates of distress | Predictors of distress |
| --- | --- |
| *Results for wives* | |

Wives agree less and are less approving of husbands

Wives show more anger and contempt

Wives appear withdrawn from the interaction

Wives appear stubborn through display of noncompliance, put-downs, commands, and complaints (GK)

Wives rate husbands' behavior less positively (FM, GBW, NVS)

Wives believe their husbands perceive them as behaving negatively (GBS, NVS)

Husbands use more neutral messages than wives

Wives use more negative messages than husbands (N) and engage in longer sequences of negative behavior (S)

*Note.* References are indicated by the following abbreviations: FM, Floyd and Markman (1983); FT, Filsinger and Thoma (1985); GBW, Gaelick, Bodenhausen, and Wyer (1985); GK, Gottman and Krokoff (1989); GMN, Gottman et al. (1977); JML, Julien et al. (1989); LG, Levenson and Gottman (1983); LG2, Levenson and Gottman (1985); N, Noller (1982); NBS, Notarius et al. (1989); NVS, Notarius, Vanzetti, and Smith (1981); S, Schaap (1982).

time), whereas distressed wives offered a positive response less than 1% of the time. Although the alternative definitions of editing offered by Gottman et al. (1977) and Notarius et al. (1989) lead to somewhat different findings, across both studies it is wives' behavior that discriminates most sharply between distressed and nondistressed couples. Such findings are consistent with the view that wives act as the "barometer" of a distressed relationship (Barry, 1970; Floyd & Markman, 1983).

It seems safest to assume at this point that there are two gender-related processes that are active in shaping the interactional behaviors of distressed and nondistressed couples in problem-solving discussion. It appears that nondistressed wives are willing and able to provide a nonnegative reply to their partners' messages that they hear as negative (Gottman et al., 1977) and that distressed wives are unwilling and/or unable to provide a positive reply to their partners' negative messages (Notarius et al., 1989). Although the magnitude of these differences between spouses is small, we believe that these subtle differences may be responsible for rather substantial differences in interactional outcomes (Notarius & Markman, 1987). An infrequent positive reply from a nondistressed wife to a negative message may be all that is required to disrupt an escalating spiral of negative exchange.

The overall negativity displayed by distressed wives (Floyd & Markman, 1983; Gottman et al., 1977; Noller, 1982; Notarius et al., 1989) is notable and deserving of explanation. One fruitful avenue of investigation might be to assess wives' attributions for marital discord in general and for their husbands' behavior in particular as a mediator of their interactional behavior (see Fincham & Bradbury, 1988). Another possibility is to consider the likely consequences of the early stages of relationship discord during which wives appear to push for engagement. Assuming a social learning model, these marriages headed for distress will be characterized by inadequate relationship skills, and wives' attempts to maintain engagement are likely to lead to greater conflict and discord, from which distressed husbands are likely to retreat. As husbands withdraw further from the relationship, their wives are likely to see this withdrawal as yet another problem with the relationship. Husbands' withdrawal is perhaps an even greater issue than the more specific disagreements that were the source of initial discord (Gottman, Notarius, Gonso, & Markman, 1976). Similarly, the press to discuss relationship difficulties and the resultant conflict that will frequently ensue may become the overriding issues for distressed husbands. For both partners, there is likely to be a profound sense of frustration: all efforts aimed at achieving harmony have failed, unresolved problems remain, and the couple identifies their marriage as unhappy and troubled.

It is at this point in their relationship that a distressed couple enters our typical research paradigm, and we ask them to identify a salient relationship problem and to "work toward a mutually satisfying solution." This task very likely creates a context that wives recognize as an opportunity to discuss relationship problems and that husbands fear as an opportunity for open conflict. In pursuit of issues that need discussion and resolution, the distressed wife is seen to be a more negative interactant, unable to edit what may well be a storehouse of gripes and frustrations. Her husband, unable to withdraw from the situation as he might do at home, is also an angry communicator, but not quite to the extent of his wife. His objective may be to keep the conversation from becoming even more negative, and so he occasionally offers a positive reply to his wife's negative messages (Notarius et al., 1989) and evaluates his wife's behavior much more positively than does an outside observer (Floyd & Markman, 1983; Notarius et al., 1989).

The distressed couple thus appears caught in a trough of dissatisfaction. With the couple lacking communication skills necessary for effective problem solving, issues mount and dissatisfaction grows. Relatively minor problems are replaced by greater concerns about the partner's capacity for maintaining the relationship. For husbands, the concern is over their wives' greater negativity and the potential for escalating conflict. For wives, the concern is over their husbands' apparent lack of investment in the relationship and lack of involvement in attempts to resolve difficulties. Neither recognizes that they are facing a common enemy: poor communication skills (Hahlweg, Revenstorf, & Schindler, 1984), destructive cognitions concerning the cause of relationship disagreements and problems (Bradbury & Fincham, 1990), and lowered expectancies for being able to resolve disagreements (Notarius & Vanzetti, 1983).

## Communication Behaviors That Predict a Decline in Satisfaction over Time

The data on predictors of marital distress can be organized around the two central themes, engagement for wives and withdrawal for husbands. Husbands who are likely to experience a decline in relationship satisfaction appear to have begun to pull back from the relationship. In a nonproblem discussion, these husbands appear to experience their wives' behavior less positively compared to husbands whose relationship satisfaction is maintained over time (Levenson & Gottman, 1983). In a problem discussion likely to generate conflict, the husbands' withdrawal is expressed as less criticism and disagreement (Gottman & Krokoff, 1989). It is as if these husbands are trying to avoid engaging in overt conflict with their wives (see Gottman & Levenson, 1988, for a speculative psychophysiological account of this hypothesis). Because this pattern is a predictor of relationship decline, the findings suggest that the relative absence of criticism and disagreements from husbands is a marker not of accord but of a decision to maintain interactional calm even if problems do not receive the attention they deserve.

The behavior of wives in relationships that predict a decline in satisfaction appears to reflect a recognition of relationship problems and an attempt to keep their husbands engaged in interaction. In nonconflict discussions and problem-solving discussions, these wives evaluate their husbands' messages more positively (Levenson & Gottman, 1983); they are more agreeing and more approving of their husbands (Gottman & Krokoff, 1989), and they are more likely to reciprocate their partners' positive behaviors (Filsinger & Thoma, 1988; Julien, Markman, & Lindhal, 1989). In essence, these wives, like their husbands, appear sensitive to relationship conflict, but rather than withdrawing, they seek to soothe the relationship through positive exchanges.

The behaviors of intimate partners in relationships that will, over time, decline in satisfaction are generally consistent with a social learning model of relationship adaptation. In the absence of relationship skills, particularly effective communication, and problem-solving skills, everyday issues are left unresolved and begin to accumulate. Early attempts to attribute difficulties to situational causes may begin to yield to more destructive thoughts that hold the partner responsible for difficulties (Kelley, Huston, & Cate, 1985). The partners are likely to feel less able to resolve relational difficulties, and in turn, lowered expectancies for successful problem solving may contribute to more destructive interpersonal processes (Notarius & Vanzetti, 1983).

## SEX-ROLE IDENTITY

The above discussion demonstrates that there are meaningful gender differences in communication behavior among married couples. Why do these differences occur, and what is the basis for them? Although some of these gender-related differences might result from biological and physiological differences (Gottman & Levenson, 1988), many of the differences likely are learned. There are many socializing factors that teach males to behave in certain ways and females to behave in other ways, and gender differences in marriage reflect, to an extent, society's norms for male/female behavior within intimate heterosexual relationships. However, within each gender, there are meaningful individual differences, and some of these individual differences probably affect relationship behavior. The field of individual differences points to a vast array of variables that could be relevant for understanding relationship behavior. The task is to identify which individual difference variables account for gender differences in marriage.

Perhaps the most central individual difference variable to consider within this context is sex-role identity. Each person develops a sense of him- or herself as a male or female, and the specifics included within this sex-role identity differ from one person to the next. Thus, differences noted among males in marital interaction may reflect these various males' beliefs about what it means to be a male within a marriage. The concept of sex-role identity can be broken down further into the variables of masculinity and femininity. Although these variables have been defined and measured differently by various investigators (e.g., Baucom, 1976; Bem, 1974; Spence, Helmreich, & Stapp, 1974), masculinity can be defined as those characteristics (behaviors, attitudes, emotions, etc.) that are typical of males and that separate them as a group from females. Likewise, femininity can be defined as those characteristics that are typical of females and that separate them as a group from males.

Traditionally, masculinity and femininity have been construed as bipolar opposites on a single dimension. As a result, any individual could be placed on this single masculinity/femininity dimension, ranging from extremely masculine at one end to extremely feminine at the other end. However, following Constantinople's (1973) recommendation, more recent investigators and theoreticians have construed masculinity and feminity as two independent unipolar dimensions. Each person can be assessed on masculinity, which ranges from "masculine" at one end to "not masculine" at the other end. The same individual also can be assessed on femininity, ranging from "feminine" to "not feminine." Although the specific attributes comprising masculinity and femininity vary somewhat according to the particular scales employed, there does seem to be some consistency in what is included within these concepts. Masculinity usually includes an instrumental, task, and achievement orientation; "masculine" persons typically have a high level of drive and ambition. They are assertive and are leaders. Femininity includes an attention to emotional and expressive aspects of life, including an emphasis on interpersonal relationships. "Feminine" individuals typically are responsible and generally have accepted society's norms for ethical behavior (Baucom, 1980).

By employing these two dimensions, each person's sex-role identity can be viewed as that individual's level of masculinity in conjunction with his or her level of femininity. Thus, an individual might be high on both masculinity and femininity; such persons have been referred to as androgynous. Similarly, an individual might be high on masculinity and low on femininity, demonstrating a stereotypic masculine-sex-typed identity. Conversely, an individual might be high on femininity and low on masculinity (feminine-sex-typed). Finally, a person might be low on both masculinity and femininity, termed undifferentiated.

By considering sex-role identity, findings that are viewed currently as reflecting sex differences in marriage can be interpreted with greater clarity. That is, investigators can evaluate whether being a member of a given gender is what is important in understanding an individual's behavior within marriage, whether a given level of masculinity and/or femininity is important, or whether gender and sex-role identity interact in some manner related to marital functioning.

## Sex-Role Identity and Marital Adjustment

The investigation of sex-role identity and marital functioning is in its infancy, and at present the most basic question is being asked: is sex-role identity related to level of marital adjustment? A number of studies show that, indeed, sex-role identity is correlated with level of marital adjustment (Antill, 1983; Baucom & Aiken, 1984; Kurdek & Schmitt, 1986; Murstein & Williams, 1983; O'Donnell & James, 1978). More specifically, higher levels of femininity are correlated with higher levels of marital adjustment, and although less consistent, greater degrees of masculinity are related to higher levels of marital adjustment. Unfortunately, these studies have been limited by at least two factors. Many of them are based on samples with a restricted range of marital adjustment and omit couples who are significantly maritally distressed. Second, the samples are often too small to investigate the simultaneous impact of both spouses' sex-role identities on either person's marital adjustment. Given the four possible sex-role types described above for an individual, there are 16 patterns of sex-role pairs when couples are considered. A recent study, based on a large number of couples ($n = 282$) sampled from the full range of marital functioning is presented briefly to exemplify the relationship between sex-role identity and marital adjustment (Peterson, Baucom, Elliott, & Aiken, in press).

All couples completed Baucom's masculinity and femininity scales (Baucom, 1976) and either the Locke–Wallace Marital Adjustment Scale (Locke & Wallace, 1959) or Spanier's Dyadic Adjustment Scale (Spanier, 1976) as measures of marital adjustment.

The findings confirmed that sex-role identity is related to level of marital functioning. Among the nondistressed community sample, androgynous–androgynous was the most frequent type of couple pair, and undifferentiated–undifferentiated couples were the least frequent. Conversely, among the couples seeking marital therapy, undifferentiated–undifferentiated was the most frequent couple type, whereas androgynous–androgynous was the least frequent.

This same pattern was confirmed when marital adjustment scores were considered rather than clinic/nonclinic status as the index of marital functioning. Higher levels of masculinity and femininity for both genders were related consistently to higher levels of marital functioning. The consistency and magnitude of these effects were striking. For example, of the 24 cells involving at least one partner with a high level of femininity, 18 had marital adjustment scores above the overall group mean. All six exceptions below the group mean involved couples in which a person high on femininity was married to an undifferentiated partner. Similarly, when persons with a high level of masculinity were considered, 17 of the 24 cells had marital adjustment scores above the overall group mean. Six of the seven exceptions involved a person high on masculinity married to an undifferentiated individual. Consequently, being married to an undifferentiated individual appears to be related to a low level of marital adjustment for both partners. In fact, of the 14 cells including an undifferentiated partner, 12 were below the group mean on marital adjustment. Similarly, two undifferentiated persons married to each other resulted in the lowest marital adjustment scores for the females and the next to lowest scores for the males. To the contrary, two androgynous persons married to each other corresponded with the highest level of marital adjustment for both males and females.

The consistent findings that sex-role identity is related to marital adjustment indicates that an understanding of gender differences in marriage can be enriched by considering sex-role identity. Yet the basis for the relationship between sex-role identity and marital adjustment is unclear. One untested hypothesis is that there are factors involved in masculinity and femininity that are adaptive for marital adjustment. Because the concepts of masculinity and femininity are rather broad, clarifying the specific factors influencing marital adjustment is crucial if the findings to date are to add to our understanding of marital functioning. At present, empirical investigations are only beginning to clarify the behavioral, cognitive, and affective correlates of sex-role identity that might influence marital functioning.

### Sex-Role Identity and Marital Behavior

As noted earlier, communication difficulties can account for a substantial portion of the variance in marital distress. Thus, one major way in which sex-role identity could influence marital functioning is via communication. At least two investigations to date confirm that sex-role identity is related to the ways that couples communicate. In both investigations, couples were instructed to resolve marital conflicts. These interactions were then coded by trained observers. Burger and Jacobson (1979) examined the frequency with which couples expressed various types of positive and negative communication and found that femininity was positively correlated with positive communications and negatively correlated with negative communications. Thus, overall, femininity was related to more effective communication between spouses.

Because negative communication appears to differentiate level of marital distress more consistently than does positive communication, Sayers and Baucom (1989) focused on couples' negative communication. They evaluated both the *frequency* of negative communication and negative communication *sequences* (i.e., negative communication from one spouse followed by negative communication from the partner) among maritally distressed couples. The results confirmed and expanded Burger and Jacobson's (1979) findings regarding the importance of femininity in marital communication. For couples that included feminine husbands, husbands and wives exhibited a lower frequency of negative communications. These same couples demonstrated fewer and shorter negative communication sequences. Finally, the more feminine the distressed wife was, the *less* likely she was to terminate a negative communication sequence. That is, feminine wives kept the negative interaction alive.

How can these findings be interpreted in light of the gender differences in communication noted earlier in the chapter? First, readers should keep in mind that the results are based on a sample of distressed couples, and comparisons are within this group only. It appears that when the husband is high on femininity, both husband and wife are less negative as they discuss problem aspects of their relationship. Such an interaction pattern is likely to lead to greater satisfaction with the communication process, although this issue has not been explored empirically. The current findings regarding feminine wives suggest that not all distressed wives respond negatively to their partners' negative messages. Instead, it is feminine distressed wives who are particularly likely to take this tack, perhaps in an attempt to reengage a withdrawing husband. Consequently, not all males and females communicate in the gender-related manner described in the first section of this chapter. Therefore, additional clarification might result from considering individuals' sex-role identities in future explorations of marital communication.

Whereas a couple's explicit attempts to communicate with each other form an important category of relationship behavior, other noncommunication behavior also is important in marital adjustment (e.g., completing household chores). For example, several investigations confirm that the frequency of various positive and negative noncommunication behaviors that occur during the day are related to relationship satisfaction (e.g., Christensen & Nies, 1980; Jacobson, Follette, & McDonald, 1982; Wills, Weiss, & Patterson, 1974). The extent to which sex-role identity is related to such daily behavior is largely unexplored. However, in a related vein, Coleman and Ganong (1985) found that androgynous persons scored higher than masculine-sex-typed and undifferentiated persons on two self-report measures of loving behavior that gave primary focus to expressing loving feelings.

## Sex-Role Identity and Cognition

In recent years, researchers from a social learning perspective have recognized that marital happiness is not merely a function of both persons' behavior. This behavior is processed cognitively by both partners, and the ways that spouses think about each other's behavior can influence their relationship satisfaction. For example, whether a husband's late arrival from the office has a positive or negative impact on his wife might be determined by her interpretation that (1) he is avoiding her and the family or (2) he is working late to make extra money to provide for the family's needs (see Fincham, Bradbury, & Scott, Chapter 4, this volume). Several categories of cognitions (including selective attention, attributions, expectancies, assumptions, and standards) appear to be related to level of marital adjustment and might therefore be examined with regard to sex-role identity (Baucom, Epstein, Sayers, & Sher, 1989).

At present there are no published investigations in this area, but recent analyses of data on causal attributions point to the potential in this domain (Baucom & Voirin, 1989). Causal attributions refer to the ways in which an individual explains why various events occur. The example provided above regarding a husband's returning late from work included two different attributions that the wife might make for his behavior. Baucom and Voirin's findings indicate that individuals' sex-role identities are correlated with the attributions they make for their partners' behavior. For example, more masculine individuals are likely to see the partner as the cause of the partner's negative behavior but at the same time to view the partner's behavior as resulting from factors that are not likely to be maintained in other situations or in the future. Feminine persons are more likely to view themselves as the causes of their partner's negative behavior. Considering positive behavior, feminine persons make attributions to themselves, their partners, and outside circumstances equally. Thus, when considering negative behavior, masculinity seems to coincide with a focus on the individual. For both positive and negative behavior, femininity corresponds to a relationship focus in interpreting the basis for an individual's behavior. Consequently, these findings suggest that it is not females *per se* that have a relationship focus but rather feminine persons who explain marital behaviors in relationship terms.

### Sex-Role Identity and Dysfunctional Emotions

Extreme or persistent negative affect in one spouse can interfere with marital functioning. For example, extreme jealousy, depression, anxiety, and anger all can have detrimental effects on the quality of a marriage. Recently, attention has been focused on the relationship between depression and marital distress because of the seeming overlap between the two. For example, Beach, Jouriles, and O'Leary (1985) report that in over half of the maritally distressed couples seeking treatment at their clinic, at least one member was clinically depressed. There is also substantial evidence that interacting with a depressed person often results in negative feelings about that individual and the relationship (see Coyne, Kahn, & Gotlib, 1987, for a recent review).

Although the interplay among sex-role identity, depression, and marital distress has not been explored, a number of studies have documented the relationship between sex-role identity and depression (e.g., Baucom & Danker-Brown, 1979) and between depression and marital discord (e.g., Beach et al., 1985; Birchler, 1986). Regarding sex-role identity and depression, correlational studies with clinically depressed patients indicate that depressed persons typically score low on measures of masculinity (e.g., Berzins, Welling, & Wetter, 1978). Similarly, experimental investigations demonstrate that individuals low on masculinity are more likely than other persons to respond to failure experiences with increases in depressed mood (e.g., Baucom, 1983; Baucom & Danker-Brown, 1984; Baucom & Weiss, 1986). Thus, given that (1) sex-role identity is related to depression and (2) depression is related to marital discord, one possible pathway through which sex-role identity might exert its influence on marital adjustment is via negative affective states such as depression. Studies that consider all three factors—sex-role identity, negative affective states, and marital adjustment—are greatly needed, and negative affective states other than depression need to be explored within this context.

## Sex-Role Identity and the Marital System

The above discussion of sex-role identity emphasized the individual rather than the couple level of analysis. Although individual characteristics are likely to impact each partner's satisfaction with the marriage, behavioral, cognitive, and affective aspects of sex-role identity may also influence the couple as a system. In order to gain a more complete understanding of how sex roles are expressed in marriage, it is important to understand how different sex-role identities might affect the marital relationship that the two individuals have developed.

Research already discussed indicates that couples with two androgynous partners are the most satisfied with their marriages, followed by couples in which one or both partners are high on masculinity and/or femininity. Couples in which one or both partners are undifferentiated are the most distressed. These findings can be understood from at least three theoretical perspectives. First, sex-role identity may serve as a normative function by regulating behavior in marriage. Second, the characteristics associated with different sex roles may be thought of as assets to be exchanged within the marital relationship. Finally, the balance of power in marriage may be affected by the partners' sex-role identities. Each of these perspectives is considered in more detail below.

### Normative Functions of Sex Roles in Marriage
Each individual in a marital relationship develops a set of norms regarding what behaviors are expected and considered acceptable

for each partner. These norms are derived from a number of sources, but they are likely to be at least partially influenced by each individual's views of male and female sex roles. According to Thibaut and Kelley (1959), the major function of norms is to increase the efficiency of interactions by providing a predictable set of responses to familiar situations. Thus, by helping to organize and constrain behavior, sex-role norms can provide guidelines for behavior when new situations are encountered. An individual who rigidly adheres to stereotyped masculine or feminine sex roles may have the skills to maintain relationship quality only within a limited range of the situations encountered in marriage. When circumstances deviate significantly from this range, the sex-typed individual's repertoire of behavioral responses may not be flexible or extensive enough to accommodate to the novel situation. An androgynous individual, however, has access to both masculine and feminine behaviors (Taylor & Hall, 1982) and has a greater chance of being able to respond adaptively to a much wider range of situational demands than a rigidly sex-typed individual (Bem & Lenny, 1976). The undifferentiated individual, with a very narrow range of behavioral options, may be predictable from a normative perspective, but he/she may make minimal contributions to the relationship because of a restricted repertoire of potentially adaptive responses.

### Exchange Value of Sex Roles in Marriage
Whereas the normative perspective emphasizes the importance of predictability and order within marriage, social exchange theory focuses on the content of what each partner has to offer in the marriage. The central tenet of social exchange theory is that partners' evaluations of the costs and benefits of maintaining their marriage determine the degree of marital quality they experience (Thibaut & Kelley, 1959). From this perspective, masculine and feminine sex-role behavior can be viewed as contributions or assets to the relationship. Thus, the greater the range of sex-role behaviors an individual possesses, the more valuable his or her sex role is to the marriage. Similarly, Thibaut and Kelley (1959) describe a relationship cost as a function of how much a relationship-enhancing behavior taxes the skill level and arouses the anxiety of a couple. Thus, relationships that require behaviors outside of the individuals' repertoire can be viewed as costs or potential sources of marital dysfunction.

An androgynous couple would, presumably, have the widest range of sex-role behaviors from which to draw in the face of the myriad of situations confronting a marriage. The advantages to be gained from the ability to exercise both masculine and feminine behaviors include enhanced access to instrumental and expressive behaviors that are important in relationship functioning. Previously discussed findings suggest that when a couple includes an undifferentiated individual who contributes neither a high level of masculine nor of feminine behavior, then both that person and that individual's spouse are likely to be dissatisfied with the relationship. Thus, the results could be interpreted to mean that each partner must be seen as making some form of significant contribution to the relationship for either person to be satisfied with the marriage.

## Sex Roles and Marital Power

Studies of power processes and marriage have consistently shown highest levels of marital satisfaction among egalitarian couples (Gray-Little & Burks, 1983). Although egalitarianism has been defined in several ways in these studies, findings indicate that compared to egalitarian decision-making strategies, coercive control techniques in decision making are clearly associated with lower marital quality ratings by both observers and couples. Although empirical investigations are still lacking in this area, it is a reasonable hypothesis that couples including two androgynous individuals are likely to be egalitarian with regard to marital power. If androgynous spouses do have a broader range of behavioral skills, then they should have a multitude of options for satisfying their own needs as well as the needs of their partners. Access to a greater number and variety of behavioral options would presumably lessen the need for coercive processes to solve relationship problems and increase the likelihood of egalitarian decision making. These couples could be expected to rely less on manipulation and coercion and more on cooperation as behavior change strategies.

## CONCLUSIONS

Although the study of gender differences and sex-role identity in marital relationships is still in its infancy, the findings to date indicate clearly that these domains of investigation warrant further consideration. Gender differences in behavior, particularly in the area of communication, suggest that males and females assume different roles as couples struggle with marital problems. The study of sex-role identity in marital relationship indicates that both masculinity and femininity can be viewed as relationship assets to couples. The behavioral, cognitive, and emotional correlates of masculinity and femininity within a marital relationship and how these might affect marital adjustment have been reviewed. Finally, the role that androgyny might play in (1) providing predictability across a range of marital situations, (2) serving as an asset in a cost/benefit analysis of the relationship, and (3) contributing to an egalitarian relationship with regard to power, has been discussed.

Admittedly, many of the theoretical interpretations provided for gender differences and sex-role findings are speculative at this time. What is critical is that we begin to realize that a consistent body of empirical findings is beginning to emerge. Consequently, now is the time to consider these findings in terms of existing theories of marital functioning and to supplement or alter these theories where necessary to recognize that gender differences and sex-role identity are likely to be major influences on couples' day-to-day functioning and long-term relationship adjustment.

# REFERENCES

Antill, J. K. (1983). Sex role complementarity versus similarity in married couples. *Journal of Personality and Social Psychology, 45*, 145–155.

Barry, W. (1970). Marriage research and conflict: An integrative review. *Psychological Bulletin, 73*, 41–54.

Baucom, D. H. (1976). Independent masculinity and femininity scales on the California Psychological Inventory. *Journal of Consulting and Clinical Psychology, 44*, 876.

Baucom, D. H. (1980). Independent CPI masculinity and femininity scales: Psychological correlates and a sex role typology. *Journal of Personality Assessment, 44*, 262–271.

Baucom, D. H. (1983). Sex role identity and the decision to regain control among women: A learned helplessness investigation. *Journal of Personality and Social Psychology, 44*, 334–343.

Baucom, D. H., & Aiken, P. A. (1984). Sex role identity, marital satisfaction and response to behavioral marital therapy. *Journal of Consulting and Clinical Psychology, 52*, 438–444.

Baucom, D. H., & Danker-Brown, P. S. (1979). Influence of sex roles on the development of learned helplessness. *Journal of Consulting and Clinical Psychology, 47*, 928–936.

Baucom, D. H., & Danker-Brown, P. (1984). Sex role identity and gender-stereotyped tasks in the development of learned helplessness in women. *Journal of Personality and Social Psychology, 46*, 422–430.

Baucom, D. H., Epstein, N., Sayers, S., & Sher, T. G. (1989). The role of cognitions in marital relationships: Definitional, methodological, and conceptual issues. *Journal of Consulting and Clinical Psychology, 57,* 31–38.

Baucom, H. H., & Voirin, D. (1989). [Sex role identity and couples' attributions for marital events.] Unpublished raw data.

Baucom, D. H., & Weiss, B. (1986). Peers' granting of control to women with different sex role identities: Implications for depression. *Journal of Personality and Social Psychology, 51,* 1075–1080.

Beach, S. R. H., Jouriles, E. N., & O'Leary, K. D. (1985). Extramarital sex: Impact on depression and commitment in couples seeking marital therapy. *Journal of Sex and Marital Therapy, 11,* 99–108.

Bem, S. L. (1974). The measurement of psychological androgyny. *Journal of Consulting and Clinical Psychology, 42,* 155–162.

Bem, S. L., & Lenney, E. (1976). Sex typing and the avoidance of cross-sex behavior. *Journal of Personality and Social Psychology, 33,* 48–54.

Berzins, J. I., Welling, M. A., & Wetter, R. E. (1978). A new measure of psychological androgyny based on the Personality Research Form. *Journal of Consulting and Clinical Psychology, 46,* 126–138.

Birchler, G. R. (1986). Alleviating depression with "marital" intervention. In A. Freeman, N. Epstein, & K. M. Simon (Eds.), *Depression in the family* (pp. 101–116). New York: Haworth Press.

Bradbury, T. N., & Fincham, F. D. (1990). Attributions in marriage: Review and critique. *Psychological Bulletin, 107,* 3–33.

Burger, A. L., & Jacobson, N. S. (1979). The relationship between sex role characteristics, couple satisfaction, and couple problem-solving skills. *American Journal of Family Therapy, 7,* 52–60.

Christensen, A., & Nies, D. C. (1980). The Spouse Observation Checklist: Empirical analysis and critique. *American Journal of Family Therapy, 8,* 69–79.

Coleman, M., & Ganong, L. H. (1985). Love and sex role stereotypes: Do macho men and feminine women make better lovers? *Journal of Personality and Social Psychology, 49,* 170–176.

Constantinople, A. (1973). Masculinity-femininity: An exception to a famous dictum? *Psychological Bulletin, 80,* 389–407.

Coyne, J., Kahn, J., & Gotlib, I. (1987). Depression. In T. Jacob (Ed.), *Family interaction and psychopathology. Theories, methods, and findings* (pp. 509–533). New York: Plenum.

Filsinger, E., & Thoma, S. (1988). Behavioral antecedents of relationship stability and adjustment: A five-year longitudinal study. *Journal of Marriage and the Family, 50,* 785–795.

Fincham, F. D., & Bradbury, T. N. (1988). The impact of attributions in marriage: Empirical and conceptual foundations. *British Journal of Clinical Psychology, 27,* 77–90.

Floyd, F., & Markman, H. (1983). Observational biases in spouse observation: Toward a cognitive/behavioral model of marriage. *Journal of Consulting and Clinical Psychology, 51,* 450–457.

Gaelick, L., Bodenhausen, G. V., & Wyer, R. S. (1985). Emotional communication in close relationships. *Journal of Personality and Social Psychology, 49,* 1246–1265.

Geiss, S. K., & O'Leary, K. D. (1981). Therapist ratings of frequency and severity of marital problems: Implications for research. *Journal of Marriage and Family Therapy, 7,* 515–520.

Gottman, J. (1979). *Marital interaction: Experimental investigations*. New York: Academic Press.

Gottman, J., & Krokoff, L. (1989). Marital interaction and satisfaction: A longitudinal view. *Journal of Consulting and Clinical Psychology, 57*, 47–52.

Gottman, J., & Levenson, R. (1988). The social psychophysiology of marriage. In P. Noller & M. A. Fitzpatrick (Eds.), *Perspectives on marital interaction* (pp. 182–200). Clevedon, UK: Multilingual Matters.

Gottman, J., Markman, H., & Notarius, C. (1977). The topography of marital conflict: A sequential analysis of verbal and non-verbal behavior. *Journal of Marriage and the Family, 39*, 461–478.

Gottman, J., Notarius, C. I., Gonso, J., & Markman, H. (1976). *A couple's guide to communication*. Champaign, IL: Research Press.

Gottman, J., & Porterfield, A. L. (1981). Communicative competence in the nonverbal behavior of married couples. *Journal of Marriage and the Family, 43*, 817–824.

Gray-Little, B., & Burks, N. (1983). Power and satisfaction in marriage: A review and critique. *Psychological Bulletin, 93*, 513–538.

Hahlweg, K., Reisner, L., Kohli, G., Vollmer, M., Schindler, L., & Revenstorf, D. (1984). Development and validity of a new system to analyze interpersonal communication: Kategoriensystem für Partnerschaftliche Interaktion. In K. Hahlweg & N. Jacobson (Eds.), *Marital interaction: Analysis and modification* (pp. 182–198). New York: Guilford Press.

Hahlweg, K., Revenstorf, D., & Schindler, L. (1984). Effects of behavioral marital therapy on couples' communication and problem-solving skills. *Journal of Consulting and Clinical Psychology, 4*, 553–566.

Jacobson, N. S., Follette, W. C., & McDonald, D. W. (1982). Reactivity to positive and negative behavior in distressed and nondistressed married couples. *Journal of Consulting and Clinical Psychology, 50*, 706–714.

Jacobson, N., & Margolin, G. (1979). *Marital therapy: Strategies based on social learning and behavioral exchange principles*. New York: Brunner/Mazel.

Julien, D., Markman, H., & Lindahl, K. (1989). A comparison of a global and a microanalytic coding system: Implications for future trends in studying interactions. *Behavioral Assessment, 11*, 81–100.

Kelley, C., Huston, T. L., & Cate, R. M. (1985). Premarital relationship corelates of the erosion of satisfaction in marriage. *Journal of Social and Personal Relationships, 2*, 167–178.

Kurdek, L. A., & Schmitt, J. P. (1986). Interaction of sex role self-concept with relationship quality and relationship beliefs in married, heterosexual cohabiting, gay, and lesbian couples. *Journal of Personality and Social Psychology, 51*, 365–370.

Levenson, R., & Gottman, J. (1983). Marital interaction: Physiological linkage and affective exchange. *Journal of Personality and Social Psychology, 45*, 587–597.

Levenson, R., & Gottman, J. (1985). Physiological and affective predictors of change in relationship satisfaction. *Journal of Personality and Social Psychology, 49*, 85–94.

Locke, H. J., & Wallace, K. M. (1959). Short marital-adjustment and prediction tests: Their reliability and validity. *Marriage and Family Living, 21*, 251–255.

Margolin, G., & Wampold, B. (1981). Sequential analysis of conflict and accord in distressed and nondistressed marital partners. *Journal of Consulting and Clinical Psychology, 46*, 1476–1486.

Murstein, B. I., & Williams, P. D. (1983). Sex roles and marriage adjustment. *Small Group Behavior, 41*, 77–94.

Noller, P. (1980). Misunderstandings in marital communication: A study of couples' nonverbal communication. *Journal of Personality and Social Psychology, 39*, 1135–1148.

Noller, P. (1982). Channel consistency and inconsistency in the communications of married couples. *Journal of Personality and Social Psychology, 43*, 732–741.

Notarius, C. I., Benson, P. R., Sloane, D., Vanzetti, N., & Hornyak, L. M. (1989). Exploring the interface between perception and behavior: An analysis of marital interaction in distressed and nondistressed couples. *Behavioral Assessment, 11*, 39–64.

Notarius, C., & Markman, H. (1987, August). *Linking research advances in understanding marital distress to clinical practice.* Paper presented in Continuing Education Program for American Psychological Association, New York.

Notarius, C. I., & Vanzetti, N. (1983). Marital Agendas Protocol. In E. Filsinger (Ed.), *A source book of marriage and family assessment* (pp. 209–227). Beverly Hills, CA: Sage Publications.

Notarius, C., Vanzetti, N., & Smith, R. (1981, November). *Assessing expectations and outcomes in marital interaction.* Paper presented at the Association for the Advancement of Behavior Therapy, Toronto.

O'Donnell, W. J., & James, C. A. (1978). *Psychological androgyny as a correlate of health and marital adjustment of career-oriented couples.* Unpublished manuscript, Department of Epidemiology, School of Public Health, University of North Carolina.

Peterson, C. D., Baucom, D. H., Elliott, M. J., & Aiken, P. A. (in press). The relationship between sex role identity and marital adjustment. *Sex Roles.*

Rubin, L. (1976). *Worlds of pain.* New York: Basic Books.

Rubin, L. (1983). *Intimate strangers.* New York: Harper & Row.

Sayers, S., & Baucom, D. H. (1989). *Sex role identity and communication among maritally distressed couples.* Manuscript submitted for publication.

Schaap, C. (1982). *Communication and adjustment in marriage.* Lisse, The Netherlands: Swets & Zeitlinger.

Spanier, G. B. (1976). Measuring dyadic adjustment: New scales for assessing the quality of marriage and similar dyads. *Journal of Marriage and the Family, 38*, 15–28.

Spence, J. T., Helmreich, R., & Stapp, J. (1974). The Personal Attributes Questionnaire: A measure of sex-role stereotypes and masculinity–femininity. *JSAS Catalog of Selected Documents in Psychology, 4*, 43. (MS No. 617)

Stoney, C., Davis, M., & Matthews, K. (1987). Sex differences in physiological responses to stress and in coronary heart disease: A causal link? *Psychophysiology, 24*, 127–131.

Taylor, M. C., & Hall, J. A. (1982). Psychological androgyny: Theories, methods, and conclusions. *Psychological Bulletin, 92*, 347–366.

Thibaut, J. W., & Kelley, H. H. (1959). *The social psychology of groups.* New York: Wiley.

Wills, T. A., Weiss, R. L., & Patterson, G. R. (1974). A behavioral analysis of the determinants of marital satisfaction. *Journal of Consulting and Clinical Psychology, 42*, 802–811.

# CHAPTER 6
# Children and Marriage

## Jay Belsky

The relationship between children and marriage is a complex one in which bidirectional relations need to be emphasized (Belsky, 1981; Lerner & Spanier, 1978). Although this means that marriages affect children (Emery, 1982) and that children affect marriages, the central focus of this chapter is on the latter phenomenon.

When we consider how children affect marriage, two contrasting views are evident. From a positive perspective, children are seen to derive from the love that spouses feel for one another and, as a result, to function as a source of joint pleasure and satisfaction that feeds back to enhance the marital relationship. The negative view conceives children as a source of stress and strain in the marriage, a barrier to intimacy, and a cause of conflict, thereby engendering disenchantment if not outright discord. Although Christensen (1968, p. 284) commented more than 20 years ago that the positive view "is part of our folklore," the large numbers of couples who today choose childlessness as a way of life certainly suggest that our folklore may be changing. In fact, the research reviewed in this chapter indicates that the contemporary negative view of children is more accurate. We discover repeatedly that children's presence and marital quality tend to be inversely related.

It is unfortunately the case that existing research has more to say about what the "effects" of children are on a marriage than it does about the processes that give rise to such effects. Few studies reveal *how* children influence marriages, and there is virtually no evidence that such effects are part of a dynamic system whereby marriage and children are reciprocally interrelated.

Many of the findings reviewed here derive from studies whose results are based on treating children, or some proxy of them (e.g., family size), as the independent variable and some index of the marriage (e.g., divorce, discord, satisfaction) as the dependent variable. To fail to recognize that what occurs within the parent-child relationship often mediates such correlational associations is to forget the fact that many spouses are also parents and that it is via the parental role that children influence marriages. In all too many cases, however, child effects are inferred from comparisons of spouses with and without children and of families in which children vary in age.

This chapter thus begins by considering the relationship between the presence of children and the probability of separation and divorce. In the second section, the effect of children on marital quality is the focus of inquiry. The third section examines processes by which children affect marriage. In the fourth section, I attempt to underscore the need for a more differentiated approach to asking questions about the effect of children on marriage by considering one source of individual differences in how marriages are affected, namely, those emanating from individual differences in children themselves. This chapter concludes with a summary of what is currently known about the effects of children on marriage.

## THE EFFECTS OF CHILDREN ON MARITAL STABILITY

It was reported nearly a century ago that the presence of children may reduce the risk of divorce in a family (Wilcox, 1891; see also Cahen, 1932), as indicated by evidence linking childlessness with increased marital instability (e.g., Bumpass & Sweet, 1972; Jacobson, 1950; Koo, Suehindran, & Griffith, 1984; Thorton, 1977; U.S. Bureau of the Census, 1971). In fact, more than a decade ago Cherlin (1977, p. 265) observed that "the most widely accepted position now is that divorce and separation are moderately lower for those who have children than for the childless." In this section we first review evidence that substantiates this claim and then consider processes that might account for the findings.

### Evidence

Cherlin's (1977) analysis of longitudinal data, involving more than 2,000 nonfarm women who reported themselves married with husband present in 1967 and who were queried 4 years later, is most frequently cited as evidence of the "braking effect" of children on divorce. After controlling for several economic variables (e.g., wage levels, savings, weeks husband and wife worked in

1966), he found, for families with at least one child younger than age 6 in 1967, that the adjusted probability of separation within the 4-year study period was one-half that for all other families (.028 vs. .056). Particularly noteworthy is the fact that this effect did not extend to households with only older offspring.

In many respects these findings are consistent with those that emerged from analyses of larger data bases. For example, by comparing the divorce rates of 2,901 mothers and 1,979 fathers who graduated from high school in 1972 with those of 2,807 married female and 2,477 married male classmates who had remained childless through 1979 (when all subjects were 24–25 years of age), Waite, Haggstrom, and Kanouse (1985) obtained "compelling evidence" that children and marital stability are positively related. Specifically, within 2 years after becoming parents only about 4% of the men and 8% of the women were divorced or separated, whereas the separation/divorce rate for nonparents was around 20% (also see White, Booth, & Edwards, 1986).

Rankin and Maneker (1985) adopted a somewhat different approach to examining the relationship between children and marital stability by studying a large sample of couples who obtained a divorce in 1977. After controlling for a variety of confounding factors (e.g., age, education, age at marriage), they determined that length of marriage was related directly to number of children. Whereas 50% of those people without children divorced within their first 5 years of marriage, only 12.2% of those people with one or more children did so. "The presence of children, therefore, does appear to delay divorce, even among couples who eventually become part of the divorcing population" (p. 47).

Even though there is an abundance of evidence linking the presence of children, particularly young children and perhaps even the number of children, with reduced risk of divorce, the data just reviewed provide little insight into the processes that might explain such findings. Before considering several possibilities, we must first entertain the prospect that the association between children and marital stability is an artifact of some third variable rather than any true effect of children *per se*. In this regard, Waite et al. (1985) observed:

> Perhaps characteristics of individuals—such as strong taste for family life or religious beliefs—simultaneously increase the chances of parenthood and decrease the chances of separation or divorce without any direct effect of having children or remaining married. Perhaps those with the most stable marriages are more willing to have children for that reason. (p. 856)

Obviously, controlling for differences between divorced and nondivorced individuals on demographic variables such as age, education, and years married does not provide assurance that the kinds of processes implied in this assessment of alternative explanations of the children–marriage stability linkage have been taken into account. It seems inappropriate, therefore, to dismiss the very real possibility that the associations under consideration reflect selection biases (to have or not have children and to remain married or to get divorced) rather than actual effects of children on marriage.

## Explanatory Mechanisms

Assuming that the linkage between children and marital stability is not an artifact of self-selection, how might the results reviewed earlier be explained? One possibility is that children enhance the quality of a marriage and thereby decrease the probability of its dissolution. However appealing this account might be, we see in the next section that, if anything, the evidence suggests just the opposite.

Other explanations of the effect of children on marital stability emphasize barriers to divorce, and one such impediment is the perceived effect of divorce on the children themselves. It is undoubtedly the case that many relationships that would otherwise dissolve remain intact "for the sake of the children."

Cherlin (1977) and others contend that economic factors are principally responsible for the effect of children on marital stability being restricted to the early childhood years, as this is the period when child care is most labor intensive and thus expensive. That is, young children prevent dissolution "not because they build new bonds between parents but rather because early child care may be too expensive and time-consuming for one spouse to manage alone" (Cherlin, 1977, p. 272).

Although there are few grounds for doubting economic explanations of the effect of children on marital stability, there is also no reason to regard the two explanations considered above as mutually exclusive. Indeed, under different economic conditions of families and psychological conditions of parents, it is likely that these two forces play different roles. And, since some couples do separate even when their children are very young, neither of the processes considered above should be regarded as insurmountable barriers to divorce by parents with young children. Moreover, given the concerns for self-selection raised earlier, it cannot be concluded that young children cause—in the strict scientific sense of the word—their parents to stay married. At best, under still unspecified conditions, children seem to delay the eventual marital dissolution of some couples.

## THE EFFECTS OF CHILDREN ON MARITAL QUALITY

The largest body of evidence pertaining to the effects of children on marriage derives from the study of the family cycle conducted principally by family sociologists. The most common focus of this body of research has been on marital satisfaction, defined in terms of subjective feelings of happiness, satisfaction, and pleasure experienced by a spouse when considering all current aspects of the marriage. Marital satisfaction is assessed routinely with self-report measures such as the Marital Adjustment Test (Locke & Wallace, 1959), the Dyadic Adjustment Scale (Spanier, 1976), or some other instrument that is usually validated by virtue of its association with such standardized measures.

The conceptual basis of research on marital satisfaction across the family life cycle is found in the writings of family development theorists, who contend that transitions in family roles of any one member foster the emergence of new family stages and can impinge on all the other role relationships in the family, including the marital union (e.g., Aldous, 1978; Duvall, 1971). What make stages different according to these theorists are the distinct role demands that they place on family members and the different patterns of family interaction that they engender. Entry of the child into the family, for example, is thought to affect marriage if only because parenthood and marriage are in competition for finite resources: "from birth of the [first] child to the time the last child leaves home, parental roles compete with marital roles for temporal and emotional priority" (Aldous, 1978, p. 158).

For the most part, family development models define stages in terms of the developmental status of either the oldest or youngest child in the family. Whereas the oldest child serves to demarcate the transition to parenthood, to school, and to adolescence, the youngest child serves as the marker for the empty nest, the stage when the last child has left home. It is as a result of the operationalization of stages in terms of children's developmental status that research on marital quality across the family life cycle can be examined from the perspective of the effects of children, particularly at different ages, on marriage. To be emphasized in considering the research reviewed here is that although most studies conceive of the child as exerting an indirect influence on the marriage, this presumed mediating path is seldom examined. In some cases, evidence is provided that illuminates processes of influence, and such data are considered only after examining the findings of cross-sectional and longitudinal studies.

## Cross-Sectional Investigations

There is no shortage of cross-sectional research highlighting an association between stages of the family life cycle, operationalized in terms of children's developmental status, and measures of marital quality (e.g., Gurin, Veroff, & Feld, 1960; Nock, 1979; Rollins & Cannon, 1974; Spanier, Sauer, & Larzelere, 1979). In many instances the nature of the association has been described as *curvilinear*, with marital quality declining continuously from the birth of the first child until the oldest child is of preschool age, in school, or an adolescent (13–17 years) and increasing thereafter (Blood & Wolfe, 1960; Burr, 1970; Rollins & Feldman, 1970; Rollins & Cannon, 1974).

Even though the cross-sectional evidence has been interpreted in terms of a curvilinear relationship between marital quality and life cycle stage, Spanier, Lewis, and Cole (1975) observed that conclusions were typically based on the visual inspection of mean differences between stages in the face of significant $F$ ratios. What were lacking, they noted, were specific assessments of the nonlinearity of the differences discerned. In an effort to redress this limitation, Spanier et al. subjected three separate sets of evidence to formal analysis, and they concluded that

> the ambiguous findings from the present data . . . indicate that claims of curvilinearity in recent articles and papers may be premature. . . . Whereas it is seemingly appropriate to conclude that couples report lower marital adjustment scores following the birth of their first child, and continuing through the early childhood years, current evidence does not yet warrant concluding that there is a leveling off followed by an increase in adjustment or satisfaction in the later years. (p. 271)

Before this conclusion is embraced, it should be noted that a further analysis of two of the sets of data (Rollins & Cannon, 1974; Rollins & Feldman, 1970) revealed a significant curvilinear pattern, even after controlling for any linear relationship (Rollins & Galligan, 1978). Also noteworthy is cross-sectional evidence of curvilinearity based on formal assessments of nonlinear trends in a study of 196 wives selected randomly from high- and low-SES neighborhoods of a midwestern city (Anderson, Russell, & Schumm, 1983) in which marital satisfaction declined through the school-age period before increasing thereafter. Regardless of how often it is replicated, the magnitude of the effect of children on marriage appears modest. Rollins and Cannon (1974) reported, for example, that family life-cycle stages accounted for less than 8% of the variance in marital satisfaction. In their independent assessment of the same issue, Anderson et al. (1983) generated a remarkably similar figure (8.4%).

### Alternative Explanations
The assumption of family-stage theorists that family life-cycle stages reflect changing roles of family members in response to childrearing demands, leads to the interpretation that changes in marriage associated with the stages are in some way a function of children's developmental status. Because of the way in which much of the data considered were gathered and analyzed, two alternative explanations of the evidence are possible, one of which still underscores the effect of children on marriage.

*Presence versus absence of children.* One possibility is that family stages merely reflect effects of presence (versus absence) of children, which, with rare exception (Marini, 1980), has been found to be related to lower marital happiness or satisfaction (Campbell, 1981; Glenn, 1975; Glenn & Weaver, 1978). In keeping with this argument, Nock (1979) reported that when the predictive power of presence/absence of children was compared to that of life-cycle stages, presence/absence of children turned out to be a somewhat stronger correlate of marital satisfaction, inclination to contemplate divorce, companionship with spouse, and sense that spouse understood respondent.

Pertinent to this discussion is research on childlessness. In a large cross-sectional sample, Renee (1970) found that couples raising children tended to be less satisfied with their marriages than were childless couples or those whose children were grown and had left home (for similar results see Feldman, 1971; Ryder, 1973). In all cases, however, voluntary childlessness was not distinguished from postponing parenthood or involuntary childlessness. Moreover, these studies did not control for relevant confounding variables (e.g., education, labor force paticipation, religious affiliation) that relate systematically not only to childlessness but to marital satisfaction as well (Houseknecht, 1979). In view of these limitations, Houseknecht (1979) examined marital satisfaction differences between 50 voluntarily childless women and 50 mothers who were similar to them in education, religion, and participation in the labor force. Childless women scored higher on overall marital satisfaction, with the greatest source of difference emerging on items tapping joint activity and conversation.

This negative effect of presence of children, although not large in absolute magnitude, has been found to be quite pervasive. Glenn and McLanahan (1982) were surprised to discover in a national sample of 1,500 respondents that the presence of children was related inversely to a single-item measure of marital happiness. This effect held among respondents of both sexes and of all races, major religious preferences, educational levels, and employment status, even after controlling for respondent age, marital age, schooling, religious attendance, family income, and occupational prestige (see also White et al., 1986). Still unclear, however, is whether children make marriages less cohesive and couples less happy or whether individuals in the most cohesive and happy relationships choose to forego bearing and rearing children.

*Years married.* Much of the effect of the life cycle, at least the downward trend in the purported curvilinear pattern, may simply be a result of the fact that over time marriages become less satisfactory. Indeed, when Miller (1976) plotted marital satisfaction in terms of years of marriage, he discovered that satisfaction declined precipitously through the first 10 years of marriage and then increased over the next 15 years—a pattern mirroring the curvilinear pattern he discerned for both marital satisfaction and companionship. Moreover, when Nock (1979) controlled for years married, he observed that the so-called "effect" of family life cycle was much attenuated, leading him to conclude that "the family life cycle has very little empirical strength of its own" (p. 24).

## Methodological Criticisms
In addition to alternative explanations of the association between family life cycle and marital quality discerned in numerous studies, two serious methodological criticisms have been raised about this body of research.

*Conventional or socially desirable responses.* One major problem is the proclivity of respondents to inflate positive and to underreport negative aspects of their marriage (Spanier et al., 1975).

Because it is more conventional to report one's marriage as doing well rather than poorly, it has been suggested that the reported increase in marital satisfaction during the empty nest years in cross-sectional studies results from the fact that older persons simply report greater marital satisfaction because they are more conventional (e.g., Rollins & Cannon, 1974; Spanier & Lewis, 1980). Consistent with this contention are Miller's (1975) findings that indicate a modest positive correlation between length of marriage and conventionalization. When Anderson et al. (1983) divided their sample into respondents scoring high and low on an index of conventionalization, however, they obtained a curvilinear relationship between stage and marital satisfaction in both subsamples. This led them to conclude that "the curvilinear trend of the family life cycle over time cannot be attributed to an artifact of marital conventionalization increasing over the later stages of the family life cycle" (p. 134).

*Cohort effects.* Cross-sectional studies of marital quality have also been criticized for selective attrition. That is, by the late stages of marriage, divorce has weeded out many of the most troubled relationships. As a result, marital quality of spouses in the later stages may be inflated relative to couples in the younger stages (Miller, 1976; Schram, 1979; Spanier et al., 1975).

Because of limits inherent to cross-sectional studies, most notably selective attrition, calls have been made for short-term longitudinal research (Klein & Aldous, 1979). Such designs involve following subjects across a transition to permit comparison of marital functioning before and after roles have changed. Also, groups that do and do not make a transition can be compared.

## Longitudinal Investigations

Short-term longitudinal investigations have become increasingly popular over the past decade. Unfortunately, most of these studies focus on the transition to parenthood. Because some relevant work has appeared pertaining to the transitions to adolescence and to the empty nest, these are considered after a summarization of the current state of knowledge with respect to the transition to parenthood.

### Transition to Parenthood

In reviewing the literature on marital change across the transition to parenthood, Belsky and Pensky (1988a) found it useful, following Huston and Robins (1982), to distinguish marital activities and interactions from more subjective feelings and attitudes regarding one's spouse and the marital relationship. The same strategy is adopted here.

*Activities and interactions.* Recent longitudinal studies indicate that the frequency, nature, and/or quality of marital interactions changes in the transition to parenthood (Engfer, 1988). In their first investigation, Belsky, Spanier, and Rovine (1983) discerned a significant decline in the expression of positive affection from the last trimester of pregnancy through 9 months post-partum as reported by both husbands and wives. In their second study, similar results were chronicled using a different set of marital questionnaires (Belsky, Lang, & Rovine, 1985). Noteworthy, too, is that these findings emerged in observational as well as self-report data.

In regard to negative interactions, conflict between spouses has been found to increase from the last trimester of pregnancy through the 9th postpartum month (Belsky & Rovine, 1990; Belsky, Rovine, & Fish, 1989; Cowan et al., 1985; Engfer, 1988). Cowan et al. discovered that although the occurrence of conflict increases for those experiencing the transition to parenthood, frequency of conflict actually decreases for those who do not become parents. In contrast, White and Booth (1985) obtained distinctly different results with their nationally representative sample, as conflict was found to increase equally for parents and nonparents. However, because the telephone interview used in this study included only four items related to conflict (two of which concerned use of violence during an argument and the presence of an alcohol problem in the family), there is reason to question the sensitivity of White and Booth's measure and, thus, the conclusions that can be drawn from their finding.

*Subjective feelings and attitudes.* In view of these changes in marital activities and interactions, it seems reasonable to expect that the feelings that a husband and wife have for each other and for their marriage should also be affected by the experience of becoming parents. A majority of studies using prepartum and postpartum marital measures reveal that marital satisfaction declines after the birth of the first child (e.g., Feldman, 1971; Feldman & Nash, 1984; Moss, Bolland, Foxman, & Owen, 1986; Ruble, Fleming, Hackel, & Stangor, 1988).

In a recent study, Cowan et al. (1985) found that unlike their husbands and control subjects, women who had become mothers showed a significant decline in marital satisfaction within the first 6 months of the infant's life. When children were 18 months of age, husbands who had become fathers also evinced pronounced declines in marital satisfaction; wives continued to decline, although not as steeply as did husbands from 6 to 18 months postpartum. Once again, husbands and wives who remained childless did not display the same degree of change. These data led Cowan et al. to conclude that "the impact of becoming a parent is felt first by women" and "only later do men feel the negative effects" (p. 469). This heightened susceptibility to negative change by women has been a persistent finding in the transition to parenthood literature for decades (e.g., Belsky et al., 1983, 1985, 1989; Waldron & Routh, 1981).

In contrast, studies by White and Booth (1985) and McHale and Huston (1985) did not find an association between the transition to parenthood and a decline in marital satisfaction. It is difficult to reconcile these conflicting results, except to note that confidential questionnaires may be more sensitive than responses given to a telephone interviewer (White & Booth, 1985) or that newlyweds may represent a unique population (McHale & Huston, 1985). It seems most appropriate to conclude that marital changes associated with the transition to parenthood probably reflect the acceleration and accentuation of developments that occur in marriages with the passage of time regardless of parental status (Belsky & Pensky, 1988b). In any event, the changes associated with the transition to parenthood are rather modest.

### Transition to Adolescence

The physiological maturation that accompanies and helps to define the period of adolescence is associated with increases in parent–child distance, adolescent autonomy, and parent–child conflict (Steinberg, 1987) and may affect the marital dyad. In addition,

> adolescents' increased involvement in social relations outside the family, including relationships with opposite-sex peers, also may affect parents' marital satisfaction by provoking concerns regarding the quality of the marital relationship, fantasies or reminiscences about alternative marital partners, or arguments over issues regarding the adolescent's social life. (Steinberg & Silverberg, 1987, p. 752)

In light of such possibilities and of cross-sectional data suggesting that adolescence may represent the low point in marital satisfaction across the family life cycle, it is surprising to discover that only two longitudinal studies have been reported examining marital change across this developmental period.

Steinberg and Silverberg (1987) found no significant change in marital satisfaction (nine-item semantic differential instrument) over a 2-year period, and, more importantly, measures of adolescent pubertal status did not forecast change in marital quality. These results can be viewed as "casting doubt on the notion that adolescent development *per se* is at the root of diminished marital satisfaction" (p. 755). The fact, however, that lack of closeness in same-sex parent–child relationships (i.e., father–son, mother–daughter) did predict decreases in marital satisfaction is consistent with the notion that child effects, even if restricted to particular dyadic constellations, are mediated via the parental experience.

Menaghan (1983) also failed to obtain a main effect of adolescent developmental status on marital quality. However, when the transition to adolescence coincided with entry of the youngest child into school, significant declines in perceived equity in the marriage emerged, accompanied by marginally significant declines in affection, even after controlling for gender of adolescent, number of children, education, and income.

Considered together, these two investigations underscore the need to think not simply in terms of the direct, unmediated effect of the adolescent on the marriage but rather on the processes by which and the conditions under which the presence of teen-agers in the family does and does not influence the spousal relationship. At best we can regard these inquiries as suggestive of future research directions.

## Transition to Empty Nest

Cross-sectional research on marital relations across the family life cycle identified the period of the empty nest as one of elevated marital satisfaction. This is consistent with studies showing that this phase of life is marked by high levels of life satisfaction and personal happiness (Glenn, 1975; Radloff, 1975). In light of this, there is reason to expect longitudinal research to reveal that marriages improve in the empty nest stage relative to early periods of the family life cycle. Unfortunately, only one investigation addresses this hypothesis.

Menaghan (1983) compared 34 adults who had their youngest child leave home with a sample of adults who also had a child leave home, but one who was not the last to depart. The transition to the empty nest was clearly associated with an increase in sense of equity in the relationship. This was not accompanied, however, by change or group difference in change in feelings of affection and fulfillment in the marriage. Such findings led Menaghan to conclude that

> the final child's departure, signaling the completion of a major task, seems to be associated with changes that lead both fathers and mothers to see their spouses as more accommodating, less insistent on their own way, and less focused on their own needs. This suggests that the final departure of children diminishes parents' feeling that their needs and wishes are being overlooked by their spouses. (p. 383)

## Conclusion

Cross-sectional and longitudinal data regarding the effect of first-born children on marriage indicate that positive interactions between spouses and marital satisfaction decrease, particularly for wives, and that conflict increases. It is important to emphasize that the changes are modest and are generally in the same direction as those that typically ensue with the mere passage of time.

The question of whether adolescence actually represents a low point in the marital life cycle, as some cross-sectional evidence suggests, remains unanswered. Although the Menaghan (1983) data suggest clearly that significant deterioration in the marriage occurs when the transition to parenthood coincides with other developmental changes among children in the family, this one study is too modest in scope to permit strong conclusions. Moreover, the conclusion it draws regarding multiple transitions is presumably not unique to adolescence.

Finally, even though only a single longitudinal investigation is available regarding the effect of children leaving home on the marriage, the fact that its findings are generally consistent with those of cross-sectional studies is noteworthy. Until evidence is reported that contests this trend, it seems reasonable to conclude that the presence of children does undermine certain aspects of the marital relationship, as evidence by the increase in equity that coincides with the departure of the last child from the home.

## PROCESSES OF INFLUENCE

It is one thing to conclude that children's presence and developmental status are associated with marital functioning and change, but quite another to account for such an empirical relationship. In this section of the chapter I consider several possible explanatory mechanisms. At the outset it should be noted that the processes to be considered are not mutually exclusive.

## Time Together and Relationship Opportunities

The most frequently cited explanation for the effect of children on marital satisfaction is that they decrease the amount of time spouses can spend together and affect adversely the nature of their interactions. Feldman (1971) reported, for example, that couples with children engaged in significantly less verbal communication and that their interaction rates were lower and involved talking more about their children and less about themselves and their relationship than was the case for childless couples (see also White et al., 1986; Rosenblatt, 1974; Ryder, 1973). Consistent with such data are those of Houseknecht (1979), which show that women with children are less likely than those who are childless by choice to engage in outside interests with their spouses, exchange stimulating ideas with their partners, calmly discuss something with them, or work with them on a project.

What remains unclear from such descriptive work is whether these patterns of spousal relations are actually the means by which children affect marital quality. A study by Miller (1976) suggests that this is the case. He found that companionship, reflecting the incidence with which spouses did things together, displayed a curvilinear pattern across the life cycle, decreasing with the arrival of children before increasing at a later point in time, and that companionship mediated the relationship between number of children in the family and marital satisfaction. Anderson et al. (1983) also found that the significant and depressing effect that presence of children had on marital satisfaction was a function principally of wives' perceived amount of discussion with their spouse. This suggests that children compete for the amount of time spouses are able to share with each other in communication. In fact, the effects of the presence of preschool children on marital satisfaction are attenuated or disappear entirely when reports of spousal discussion (Schumm & Bugaishis, 1986) and of marital interaction (White et al., 1986) are statistically controlled. Thus, it appears that not only do couples with children spend less time together as a couple, communicate less, and focus more of their interactions on the children than on their relationship, but these effects of children on spousal interaction are responsible in part for the inverse relationship between children and marital satisfaction.

## Childrearing Disagreements

Throughout childhood parents are forced to make many decisions regarding their offspring that offer ample opportunity for disagreement and conflict between spouses. To the extent that couples have difficulty resolving such disagreements, children may serve inadvertently to undermine marital quality. Entirely consistent with this argument is Block, Block, and Morrison's (1981) discovery that couples who disagreed more on childrearing attitudes and values when their children were preschoolers were significantly more likely to be divorced a decade later.

Consideration of the role of parental disagreements over childrearing should again alert us to the problem of self-selection and the difficulty of drawing causal inferences. That is, couples for whom communication is problematic to begin with may well be most likely to experience conflict over issues pertaining to childrearing. It might thus be better to view children less as a cause of marital conflict and more as stimuli that promote the manifestation of latent or preexisting communication difficulties. Thus, by providing some couples with another topic on which to disagree, children may contribute to the deterioration of marital relations.

## Division of Labor

Another potential source of conflict concerns division of household labor. There is some evidence that coincident with the arrival of children is the traditionalization of family roles, a situation that is a source of serious concern for many wives (Hoffman & Manis, 1978; Belsky et al., 1985; Cowan et al., 1985; White et al., 1986; but see Goldberg, Michaels, & Lamb, 1985). Data suggesting that family roles become more traditional take on added meaning in light of related evidence linking division of labor to marital satisfaction. Most noteworthy, perhaps, is the finding of White et al. (1986) that household division of labor and satisfaction with division of labor are important mediators of the relationship between children's presence and lower marital happiness in the case of women. Husbands also can be influenced by the division of labor, as men who did more feminine chores and house tasks early in the infant's first year in one study reported lower marital adjustment and more marital difficulties stemming from adjustment to the baby (Goldberg et al., 1985).

## Psychological Well-Being

The presence of children is related not only to lower levels of marital satisfaction but also to less psychological well-being. A comprehensive review of the relevant literature led McLanahan and Adams (1987) to conclude that the presence of children appears to be associated with lower levels of happiness and satisfaction and with higher levels of psychological distress for both women and men. Of special interest is the fact that whereas the effects of children seem more negative for women, and the differences in well-being of parents and nonparents appear to be relatively small, a historical perspective suggests that they have increased since the 1950s.

Because at least two surveys indicate that psychological distress is greater among wives when husbands do not assist with housework (Kessler & McRae, 1982; Ross, Mirowsky, & Huber, 1983), it seems necessary to reconsider the role of division of labor to understand the process by which children affect marriage. Conceivably, by traditionalizing the division of labor, children could increase wives' psychological distress and thereby exert an adverse impact on marital relations. Of course, this is not the only path by which these multiple determinants of marital quality might be configured. Equally conceivable is that it is the effect of children on marriage, perhaps mediated by the division of labor, that affects psychological well-being. Data are not yet available, however, to distinguish between these alternatives.

In closing, it is perhaps wisest to emphasize the multiple means by which children can influence marriages. Ultimately it must be acknowledged that because children are not randomly assigned to couples, any effects of children on marriages or on the processes considered to mediate such effects cannot be thought of in narrowly causal terms.

## INDIVIDUAL DIFFERENCES IN CHILDREN

With the exception of the developmental status of the oldest (or youngest) child in the family, investigators have tended to treat all children as if they were the same in their attempts to discern the effects of children on marriage (Belsky, 1981). In this section, we consider three general parameters of individual differences (gender, temperament, and handicap/disability) on which some data exist to illuminate the issue of whether child effects on marriage vary as a function of characteristics of the child.

## Gender

Worldwide surveys on the value of children reveal a near universal preference for sons over daughters (Hoffman & Hoffman, 1973), and it appears that child gender influences divorce practices in the United States (Spanier & Glick, 1981). Morgan, Lye, and Condran (1988) reported that

> for couples with one child, the . . . risk of [marital] disruption is 9% higher for those with a daughter than for those with a son. For two child families, the risk of disruption is lowest for couples with two sons, followed by those with one son and one daughter (9% higher), and the highest observed risk is for couples with two daughters (18% higher). (p. 115)

Although these figures pertain only to Caucasian women, they are basically the same for blacks. In attempting to account for these gender-related divorced statistics, Morgan et al. (1988) concluded that "sons promote greater [marital] stability than daughters because they elicit a greater investment and involvement from fathers" (p. 124).

Even though sons may function to keep marriages intact, their presence is not associated consistently with higher levels of marital quality. For example, Farber and Blackman (1956) and Luckey and Bain (1970) failed to find a relationship between gender of child and marital adjustment. In contrast, Easterbrooks and Emde (1986) determined that mothers (but not fathers) of 6-month-old daughters were significantly less satisfied than were mothers of sons. Perhaps most noteworthy are their observational findings that girls made more demands on their parents when spouses were engaged in a marital communication task.

Further evidence for the importance of child gender was provided by Abbott and Brody (1985), who studied middle-class, Caucasian women from maritally intact families who were working and raising one or two male or female children under 2 years or between 3 and 5 years of age. When comparisons were made between these women and a group of childless wives, it was discovered that the significant difference in favor of childless women on marital adjustment was principally a function of women with two male children, one an infant and one a preschool child. Whereas such mothers scored significantly lower on marital adjustment than childless women, mothers with female children (especially female infants) were not different from women without children.

At first glance these findings appear inconsistent with those reported by Easterbrooks and Emde, which implicated female offspring as a correlate of lower marital satisfaction. The fact that mothers in the Abbott and Brody (1985) investigation were rearing two very young children *and* working suggests, however, that what is really being discerned in this inquiry is the effect of multiple stressors. This notion is consistent with Glenn and McLanahan's (1982) findings that the negative association between children and wives' marital happiness is more pronounced among white women when they are employed full-time. The fact that sons tend to be more active, fussy, and difficult to manage than young girls (Maccoby, 1980; Thomas & Chess, 1977) and that mothers of preschool-aged boys experience more stress than those with girls of the same age (Halverson & Martin, 1981) suggests clearly why working and having two sons may make the marriage particularly vulnerable. Consider, too, the possibility that as a result of fathers' greater involvement with sons, husbands are more likely in the case of male offspring to question their wives' childrearing practices and thereby engender marital tension. More research regarding gender and marital quality is needed before any definitive conclusions can be drawn, however, and greater efforts must be made to understand the processes by which influences are exerted.

## Temperament

Over the past two decades developmental psychology has witnessed an explosion of interest in child temperament. In large measure this interest has its roots in efforts to understand how children shape the parental care they receive in their families and their social experiences more generally. As work on child effects has grown, it is not surprising that family researchers have endeavored to understand how individual differences in child temperament influence marital quality (Lerner & Spanier, 1978).

Evidence exists linking an active–negative or difficult child temperament with compromised parent–child interaction (e.g., Buss, 1981; Campbell, 1979; Maccoby, Snow, & Jacklin, 1984), conflicted sibling relations (Brody, Stoneman, & Burke, 1987), and even with parental depression (Cutrona & Troutman, 1986;

Wilkie & Ames, 1986). These data lead to the hypothesis that such a behavioral style should also be related to troubled, stressed, or less satisfied marital relations. One of the first investigations to provide evidence consistent with such reasoning revealed that when babies were particularly demanding (i.e., cried frequently, often "on the move," had feeding problems), spouses experienced more difficulty in the transition to parenthood (Russell, 1974).

A more compelling set of findings shows that parental reports of infant temperament predict *change* in marital satisfaction from the last trimester of pregnancy through 4 months post-partum. Specifically, McMillan and Jacobson (1986) found that husbands and wives with babies they described as easy underwent no change in marital satisfaction, but those with babies classified as difficult declined an average of 15 points. The fact that postpartum temperament ratings were unrelated to prenatal marital satisfaction ratings increases confidence in the interpretation that child characteristics—at least as experienced by parents—affected the marital relationship.

In a most interesting report, Brody et al. (1987) astutely observed that virtually all the work on temperament and marriage, like that on temperament and parent–child relationships, pertains to the behavioral characteristics of only one child in the family. In multichild families, they note, it is likely to be the constellation of temperamental features of the children that will prove most influential. Their analyses of temperamental reports on two-son and two-daughter families in which the older child was between 7 and 9 years of age and the younger between 4.5 and 6.5 showed that fathers were least satisfied with their marriages and reported more conflict with their wives when both their sons had active–emotional temperaments. Maternal marital satisfaction was most vulnerable when both daughters were active–emotional (or when this was true of just the elder daughter). The fact that the marital-temperament associations were gender specific (i.e., mothers and daughters, fathers and sons) serves to underscore the complexity of relations that are likely to exist between child characteristics and marital relationships.

The findings reviewed to this point provide little insight into the processes by which temperament influences the marriage. Fortunately, a series of related studies are beginning to illuminate some of the potential mediators of these temperament effects, especially parents' psychological well-being (Levitt, Weber, & Clark, 1986; Wilkie & Ames, 1986). For example, Engfer (1988) found that the degree to which a child was difficult at 18 months was highly related to maternal irritability, which strongly predicted marital conflict at 43 months. Moreover, with maternal psychological functioning controlled, the bivariate relationship between difficultness and marital conflict was reduced to zero. Before concluding that processes of influence in the family are unidirectional rather than reciprocal, it should be noted that findings from an earlier report indicated that marital conflict and communication at 4 months significantly predicted infant difficultness 14 months later (Engfer, 1985). Thus, the possibility must be entertained that the discerned (and mediated) effects of temperament on marriage via spouses' psychological well-being may themselves have their origins in earlier family processes (Belsky, 1981).

At a more microanalytic level, Easterbrooks and Emde's (1986) study found that the mothers of highly intrusive 6-month-old infants who made frequent bids to parents during a marital discussion task via positive (pleasure vocalizations, directed smiles) *and* negative means (crying, pulling clothes) reported lower marital satisfaction. Women who perceived their infants as more easily frustrated and as more angry also reported lower satisfaction. The fact that demanding infant behaviors served to disrupt marital communications and that less satisfied mothers were more responsive to their infants' bids is clearly consistent with the notion that marital and parent–child subsystems of the family are often in competition and that children affect marriages by affecting spousal interactions.

One of the major concerns that can be raised about much of the research in this area involves the possibility that the associations between child temperament and marital quality may simply be an artifact of method variance, since both constructs are often measured using questionnaires completed by the same respondent. The availability of observational as well as parent-report data in the original Easterbrooks and Emde (1986) study and in a follow-up investigation (when infants were 18 and 24 months) does much to ameliorate such concern. At 6 months the association between temperament and marriage also emerged in a rating of marital harmony based on observation of spousal communication in the laboratory; and at 18 and 24 months, toddler behavior (i.e., compliance) observed in the laboratory was associated positively with the rating of marital harmony (Easterbrooks & Emde, 1988). Because such findings reflect contemporaneous rather than longitudinal associations, the wisest course continues to be to entertain multiple and reciprocal processes of influence linking temperament and marital quality rather than to assume that one or another is preeminent.

## Handicap/Disability

The contention that children affect marriages via the demands they place on adults in their parental roles leads to the expectation that children whose care ought to be especially demanding, namely, those with some kind of handicap or disability (including mental retardation), should create stress if not outright marital dissatisfaction. The available evidence provides empirical support for this notion and also highlights the complexity of child effects on marriage.

After reviewing the relevant literature on mentally retarded children and marriage, Crnic, Friedrich, and Greenberg (1983) observed that "research to date does not present a clear picture" (p. 128). For example, Waisbren (1980) found that the presence of a developmentally delayed infant was not related to marital satisfaction, whereas Friedrich and Friedrich (1981) found that mothers with a school-age handicapped child were less satisfied than mothers who did not have such a child. One factor that may account for such inconsistent findings is the age of the child, insofar as some child effects on marriages may take time to emerge (Crnic et al., 1983). Consistent with this proposition are Bristol, Gallagher, and Shopler's (1988) recent findings that mothers and fathers of developmentally disabled, mentally delayed, 2- to 6-year-old boys, in comparison to parents of matched, nondisabled children, scored significantly lower on the Locke–Wallace Marital Adjustment Test.

The fact that Friedrich, Wilturner, and Cohen (1985) recently observed that degree of mental retardation was related inversely to wives' marital happiness underscores the need to move beyond mere presence versus absence of a handicapping condition. Nonetheless, despite these eminently meaningful results, studies of both disabled (Bristol, 1987) and chronically ill children (Kazak, 1986) demonstrate that severity of the child's disorder alone is not a strong predictor of family adaptation (Bristol et al., 1988).

It is now well recognized that families respond differently to children's handicapping conditions and characteristics and that additional factors in the ecology of the family need to be considered (Howard, 1978; Korn, Chess, & Ferndandez, 1978) including parental coping skills, economic resources, and attitudes and values (Bristol et al., 1988; Crnic et al., 1983). For example, Bristol

(1987) found that social support, active coping strategies, and maternal beliefs increased substantially the variance explained in marital adjustment over and above that caused by child characteristics. Relatedly, Korn et al. (1978) found that marital conflict and family stress were less pronounced when medical services were available to families whose child had suffered a congenital disability as a result of a rubella epidemic.

A critical factor that must be taken into consideration is the relationship that exists between spouses prior to the handicapped/disabled child's birth. In fact, Korn et al. (1978) noted that "in some cases, the handicapped child and the challenges involved were seen as a rewarding experience that actually strengthened the marriage and family" (p. 307). Perhaps the clearest evidence of such an effect can be found in Gath's (1978) longitudinal investigation of individual differences among Down syndrome infants and a matched sample of families bearing normal infants. Although Gath observed that "the most striking difference" between the families was the greater "number of broken or disharmonious marriages in the mongol group" (p. 105), the fact that an equal number of marriages in the two groups were rated as good (but not fair or poor) led the author to conclude that the arrival of a baby with a congenital handicap may not so much hamper a good marriage as "disrupt the balance of a moderate or more vulnerable marriage" (Gath, 1978, p. 105). Indeed, the finding that a *greater* number of couples bearing a Down syndrome infant were rated as high on warmth displayed in marital interviews supports the notion that, under some circumstances, the birth of an abnormal child can bring spouses closer together.

The more general point to draw from this discussion is that whatever the child's characteristics, they exist in the context of a family and that effects of the child are likely to be dependent on this broader family context.

## Conclusion

In an earlier paper (Belsky, 1981), I bemoaned the fact that we knew little about how child characteristics influenced marital relations. As this section of the chapter should make evident, things have changed. Not only are gender effects on marital stability and quality under investigation, but so too are more process-oriented dimensions of child behavior and development. It is clear that although the effects of child gender on marriage remain uncertain, there is consistent evidence that children with difficult temperaments place real stresses on marriages. Still unclear, however, is the extent to which such temperamental difficulties are organismically based or family generated.

In any event, there is a need to reiterate continually a core theme, namely, that reciprocal rather than unidirectional processes of influence characterize child development in the family system. Moreover, such bidirectional processes of influence need to be considered within developmental, family, and community contexts. How individual differences in children affect marriages depends on the affective status of the marital relationship prior to the child's arrival and the other stressors and supports that exist within and beyond the household. When multiple stressors exist, it is easy to imagine how marriages are negatively affected by a handicapped or temperamentally difficult child. On the other hand, when instrumental and emotional supports are available to relieve stressed parents, especially demanding children need not adversely affect the husband–wife bond. Perhaps most heartening is the evidence showing that even in the face of child stressors, some marriages can thrive and prosper. It is therefore clear that process and context must be considered in order to understand the effects of individual differences of children on the marriage.

## GENERAL CONCLUSION

To summarize, the available evidence indicates (1) that the presence of young children in the family fosters marital stability by inhibiting marital dissolution; (2) that cross-sectional research reveals that marital quality tends to decline with the arrival of a first child and continues in this direction or levels off until children leave the home, at which time it increases; (3) that whereas these cross-sectional findings may be in part a function of cohort effects and of the selective attrition of the most troubled marriages from samples by the time of the empty nest, short-term longitudinal research indicates that marital quality does decline across the transition to parenthood, although such change probably reflects an acceleration and accentuation of normative changes that take place over time irrespective of children, and in some respects (e.g., equity), marital quality does improve once children leave home; (4) that reduced spousal companionship, disagreements over childrearing, the traditionalizing effect of children on the household division of labor, and the adverse effects of children on psychological well-being most likely mediate the marital changes associated with children just summarized; and (5) that children who are (or who are perceived to be) temperamentally difficult or handicapped/disabled place greater stress on marital relationships, although the actual effects of such child characteristics are dependent on a variety of other factors that function either to buffer the marriage from such stress or to accentuate it.

In considering these conclusions, we must keep two critical points in mind. First, in no investigation have child effects been large. Thus, even though the overall effect of children seems to result in greater spousal conflict, less interaction, and lower satisfaction with the relationship, it would be erroneous to conclude that children ruin marriages. In fact, young children seem to keep marriages intact, and parents themselves do not uniformly view children as harmful to their marriage (see Hoffman & Manis, 1978).

The second point to be made in qualifying the conclusions drawn above is that the available evidence does not reveal, in the strict scientific sense of the word, child "effects." Even in the best studies, when statistical controls are included for demographic variables, other important and unmeasured constructs (i.e., motivation to have children) remain to exert an influence. Without random assignment of children to marriages, it is difficult to imagine how pure effects could be evaluated. Similarly, until more objective assessments of child temperament are included in studies, or factors that might influence parents' perceptions of their children are controlled, it is inappropriate to assume that such characteristics of children affect marriages in any unidirectional manner. It seems best, therefore, to view children and their "effects" on marriages in systems' terms where the emphasis is on interdependency and reciprocal influence rather than on linear causation.

# ACKNOWLEDGMENTS

Work on this chapter was supported by a grant from the National Institute of Child Health and Human Development (R01HD15496) and by an NIMH Research Scientist Development Award (K02MH00486). Special thanks are extended to the editors of this volume for helping me to reduce the length of the original version of this chapter.

# REFERENCES

Abbott, D., & Brody, G. (1985). The relation of child age, gender, and number of children to the marital adjustment of wives. *Journal of Marriage and the Family, 47,* 77–84.

Aldous, J. (1978). *Family careers: Developmental change in families.* New York: Wiley.

Anderson, A., Russell, C., & Schumm, W. (1983). Perceived marital quality and family life cycle categories: A further analysis. *Journal of Marriage and the Family, 45,* 127–139.

Belsky, J. (1981). Early human experience: A family perspective. *Developmental Psychology, 17,* 3–23.

Belsky, J., Lang, M., & Rovine, M. (1985). Stability and change in marriage across the transition to parenthood: A second study. *Journal of Marriage and the Family, 47,* 855–866.

Belsky, J., Pensky, E. (1988a). Developmental history, personality, and family relationships: Toward an emergent family system. In R. Hinde & J. Stevenson-Hinde (Eds.), *Relationships within families* (pp. 193–217). London: Cambridge University Press.

Belsky, J., & Pensky, E. (1988b). Marital change across the transition to parenthood. *Marriage and Family Review, 12,* 133–156.

Belsky, J., & Rovine, M. (1990). Patterns of marital change across the transition to parenthood. *Journal of Marriage and the Family, 52,* 109–123.

Belsky, J., Rovine, M., & Fish, M. (1989). The developing family system. In M. Gunnar (Ed.), *Systems and development* (Vol. 22, *Minnesota symposia on child psychology;* pp. 119–166). Hillsdale, NJ: Erlbaum.

Belsky, J., Spanier, G. B., & Rovine, M. (1983). Stability and change in marriage across the transition to parenthood. *Journal of Marriage and the Family, 45,* 553–556.

Block, J. H., Block, J., & Morrison, J. (1981). Parental agreement–disagreement on child-rearing orientations and gender-related personality correlates in children. *Child Development, 52,* 965–974.

Blood, R., & Wolfe, D. (1960). *Husbands and wives: The dynamics of married living.* Glencoe, IL: The Free Press.

Bristol, M. M. (1987). Mothers of children with autism or communication disorders: Successful adaptations and the double ABCX model. *Journal of Autism and Developmental Disabilities, 17,* 469–486.

Bristol, M., Gallagher, J., & Schopler, E. (1988). Mothers and fathers of young developmentally disabled and nondisabled boys: Adaptation and spousal support. *Developmental Psychology, 24,* 441–451.

Brody, G. H., Stoneman, Z., & Burke, M. (1987). Child temperaments, maternal differential behavior, and sibling relationships. *Developmental Psychology, 23,* 354–362.

Bumpass, L. L., & Sweet, J. A. (1972). Differentials in marital instability: 1970. *American Sociological Review, 37,* 754–766.

Burr, W. R. (1970). Satisfaction with various aspects of marriage over the life cycle sample. *Journal of Marriage and the Family, 26,* 29–37.

Buss, D. M. (1981). Predicting parent–child interactions from children's activity level. *Developmental Psychology, 17,* 59–65.

Cahen, A. (1932). *Statistical analysis of American divorce.* New York: Columbia University Press.

Campbell, A. (1981). *The sense of well-being in America.* New York: McGraw-Hill.

Campbell, S. B. G. (1979). Mother–infant interaction as a function of maternal ratings of temperament. *Child Psychology and Human Development, 10,* 67–76.

Cherlin, A. (1977). The effect of children on marital dissolution. *Demography, 14,* 265–272.

Christensen, H. T. (1968). Children in the family: Relationship of number and spacing to marital success. *Journal of Marriage and the Family, 30,* 283–285.

Cowan, C., Cowan, P., Heming, G., Garrett, E., Coysh, W., Curtis-Boles, H., & Boles, A. (1985). Transitions to parenthood: His, hers, and theirs. *Journal of Family Issues, 6,* 451–482.

Crnic, K., Friedrich, W., & Greenberg, M. (1983). Adaptation of families with mentally retarded children: A model of stress, coping, and family ecology. *American Journal of Mental Deficiency, 88,* 125–138.

Cutrona, C. E., & Troutman, B. R. (1986). Social support, infant temperament, and parenting self-efficacy. A medical model of postpartum depression. *Child Development, 57,* 1507–1518.

Duvall, E. M. (1971). *Family development* (4th ed.). Philadelphia: Lippincott.

Easterbrooks, A., & Emde, R. (1986, April). *Marriage and infant: Different systems linkages for mothers and fathers.* Paper presented at the International Conference on Infant Studies, Beverly Hills, CA.

Easterbrooks, M. A., & Emde, R. (1988). Marital and parent–child relationships: The role of affect in the family system. In R. Hinde & J. Stevenson-Hinde (Eds.), *Relationships in families: Mutual influences* (pp. 83–103). Oxford: Oxford University Press.

Emery, R. E. (1982). Interparental conflict and the children of discord and divorce. *Psychological Bulletin, 92,* 310–330.

Engfer, A. (1985, July). *Antecedents of perceived behavior problems in children four and 18 months of age: A longitudinal study.* Paper presented at conference on Temperament and Development in Childhood, Leiden, The Netherlands.

Engfer, A. (1988). The interrelatedness of marriage and the mother–child relationship. In R. Hinde & J. Stevenson-Hinde (Eds.), *Relationships with families: Mutual influences* (pp. 104–118). Oxford, England: Oxford University Press.

Farber, B., & Blackman, L. (1956). Marital role tensions and number and sex of children. *American Sociological Review, 21,* 596–601.

Feldman, H. (1971). The effects of children on the family. In A. Michel (Ed.), *Family issues of employed women in Europe and America* (pp. 41–50). Leiden, The Netherlands: E. J. Brill.

Feldman, S., & Nash, S. (1984). The transition from expectancy to parenthood: Impact of the firstborn child on men and women. *Sex Roles, 11,* 84–96.

Friedrich, W. N., & Friedrich, W. L. (1981). Comparison of psychosocial assets of parents with a handicapped child and their normal controls. *American Journal of Mental Deficiency, 85,* 551–553.

Friedrich, W., Wilturner, L., & Cohen, D. (1985). Coping resources and parenting mentally retarded children. *American Journal of Mental Deficiency, 90,* 130–139.

Gath, A. (1978). *Down's syndrome and the family: The early years.* London: Academic Press.

Glenn, N. (1975). Psychological well-being in the postparental stage: Some evidence from national surveys. *Journal of Marriage and the Family, 37,* 105–110.

Glenn, N., & McLanahan, S. (1982). Children and marital happiness: A further specification of relationships. *Journal of Marriage and the Family, 44,* 63–72.

Glenn, N. D., & Weaver, C. N. (1978). A multivariate, multisurvey study of marital happiness. *Journal of Marriage and the Family, 40*(May), 269–282.

Goldberg, W., Michaels, G., & Lamb, M. (1985). Husbands' and wives' adjustment to pregnancy and first parenthood. *Journal of Family Issues, 6,* 483–504.

Gurin, G., Veroff, V., & Feld, S. (1960). *Americans view their mental health.* New York: Basic Books.

Halverson, L. F., & Martin, C. L. (1981, April). *Parent–child stability over time.* Paper presented at the annual meeting of the Society for Research in Child Development, Boston.

Hoffman, L., & Hoffman, M. (1973). The value of children to parents. In J. T. Fawcett (Ed.), *Psychological perspectives on population* (pp. 106–151). New York: Basic Books.

Hoffman, L., & Manis, J. (1978). Influences of children on marital interaction and parental satisfactions and dissatisfactions. In R. Lerner & G. Spanier (Eds.), *Child influences on marital and family interaction: A life-span perspective* (pp. 165–213). New York: Academic Press.

Houseknecht, S. K. (1979). Childlessness and marital adjustment. *Journal of Marriage and the Family, 41,* 259–265.

Howard, J. (1978). The influence of children's developmental dysfunctions on marital quality and family interaction. In R. Lerner & G. Spanier (Eds.), *Child influences on marital and family interaction: A life-span perspective* (pp. 275–298). New York: Academic Press.

Huston, T., & Robins, E. (1982). Conceptual and methodological issues in studying close relationships. *Journal of Marriage and the Family, 44,* 901–925.

Jacobson, P. (1950). Differentials in divorce by duration of marriage and size of family. *American Sociological Review, 15,* 235–244.

Kazak, A. E. (1986). Stress in families of children with myelomeningocele. *Developmental Medicine and Child Neurology, 28,* 220–228.

Kessler, R., & McRae, J. (1982). The effects of wives' employment on the mental health of married men and women. *American Sociological Review, 47,* 216–227.

Klein, D., & Aldous, J. (1979). Three blind mice: Misleading criticisms of the family life cycle concept. *Journal of Marriage and the Family, 41,* 689–691.

Koo, H., Suehindran, C., & Griffith, J. (1984). The effects of children on divorce and remarriage: A multivariate analysis of life table probabilities. *Population Studies, 38,* 451–471.

Korn, S., Chess, S., & Fernandez, P. (1978). The impact of children's physical handicaps on marital quality and family interaction. In R. Lerner & G. Spanier (Eds.), *Child influences on marital and family interaction: A life-span perspective* (pp. 299–326). New York: Academic Press.

Lerner, R., & Spanier, G. (1978). *Child influences on marital and family instruction.* New York: Academic Press.

Levitt, M., Weber, R., & Clark, M. (1986). Social network relationships as sources of maternal support and well-being. *Developmental Psychology, 22,* 310–316.

Locke, H., & Wallace, K. (1959). Short marital adjustment and prediction tests: Their reliability and validity. *Marriage and Family Living, 21,* 251–255.

Luckey, E. B., & Bain, J. K. (1970). Children: A factor in marital satisfaction. *Journal of Marriage and the Family, 28,* 43–44.

Maccoby, E. E. (1980). *Social development.* New York: Harcourt Brace Jovanovich.

Maccoby, E. E., Snow, M. E., & Jacklin, C. N. (1984). Children's dispositions and mother–child interaction at 12 and 18 months: A short-term longitudinal study. *Developmental Psychology, 20,* 459–472.

Marini, M. (1980). Effects of number and spacing of children on marital and parental satisfaction. *Demography, 17,* 225–242.

McHale, S., & Huston, T. (1985). The effect of the transition to parenthood on the marriage relationship. *Journal of Family Issues, 6,* 409–434.

McLanahan, S., & Adams, J. (1987). Parenthood and psychological well being. *Annual Review of Immunology, 5,* 237–257.

McMillan, M., & Jacobson, J. (1986, August). *The relationship between infant temperament and the adjustment of first-time parents.* Paper presented at the 94th annual convention of the American Psychological Association, Washington, DC.

Menaghan, E. (1983). Marital stress and family transitions: A panel analysis. *Journal of Marriage and the Family, 45,* 371–386.

Miller, B. C. (1975). Studying the quality of marriage cross-sectionally. *Journal of Marriage and the Family, 37,* 11–12.

Miller, B. C. (1976). A multivariate developmental model of marital satisfaction. *Journal of Marriage and the Family, 38,* 643–658.

Morgan, S., Lye, D., & Condran, G. (1988). Sons, daughters, and divorce: Does the sex of children affect the risk of divorce. *American Journal of Sociology, 94,* 110–129.

Moss, P., Bolland, G., Foxman, R., & Owen, C. (1986). Marital relations during the transition to parenthood. *Journal of Reproductive and Infant Psychology, 4,* 57–67.

Nock, S. L. (1979). The family life cycle: Empirical or conceptual tool? *Journal of Marriage and the Family, 41,* 15–26.

Radloff, L. S. (1975). Sex differences in depression: The effects of occupation and marital status. *Sex Roles, 1,* 249–265.

Rankin, R., & Maneker, J. (1985). The duration of marriage in a divorcing population: The impact of children. *Journal of Marriage and the Family, 47,* 43–52.

Renee, K. (1970). Correlates of dissatisfaction in marriage. *Journal of Marriage and the Family, 32,* 54–66.

Rollins, B. C., & Cannon, K. L. (1974). Marital satisfaction over the family life cycle: A re-evaluation. *Journal of Marriage and the Family, 36,* 271–283.

Rollins, B. C., & Feldman, H. (1970). Marital satisfaction over the life cycle. *Journal of Marriage and the Family, 32,* 20–28.

Rollins, B., & Galligan, R. (1978). The developing child and marital satisfaction of parents. In R. Lerner & G. Spanier (Eds.), *Child influences on marital and family interaction: A life-span perspective* (pp. 71–105). New York: Academic Press.

Rosenblatt, P. C. (1974). Behavior in public places: Comparison of couples accompanied and unaccompanied by children. *Journal of Marriage and the Family, 36,* 750–755.

Ross, C., Mirowsky, J., & Huber, J. (1983). Marriage patterns and depression. *American Sociological Review, 48,* 809–823.

Ruble, D., Fleming, A., Hackel, L., & Stangor, C. (1988). Changes in the marital relationship during the transition to first-time motherhood: Effects of violated expectations concerning division of household labor. *Journal of Personality and Social Psychology, 55,* 78–87.

Russell, C. (1974). Transition to parenthood: Problems and gratifications. *Journal of Marriage and the Family, 36,* 294–301.

Ryder, R. G. (1973). Longitudinal data relating marriage satisfaction and having a child. *Journal of Marriage and the Family, 35*, 604-606.

Schram, R. W. (1979). Marital satisfaction over the family life cycle: A critique and proposal. *Journal of Marriage and the Family, 41*, 7-12.

Schumm, W., & Bugaishis, M. (1986). Marital quality over the marital career: Alternative explanations. *Journal of Marriage and the Family, 48*, 165-168.

Spanier, G. B. (1976). Measuring dyadic adjustment: New scales for assessing the quality of marriage and similar dyads. *Journal of Marriage and the Family, 38*, 15-28.

Spanier, G., & Glick, P. (1981). Marital instability in the United States: Some correlates and recent changes. *Family Relations, 31*, 329-338.

Spanier, G. B., & Lewis, R. A. (1980). Marital quality: A review of the seventies. *Journal of Marriage and the Family, 42*, 825-839.

Spanier, G. B., Lewis, R. A., & Cole, C. L. (1975). Marital adjustment over the family life cycle: The issue of curvilinearity. *Journal of Marriage and the Family, 31*, 263-268.

Spanier, G. B., Sauer, W., & Larzelere, R. (1979). An empirical evaluation of the family life cycle. *Journal of Marriage and the Family, 41*, 27-38.

Steinberg, L. (1987). The impact of puberty on family relations. *Developmental Psychology, 23*, 451-460.

Steinberg, L., & Silverberg, S. (1987). Influences on marital satisfaction during the middle stages of the family life cycle. *Journal of Marriage and the Family, 49*, 751-760.

Thomas, A., & Chess, S. (1977). *Temperament and development.* New York: Brunner/Mazel.

Thorton, A. (1977). Children and marital stability. *Journal of Marriage and the Family, 39*, 531-540.

U.S. Bureau of the Census (1971). *Social and economic variations in marriage, divorce, and remarriage: 1967.* Current Population Reports, Series P-20, Number 223. Washington, DC: U.S. Government Printing Office.

Waisbren, S. E. (1980). Parents reactions after the birth of a developmentally disabled child. *American Journal of Mental Deficiency, 84*, 345-351.

Waite, L., Haggstrom, G., & Kanouse, D. (1985). The consequences of parenthood for the marital stability of young adults. *American Sociological Review, 50*, 850-857.

Waldron, H., & Routh, D. (1981). The effect of the first child on the marital relationship. *Journal of Marriage and the Family, 43*, 785-788.

White, L., & Booth, A. (1985). The transition to parenthood and marital quality. *Journal of Family Issues, 6*, 435-449.

White, L., Booth, A., & Edwards, J. (1986). Children and marital happiness: Why the negative correlation. *Journal of Family Issues, 7*, 131-147.

Wilcox, W. (1891). *The divorce problem: A study in statistics.* New York: Columbia University Press.

Wilkie, C., & Ames, E. (1986). The relationship of infant crying to parental stress in the transition to parenthood. *Journal of Marriage and the Family, 48*, 545-550.

# CHAPTER 7

# Employment and Marital Functioning

## Julian Barling

The relationship between employment and marital functioning has been the focus of research and theorizing for some time (Dyer, 1956; Locke & Mackeprang, 1949). Earlier writers assumed that family functioning would affect work performance (Hoppock, 1935). Later, there was some disagreement regarding both the nature and direction of this relationship (Friend & Haggard, 1948), and Parsons (1959) went on to postulate that within industrialized societies, "the direct integration of occupational function with the kinship system, as it occurs in many nonliterate and peasant societies, is quite impossible. . . . Familial and occupational roles are sharply segregated from each other" (p. 263). Yet by the 1970s, consensus had emerged that work and family roles are intertwined (Kanter, 1977; Voydanoff, 1987), especially for women (Hall, 1972).

There is now a large literature on the relationship between employment and marital functioning. This literature reflects the contributions of a wide variety of researchers within the social sciences who have tended to assume that employment characteristics exert a unidirectional and negative influence on marital functioning. In addition, the majority of this research has focused on the possible effects of temporal or objective characteristics of employment on marital functioning. Only recently has this focus been broadened to include an examination of the effects of the subjective meaning of employment on marriage.

The goal of this chapter is to provide an integrated perspective on the influence of employment characteristics on marital functioning. The possible effects of temporal employment characteristics and the effects of the subjective meaning of employment and unemployment on marital functioning are discussed in the first two sections, respectively. The third section reviews data suggesting that marital functioning influences work. In the fourth section, the question of whether employment characteristics exert a meaningful or clinical effect on marital functioning (as opposed to a statistical effect) is considered. Conceptual and methodological directions appropriate for further research are identified in the fifth section, and the chapter concludes with a summary of what is known about the interdependence of employment and marital functioning.

## TEMPORAL EMPLOYMENT CHARACTERISTICS AND MARITAL FUNCTIONING

There are two temporal dimensions along which employment characteristics can vary, namely, the *amount* of time spent working and the *scheduling* of that time. The possible effects of both these dimensions have been the focus of numerous empirical investigations. Based on findings showing that prolonged absence from the marriage can exert negative effects on the remaining spouse and family members (Biller, 1974), the overriding assumption in research is that absence from the marriage, especially by the wife, is inevitably harmful for the remaining partner (Laws, 1971).

Piotrkowski and Gornick (1987) have suggested that our understanding of work-related absences is facilitated by categorizing the absence as ordinary or extraordinary. Unlike extraordinary absences, ordinary absences are typically brief, involving regular and predictable departure and reunion rituals that help other family members understand and cope with the absence. Thus, within this framework, both regular work and nonrotating shift-work schedules constitute ordinary work absences. In contrast, protracted work-related absences, whether or not they are regular and predictable, such as 3-month tours of duty for naval personnel (Marsella, Dubanoski, & Mohs, 1974), are considered to be extraordinary. Likewise, irregular or nonstandard shift-work schedules constitute extraordinary work absences because they are unpredictable.

On the basis of the distinction between ordinary and extraordinary work-related absence, three hypotheses have been supported concerning the effects of work absence on different aspects of marital functioning. The aspects of marital functioning investigated are marital role performance (an objective index of the number of formal and informal activities necessary to ensure that marital obligations are fulfilled), interference between work and family roles (a subjective description of the conflict experienced between these two roles), and marital satisfaction or adjustment.[1] The first hypothesis is that ordinary work-related absence exerts no meaningful influence on marital functioning. Second, extraordinary work-related absence affects marital role performance negatively and increases the perceived interference between work and family roles. Third, neither ordinary nor extraordinary work-related absence exerts a direct influence on marital satisfaction. However, chronic unsatisfactory marital role performance or high levels of felt interference between work and family roles resulting from prolonged or extraordinary work-related absence influence marital satisfaction directly. Empirical evidence addressing these hypotheses is now considered.

## Ordinary Work-Related Absences

### *The Amount of Time Spent Working*
The hypothesis that ordinary work-related absence is not associated directly with marital satisfaction has been supported by studies showing that the amount of time spent working by the husband on a regular basis is not related either to his own (Clark, Nye, & Gecas, 1978) or his spouse's marital satisfaction (Greenhaus, Bedeian, & Mossholder, 1987). In contrast, the total number of hours spent at work is related inversely to the amount of time either spouse can devote to household responsibilities (Staines & Pleck, 1984), their belief that they can manage the conflict between work and family roles (Voydanoff, 1988), and their satisfaction with family activities (Voydanoff & Kelly, 1984). However, the meaning of such findings is questionable. First, the amount of variance accounted for is usually small (e.g., less than 1.3% in Voydanoff and Kelly's [1984] study). Second, other studies have failed to find an association between amount of time spent working and marital role performance (Clark et al., 1978; Jackson, Zedeck, & Summers, 1985).

---

[1]For the purposes of this chapter, marital satisfaction or adjustment is viewed as a global, subjective evaluation of the extent to which an individual's expectations from the marriage are met.

Another potential effect of the amount of time spent working on marital functioning is manifest in overtime work (i.e., work beyond that normally required). Studies of overtime show that, independent of the number of regular hours worked per week, the number of hours worked overtime per week is not associated with marital role performance (e.g., assisting with household activities, discussions on personal and family problems; Jackson et al., 1985) or marital satisfaction (Staines & Pleck, 1984). However, because relatively few people work overtime, and there is a limited amount of time that people can work overtime, range restriction limits the extent to which statistically significant relationships might emerge.

The amount of time actually spent working (whether on a regular or overtime basis) provides a truncated perspective of the amount of time individuals spend away from their families for employment-related purposes. Consistent with the movement of families away from urban centers toward the suburbs, increasing amounts of time are necessary for commuting to and from work. Assessing the effects of commuting becomes even more interesting when the stressful nature of the commuting experience is appreciated (Schaeffer, Street, Singer, & Baum, 1988). Only two studies have focused on commuting and marital functioning, and their results are contradictory. Jackson et al. (1985) showed that the amount of time spent commuting (an average of 55.34 minutes per day) was associated significantly with self-reported dissatisfaction with the congruence between work and family roles. On the other hand, Pleck, Staines, and Lang (1980) showed that neither the amount of time spent commuting nor commuting-related problems were associated with conflict between work and family roles. Although neither of these two studies suggests that commuting exerts a substantive influence on marital functioning, a different approach may be necessary to reveal any negative effects of commuting. Specifically, both these studies assume that commuting is a chronic stressor, yet a daily stressor model may be more appropriate (Pratt & Barling, 1988). Individuals may adapt to the persistent nature of commuting and become unsettled only by unpredictable and uncontrollable daily events encountered while doing so.

Most of the aforementioned research has focused on the temporal work characteristics of the husband. Another way to understand how the amount of time spent working influences marital functioning is by assessing the association between marital functioning and the wife's employment status. Central to the large body of research investigating this issue is the assumption that the amount of time spent working by the wife detracts from her availability to her husband and that this exerts negative effects on his marital satisfaction (see Barling, 1990).

Initial fears that the wife's employment would exert negative effects on her husband's marital functioning were probably maintained by the results of Burke and Weir's (1976) early study, which showed that husbands of employed wives were more maritally dissatisfied than husbands of homemakers. Nonetheless, the external validity of their findings is questionable. First, their study was fraught with methodological problems (see Barling, 1990). Second, numerous studies have failed to replicate their findings when specific facets of marital satisfaction have been assessed (e.g., Booth, 1979; Locksley, 1980). The possibility that wives' employment exerts no negative effects on marital functioning is strengthened when their own marital functioning is investigated. Employed wives experience no more marital dissatisfaction than homemakers (Locksley, 1980), and when husbands support their wives' decision to work outside of the home (Houseknecht & Macke, 1981) or hold positive attitudes to wives' employment (Spitze & Waite, 1981), employed wives report higher levels of marital satisfaction than nonemployed wives.

If equal participation by both spouses in household responsibilities is a valued social goal, then it can be argued that wives' employment may enhance some aspects of husbands' marital functioning. When specific marital role responsibilities are examined, the benefits of employment for the wife become apparent. Although wives still complete substantially more household chores than their husbands (perhaps six times as many, according to Moore & Hofferth, 1979), employed wives complete significantly fewer household chores than their nonemployed counterparts (Presland & Antill, 1987). Thus, even though household and childcare responsibilities are still not shared equally between spouses (Spitze, 1988), employment helps wives attain greater equity in the marital relationship.

A remaining possibility is that an indirect relationship exists between the total amount of time worked and marital satisfaction (Mortimer, 1980). Although there is no direct relationship between the amount of time spent working and marital adjustment, the conflict between work and family roles is elevated when individuals work longer hours *and* experience greater job-related time pressures (Mortimer, 1980). In turn, both the conflict between work and family roles (Barling, 1986; Suchet & Barling,

1986) and an unequal distribution of housework (Yogev & Brett, 1985) predict marital dissatisfaction for males and females. This process becomes all the more plausible because, using longitudinal data, MacEwen and Barling (1988a) showed that the alternative hypothesis that marital dissatisfaction induces change in interrole conflict can be excluded. Mortimer (1980) explicitly tested such a process model in a single study. Her data show that although there is no direct relationship between objective and subjective work-related time demands and marital adjustment, such time demands influenced work-related family strain and wives' supportive behaviors, which in turn affected marital adjustment.

## The Scheduling of Work Time

The second temporal axis along which work varies is the *scheduling* of work time, or the shift-work schedule. The literature on this topic does not support the assumption that employment (in this instance, involvement in shift-work schedules) affects family functioning negatively. For example, a regular shift schedule that includes days worked on weekends is associated with 2.4 hours *less* spent on housework per week by the husband (Staines & Pleck, 1984). Likewise, involvement in a rotating shift schedule is also associated with less satisfactory marital role performance. Yet when the pattern of hours rather than days is varied, a different perspective emerges (see Mott, Mann, McLoughlin, & Warwick, 1965). Involvement in an afternoon or night shift results in *more* time per week devoted to household responsibilities per week (6.2 hours and 4 hours, respectively, per week in Staines and Pleck's [1984] study). Similar differences also emerge when workers accept longer work hours per day (10) in exchange for fewer days at work (4) per week. This work schedule also provides an opportunity to disentangle the effects of the amount of work from its scheduling, because the number of hours worked per week remains constant, although the scheduling of the hours changes.

Maklan (1977) showed that there were no substantial differences in the amount of traditionally female gender-typed household chores engaged in by husbands in 4- to 5-day work weeks. Differences did emerge, however, when traditionally male-oriented household responsibilities (such as home repairs and maintenance) were considered: husbands in the 4-day week engaged in substantially more of these behaviors than their counterparts on a 5-day schedule. Thus, involvement in nonregular shift-work schedules need not exert a detrimental influence on the first aspect of marital functioning, namely, objective indices of marital role performance. Instead, under certain schedules, the number of marital roles completed increases. As regards marital adjustment, Maklan (1977) found no differences between individuals involved in a 4-day or 5-day work week. Nevertheless, there were interesting distributional differences between the marital adjustment scores of these two groups. Specifically, individuals involved in the 4-day work week yielded far more extreme scores (both positive and negative) than their counterparts engaged in a more regular 5-day work week.

In summary, there is very little support for the notion that ordinary work-related absences exert any direct negative influence on marital functioning. This is consistent with data obtained from five separate national random samples conducted between 1973 and 1980, from which Lacy, Bokemeier, and Shepard (1983) have shown that respondents consistently rank the amount of time spent working as the least important job-related attribute when contrasted with aspects such as the meaning of work, promotion, income, and security.

## Extraordinary Work-Related Absences

Nonstandard shift schedules constitute extraordinary work absences because they are irregular and less predictable. A different pattern emerges when the effects of nonstandard work schedules on one aspect of marital functioning are considered, namely, subjective reports of interference between work and family roles. Working either on weekends or holidays (Shamir, 1983; Staines & Pleck, 1984) or the late afternoon/early evening shift (Shamir, 1983) is associated with significantly greater levels of work–family interference. Involvement in any of these shift schedules removes these individuals from the family context at precisely those times when their presence is most required. Hence, a paradox emerges because marital role performance (the objective number of role obligations fulfilled) and work–family interference (the subjective report of conflict between these two roles) are influenced differently by shift work in general and by the afternoon shift in particular—in other words, by ordinary and extraordinary work absences.

Consequently, shift-work exerts a different effect on the quantity versus the quality of marital functioning. Whereas working a nonday shift facilitates greater involvement in various aspects of marital role performance (an index of the quantity of marital functioning), it is also associated with the experience of higher levels of conflict between work and marital role fulfillment (an index of the quality of marital functioning). As was the case when considering the effects of ordinary work-related absences, there is no consistent support for the notion that marital adjustment or satisfaction is affected directly by extraordinary work-related absences.

In summarizing the effects of ordinary and extraordinary work-related absences on marital functioning, the hypotheses outlined earlier are supported. That is, ordinary work-related absence exerts no detrimental effect on marital functioning, extraordinary work-related absences interfere with the sensitive balance between work and family roles, and neither ordinary nor extraordinary work-related absences directly influence marital satisfaction. Instead, marital dissatisfaction is a distal outcome of temporal work characteristics and will become manifest only where temporal characteristics exert enduring effects on marital role performance and/or work–family conflict.

## SUBJECTIVE EMPLOYMENT EXPERIENCES AND MARITAL FUNCTIONING

Research on subjective employment experiences has been influenced by theorizing about work stressors. It has been hypothesized that the effects of a work stressor will endure as long as the stressor itself is present or there is some concern that its effects linger (Pratt & Barling, 1988). Extending this argument to predict the effects of subjective employment characteristics (as opposed to temporal aspects of employment) on marital functioning, it is thought that enduring rather than episodic work experiences will influence marital functioning and that the direction of the influence will be consistent with the nature of the work experience. Thus, negative work experiences will exert a harmful effect on marital functioning. It is frequently overlooked, however, that this relationship also implies that positive work experiences wield a positive influence on marital functioning. Also, personal or contextual factors moderate this relationship. There is a considerable body of data to support these arguments across diverse subjective employment experiences, such as chronic work stressors, participation in decision making, and job dissatisfaction. The possible effects of each of the employment experiences are discussed in turn.

Intrarole conflict[2] is a chronic work stressor experienced by approximately one-third of the population (Kahn, Wolfe, Quinn, Snoek, & Rosenthal, 1964), and a husband's intrarole conflict is associated with both his own (Barling, 1986; Greenhaus et al., 1987) and his wife's (Burke, Weir, & DuWors, 1980) marital satisfaction. When the chronic work stressor is severe, a significant relationship emerges between the negative experience of chronic work stress and spouse abuse, both in cross-sectional (Barling & Rosenbaum, 1986) and in longitudinal (MacEwen & Barling, 1988b) studies. Nevertheless, MacEwen and Barling (1988b) propose that a different model of stress may be more appropriate to understanding the relationship between work stressors and spouse abuse. Specifically, they suggest that marital aggression may be more a function of daily or acute work stressors because of their sudden, unpredictable, and typically infrequent nature.

Limiting attention to the relationship between work stressors and marital functioning would result in a truncated and unnecessarily pessimistic view of work experiences, because the work context also provides ample opportunities for positive experiences (Broadbent, 1985). It is critical, therefore, to investigate other subjective work experiences such as participation in decision making and job satisfaction to understand more fully the possible effects of employment experiences on family functioning.

Price (1985) has suggested that participation in decision making increases workers' feelings of autonomy, and because of its intrinsically reinforcing nature, the effects of participation in decision making would generalize to nonwork spheres. Two studies support Price's assertion. Piotrkowski (1979) found that work that did not offer the possibility of participation in decision making was associated with patterns of nonparticipation in the family among a sample of blue-collar workers. Using a qualitative approach involving in-depth interviews, Crouter (1984a) found that the effects of participation in decision making can be positive. For example, one participant stated that: "Working here takes more time away from my personal and family life, but it has helped in terms of dealing with my family. I'm more willing to get their opinions. We hold 'team meetings' at home to make decisions"

---

[2]Intrarole conflict refers to the conflict within a single role such as the individual's work role. Thus, for example, an individual would experience intrarole conflict when he or she reports to two or more individuals for the same function, each of whom hold differing expectations of what successful performance entails. On the other hand, interrole conflict emerges when an individual tries to satisfy incompatible roles from two different domains such as work and family.

(Crouter, 1984a, p. 82). However, not all the spouses in Crouter's (1984a) study reacted as positively. For example, another employee stated: "My husband can't understand why I like it here so much and why I'd want to work later [longer hours]. He thinks I've become terribly independent. It bothered him at first . . . I felt part of a team. He had trouble understanding that and felt left out" (Crouter, 1984a, p. 82).

Some pertinent issues emerge. First, it is apparent that what might be beneficial for one spouse may well exert negative effects on the other spouse. This could occur when the democratic ethic demanded by participatory work environments is inconsistent with the authoritarian climate inherent in many blue-collar marriages (Komarovsky, 1987). Second, it does not follow that one spouse should be denied opportunities for participating in decision making because of possibly negative effects on the other spouse or on the marriage. Instead, it behooves employers to introduce organizational structures that are most likely to enhance individuals' psychological well-being and to ensure greater symmetry between organizational or work structures, on the one hand, and family structures on the other in an attempt to reduce negative effects of work on marital functioning.

Turning to a different subjective factor, job satisfaction, we can discern that its association with marital satisfaction is apparently dependent on moderating conditions or situations. Although positive correlations emerge frequently between work and nonwork satisfaction (including marital satisfaction), negative relationships also emerge under specific circumstances. For example, a negative correlation between work satisfaction and marital satisfaction is most likely when an individual lacking gratification in one domain (e.g., work) seeks fulfillment in another (e.g., marriage) or when the activities necessary for success in one domain are incompatible with those in the other domain (Pond & Green, 1983).

### Comparing Temporal Attributes and Subjective Employment Experiences

Our discussion of temporal and subjective employment characteristics raises the question of whether they have comparable effects on marital functioning. There are a few studies that directly contrast the effects of temporal and subjective employment characteristics, and inferences about their relative effects can also be drawn from two different research spheres, namely, research on flexible work schedules and research on wives' employment.

Two different aspects of work schedule flexibility have been considered: temporal characteristics of the schedule and individuals' perceptions of the extent to which they exert control over the amount and scheduling of their work time. These two aspects exert neither consistent nor similar effects on marital functioning. First, individuals involved in flexible work schedules devote significantly more of their nonwork time to family responsibilities than do individuals who do not have access to flexible work schedules (Winett & Neale, 1980). Yet the extent to which individuals perceive that they exert some control over the flexibility of the schedule is not associated with marital role performance (Staines & Pleck, 1984). In a later analysis, perceived control over the schedule was shown to fulfill another role. Specifically, Staines and Pleck (1986) showed that the relationship between nonstandard work schedules and marital functioning was moderated by perceived schedule flexibility. Second, objective involvement in and perceived control over one's work schedule are both negatively correlated with the conflict between work and family roles (Staines & Pleck, 1984). Third, Staines and Pleck (1984) showed that perceived control over work schedule flexibility was positively associated with their measure of family adjustment (a three-item measure, two of which assessed marital adjustment). Fourth, subjective work experiences predict work–family conflict even after controlling for temporal characteristics of employment (Voydanoff, 1988).

A second difference between the effects of temporal and subjective employment characteristics on marital functioning is documented in research on wives' employment status. As noted previously, wives' employment status has no direct association with their own or their spouse's marital satisfaction (Locksley, 1980; Staines et al., 1978). On the contrary, the meaning of the wife's employment can exert important effects on the marriage when the wife's employment is cast within the context of the relative occupational prestige of each of the partners. Marital dissatisfaction is heightened among those couples where the wife's job is associated with greater occupational prestige than her husband's job (Hornung & McCullough, 1981). The importance of this effect is suggested by four factors. First, occupational prestige relative to one's partner exerts a greater effect on marital dissatisfaction than the effects of occupational prestige for either spouse taken in isolation. Second, these findings are probably somewhat conservative because only those marriages that had endured the stresses of incompatibility were included; status incompatibility that may have resulted in prior dissolution of the marriage was not taken into account (Hornung & McCullough, 1981). Third, Philliber and Hiller (1983) showed that the likelihood of marital dissolution was greater when the wife had a job that reflected greater occupational attainment than that of her husband. Similarly, Hornung, McCullough, and Sugimoto (1981) showed that three forms of marital aggression (namely, psychological and physical aggression and life-threatening behavior) were greater when occupational status incompatibility was high or the wife held a nontraditional or blue-collar job. Fourth, the effects of status incompatibility on marital dissatisfaction are more pronounced when wives' commitment to job advancement is high.

Two conclusions can be derived from the data on the relationship between wives' employment and either occupational status incompatibility or work schedule flexibility. First, temporal or objective work characteristics and subjective employment attributes may exert different effects on marital functioning. Second, when the relative effects of these employment attributes are contrasted, the subjective meaning of employment appears to exert a greater effect than temporal components. This is again consistent with the findings of Lacy et al. (1983) that individuals accord more importance to the subjective than to the temporal characteristics of their jobs.

Finally, it should be noted that research has investigated husbands' subjective employment experiences. However, the results of studies focusing on wives suggest strongly that employment experiences that are common to both spouses (thereby excluding experiences such as occupational status inconsistency because of its unique meaning to the couple) affect their marital satisfaction equally. Consequently, concerns that husbands' and wives' employment status and employment experiences exert different effects on marital functioning are not consistent with the data currently available.

## Unemployment and Marital Functioning

Any analysis of employment and marital functioning would be incomplete without considering the consequences of unemployment for the marital relationship. Much of the considerable research on this topic was generated from data collected during the

1930s. However, whether the results from such studies can be generalized to the present time is open to question. The experience of unemployment was arguably different during that period because of high rates of unemployment throughout the industrialized world and the extensive financial hardship that individuals and families experienced when the breadwinner was unemployed (Jahoda, 1982). In addition, most reports were case studies with no comparison groups. Consequently, only recent studies that used control group designs are considered here.

Given the widespread belief that unemployment exerts negative effects on the family and the plethora of studies on unemployment and psychological well-being (e.g., Fryer & Payne, 1986), there is surprisingly little recent research on unemployment and marital functioning. Two studies have investigated the relationship between unemployment and marital adjustment. First, Brinkerhoff and White (1978) showed that neither employed nor unemployed individuals, nor their spouses, differed in their level of marital satisfaction. Although there was also no relationship between income and marital satisfaction, Brinkerhoff and White (1978) did show that unemployed husbands with low family income were significantly more dissatisfied with their marriages. In a second study, Larson (1984) showed that employed and unemployed males differed in marital adjustment. He also obtained some evidence to suggest that this difference might result from more disagreements and arguments in relationships in which the husband is unemployed.

There are also some studies investigating the association between unemployment and two specific aspects of marital functioning, namely, marital role performance and spouse abuse. Warr and Payne (1983) and Shamir (1986) contrasted the extent to which employed and unemployed men share in household tasks. These studies found that unemployed men complete more household tasks, a finding that is particularly important for two reasons. First, it generalizes across both working-class and middle-class men (Warr & Payne, 1983). Second, Shamir (1986) showed that over a 6-month period reemployed men and women decrease their participation in household tasks. It remains for future research to assess why unemployed individuals participate more in household activities, especially in view of data to show that men who work a night shift and are alone at home during the day also increase the number of household tasks completed (Staines & Pleck, 1984). Taken together, these findings raise the possibility that it is neither unemployment nor the nature of the shift *per se* that is important but, rather, the increased amount of solitary time the husband passes at home.

With regard to spouse abuse, the two different methodologies used to investigate its relationship to unemployment (i.e., the study of abused samples versus random samples of the normal population) provide some empirical support for an association between these two variables. The belief that unemployment is related to spouse abuse gained considerable credibility from studies showing a disproportionate number of unemployed men in samples of abusive husbands (Gayford, 1975; Lewis, 1987). For example, Gayford (1975) studied 100 women who had been severely beaten by their husbands and found that 29% of the wives reported that their husbands were unemployed. The interpretation of this finding is limited by several factors including (1) the use of a self-selected sample derived primarily from a social welfare agency, (2) uncertainty regarding whether husbands were currently unemployed, and (3) a definition of abuse that involved more frequent and severe aggression than that typically required in standard definitions (O'Leary et al., 1989).

It is important to note, therefore, that the association between unemployment and spouse abuse has been found in random samples of the normal population. Several features of this relationship emerged from Straus, Gelles, and Steinmetz's (1980) study of a national probability sample of 2,143 intact families in the United States. First, using an index of physical aggression that included non-life-threatening behaviors such as pushing, shoving, and throwing objects, Straus et al. (1980) found that the extent of husband-to-wife violence was double (8% versus 4%) when the husband was unemployed rather than employed. Second, although it is not possible to identify precipitating causes, physical aggression inflicted on husbands by wives occurred in 14% of marriages where the husband was unemployed (contrasted with 4% when the husband was employed). Third, physical aggression between spouses, whether husband to wife (12%) or wife to husband (13%), was greater when the husband was employed on a part-time rather than a full-time basis. A decade later, Straus and Gelles (1986) again analyzed spouse abuse using a national probability sample of 3,250 intact couples. Even though the unemployment rate was lower when they had interviewed subjects in 1985, Straus and Gelles (1986) maintain that the same relationship between unemployment and spouse abuse was replicated.

Despite the apparent consistency in findings obtained from

these two different methodologies, a number of questions remain unanswered. First, the causal role of unemployment is not addressed. For example, does unemployment precipitate physical aggression in previously nonaggressive couples, or does unemployment exacerbate existing problems? This is especially relevant because Komarovsky (1940) noted that those marriages most at risk following unemployment manifested most problems before the husband became unemployed. Second, research is needed to investigate whether and how the psychological experience of unemployment (e.g., daily time structure, sense of purpose, sense of community, the ability to use one's skills; Jahoda, 1982) is associated with spouse abuse. Third, not all individuals who lose their jobs become maritally dissatisfied or physically aggressive. What factors enhance resilience in those who do not? Finally, the vast majority of unemployment research still focuses on men only, despite the fact that relative to the total number of employed men and women, more women are unemployed than men.

## INFLUENCE OF MARITAL FUNCTIONING ON WORK

Most of the research reviewed thus far assumes that employment (and unemployment) characteristics and experiences influence marital functioning. Kanter (1977) has referred to this assumption as "economic determinism," or the belief that work inevitably influences the family. Yet it is clear that such an assumption is inadequate for capturing fully the interdependence between work and family. Crouter (1984b) showed in a qualitative study of 55 workers that workers themselves realize that family issues affect their work performance. Importantly, this spillover could be positive (e.g., "I can see other people's personal problems, I didn't much when I was single. Now I know what they're going through, and I'm more understanding" [Crouter, 1984b, p. 431]) or negative ("When there's strife at home, I have to consciously put it in the back of my mind. My son had a serious motorcycle accident last year and could have died. That took its toll on my abilities to concentrate. Arguments do that, too" [Crouter, 1984b, p. 432]). Interestingly, it appears that expressions of positive spillover are more characteristic of males, and experiences of negative spillover are more frequent for females (Crouter, 1984b).

There are data from which it can be inferred that both structural and functional aspects of marriage influence employment characteristics and experiences. For example, childbirth and child-rearing by the mother limit her decisions concerning entry, exit, and reentry into the labor force (Hock, Morgan, & Hock, 1985). Likewise, women are more likely to engage in training courses for male-dominated vocations if the significant men in their lives support such a decision (Houser & Garvey, 1983).

Over and above the effects of the marriage on such structural employment characteristics, there are also data indicating that marital functioning influences diverse aspects of work performance and satisfaction. First, Guest and Williams (1973) suggested that pressures arising in the home influence accidents and absenteeism, and Kriegsmann and Hardin (1974) found some evidence that the process of a divorce negatively affects work performance, absenteeism, and turnover. Second, Rudd and McKenry (1986) showed that even after controlling statistically for five demographic variables and one organizational variable (workload), the extent to which mothers' employment aspirations were perceived as supported by children and fathers significantly influenced their job satisfaction. Third, the best predictor of a husband's intention to accept his company's offer to relocate was his spouse's willingness to move (Brett & Reilly, 1988).

Yet these studies suffer from the same defects as those relating to the influence of employment/unemployment characteristics and experiences on marital functioning. Specifically, most of the conclusions concerning causality are based on cross-sectional data and therefore must remain inconclusive. One study used a short-term longitudinal design to address this deficiency. Barling and Mac-Ewen (1989) developed a process model specifying that the stress required in balancing work and family (rather than marital) roles would exert an indirect influence on performance (proofreading) through their direct influence on attentional and concentration problems. Although not conclusive, the data support their model and provide sufficient incentive to investigate further how marital functioning influences different aspects of work performance.

## EMPLOYMENT AND MARITAL FUNCTIONING: STATISTICAL VERSUS CLINICAL EFFECTS

Our review shows that with few exceptions, the relationship between employment or unemployment characteristics or experiences on the one hand and marital functioning on the other are modest in magnitude. Even when multivariate analyses are conducted and the joint effects of different employment experiences are considered (e.g., Barling, 1984), the amount of variance explained in marital functioning is still limited. Some comments concerning this observation are in order.

First, because employment is only one of the multiple predictors of marital functioning, it alone should not account for a substantial portion of the variance in marital functioning. Yet there are exceptions to the typically modest relationship between employment/unemployment experiences and marital functioning. Three examples will suffice, namely, the effects of interrole conflict on marital satisfaction, of status incongruency on physical aggression, and of work stress on physical aggression within the marital relationship.

Two studies have shown that interrole conflict experienced by husbands and wives is associated with marital dissatisfaction scores indicative of a marriage "at risk." Barling (1986) found that fathers experiencing high interrole conflict and who were low in personality hardiness (a personality construct embracing a perception of external events as challenges rather than threats, a feeling of commitment rather than alienation, and perceived control rather than powerlessness; Kobasa, 1982) scored in the distressed range (81.9) on the Short Marital Adjustment Test (SMAT; Locke & Wallace, 1959). In contrast, the marital satisfaction of husbands experiencing high levels of interrole conflict and high personality hardiness or low levels of interrole conflict irrespective of their personality hardiness was satisfactory (all $Ms > 106.61$). Likewise, Suchet and Barling (1986) showed that employed mothers who experienced elevated levels of interrole conflict and received minimal emotional and instrumental support from their husbands also yielded scores indicative of a marriage "at risk" ($M = 79.67$ on the SMAT). Regardless of levels of support, employed wives low in interrole conflict, like employed wives high in interrole conflict who received support, showed satisfactory marital adjustment (all $Ms > 103.27$). Although conclusions about causal direction are limited by the cross-sectional nature of these two studies, short-term longitudinal data did not support the alternative hypothesis that marital dissatisfaction increases feelings of interrole conflict (MacEwen & Barling, 1988a).

Second, the increasing number of women entering the labor force over the past two decades has led to an increase in the number of marriages where the wife is employed. Although several aspects of labor-force participation by women have been identified as risk factors for physical abuse by husbands (Hornung et al., 1981), it is clear that wife's occupational status *per se* is not a risk factor. Instead, the risk for experiencing psychological and physical abuse and life-threatening behavior increases when the wife holds a job of higher occupational prestige than her spouse. For example, data of Hornung et al. (1981) show that when the man is an "overachiever," the relative risk of psychological and physical abuse and life-threatening behavior is 0.97, 0.69, and 0.17, respectively.[3] Yet the relative risk of the wife experiencing these same forms of aggression when her occupational achievement surpasses that of her husband increases to 1.03, 1.29, and 1.46, respectively (Hornung et al., 1981). One potential limitation to the generalizability of these studies on status incompatibility is that the data were collected some time ago (e.g., 1973–1974; Hornung & McCullough, 1981), and attitudes to employed women have since changed.

Third, as noted previously, there is some empirical support for the idea that work stressors are associated with spouse abuse by males (Barling & Rosenbaum, 1986) and females (MacEwen & Barling, 1988b). Even though the amount of variance explained in marital aggression was low in both studies, the fact that prior global stress (which included work and life stress) accounted for 1% of the variance in women's marital aggression in MacEwen and Barling's (1988b) study may be meaningful for two reasons. First, apart from the statistical significance of this finding, there was a 1-year time lag between the assessment of stress and marital aggression. Second, despite the fact that marital aggression is a relatively stable phenomenon (O'Leary et al., 1989), the initial stress accounted for 1% of the variance in subsequent aggression even after removing the variance (51%) attributable to prior levels of marital aggression. Consequently, the relationship between stress and marital aggression may be relatively robust.

Nonetheless, the findings from most studies of employment and unemployment factors and marital functioning do raise a major question that should be the focus of future research. Does the presence of multiple risk factors increase the risk of marital problems? Thus, future research should concentrate on distinguishing the *relative* role of employment factors in predicting

[3]The concept of relative risk in this context would indicate, for example, that where the inconsistency emerges because the wife is "occupation-high" (compared to her spouse), she is 1.46 times more likely to suffer at least one instance of life-threatening behavior than in those situations where there is occupation consistency between the partners.

marital dysfunction. To do so would require a research strategy in which different categories of predictor variables (e.g., employment experiences, depression, life stress) are analyzed within a multivariate design.

## PRIORITIES FOR FURTHER RESEARCH
## ON EMPLOYMENT AND MARITAL FUNCTIONING

Although research and speculation on employment and the family are increasing exponentially, it is apparent that critical questions remain unanswered. First, with few exceptions (MacEwen & Barling, 1988a, 1988b), the majority of studies focusing on employment and unemployment and marital functioning have relied predominantly on cross-sectional nonexperimental data. The obvious limitation that arises from a failure to use experimental designs and/or longitudinal data is that statements regarding causal priority are tenuous. A critical need for future research, therefore, is to address causal questions directly. Given the difficulty of using true experimental designs in studying employment and family functioning, the importance of data collected longitudinally as a basis for subsequent causal inferences increases.

Second, research should investigate why a relationship exists between employment and marital functioning. In other words, the research agenda should be broadened to focus on mediating variables. Such an approach has proved useful in the related area of mothers' role satisfaction and their children's behavior (Lerner & Galambos, 1985; MacEwen & Barling, 1990) as well as showing how mothers' personal strain and mother–child interactions mediate the relationship between maternal interrole conflict and children's behavior problems (MacEwen & Barling, 1990). By a similar approach, factors that mediate the relationship between temporal work requirements and marital satisfaction (e.g., work–family interrole conflict and spouse support; Mortimer, 1980) have been identified.

Third, most research has focused on young or middle-aged couples, and hence relatively little is known about marital satisfaction in older couples or about the relationship between employment and marital functioning in older couples. Specifically, what are the potential effects of retirement on marital functioning? Given literature showing (1) that employment offers a means of achieving psychological well-being and (2) that job loss may affect marital functioning, this may represent a productive research direction.

Fourth, it is important to investigate the marital functioning of housewives (Hornung et al., 1981). However, instead of focusing merely on employment or unemployment status, the consequences of housewives' aspirations for or commitment to employment on marital functioning might be investigated (Barling, Fullagar, & Marchl-Dingle, 1988). Finally, research is also needed to investigate the effects of part-time employment on marital functioning. This is the fastest growing segment of the work force, and there are data showing that marital functioning may be associated with part-time employment status. For example, physical aggression within marriage is significantly higher among part-time employees than either their full-time or unemployed counterparts (Straus et al., 1980).

## CONCLUSION

A number of conclusions can be drawn concerning the relationship between employment and marital functioning. First, consistent with common assumptions, there are statistical associations between employment experiences and marital functioning. Contrary to popular belief, however, neither work in general nor the amount of time devoted to work in particular inevitably exerts negative effects on marital functioning. Instead, when any negative effect does emerge, it is typically because extraordinary work absences diminish marital role performance and increase interrole conflict, which in turn affect marital dissatisfaction. Moreover, positive employment experiences are associated with positive marital functioning, whereas negative employment experiences or high levels of work stressors are associated with negative marital functioning. Second, subjective employment experiences are more predictive of marital functioning than are temporal employment attributes. This is important given that most research and theory continue to focus on temporal employment attributes. Third, unemployed individuals are more likely to abuse their spouses than are their employed counterparts, yet differences between these two groups in marital adjustment are not as clear-cut. Finally, despite the fact that findings from empirical research have provided refinements in understanding the relationship between employment (and unemployment) and marital functioning, the issue of causal direction in this relationship remains ambiguous, and more attention should be focused on the meaning of all these relationships from a clinical perspective.

## A C K N O W L E D G M E N T S

Completion of this chapter was supported by grants from the Social Sciences and Humanities Research Council of Canada (Grant No: 410-88-0891) and Imperial Oil. The author expresses considerable appreciation to Karyl MacEwen for constructive comments regarding earlier versions of this chapter.

## R E F E R E N C E S

Barling, J. (1984). Effects of husbands' work experiences on wives' marital satisfaction. *Journal of Social Psychology, 124*, 219-225.

Barling, J. (1986). Interrole conflict and marital functioning amongst employed fathers. *Journal of Occupational Behaviour, 7*, 1-8.

Barling, J. (1990). *Employment, stress and family functioning*. London: Wiley.

Barling, J., Fullagar, C., & Marchl-Dingle, J. (1988). Employment commitment as a moderator of the maternal employment status/child behaviour relationship. *Journal of Organizational Behaviour, 9*, 113-122.

Barling, J., & MacEwen, K. E. (1989). *Effects of maternal employment role experiences on behavioral performance*. Manuscript submitted for publication.

Barling, J., & Rosenbaum, A. (1986). Work stressors and wife abuse. *Journal of Applied Psychology, 71*, 346-348.

Biller, H. B. (1974). *Paternal deprivation*. Lexington, MA: Lexington Books.

Booth, A. (1979). Does wives' employment cause stress for husbands? *The Family Coordinator, 28*, 445-449.

Brett, J. M., & Reilly, A. H. (1988). On the road again: Predicting the job transfer decision. *Journal of Applied Psychology, 73*, 614-620.

Brinkerhoff, D. B., & White, L. K. (1978). Marital satisfaction in an economically marginal population. *Journal of Marriage and the Family, 40*, 259-267.

Broadbent, D. E. (1985). The clinical impact of job design. *British Journal of Clinical Psychology, 24*, 33-44.

Burke, R. J., & Weir, T. (1976). Some personality differences between members of one-career and two-career families. *Journal of Marriage and the Family, 38*, 453-459.

Burke, R. J., Weir, T., & DuWors, R. E. (1980). Work demands on administrators and spouse well-being. *Human Relations, 33*, 253-278.

Clarke, R. A., Nye, F. I., & Gecas, V. (1978). Husbands' work involvement and marital role performance. *Journal of Marriage and the Family, 40*, 9-21.

Crouter, A. C. (1984a). Participative work as an influence on human development. *Journal of Applied Developmental Psychology, 5*, 71-90.

Crouter, A. C. (1984b). Spillover from family to work: The neglected side of the work-family interface. *Human Relations, 37*, 425-442.

Dyer, W. G. (1956). A comparison of families of high and low job satisfaction. *Marriage and Family Living, 18,* 58-60.

Friend, J. G., & Haggard, E. A. (1948). *Work adjustment in relation to family background: A conceptual basis for counseling.* Oxford: Oxford University Press.

Fryer, D., & Payne, R. (1986). Being unemployed: A review of the literature on the psychological experience of unemployment. In C. L. Cooper & I. T. Robertson (Eds.), *International review of industrial and organizational psychology 1986* (pp. 235-278). London: Wiley.

Gayford, J. J. (1975). Wife battering: A preliminary survey of 100 cases. *British Medical Journal, 1,* 194-197.

Greenhaus, J. H., Bedeian, A. G., & Mossholder, K. W. (1987). Work experiences, job performance, and feeling of personal and family well-being. *Journal of Vocational Behavior, 31,* 200-215.

Guest, D., & Williams, R. (1973). How home affects work. *New Society, January,* p. 18.

Hall, D. T. (1972). A model of coping with role conflict: The role behavior of college educated women. *Administrative Science Quarterly, 17,* 471-486.

Hock, E., Morgan, K. C., & Hock, M. D. (1985). Employment decisions made by mothers of infants. *Psychology of Women Quarterly, 9,* 383-402.

Hoppock, R. (1935). *Job satisfaction.* New York: Harper.

Hornung, C. A., & McCullough, B. C. (1981). Status relationships in dual employment marriages: Consequences for psychological well-being. *Journal of Marriage and the Family, 43,* 125-141.

Hornung, C. A., McCullough, B. C., & Sugimoto, T. (1981). Status relationships in marriage: Risk factors in spouse abuse. *Journal of Marriage and the Family, 43,* 675-692.

Houseknecht, S. K., & Macke, A. S. (1981). Combining marriage and career: The marital adjustment of professional women. *Journal of Marriage and the Family, 43,* 651-661.

Houser, B. B., & Garvey, C. (1983). The impact of family, peers and educational personnel upon career decision making. *Journal of Vocational Behavior, 23,* 35-44.

Jackson, S., Zedeck, S., & Summers, E. (1985). Family life disruptions: Effects of job-induced structural and emotional interference. *Academy of Management Journal, 28,* 574-586.

Jahoda, M. (1982). *Employment and unemployment: A social psychological analysis.* Cambridge: Cambridge University Press.

Kahn, R. L., Wolfe, D. M., Quinn, R. P., Snoek, J. D., & Rosenthal, R. A. (1964). *Role stress: Studies in role conflict and ambiguity.* New York: Wiley.

Kanter, R. M. (1977). *Work and family in the United States: A critical review and agenda for research and policy.* New York: Russell Sage.

Kobasa, S. C. (1982). The hardy personality: Toward a social psychology of stress and health. In G. S. Sanders & J. Suls (Eds.), *Behavioral medicine: Work, stress and health.* Dordrecht, The Netherlands: Martinus Nijhoff.

Komarovsky, M. (1940). *The unemployed man and his family.* New York: Dryden.

Komarovsky, M. (1987). *Blue-collar marriage.* New Haven, CT: Yale University Press.

Kriegsmann, J. K., & Hardin, D. R. (1974). Does divorce hamper job performance? *The Personnel Administrator, 19,* 26-29.

Lacey, W. B., Bokemeier, J. L., & Shepard, J. M. (1983). Job attribute preferences and work commitment of men and women in the United States. *Personnel Psychology, 36,* 315–329.

Larson, J. H. (1984). The effects of husband's unemployment on marital and family relations in blue-collar families. *Family Relations, 33,* 503–511.

Laws, J. L. (1971). A feminist review of marital adjustment literature: The rape of the Locke. *Journal of Marriage and the Family, 33,* 483–519.

Lerner, J. V., & Galambos, N. L. (1985). Maternal role satisfaction, mother–child interaction and child temperament: A process model. *Developmental Psychology, 21,* 1157–1164.

Lewis, B. Y. (1987). Psychosocial factors related to wife abuse. *Journal of Family Violence, 2,* 1–10.

Locke, H. J., & Mackeprang, M. (1949). Marital adjustment and the employed wife. *American Journal of Sociology, 54,* 536–538.

Locke, H. J., & Wallace, K. M. (1959). Short marital adjustment and prediction tests: Their reliability and validity. *Marriage and Family Living, 21,* 251–255.

Locksley, A. (1980). On the effect of wives' employment on marital adjustment and companionship. *Journal of Marriage and the Family, 42,* 337–345.

MacEwen, K. E., & Barling, J. (1988a). Interrole conflict, family support and marital adjustment of employed mothers: A short term, longitudinal study. *Journal of Organizational Behavior, 9,* 241–250.

MacEwen, K. E., & Barling, J. (1988b). Multiple stressors, violence in the family of origin, and marital aggression: A longitudinal investigation. *Journal of Family Violence, 3,* 73–88.

MacEwen, K., & Barling, J. (1990). *Maternal employment experiences, parenting and children's behavior.* Manuscript submitted for publication.

Maklan, D. M. (1977). *The four-day workweek: Blue collar adjustment to a nonconventional adjustment arrangement of work and leisure time.* New York: Praeger.

Marsella, A. J., Dubanoski, R. A., & Mohs, K. (1974). The effects of father presence and absence upon maternal attitudes. *Journal of Genetic Psychology, 125,* 257–263.

Moore, K. A., & Hofferth, S. L. (1979). Effects of women's employment on marriage: Formation, stability and roles. *Marriage and Family Review, 2,* 27–36.

Mortimer, J. T. (1980). Occupation–family linkages as perceived by men in the early stages of professional and managerial careers. In H. Z. Lopata (Ed.), *Research in the interweave of social roles: Women and men* (vol. 1, pp. 99–117). Greenwich, CT: JAI Press.

Mott, P. E., Mann, F. C., McLoughlin, Q., & Warwick, D. P. (1965). *Shift work: The social, psychological, and physical consequences.* Ann Arbor, MI: University of Michigan Press.

O'Leary, K. D., Barling, J., Arias, I., Rosenbaum, A., Malone, J., & Tyree, A. (1989). Prevalence and stability of marital aggression: A longitudinal investigation. *Journal of Consulting and Clinical Psychology, 57,* 263–268.

Parsons, T. (1959). The social structure of the family. In R. N. Anshem (Ed.), *The family: Its function and destiny* (rev. ed.; pp. 241–274). New York: Harper.

Philliber, W. W., & Hiller, D. V. (1983). Relative occupational attainments of spouses and later changes in marriage and wife's work experience. *Journal of Marriage and the Family, 45,* 161–170.

Piotrkowski, C. S. (1979). *Work and the family system.* New York: Macmillan.

Piotrkowski, C. S., & Gornick, L. K. (1987). Effects of work-related separations on children and families. In J. Bloom-Feshback & S. Bloom-Feshback (Eds.), *The psychology of separation and loss* (pp. 267–299). San Francisco: Jossey-Bass.

Pleck, J. H., Staines, G. L., & Lang, L. (1980). Conflicts between work and family life. *Monthly Labor Review, 103,* 29–32.

Pond, S. B., & Green, S. B. (1983). The relationship between job and marriage satisfaction within and between spouses. *Journal of Occupational Behaviour, 4,* 145–155.

Pratt, L. I., & Barling, J. (1988). Differentiating between daily events, acute and chronic stressors: A framework and its implications. In J. J. Hurrell, L. R. Murphy, S. L. Sauter, & C. L. Cooper (Eds.), *Occupational stress: Issues and developments in research* (pp. 41–53). London: Taylor & Francis.

Presland, P., & Antill, J. K. (1987). Household division of labour: The impact of hours worked in paid employment. *Australian Journal of Psychology, 39,* 273–291.

Price, R. H. (1985). Work and community. *American Journal of Community Psychology, 13,* 1–12.

Rudd, N. M., & McKenry, P. C. (1986). Family influence on the job satisfaction of employed mothers. *Psychology of Women Quarterly, 10,* 363–372.

Schaeffer, M. H., Street, S. W., Singer, J. E., & Baum, A. (1988). Effects of control on the stress reactions of commuters. *Journal of Applied Social Psychology, 18,* 944–957.

Shamir, B. (1983). Some antecedents of work-nonwork conflict. *Journal of Vocational Behavior, 23,* 98–111.

Shamir, B. (1986). Unemployment and household division of labor. *Journal of Marriage and the Family, 48,* 195–206.

Spitze, G. (1988). Women's employment and family relations: A review. *Journal of Marriage and the Family, 50,* 595–618.

Spitze, G., & Waite, L. J. (1981). Wives' employment: The role of husbands' perceived attitudes. *Journal of Marriage and the Family, 43,* 117–124.

Staines, G. L., & Pleck, J. H. (1984). Nonstandard work schedules and family life. *Journal of Applied Psychology, 69,* 515–523.

Staines, G. L., & Pleck, J. H. (1986). Work schedule flexibility and family life. *Journal of Occupational Behaviour, 7,* 147–154.

Staines, G. L., Pleck, J. H., Shepard, L. J., & O'Connor, P. (1978). Wives' employment status and marital adjustment: Yet another look. *Psychology of Women Quarterly, 3,* 90–120.

Straus, M. A., & Gelles, R. J. (1986). Societal change and change in family violence from 1975 to 1985 as revealed by two national surveys. *Journal of Marriage and the Family, 48,* 465–479.

Straus, M. A., Gelles, R. J., & Steinmetz, S. K. (1980). *Behind closed doors: Violence in the American family.* New York: Anchor Press.

Suchet, M., & Barling, J. (1986). Employed mothers: Interrole conflict, spouse support and marital functioning. *Journal of Occupational Behaviour, 7,* 167–178.

Voydanoff, P. (1987). *Work and family life.* Newbury Park, CA: Sage.

Voydanoff, P. (1988). Work role characteristics, family structure demands and work/family conflict. *Journal of Marriage and the Family, 50,* 749–762.

Voydanoff, P., & Kelly, R. F. (1984). Determinants of work-related family problems among employed parents. *Journal of Marriage and the Family, 46,* 881–892.

Warr, P. B., & Payne, R. L. (1983). Social class and reported changes after job loss. *Journal of Applied Social Psychology, 13,* 206–222.

Winett, R. A., & Neale, M. S. (1980). Modifying settings as a strategy for permanent, preventive behavior change. In P. Karoly & J. J. Steffen (Eds.), *Improving long-term effects of psychotherapy.* New York: Gardner Press.

Yogev, S., & Brett, J. (1985). Perceptions of the division of housework and child care and marital satisfaction. *Journal of Marriage and the Family, 47,* 609–618.

# CHAPTER 8

# Marriage and Psychopathology

Ian H. Gotlib
Scott B. McCabe

Over the past 15 years we have witnessed a dramatic surge of interest in interpersonal factors involved in the etiology and maintenance of emotional disorders. There are now detailed interpersonally based theoretical conceptualizations of such disorders as depression (Gotlib & Hooley, 1988), anxiety or agoraphobia (Kleiner & Marshall, 1985), alcoholism (Jacob & Seilhamer, 1987), and schizophrenia (Goldstein, Hand, & Hahlweg, 1986). Paralleling these developments is a growing body of research documenting the efficacy of interventions derived from these formulations, including interpersonally oriented approaches for the treatment of depression (Gotlib & Colby, 1987), agoraphobia (Barlow, O'Brien, & Last, 1984), alcoholism (O'Farrell, 1986), and schizophrenia (Leff, Kuipers, Berkowitz, Eberlein-Vries, & Sturgeon, 1982).

Although this literature highlights the theoretical and therapeutic importance of focusing on the families and social systems of disordered persons, attention has begun to be paid more specifically to the spouses of these individuals and to the quality of their marriages. There is now an expanding literature concerning the psychosocial functioning of couples in which one spouse is suffering from a psychiatric disorder, and it is clear from the results of these investigations that there is a strong and consistent relationship between psychopathology and a number of aspects of marriage and marital functioning. Indeed, findings from these studies are beginning to guide the strategies used by marital therapists in treating psychopathology.

Unfortunately, there is no single, concise source to which interested researchers and therapists can turn for information concerning the association between marriage and psychopathology. The purpose of this chapter, therefore, is to provide the reader with an overview of the findings of research conducted in this area. In presenting this overview, we draw on three broad bodies of research. We begin with an examination of the literature concerning the relationship between marital status and psychopathology; we then turn to research examining the quality of marriages and marital interactions of couples in which one spouse is exhibiting an emotional disorder; third, research concerning the application of marital therapy to the treatment of psychopathology is examined. In discussing these three literatures, we present the results of relevant investigations in the areas of depression, anxiety, alcoholism, and, where possible, schizophrenia. We conclude the chapter by outlining what we believe are critical issues and fruitful directions for future research in the study of marriage and psychopathology.

## MARITAL STATUS AND PSYCHOPATHOLOGY

Epidemiologists have consistently demonstrated an association between psychiatric disturbance and marital status (Bebbington, 1987; Odegaard, 1946). With remarkably few exceptions, the highest rates of psychological distress have been reported for unmarried individuals (i.e., those separated, divorced, widowed, and never married), whereas currently married persons evidence the lowest rates of distress (Bachrach, 1975). Indeed, Gove, Hughes, and Styles (1983) found that marital status was a more powerful predictor of mental health than education, income, age, race, or childhood background. Interestingly, this effect remains essentially unaffected by the social class of the sample, the type of sample examined (e.g., psychiatric patients, unselected community residents), or the dependent variable that is assessed (e.g., depression, anxiety, and mental illness, psychiatric hospitalization).

Although the association between marital status and psychopathology is well established, it is not yet clear *why* married people are more likely to be free of psychopathology than are their unmarried counterparts. Nevertheless, three major hypotheses have been proposed to account for this association. The *selection* hypothesis proposes that individuals who display psychiatric symptomatology are less desirable and, therefore, are less likely to marry than are their emotionally healthier counterparts. In contrast, the *causation* hypothesis posits that marriage either protects the individual from psychopathology or is an etiological factor in the disturbance. Finally, the *utilization* hypothesis proposes that the relationship between marital status and psychopathology is an artifact of married and unmarried individuals having different rates of hospitalization. Because of their importance in furthering our understanding of the nature of the relationship between marriage and psychopathology, we discuss each explanation in turn.

## Selection Hypothesis

According to the selection hypothesis, individuals who exhibit symptoms of psychopathology are less likely to get married than are emotionally healthier people. Moreover, if such people do get married, they are expected to demonstrate relatively high rates of divorce. Proponents of the selection hypothesis argue that marriage requires initiative, social skills, and an integrated personality. Individuals who are symptomatic or who are not currently symptomatic but have a vulnerability to develop a psychiatric disorder and therefore display behavioral anomalies, withdrawal, and a lack of social skills are less likely to develop intimate relationships. Consequently, these individuals are either selected out of the "marital pool" or marry individuals who are also impaired (cf. Merikangas, 1982). Not surprisingly, given the greater assertiveness and independence required of the traditional male role in courtship, this selection process is hypothesized to affect males more than females.

The success of the selection hypothesis is most apparent in schizophrenic and alcoholic populations. For example, on the basis of five epidemiological studies, Eaton (1975) concluded that the highest rates of hospitalization for schizophrenic disorders are for never-married individuals. Further, in all five of the studies, the hospitalization rates for never-married males were consistently greater than were the rates for never-married females, indicating that female schizophrenics are more likely to find mates than are their male counterparts. This pattern of findings, which is clearly consistent with the selection hypothesis, has also been reported by a number of other investigators. For example, Bachrach (1975), Farina, Garmezy, and Barry (1963), and Turner, Dopkech, and Labreche (1970) found not only that unmarried individuals had a higher proportion of psychiatric admissions for schizophrenia than did married persons but, further, that never-married males had a higher proportion of admissions and readmissions for schizophrenia than did never-married females. Finally, both Robertson (1974) and Reich and Thompson (1985) reported comparable findings for referrals for alcoholism. Indeed, Robertson found that the referral rate for never-married males was almost twice that for married males. In contrast, rates for females were consistently low and were undifferentiated for never-married and married categories in terms of referral for alcoholism.

## Causation Hypothesis

In contrast to the notion that emotional distress or psychiatric disorder prevents individuals from marrying, the causation hypothesis suggests that marriage itself either causes or protects against psychopathology. Thus, the different lifestyles associated with the various marital statuses produce different levels of stress, resulting in different rates of emotional disorder. According to the causation hypothesis, the finding that married persons have lower rates of emotional disturbance than do nonmarried individuals is the result of the increased social support available from the spouse (cf. Brown & Harris, 1978) and/or the increased stress of being single, separated, divorced, or widowed. Indeed, Gove (1973) has suggested that marriage offers spouses an enhanced sense of meaning and importance and that married persons are more likely than their unmarried counterparts to have someone who regulates their behavior in an adaptive way.

In one of the most comprehensive investigations of the causation hypothesis, Pearlin and Johnson (1977) examined the relationship between life strains and psychological distress in a large sample of married and unmarried persons. They found not only that a greater proportion of unmarried than married individuals experienced life strains (e.g., economic hardship, social isolation) but, further, that life strains had an unequal effect on these two groups of people. In summarizing their results, Pearlin and Johnson suggested that "marriage can function as a protective barrier against the distressful consequences of external threats. Marriage does not prevent economic and social problems from invading life, but it apparently can help people fend off the psychological assaults that such problems otherwise create" (p. 714).

Although the results of this study begin to elucidate the processes that may lead to the differential incidence of distress and psychopathology among married and unmarried individuals, it is important to note that a number of investigators have found that females generally exhibit higher rates of distress and disorder than do males (Gove & Tudor, 1973; Weissman & Klerman, 1977). More specifically, however, these gender differences seem to be largest among married persons. For example, using a sample of psychiatric inpatients with a variety of diagnoses, Kirshner and Johnston (1983) found that married women demonstrated significantly lower scores than did married men on the Global Assessment Scale (Endicott, Spitzer, Fleiss, & Cohen, 1976), whereas the scores of unmarried men and women did not differ. Thus, whereas marriage appears to be beneficial for men, married women have been found to exhibit greater psychopathology and distress than have both unmarried women and married men (see also Roberts & O'Keefe, 1981; Walker, Bettes, Kain, & Harvey, 1985).

In attempting to explain these gender differences, several investigators have invoked the concept of sex-role stereotypes. For example, Gove (1972) argues that marriage provides greater emotional satisfaction for men than it does for women, because men traditionally hold a number of major roles (e.g., head of household, primary wage earner) that are typically rewarding and socially desirable. In contrast, women tend to hold only one major role, that of housewife, and this role tends to be devalued in our society, is often frustrating and economically unrewarding, and limits women's capacity to maintain control over their lives (cf. Bernard, 1972). Gove suggests further that because it is relatively unstructured and offers no economic return, household-related work provides more time for women to brood and leaves them vulnerable and dependent on their husbands for economic support. Thus, married men and women are hypothesized to be differentially protected against psychopathology and emotional disorder by virtue of the number of roles associated with each gender and the amount of gratification these roles provide.

In support of this position, a number of investigators have demonstrated that women who are employed outside of the home have lower levels of psychiatric symptomatology and distress than do women in more traditionally female roles (Radloff, 1975). Weissman, Pincus, Radding, Lawrence, and Siegel (1973), for example, found that as women gained employment, they became less depressed. In a recent prospective study of postpartum depression conducted in our own laboratory (Gotlib, Whiffen, Mount, Milne, & Cordy, 1989), we found similar evidence of the potentially detrimental effects of traditional female roles. Studying a large sample of pregnant women, we found that those who did not work outside of the home were significantly more likely to become depressed following the birth of a child than were those who were employed. Thus, although there have also been negative results in this area (Lennon, 1987), it appears that gender roles may mediate the relationship between marital status and psychopathology.

Finally, it is important to note that, although the results of these studies suggest that stereotypic female roles may exacerbate psychiatric symptomatology, this explanation does not account adequately for the high level of separated and divorced individuals who experience distress and who seek psychological or psychiatric treatment. Hirschfeld and Cross (1981), for example, note that separated and divorced women report the highest levels of depressive symptoms. In a variant of the causation hypothesis designed to explain results such as these, Bloom, Asher, and White (1978) and Ensel (1986) suggest that the *change* from being married to becoming separated, divorced, or widowed represents a stressful life event in which self-conceptions may be challenged and social networks dissolved, thereby leading to increased distress and emotional disorder. Further, one of the common consequences of divorce for women, and especially for women with young children, is a diminished socioeconomic status. Consequently, not only is the role of unmarried mother potentially stressful and unrewarding following divorce but, further, the associated stressors may be magnified.

## Utilization Hypothesis

According to the differential utilization hypothesis, although single and married individuals demonstrate essentially equivalent levels of psychopathology, single people are more likely to be hospitalized, whereas married individuals enter into treatment less frequently or utilize alternative treatments. For example, Hammer (1963) suggested that married persons with schizophrenic symptoms may be less likely than unmarried persons to utilize treatment facilities because their spouses may care for them and mediate their relationship to the community.

In a study described earlier, Eaton (1975) evaluated the utilization hypothesis in regard to schizophrenia. Eaton argued that widowed persons may have higher rates of first admission to hospital than married persons because of etiological factors *or* differential utilization. If widowed persons have longer treatment durations than do married persons, however, it is likely because of differential utilization. Thus, Eaton calculated a ratio comparing the duration of psychiatric hospitalization of currently married and widowed individuals, matched for age. If the utilization theory were correct, the ratio of duration of widowed to married persons would be greater than 1.00. In fact, Eaton found the ratio to be greater than 1.00 for males and females in 9 out of 10 comparisons, providing strong support for the utilization hypothesis.

Robertson (1974) also examined the differential utilization hypothesis for a large sample of first admissions to hospital between 1963 and 1967 by comparing the marital status of hospital admission with the marital status of referrals to extramural psychiatric services. Consistent with the utilization hypothesis, Robertson found that unmarried persons with mental disorders are more likely to be admitted to hospitals than their married counterparts, who are more likely to be referred to extramural psychiatric services in the community. Similar results were reported by Franklin, Kittredge, and Thrasher (1975), who found that, compared with married patients, a higher proportion of single, separated, and divorced patients were readmitted to hospital within 1 year of discharge from their initial hospitalization. Because of the differential hospitalization of the single and married, these investigators caution that reliable judgments about the incidence of psychopathology in different marital groups cannot be made on the basis of hospital admission studies alone.

## Summary

We have seen, therefore, that the selection, causation, and differential utilization hypotheses all offer feasible explanations for the general finding of the greater incidence of psychopathology among the unmarried. Indeed, it may well be the case that different theories must be invoked when we consider different types of categories of psychopathology. The selection hypothesis, for example, may be a better explanation when considering more severe psychiatric disorders, such as schizophrenia and alcoholism, whereas the causation hypothesis may provide a better explanation for the elevated incidence of depressive symptoms among married women. Although these theories each provide a partial explanation of the relationship among marital status, gender, and psychopathology, they become less satisfactory when more complex associations are considered, which include age, education, and employment status. And as Walker et al. (1985) have pointed out, despite the number of studies examining marital status and psychopathology, the percentage of variance in psychopathology accounted for by marital status and gender interactions is typically quite small.

One of the primary difficulties in examining the role of marital status in psychopathology involves the relatively superficial and insensitive nature of this construct. In particular, marital status fails to consider the quality of the marital relationship, which may mediate the association between marriage and psychopathology. Indeed, Renne (1971) found that both males and females who are dissatisfied with their marriages are in poorer mental health than are their separated and divorced counterparts: "Unhappily married persons are more susceptible than other married persons or divorced persons to physical and psychological health problems . . . because marriage itself affects health" (p. 338). As we see in the following sections, research examining the quality of marriages in which one spouse is suffering from a psychiatric disturbance indicates clearly that these marriages are characterized by elevated levels of tension and distress and are at increased risk for divorce. Thus, it is to the relationship between marital distress and psychopathology that we now turn.

## MARITAL DISTRESS AND PSYCHOPATHOLOGY

The association between marital distress and psychopathology has been the focus of considerable research by psychologists in recent years, and a number of investigations implicate marital distress and dysfunction in both the etiology and course of emotional disorder. Sager, Gundlach, and Kremer (1968), for example, estimated that 50% of all patients who seek psychotherapy do so because of marital problems. A growing body of literature also demonstrates that treatment outcome is less favorable in couples who are experiencing marital distress and that relapse is more likely for those patients who return to unsatisfying marriages (Hooley, 1986).

Evidence from a variety of sources has long indicated that living with a psychiatrically disturbed person exerts a significant toll on the individual's spouse and family, financially, emotionally, and physically (Claussen & Yarrow, 1955; Noh & Avison, 1988). Targum, Dibble, Davenport, and Gershon (1981), for example, found that over half of the spouses of bipolar depressed patients indicated that they regretted having married. More recently, Noh and Turner (1987) reported that the perception of the psychiatric patient as a burden was one of the most important correlates of psychologial distress among their spouses. Indeed, Coyne, Kessler, et al. (1987) found that 40% of the spouses of depressed persons were themselves sufficiently distressed to warrant referral for psychotherapy.

In the following sections, we review representative research examining the relationship between marital distress and depression, anxiety, alcoholism, and schizophrenia. There are remarkable similarities in the results of these studies, indicating that all of these forms of psychopathology may be characterized by dysfunctional marriages.

## Marital Distress and Depression

The association between depression and marital quality has generated the greatest interest of any disorder, not only because of the consistent epidemiological finding of a high rate of depression among married women (Radloff, 1975) but also because of the growing recognition of the importance of the interpersonal context of this disorder (Brown & Harris, 1978; Coyne, Kahn, & Gotlib, 1987; Gotlib & Whiffen, in press).

Considerable and varied evidence attests to the relationship between marital distress and depression. For example, Paykel et al. (1969) found that the most frequent life event preceding the onset of depression was an increase in arguments with the spouse. Similarly, Vaughn and Leff (1976) found that depressives are more vulnerable than schizophrenics to hostile statements made by family members, and Schless, Schwartz, Goetz, and Mendels (1974) demonstrated that this vulnerability to marriage-related stresses persists after depressed patients recover. Indeed, Merikangas (1984) reported a divorce rate in depressed patients 2 years after discharge that was nine times that of the general population. Finally, recent investigations have reported that the lack of an intimate, confiding relationship with a spouse or boyfriend increased women's vulnerability for depression (Brown & Harris, 1978; Costello, 1982).

The results of these investigations have provided the foundation for studies examining more systematically the marital relationships of depressed persons. Weissman and her colleagues (Rounsaville, Weissman, Prusoff, & Herceg-Baron, 1979; Weissman & Paykel, 1974) conducted structured interviews with 40 depressed female psychiatric outpatients over the course of their treatment. Weissman found that these patients reported greatest impairment as wives and mothers, expressing problems in the areas of affection, dependency, sexual functioning, and communication. The marital relationships of the depressed women were characterized by friction and hostility, and the women tended to be less assertive and less affectionate toward their spouses than were matched normal controls. Interestingly, marital disputes were an important determinant of treatment outcome for these women: those who reported having marital disputes demonstrated little improvement in their symptoms and social functioning following individual therapy. Furthermore, at a 4-year follow-up, marital problems were found to persist, even though the women were no longer severely depressed (Bothwell & Weissman, 1977; see also Gotlib & Lee, 1989).

Although Weissman's results were corroborated by other investigators (Freden, 1982), the validity of findings obtained with self-report data has been questioned, particularly in light of the depression-associated cognitive distortion posited by Beck's model of depression (Beck, 1967; Beck, Rush, Shaw, & Emery, 1979). To address this concern, investigators have begun to utilize direct observational methods.

In one of the first such observational studies, Hinchliffe, Hooper, and Roberts (1978) examined the behavior of 20 depressed patients interacting with their spouses and with opposite-sex strangers. Compared to the interactions of nondepressed surgery control patients, couples with a depressed spouse showed greater conflict, tension, and negative expressiveness. The interactions of the depressed patients were also characterized by a greater number of interruptions and a greater frequency of pauses. After recovery, the interactions of the 10 male depressed patients were less negative and resembled those of the surgical controls; consistent with Weissman and Paykel's (1974) findings, however, the depressed women continued to show high levels of tension and negative expressiveness.

Several other groups of investigators have found the interactions of depressed persons and their spouses to be characterized by hostility. Arkowitz, Holliday, and Hutter (1982), for example, found that following interactions with their wives, husbands of depressed women reported feeling more hostile than did husbands of psychiatric and nonpsychiatric control subjects. Similarly, Kahn, Coyne, and Margolin (1985) reported that couples with a depressed spouse were sadder and angrier following marital interactions and experienced each other as more negative, hostile, mistrusting, and detached than did nondepressed couples.

Two studies conducted in our laboratory provide further evidence of the negative marital interactions of depressed persons. In the first, Kowalik and Gotlib (1987) had depressed and nondepressed psychiatric outpatients and nondepressed nonpsychiatric controls interact with their spouses while they simultaneously coded both the intended impact of their own behavior and their perceptions of their spouses' behavior. Compared with the nondepressed controls, the depressed patients were found to code a lower percentage of their messages as positive and a higher percentage as negative, indicating that they perceived the interactions and their spouses as problematic. Interestingly, however, behavioral ratings made by observers did not differentiate among the three groups of subjects and spouses. In the second study, Gotlib and Whiffen (1989) examined marital satisfaction and interpersonal behavior in groups of depressed psychiatric inpatients, nondepressed medical patients, and nondepressed community controls. Subjects and their spouses completed measures of marital satisfaction and then participated in a 20-minute marital interaction task. Both the depressed and the medical patients and their spouses reported significantly lower marital satisfaction than did the community control couples. Furthermore, during the marital interaction, couples in both patient groups smiled less, exhibited less pleasant facial expression, and maintained eye contact less frequently than did the nonpatient control couples. The results of these studies suggest, therefore, that depressed persons and their spouses perceive their marital interactions to be marked by tension and hostility.

Subsequent investigations have attempted to separate the disruptive effects of marital distress from those of depression. Hautzinger, Linden, and Hoffman (1982) examined 26 couples seeking marital therapy, in which half had a depressed spouse and the others did not. Hautzinger et al. found that the communication patterns of the depressed–distressed couples were more uneven, negative, and asymmetric than were the communications of the distressed–nondepressed couples, suggesting an additive effect of marital distress and depression.

Biglan and Hops and their colleagues (Biglan et al., 1985; Hops et al., 1987) compared the marital interactions of couples who were neither depressed nor maritally distressed with those of two groups of couples in which the wife was clinically depressed.

In one of these two groups the couples were also reporting marital distress, whereas in the other the level of marital distress was relatively low. Biglan et al. found that, regardless of level of marital distress, depressed women exhibited higher rates of depressive affect and behavior and lower rates of problem-solving behavior than did either their husbands or the nondepressed control spouses. Moreover, in examining the conditional probabilities of these interactional behaviors, Biglan and Hops found that the depressed wives' dysphoric displays served to reduce the likelihood of their husbands' aversive behaviors.

Finally, Ruscher and Gotlib (1988) examined the effects of marital distress and depression on the marital interactions of mildly depressed couples from the community and nondepressed control couples. The results indicated that, compared with nondepressed couples, couples in which one partner was depressed emitted a lower proportion of positive verbal behaviors and a greater proportion of negative verbal and nonverbal behaviors. Interestingly, this pattern of results was no longer significant when level of marital satisfaction was covaried, suggesting that the interactional effects of depression obtained in this sample were a function of marital distress.

The results reviewed above suggest that the marriages of depressed persons are dysfunctional. Moreover, there is evidence to suggest that problematic marital interactions and low marital satisfaction may not be specific to depression but, rather, may be characteristic of couples in which one spouse is experiencing any form of disorder. As we discuss below, marital dysfunction is also associated with agoraphobia, alcoholism, and schizophrenia.

## Marital Distress and Anxiety

In a recent epidemiological study, Myers et al. (1984) found that the most frequently treated anxiety disorders were phobic reactions. Interestingly, although simple phobias have the highest incidence of all phobias in the general population, agoraphobia is the most common complaint of those individuals seeking treatment. Because agoraphobia is most prevalent in married women (Hafner, 1986), it is not surprising to find that most of the theory and research in this area have focused on women and their marital relations. In this section, therefore, we examine studies of marital quality among agoraphobic female patients and their spouses.

The importance of the marital relationship in the etiology, maintenance, and recovery from agoraphobic conditions has been highlighted by a number of theorists and researchers. Goldstein (1970; Chambless & Goldstein, 1981), for example, posited that most agoraphobics are in unsatisfying relationships from which they wish to flee, but they do not leave because they fear independence. Similarly, Fodor (1974) suggested that agoraphobic women have been reinforced for extreme stereotypic female behavior and, consequently, become especially helpless, fearful, and dependent. Consistent with these postulations, Hand, Lamontagne, and Marks (1974) estimated that as many as 67% of agoraphobic women experience significant marital distress. It is important to note, however, that these formulations and statistics are derived largely from case studies and uncontrolled investigations (Fry, 1962; Goodstein & Swift, 1977).

The results of better-controlled empirical examinations of marital distress and agoraphobia are less consistent in implicating marital dissatisfaction in this disorder. Buglass et al. (1977) examined the marital relationships of a group of agoraphobic women and a nonpsychiatric control group and found that, although a small number of the marriages of the agoraphobic women were clearly problematic, most were comparable to those of the control women with respect to social, domestic, and decision-making activities. In a similar investigation, Arrindell and Emmelkamp (1986) assessed marital adjustment and intimacy in female agoraphobic patients and their spouses as well as in nonphobic female psychiatric patients and their husbands, maritally distressed couples, and happily married couples. Although agoraphobic patients and their partners rated their marriages as somewhat less satisfactory than did the happily married controls, they nevertheless reported significantly greater marital satisfaction than did both the psychiatric control couples and the maritally distressed controls. Both of these studies, therefore, indicate that agoraphobic couples report equivalent levels of marital satisfaction to those of nonpsychiatric, nondistressed couples.

In evaluating this body of literature, it is important to realize that agoraphobic patients who also exhibited marked depressive mood were excluded from these studies. For example, whereas Buglass et al. (1977) explicitly excluded agoraphobics with depressed mood, Arrindell and Emmelkamp (1986) used DSM-III criteria for agoraphobia, which calls for rejection of a diagnosis of agoraphobia if there is also a major affective disorder that appeared to have preceded the agoraphobic symptoms. Given the high prevalence of depressive disorders among agoraphobic patients (Chambless & Goldstein, 1981), it is likely that the subjects in these studies represent a select subsample of women with minimal levels of depression. Moreover, given the association described earlier between depression and marital distress, this exclusion criterion probably also eliminated maritally distressed agoraphobic women from the studies. Thus, the results of these studies should be interpreted with some caution. Finally, although a change in diagnostic criteria in DSM-III-R now permits a diagnosis of agoraphobia in the presence of a coexisting depressive disorder, there have been no studies of the marriages of agoraphobic patients using these criteria. It is clear, however, that future studies in this area have the potential to elucidate the nature of the relationship among depression, anxiety, and marital dysfunction.

## Marital Distress and Alcoholism

Compared with depression and agoraphobia, the alcoholism literature is in a relatively early stage with respect to the study of marital interactions and adjustment. Despite its extensive effects on the family, alcoholism has been viewed traditionally as an individual problem. In fact, research examining the family interactions of alcoholics has resulted in fewer than a dozen published studies between 1974 and 1987, and even fewer investigations have examined the relationship between marital satisfaction and alcoholism.

The results of studies using retrospective reports are often contradictory. Davis (1976) and Tamerin, Toler, DeWolfe, Packer, and Neuman (1973), for example, found that alcoholic patients and their spouses described the alcoholic in positive terms when he was sober and negatively when he was intoxicated. Wiseman (1981) interviewed wives of alcoholics and found that, in contrast to the results reported by Davis and Tamerin et al., periods of sobriety were associated with increased levels of marital tension in which the wives were frequently critical of their husbands. Wiseman noted that the alcoholic husbands were less likely to be reinforced for sobriety, thereby perpetuating the alcoholism. Moreover, at least for the alcoholic spouse, marital satisfaction may be increased during intoxicated periods because of decreased levels of criticism (O'Farrell & Birchler, 1987).

These discrepancies between reports of sober and intoxicated conditions led researchers to include direct observations of couples while the alcoholic spouse was sober and intoxicated. In one of the first such studies, Steinglass, Davis, and Berenson (1977) found that during periods of intoxication, interpersonal behavior became more exaggerated or amplified and restricted or narrow in range. Moreover, the behaviors that emerged during these periods were often more positive than those observed when the couple was sober. Jacob, Dunn, and Leonard (1983) similarly found that increased use of alcohol was associated with greater levels of marital satisfaction. Thus, according to these studies, alcohol use appears to provide a temporary solution to a dysfunctional marital system.

Billings, Kessler, Gomberg, and Weiner (1979) examined the marital interactions of alcoholic, nonalcoholic but maritally distressed, and normal couples under drinking and nondrinking conditions. The results of this study indicated that both alcoholic and maritally distressed nonalcoholic couples displayed more negative behavior and greater hostility than did the nondistressed, nonalcoholic controls. Moreover, the availability of alcohol had little effect on the interaction. As Jacob and Seilhamer (1987) note, however, because the drinking manipulation in this study was extremely weak (e.g., only half of the alcoholic couples chose to drink during the drinking session), the results tell us little about the impact of alcohol ingestion on marital interaction.

The findings of studies that used more effective drinking manipulations are inconsistent. Frankenstein, Hay, and Nathan (1985) found that more positive verbalizations were expressed in the alcohol than in the no-alcohol sessions. Indeed, the nonalcoholic spouses doubled their rate of positive verbal behaviors when their alcoholic spouses were intoxicated. In contrast, however, Jacob and his colleagues (Jacob & Krahn, 1988; Jacob, Ritchey, Cvitkovic, & Blane, 1981) found that alcohol increased *negative* behaviors in interactions of alcoholics and their spouses. Jacob and Seilhamer (1987) discuss possible reasons for these discrepant findings, which include differences in level of intoxication and in subject selection criteria. In particular, Jacob and Seilhamer emphasize the importance of distinguishing between binge drinkers and steady drinkers (Dunn, Jacob, Hummon, & Seilhamer, 1987; Jacob et al., 1983). For example, Jacob and Leonard (1988) found different patterns of marital interactions for binge versus steady drinkers. Clearly, therefore, future studies must consider more explicitly the alcoholic spouse's drinking behavior.

Finally, the long-term outcome for marital satisfaction in relationship to alcohol consumption must be examined to determine how these factors affect the alcoholics' marriages over time. In this regard, Moos, Finney, and Gamble (1982) compared remitted alcoholics and relapsed alcoholics to a group of matched community control subjects on a variety of sociodemographic, coping, social, health-related, and family and work environment measures. Moos et al. found few differences between spouses of recovered alcoholics and community control spouses. In contrast, compared to control spouses, spouses of relapsed or nonrecovered alcoholics experienced more negative life events, drank more alcohol, participated in fewer social activities, had less family cohesiveness, and participated in fewer recreational activities with their families. It appears from this study, therefore, that marital adjustment improves over time for alcoholics and their spouses who recover from the disorder.

## Marital Distress and Schizophrenia

The literature examining the relationship of schizophrenic disorders and marital distress is virtually nonexistent. As we noted earlier, the large proportion of schizophrenic individuals are unmarried, particularly if the patient is male. Consequently, most of the literature examining the interactions of schizophrenic patients with others is restricted to interactions with parents. One notable exception is research conducted by Hooley, Richters, Weintraub, and Neale (1987), in which married subjects from the Stony Brook High Risk Project were selected and data on level of marital distress, DSM-III diagnosis, and associated symptoms were obtained. No difference in the level of spouse's marital satisfaction was found among schizophrenic, depressed, and impulse-control disorders. When subjects were reclassified into groups based on symptom profiles, however, significant differences in marital satisfaction emerged. In this reclassification, subjects were assigned to groups based on their predominant positive or negative symptom patterns (see Andreasen, 1982). Whereas positive symptoms were defined as florid symptomatology or behavioral excesses (e.g., hallucinations, delusions), negative symptoms were described as a lack or deficit in normal functioning (e.g., self-neglect, apathy).

Hooley et al. (1987) proposed a symptom controllability model in which symptoms that are perceived by others as behavioral excesses or as out of patient control (i.e., positive symptoms) would be associated with less marital distress, whereas symptoms that are viewed as deficits in normal behavior (i.e., negative symptoms) would be associated with greater levels of marital dissatisfaction. When patients were categorized on the basis of their predominant symptomatology, Hooley et al. found that spouses of patients with positive symptom profiles reported higher marital satisfaction than did spouses of patients with negative profiles. Thus, even though the patients who were identified as positive-symptom patients were rated by clinicians as significantly more disturbed than were negative-symptom patients, their spouses were less likely to be maritally distressed. The results of this study suggest, therefore, that level of marital functioning may play a role in schizophrenia. Despite these promising findings, however, it is clear that until additional research is conducted in this area, we can say little regarding the relationship between marital functioning and schizophrenia.

## Summary

The investigations examined in this section were concerned with very different disorders. Although there is some overlap in the symptom patterns exhibited by individuals diagnosed as depressed, anxious, alcoholic, and schizophrenic (Gotlib & Cane, 1989), there are clearly behavioral differences among these disorders. Nevertheless, there is remarkable similarity in both the concepts and the results described by researchers in this field. Marriages of couples in which one spouse is exhibiting a psychiatric or emotional disturbance have been found to be characterized by elevated levels of negative affect, conflict, tension, hostility, and marital distress. Moreover, this pattern of results has been obtained both with self-report and with observational methodologies. Indeed, the consistency of findings indicating an association of marital distress and psychopathology has led investigators to examine the efficacy of intervention strategies for psychiatric disorders that involve focusing on the marriage and/or simply including the spouse in therapy. In the final major section of this chapter, therefore, we present an overview of research examining the effectiveness of marital and spouse-involved treatments for depression, agoraphobia, alcoholism, and schizophrenia.

## MARITAL THERAPY AND PSYCHOPATHOLOGY

Only recently has marital therapy begun to be utilized in the treatment of emotional disorders (Gotlib & Colby, 1987). As Jacobson, Holtzworth-Munroe, and Schmaling (1989) have noted, there are three rationales for using marital therapy or, at the least, for involving the spouse in treatment. First, family therapists typically view psychiatric disorder as resulting from a disturbed family environment; consequently, change in the marital system is a necessary prerequisite to change in the patient. Second, proponents of a social–environmental perspective consider the higher rates of emotional disturbance in women to be a function of their stereotypic marital role and call for the involvement of the spouse in therapy. Finally, a growing number of cognitive and behavioral therapists are recognizing the support and resource value of the spouse as an adjunct to treatment. Thus, for a number of reasons, there is now an increasing body of literature concerning the efficacy of marital therapy or spouse involvement for the treatment of emotional disorders. In the sections that follow we present the results of relevant research in the areas of depression, agoraphobia, alcoholism, and schizophrenia.

## Marital Therapy and Depression

The consistent association between depression and marital distress has led investigators to examine the efficacy of marital therapy in the treatment of this disorder. As we shall see, the results of these studies highlight the need to treat not only the symptoms of depression but the marital relationship as well.

Based on an early series of case studies, Lewinsohn and his colleagues (Lewinsohn & Atwood, 1969; Lewinsohn & Schaffer, 1971) suggested that providing patients and their spouses with feedback about their interpersonal behaviors can result in a decrease in depression and an improvement in their marital relationships. In a more controlled investigation, McLean, Ogston, and Grauer (1973) examined the effects of conjoint marital therapy on the valence of communications in depressed patients and their spouses. Couples were trained to monitor the feedback they were giving to their spouses. At a 3-month follow-up, depressed couples receiving this marital therapy demonstrated significant reductions in their depressed mood and in the frequency of their negative interactions.

Friedman (1975) described encouraging results of a marital/family treatment for depression. Both drug and marital therapy showed substantial advantages over placebo conditions. Moreover, whereas drug therapy was associated with early improvement in clinical symptoms, marital therapy led to longer-term improvement in the patient's participation and performance in family role tasks, a reduction in interpersonal hostility, and improvement in their perceptions of the quality of their marriages. Similar results were also reported by Beach and O'Leary (1986), who examined the relative efficacy of conjoint behavior marital therapy, individual cognitive therapy, and a waiting-list control condition for the treatment of depression. Because their report is based on only eight subjects, it is inappropriate to draw firm conclusions about the differential effectiveness of these intervention approaches. Nevertheless, it is noteworthy that only the wives who received marital therapy demonstrated both clinically significant reductions in depressive symptomatology and a marked reduction in marital functioning.

The results of Friedman's (1975) and Beach and O'Leary's (1986) studies are consistent with Weissman's (1979) observations that, whereas antidepressant medication combined with individual psychotherapy can reduce depressive symptoms, it appears to have little effect on marital difficulties. Indeed, Weissman and Klerman (1973) reported that despite symptomatic improvement, marital difficulties were the single problem area discussed most frequently by depressed women in maintenance therapy. Moreover, in a 4-year follow-up of these women, Bothwell and Weissman (1977) reported that although the women were asymptomatic with respect to depression, they continued to report problems with marital disputes.

Three recently developed interpersonal approaches to therapy for depression have yielded promising results. First, Klerman, Weissman, Rounsaville, and Chevron (1984) have described their Interpersonal Psychotherapy (IPT), which is based on the assumption that depression results from difficulties in the interpersonal relationships between depressed persons and their significant others. Interpersonal Psychotherapy, therefore, attempts to improve interpersonal functioning and to alleviate depressive symptoms by concentrating on how the patient is coping with current interpersonal stressors. DiMascio et al. (1979) and Weissman et al. (1979) have demonstrated that IPT is as effective as pharmacotherapy in reducing depressive symptomatology and is more effective in improving interpersonal functioning. Furthermore, at a 1-year follow-up, patients who had received IPT alone or in combination with pharmacotherapy demonstrated significantly better social functioning than did patients who had received pharmacotherapy alone (Weissman, Klerman, Prusoff, Sholomskas, & Padian, 1981).

The second interpersonal approach to therapy is Inpatient Family Intervention (IFI), described by Clarkin et al. (1986) for the treatment of hospitalized depressed patients. Patients and relevant family members meet regularly during the patient's hospitalization with a family therapist and the patient's primary therapist acting as cotherapists. The IFI is aimed at helping patients and their families accept and understand the current illness and at identifying possible precipitating stressors, both within and outside of the family; IFI also attempts to identify family interaction patterns that may produce stress for the patient and to plan strategies to minimize potential stressors. Glick et al. (1985) reported that both depressed and schizophrenic patients demonstrated favorable short-term response to IFI with respect to clinical symptomatology. Haas et al. (1988) found subsequently that depressed female patients appeared to benefit more from IFI treatment than did depressed males in terms of both clinical symptoms and family functioning, and Spencer et al. (1988) have documented the persistence of these effects 6 months later.

Finally, Gotlib and Colby (1987) have presented an interpersonal systems approach to the conceptualization of depression and have outlined explicit strategies and procedures to be used in assessing and treating depressed patients and their spouses. Gotlib and Colby delineate circumstances under which the spouses or relatives of depressed individuals should be involved in therapy and describe the effective use of such therapeutic procedures as joining, enactment, reframing, restructuring, and altering family boundaries. Although additional empirical work is required to refine the techniques described and to further validate the efficacy of this intervention, the results of initial studies utilizing this interpersonal approach to the treatment of depression are promising.

## Marital Therapy and Agoraphobia

Agoraphobia has been conceptualized historically as a systemic difficulty in which domineering men, typically raised in father-absent families, marry dependent women. The males in such marriages are hypothesized to identify with the stereotypic male sex roles as a consequence of father absence and to reinforce their wives' dependency and agoraphobic symptomatology in order to maintain their own sense of self. Thus, as we note earlier in the chapter, wives in these marriages are believed to hold stereotypic female sex-role perspectives that lead to marital difficulties (cf. Hafner, 1986). Moreover, theorists have suggested that husbands may reinforce their wives' agoraphobic symptomatology and that poor levels of marital adjustment will play an etiological role in these marriages. Indeed, some investigators have suggested that symptomatic reduction in agoraphobic wives may have a *negative* impact on the husbands' own psychological well-being and/or result in greater levels of marital distress.

A number of studies have examined marital distress and treatment outcomes in agoraphobic patients who were treated either alone or together with their spouses. Because of the importance attached to marital satisfaction in agoraphobia, researchers have examined levels of marital distress before and after treatment (Buglass et al., 1977; Cobb, McDonald, Marks, & Stern, 1980). However, evidence for the existence of marital distress prior to treatment has not been found consistently (Barlow et al., 1984; Cerny, Barlow, Craske, & Himadi, 1988), and findings concerning posttreatment levels of marital satisfaction have also been inconsistent. Whereas some investigators have reported increased levels of marital satisfaction accompanying reduction in agoraphobic symptomatology (Barlow et al., 1984; Himadi, Cerny, Barlow, Cohen, & O'Brien, 1986), others have found the husband's levels of marital satisfaction and psychological well-being to *decrease* following improvement in the wives (Hafner, 1977; Milton & Hafner, 1979). Indeed, only Barlow et al. (1984) found that including the spouse in treatment resulted in better and quicker symptomatic improvement than did treatment not involving the spouse.

Finally, a number of studies have examined how levels of marital satisfaction affect treatment outcome, again with inconsistent results. For example, whereas Himadi et al. (1986) found that pretreatment levels of marital satisfaction had no impact on treatment outcome, Milton and Hafner (1979) found that marriages characterized by lower marital satisfaction improved less in treatment and were more likely to relapse during follow-up. Similarly, Monteiro, Marks, and Ramm (1985) found that patients with better initial marital adjustment improved more than did patients with lower initial levels of marital adjustment; nevertheless, even the patients with poor marital adjustment improved significantly.

In general, therefore, studies that have involved the spouse in the treatment of agoraphobia have yielded equivocal results. Himadi et al. (1986) have speculated that the sometimes-reported negative results on husbands' mental health might be related to the fact that there were significant changes in the patients' behaviors that the spouse did not understand. They suggested that the negative effects on spouses may have resulted from their lack of involvement in the therapeutic process. Nevertheless, it is clear that much more research is required examining the effects of marital or spouse-involved treatment on agoraphobic symptoms and marital distress.

## Marital Therapy and Alcoholism

As we noted earlier, the alcoholism literature has evolved from studies designed to assess family interactions and drinking behavior. These early studies suggested that drinking stabilized dysfunctional families, allowing the expression of previously repressed behaviors or feelings. Subsequent examination of marital interactions and experimentally induced drinking have provided some support for these notions (e.g., Frankenstein et al., 1985), although the findings of other investigations stand in direct contrast (Jacob et al., 1981). In any case, marital therapy is now being used increasingly in the treatment of alcoholism.

At least two studies examining the treatment efficacy of marital therapies for alcoholism have been reported. O'Farrell, Cutter, and Floyd (1985) compared the effects of behavioral marital therapy and interactional couples therapy groups to an individual-counseling, no-marital-treatment control group. Overall, O'Farrell et al. found that, although drinking behavior decreased in all three groups, marital satisfaction improved most in the behavioral marital therapy group. In a 2-year follow-up of these patients conducted to assess their attributions for subsequent drinking relapse, Maisto, O'Farrell, Connors, McKay, and Pelcovits (1988) found that a high proportion of the patients (and particularly those who had received marital therapy) reported that their spouses contributed to their subsequent relapses. As Maisto et al. state, "the findings were consistent with the assumptions of marital therapy for alcoholism in suggesting that spouse and other family members are viewed by many patients as influencing both their resumption of drinking and the termination of relapse episodes" (p. 82).

In the second controlled investigation in this area, McCrady et al. (1986) compared three approaches to the treatment of alcoholics and their spouses. In one condition, the spouse was required to be present but was asked not to participate actively in treatment. The second condition included some marital therapy that was restricted to alcohol-related issues. Finally, the third condition included these components as well as behavioral marital therapy. McCrady et al. found that subjects in all three groups demonstrated marked decreases in the frequency of their drinking as well as increases in their levels of marital satisfaction. Consistent with the results of the O'Farrell et al. (1985) study, subjects in the behavioral marital therapy condition demonstrated more rapid drinking reductions, relapsed less rapidly after treatment, and maintained their marital satisfaction longer than did subjects in the alcohol-focused spouse-involvement group. Although both studies suggest that behavioral marital therapy may be an important adjunct to traditional treatments for alcoholism, this conclusion awaits further research.

## Marital Therapy and Schizophrenia

Because schizophrenia is characterized by a preponderance of unmarried individuals, marital treatment for this disorder is less common than is the case for other disorders. In fact, we were able to find only one controlled investigation examining the efficacy of marital therapy in the treatment of schizophrenia. Alanen and Kinnunen (1975) studied 30 married couples in which one spouse was diagnosed as schizophrenic and had become ill subsequent to the marriage. In half of the couples the index patient was the husband, and in the other half the wife. Eight female patients and their spouses and 10 male patients and their spouses participated in the conjoint marital therapy component of this study. Alanen and Kinnunen examined a number of variables and present a complex and interesting series of discussions concerning the patients' and spouses' prepsychotic personalities, psychometric testing, and subclassification of marital dyads based on patterns of marital interactions. Overall, the outcome of marital therapy was rated by the therapists as favorable for 10 of the couples; ambiguous or little change was found for the other eight couples. Furthermore, based on the subclassifications derived from the interaction patterns, Alanen and Kinnunen found marital therapy to be more effective in couples whose interaction was characterized by the patient's superficial domination and the spouse's passive but supportive style than in marriages that were characterized by passive–dependent patients and dominating and unempathic spouses.

More research is needed to examine the value of marital therapy in the treatment of schizophrenic disorders, particularly given the role that critical interpersonal styles of significant family members have been found to play in the relapse of schizophrenics (Vaughn & Leff, 1976). We must also acknowledge, however, that of the disorders examined in this chapter, it is likely that the exclusive use of marital therapy will be least beneficial in the treatment of schizophrenia.

## Summary

There is growing evidence that marital therapy or spouse involvement represents a promising direction in the treatment of psychopathology. Although individual therapy has been found to be effective in reducing the level of symptomatology in a number of disorders, it is less effective in ameliorating difficulties in marital functioning. In both depression and anxiety, marital therapy has been demonstrated to achieve both symptom relief and a reduction in marital discord. As Jacobson et al. (1989) note, however, the literature in this area is still in its early stages, and firm conclusions await further research.


## CONCLUDING COMMENTS

We have attempted in this chapter to provide an overview of research examining the relationship between marriage and psychopathology. Three distinct bodies of literature attest to the strength and consistency of this relationship. First, studies examining the association between marital status and psychopathology indicate that unmarried individuals generally exhibit higher rates of emotional disorder than do their married counterparts. Although the presence of psychopathology probably prevents a significant number of people from marrying and thereby contributes to the higher rate of disorder among the unmarried, we have also reviewed evidence that marriage itself may serve either to protect individuals from psychopathology or, in the case of depression and women, to contribute to the development of disorder. Indeed, it is probable that both these explanations are viable, depending on the particular disorder under investigation.

Second, there is little question that individuals who exhibit symptoms of psychopathology also experience significant levels of marital distress. Across a number of disorders, investigators using both self-report and observational methodologies have consistently found the marriages of psychiatrically disturbed individuals to be characterized by negative interactions, hostility, and increased levels of conflict. Moreover, there is growing evidence that these marital difficulties persist long after the individual is no longer symptomatic and that patients who return from hospital to problematic marriages have a higher rate of relapse than do individuals whose marriages are more satisfying.

The third body of research examined in this chapter concerns the efficacy of marital therapy or spouse involvement in the treatment of psychiatric disorder. Although this literature is significantly smaller than the other two areas, the results of the studies that have been conducted indicate that marital therapy may be a promising approach to the treatment of these disorders; this is particularly true for studies involving depressed and agoraphobic patients.

Given the diversity of studies and areas that we have considered here, it is difficult to identify key issues and to make recommendations for future research. Nevertheless, one issue in particular that cuts across research in all of these areas concerns the causal nature of the relationship between marriage and psychopathology. For example, we have highlighted theories that seek to explain the association between psychopathology and marital status. Thus, whereas the selection hypothesis proposes that psychopathology leads to differences in marital status, the causation hypothesis posits that, because of their different associated lifestyles and stressors, different marital statuses result differentially in psychopathology. Similarly, with respect to marital satisfaction, it is as plausible to posit that marital distress leads to psychopathology as it is to suggest that psychopathology in one spouse results in decreased marital satisfaction for the couple (Gotlib & Hooley, 1988). Finally, although there are investigators who would interpret the positive effects of marital therapy on psychopathology as evidence of a causal link between marital functioning and emotional disorder, it is apparent that there are a number of alternative explanations for these results, none of which necessarily implies a causal relationship.

It is clear from this brief discussion and from the research reviewed in this chapter that we are still far from being able to resolve this issue. In this regard, we believe that the greatest need in this field is for longitudinal, prospective studies of marriage and psychopathology. Although such investigations will undoubtedly be difficult to design and execute, the rewards in terms of furthering our understanding of the relationship between marriage and psychiatric disorder will be considerable. It is our hope that the research and issues presented in this chapter will serve to stimulate such investigations.

# ACKNOWLEDGMENTS

Preparation of this chapter was facilitated by Grants MA-8574 from the Medical Research Council of Canada and 6606-3465-46 from Health and Welfare Canada to Ian H. Gotlib.

# REFERENCES

Alanen, Y. O., & Kinnunen, P. (1975). Marriage and the development of schizophrenia. *Psychiatry, 38,* 346–365.

Andreasen, N. C. (1982). Negative symptoms in schizophrenia: Definition and reliability. *Archives of General Psychiatry, 39,* 784–788.

Arkowitz, H. S., Holliday, S., & Hutter, M. (1982). *Depressed women and their husbands: A study of marital interaction and adjustment.* Paper presented at the Annual Meeting of the Association for Advancement of Behavior Therapy, Los Angeles.

Arrindell, W. A., & Emmelkamp, P. M. G. (1986). Marital adjustment, intimacy and needs in female agoraphobics and their partners: A controlled study. *British Journal of Psychiatry, 149,* 592–602.

Bachrach, L. L. (1975). *Marital status and mental disorder: An analytical review.* National Institute of Mental Health, DHEW Publication No. (ADM) 75-217. Washington, DC: U.S. Government Printing Office.

Barlow, D.H., O'Brien, G. T., & Last, C. G. (1984). Couples treatment of agoraphobia. *Behavior Therapy, 15,* 41–58.

Beach, S. R. H., & O'Leary, D. K. (1986). The treatment of depression occurring in the context of marital discord. *Behavior Therapy, 17,* 43–50.

Bebbington, P. (1987). Marital status and depression: A study of English national admission statistics. *Acta Psychiatrica Scandanavica, 75,* 640–650.

Beck, A. T. (1967). *Depression: Clinical, experimental, and theoretical aspects.* New York: Harper & Row.

Beck, A. T., Rush, A. J., Shaw, B. F., & Emery, G. (1979). *Cognitive therapy of depression.* New York: Guilford Press.

Bernard, J. (1972). *The future of marriage.* New York: Bantam Books.

Biglan, A., Hops, H., Sherman, L., Friedman, L. S., Arthur, J., & Osteen, V. (1985). Problem-solving interactions of depressed women and their husbands. *Behavior Therapy, 16,* 431–451.

Billings, A. G., Kessler, M., Gomberg, C. A., & Weiner, S. (1979). Marital conflict resolution of alcoholic and nonalcoholic couples during drinking and non-drinking sessions. *Journal of Studies on Alcohol, 40,* 183–195.

Bloom, B., Asher, S. J., & White, S. W. (1978). Marital disruption as a stressor: A review and analysis. *Psychological Bulletin, 85,* 867–894.

Bothwell, S., & Weissman, M. M. (1977). Social impairments four years after an acute depressive episode. *American Journal of Orthopsychiatry, 47,* 231–237.

Brown, G. W., & Harris, T. (1978). *Social origins of depression.* New York: Free Press.

Buglass, D., Clarke, A. J., Henderson, A. S., Kreitman, A., Kreitman, N., & Presley, A. S. (1977). A study of agoraphobic housewives. *Psychological Medicine, 7,* 73–86.

Cerny, J. A., Barlow, D. H., Craske, M. G., & Himadi, W. G. (1988). Couples treatment of agoraphobia: A two-year follow-up. *Behavior Therapy, 18,* 401–416.

Chambless, D. L., & Goldstein, A. J. (1981). Clinical treatment of agoraphobia. In M. Mavissakalian & D. H. Barlow (Eds.), *Phobia: Psychological and pharmacological treatment* (pp. 103–144). New York: Guilford Press.

Clarkin, J. F., Spencer, H. H., Lestelle, V., Peyser, J., DeMane, N., Haas, G. L., & Glick, I. D. (1986). *IFI for affective disorder: A manual of inpatient family intervention.* Unpublished manuscript, Cornell University Medical College, New York.

Claussen, J., & Yarrow, M. (1955). Introduction: Mental illness and the family. *Journal of Social Issues, 11,* 3–5.

Cobb, J., McDonald, R., Marks, I., & Stern, R. (1980). Marital versus exposure treatment for combined marital and phobic–obsessive problems. *Behaviour Analysis and Modification, 4,* 3–16.

Costello, C. G. (1982). Social factors associated with depression: A retrospective community study. *Psychological Medicine, 12,* 329–339.

Coyne, J. C., Kahn, J., & Gotlib, I. H. (1987). Depression. In T. Jacob (Ed.), *Family interaction and psychopathology* (pp. 509–533). New York: Plenum.

Coyne, J. C., Kessler, R. C., Tal, M., Turnbull, J., Wortman, C. B., & Greden, J. F. (1987). Living with a depressed person. *Journal of Consulting and Clinical Psychology, 55,* 347–352.

Davis, D. I. (1976). Changing perception of self and spouse from sober to intoxicated state: Implications for research in family factors that maintain alcohol abuse. *Annals of the New York Academy of Science, 273,* 497–506.

DiMascio, A., Weissman, M. M., Prusoff, B. A., Neu, C., Zwilling, M., & Klerman, G. L. (1979). Differential symptom reduction by drugs and psychotherapy in acute depression. *Archives of General Psychiatry, 36,* 1450–1456.

Dunn, N., Jacob, T., Hummon, N., & Seilhamer, R. (1987). Marital stability in alcoholic–spouse relationships as a function of drinking pattern and location. *Journal of Abnormal Psychology, 96,* 99–107.

Eaton, W. W. (1975). Marital status and schizophrenia. *Acta Psychiatrica Scandinavica, 52,* 320–329.

Endicott, J., Spitzer, R. L., Fleiss, J. L., & Cohen, J. (1976). The Global Assessment Scale: A procedure for measuring overall severity of psychiatric disturbance. *Archives of General Psychiatry, 33,* 766–771.

Ensel, W. M. (1986). Sex, marital status, and depression: The role of life events and social support. In N. Lin, A. Dean, & W. M. Ensel (Eds.), *Social support, life events, and depression* (pp. 231–247). Montreal: Academic Press.

Farina, A., Garmezy, N., & Barry, H. (1963). Relationship of marital status to incidence and prognois of schizophrenia. *Journal of Abnormal Social Psychology, 67,* 624–630.

Fodor, I. (1974). The phobic syndrome in women. In V. Franks & V. Burtle (Eds.), *Women in therapy* (pp. 132–168). New York: Brunner/Mazel.

Frankenstein, W., Hay, W. M., & Nathan, P. E. (1985). Effect of intoxication on alcoholics' marital communication and problem solving. *Journal of Studies on Alcohol, 46,* 1–6.

Franklin, J. I., Kittredge, L. D., & Thrasher, J. H. (1975). A survey of factors related to mental hospital readmissions. *Hospital and Community Psychiatry, 11,* 749–751.

Freden, L. (1982). *Psychosocial aspects of depression.* Chichester: Wiley.

Friedman, A. S. (1975). Interaction of drug therapy with marital therapy in depressive patients. *Archives of General Psychiatry, 32*, 619–637.

Fry, W. (1962). The marital context of an anxiety syndrome. *Family Process, 1*, 245–252.

Glick, I. D., Clarkin, J. F., Spencer, J. H., Haas, G. L., Lewis, A. B., Peyser, J., DeMane, N., Good-Ellis, M., Harris, E., & Lestelle, V. (1985). A controlled evaluation of inpatient family intervention: I. Preliminary results of the six-month follow-up. *Archives of General Psychiatry, 42*, 882–886.

Goldstein, A. (1970). Case conference: Some aspects of agoraphobia. *Journal of Behavior Therapy and Experimental Psychiatry, 1*, 305–313.

Goldstein, M. J., Hand, I., & Hahlweg, K. (1986). *Treatment of schizophrenia: Family assessment and intervention.* Berlin, Heidelberg: Springer-Verlag.

Goodstein, R., & Swift, K. (1977). Psychotherapy with phobic patients: The marriage relationship as the source of symptoms and focus of treatment. *American Journal of Psychotherapy, 31*, 285–292.

Gotlib, I. H., & Cane, D. B. (1989). Self-report assessment of depression and anxiety. In P. C. Kendall & D. Watson (Eds.), *Anxiety and depression: Distinctive and overlapping features* (pp. 131–169). Orlando, FL: Academic Press.

Gotlib, I. H., & Colby, C. A. (1987). *Treatment of depression: An interpersonal systems approach.* New York: Pergamon Press.

Gotlib, I. H., & Hooley, J. M. (1988). Depression and marital distress: Current status and future directions. In S. W. Duck (Ed.), *Handbook of personal relationships* (pp. 543–570). Chichester, England: Wiley.

Gotlib, I. H., & Lee, C. M. (1989). The social functioning of depressed patients: A longitudinal assessment. *Journal of Social and Clinical Psychology, 8*, 223–237.

Gotlib, I. H., & Whiffen, V. E. (1989). Depression and marital functioning: An examination of specificity and gender differences. *Journal of Abnormal Psychology, 98*, 23–30.

Gotlib, I. H., & Whiffen, V. E. (in press). The interpersonal context of depression: Implications for theory and research. In W. H. Jones & D. Perlman (Eds.), *Advances in personal relationships* (vol. 3). Greenwich, CT: JAI Press.

Gotlib, I. H., Whiffen, V. E., Mount, J. H., Milne, K., & Cordy, N. I. (1989). Prevalence rates and demographic characteristics associated with depression in pregnancy and the postpartum. *Journal of Consulting and Clinical Psychology, 57*, 269–274.

Gove, W. R. (1972). The relationship between sex roles, marital status, and mental illness. *Social Forces, 51*, 34–44.

Gove, W. R. (1973). Sex, marital status, and mortality. *American Journal of Sociology, 79*, 45–67.

Gove, W. R., Hughes, M., & Styles, C. B. (1983). Does marriage have positive effects on the psychological well-being of the individual? *Journal of Health and Social Behavior, 24*, 122–132.

Gove, W. R., & Tudor, J. F. (1973). Adult sex roles and mental illness. *American Journal of Sociology, 78*, 812–835.

Haas, G. L., Glick, I. D., Clarkin, J. F., Spencer, J. H., Lewis, A. B., Peyser, J., DeMane, N., Good-Ellis, M., Harris, E., & Lestelle, V. (1988). Inpatient family intervention: A randomized clinical trial. II. Results at hospital discharge. *Archives of General Psychiatry, 45*, 217–224.

Hafner, R. J. (1977). The husbands of agoraphobic women and their influence on treatment outcome. *British Journal of Psychiatry, 131*, 289–294.

Hafner, R. J. (1986). *Marriage and mental illness: A sex-roles perspective.* New York: Guilford Press.

Hammer, M. (1963). Influences of small social networks as factors on mental hospital admission. *Human Organization, 22,* 243–251.

Hand, I., Lamontagne, Y., & Marks, I. M. (1974). Group exposure (flooding) *in vivo* for agoraphobics. *British Journal of Psychiatry, 124,* 588–602.

Hautzinger, M., Linden, M., & Hoffman, N. (1982). Distressed couples with and without a depressed partner: An analysis of their verbal interaction. *Journal of Behavior Therapy and Experimental Psychiatry, 13,* 307–314.

Himadi, W. G., Cerny, J. A., Barlow, D. H., Cohen, S., & O'Brien, G. T. (1986). The relationship of marital adjustment to agoraphobic outcome. *Behaviour Research and Therapy, 24,* 107–115.

Hinchliffe, M., Hooper, D., & Roberts, F. J. (1978). *The melancholy marriage.* New York: Wiley.

Hirschfeld, R. M. A., & Cross, C. K. (1981). Epidemiology of affective disorders. *Archives of General Psychiatry, 39,* 35–46.

Hooley, J. M. (1986). Expressed emotion and depression: Interactions between patients and high-versus-low-expressed emotion spouses. *Journal of Abnormal Psychology, 95,* 237–246.

Hooley, J. M., Richters, J. E., Weintraub, S., & Neale, J. M. (1987). Psychopathology and marital distress: The positive side of positive symptoms. *Journal of Abnormal Psychology, 96,* 27–33.

Hops, H., Biglan, A., Sherman, L., Arthur, J., Friedman, L., & Osteen, V. (1987). Home observations of family interactions of depressed women. *Journal of Consulting and Clinical Psychology, 55,* 341–346.

Jacob, T., Dunn, N. J., & Leonard, K. (1983). Patterns of alcohol abuse and family stability. *Alcoholism: Clinical and Experimental Research, 7,* 382–385.

Jacob, T., & Krahn, G. L. (1988). Marital interactions of alcoholic couples: Comparison with depressed and nondistressed couples. *Journal of Consulting and Clinical Psychology, 56,* 73–79.

Jacob, T., & Leonard, K. E. (1988). Alcoholic-spouse interaction as a function of alcoholism subtype and alcohol consumption interaction. *Journal of Abnormal Psychology, 97,* 231–237.

Jacob, T., Ritchey, D., Cvitkovic, J. F., & Blane, H. T. (1981). Communication styles of alcoholic and nonalcoholic families when drinking and not drinking. *Journal of Studies on Alcohol, 42,* 466–482.

Jacob, T., & Seilhamer, R. (1987). Alcoholism and family interaction. In T. Jacob (Ed.), *Family interaction and psychopathology: Theories, methods and findings* (pp. 535–580). New York: Plenum Press.

Jacobson, N. S., Holtzworth-Munroe, A., & Schmaling, K. B. (1989). Marital therapy and spouse involvement in the treatment of depression, agoraphobia, and alcoholism. *Journal of Consulting and Clinical Psychology, 57,* 5–10.

Kahn, J., Coyne, J. C., & Margolin, G. (1985). Depression and marital disagreement: The social construction of despair. *Journal of Social and Personal Relationships, 2,* 447–461.

Kirshner, L. A., & Johnston, L. (1983). Effects of gender on inpatient psychiatric hospitalization. *Journal of Nervous and Mental Disease, 171,* 651–657.

Kleiner, L., & Marshall, W. L. (1985). Relationship difficulties and agoraphobia. *Clinical Psychology Review, 5,* 581–595.

Klerman, G. L., Weissman, M. M., Rounsaville, B. J., & Chevron, E. (1984). *Interpersonal psychotherapy of depression.* New York: Basic Books.

Kowalik, D. L., & Gotlib, I. H. (1987). Depression and marital interaction: Concordance between intent and perception of communication. *Journal of Abnormal Psychology, 96*, 127-134.

Leff, J. P., Kuipers, L., Berkowitz, R., Eberlein-Vries, R., & Sturgeon, D. (1982). A controlled trial of social intervention in the families of schizophrenic patients. *British Journal of Psychiatry, 141*, 121-134.

Lennon, M. C. (1987). Sex differences in distress: The impact of gender and work roles. *Journal of Health and Social Behavior, 28*, 290-305.

Lewinsohn, P. M., & Atwood, G. E. (1969). Depression: A clinical research approach. *Psychotherapy: Theory, Research, and Practice, 6*, 166-171.

Lewinsohn, P. M., & Schaffer, M. (1971). The use of home observations as an integral part of the treatment of depression: Preliminary report of case studies. *Journal of Consulting and Clinical Psychology, 37*, 87-94.

Maisto, S. A., O'Farrell, T. J., Connors, G. J., McKay, J. R., & Pelcovits, M. (1988). Alcoholics' attributions of factors affecting their relapse to drinking and reasons for terminating relapse episodes. *Addictive Behaviors, 13*, 79-82.

McCrady, B. S., Noel, N. E., Abrams, D. B., Stout, R. L., Nelson, H. F., & Hay, W. M. (1986). Comparative effectiveness of three types of spouse involvement in outpatient behavioral alcoholism treatment. *Journal of Studies on Alcohol, 47*, 459-467.

McLean, P. D., Ogston, L., & Grauer, L. (1973). Behavioral approach to the treatment of depression. *Journal of Behaviour Therapy and Experimental Psychiatry, 4*, 323-330.

Merikangas, K. R. (1982). Assortative mating for psychiatric disorders and psychological traits. *Archives of General Psychiatry, 39*, 1173-1180.

Merikangas, K. R. (1984). Divorce and assortative mating among depressed patients. *American Journal of Psychiatry, 141*, 74-76.

Milton, F., & Hafner, R. J. (1979). The outcome of behavior therapy for agoraphobia in relation to marital adjustment. *Archives of General Psychiatry, 36*, 807-811.

Monteiro, W., Marks, I. M., & Ramm, E. (1985). Marital adjustment and treatment outcome in agoraphobia. *British Journal of Psychiatry, 146*, 383-390.

Moos, R. H., Finney, J. W., & Gamble, W. (1982). The process of recovery from alcoholism: II. Comparing spouses of alcoholic patients and spouses of matched community controls. *Journal of Studies on Alcohol, 43*, 888-909.

Noh, S., & Avison, W. R. (1988). Spouses of discharged psychiatric patients: Factors associated with their experience of burden. *Journal of Marriage and the Family, 50*, 377-389.

Noh, S., & Turner, R. J. (1987). Living with psychiatric patients: Implications for the mental health of family members. *Social Science and Medicine, 25*, 263-271.

Odegaard, O. (1946). Marriage and mental disease: A study in social psychopathology. *Journal of Mental Science, 92*, 35-59.

O'Farrell, T. J. (1986). Marital therapy in the treatment of alcoholism. In N. S. Jacobson & A. S. Gurman (Eds.), *Clinical handbook of marital therapy* (pp. 513-535). New York: Guilford Press.

O'Farrell, T. J., & Birchler, G. R. (1987). Marital relationships of alcoholic, conflicted, and nonconflicted couples. *Journal of Marital and Family Therapy, 13*, 259-274.

O'Farrell, T. J., Cutter, H. S. G., & Floyd, F. J. (1985). Evaluating behavioral marital therapy for male alcoholics: Effects on marital adjustment and communication from before to after treatment. *Behavior Therapy, 16*, 147-167.

Paykel, E. S., Myers, J. K., Dienelt, M. N., Klerman, G. L., Lindenthal, J. J., & Pepper, M. P. (1969). Life events and depression: A controlled study. *Archives of General Psychiatry, 21*, 753-760.

Pearlin, L. I., & Johnson, J. S. (1977). Marital status, life-strains, and depression. *American Sociological Review, 42*, 704-715.

Radloff, L. (1975). Sex differences in depression: The effects of occupation and marital status. *Sex Roles, 1*, 249-265.

Reich, J., & Thompson, W. D. (1985). Marital status of schizophrenic and alcoholic patients. *Journal of Nervous and Mental Disease, 173*, 499-502.

Renne, K. S. (1971). Health and marital experience in an urban population. *Journal of Marriage and the Family, 33*, 338-350.

Roberts, R. E., & O'Keefe, S. J. (1981). Sex differences in depression reexamined. *Journal of Health and Social Behavior, 22*, 394-400.

Robertson, N. C. (1974). The relationship between marital status and the risk of psychiatric referral. *British Journal of Psychiatry, 124*, 191-202.

Rounsaville, B. J., Weissman, M. M., Prusoff, B. G., & Herceg-Baron, R. L. (1979). Marital disputes and treatment outcome in depressed women. *Comprehensive Psychiatry, 20*, 483-489.

Ruscher, S. M., & Gotlib, I. H. (1988). Marital interaction patterns of couples with and without a depressed partner. *Behavior Therapy, 19*, 455-470.

Sager, C. J., Gundlach, R., & Kremer, M. (1968). The married in treatment. *Archives of General Psychiatry, 19*, 205-217.

Schless, A. P., Schwartz, L., Goetz, C., & Mendels, J. (1974). How depressives view the significance of life events. *British Journal of Psychiatry, 125*, 406-410.

Spencer, J. H., Glick, I. D., Haas, G. L., Clarkin, J. F., Lewis, A. B., Peyser, J., DeMane, N., Good-Ellis, M., Harris, E., & Lestelle, V. (1988). A randomized clinical trial of Inpatient Family Intervention, III: Effects at 6-month and 18-month follow-ups. *American Journal of Psychiatry, 145*, 1115-1121.

Steinglass, P., Davis, D., & Berenson, D. (1977). Observations of conjointly hospitalized "alcoholic couples" during sobriety and intoxication: Implications for theory and therapy. *Family Process, 16*, 1-16.

Tamerin, J. S., Toler, A., DeWolfe, J., Packer, L., & Neuman, C. P. (1973). Spouses' perception of their alcoholic partners: A retrospective view of alcoholics by themselves and their spouses. In *Proceedings of the Third Annual Alcoholism Conference of the National Institute on Alcohol Abuse and Alcoholism* (pp. 33-49). Washington, DC: NIAAA.

Targum, S. D., Dibble, E. D., Davenport, Y. B., & Gershon, E. S. (1981). Family attitudes questionnaire: Patients and spouses view bipolar illness. *Archives of General Psychiatry, 38*, 562-568.

Turner, R. J., Dopkech, L. S., & Labreche, G. P. (1970). Marital status and schizophrenia: A study of incidence and outcome. *Journal of Abnormal and Social Psychology, 76*, 110-116.

Vaughn, C. E., & Leff, J. P. (1976). The influence of family and social factors on the course of psychiatric illness: A comparison of schizophrenic and depressed neurotic patients. *British Journal of Psychiatry, 129*, 125-137.

Walker, E., Bettes, B. A., Kain, E. L., & Harvey, P. (1985). Relationship of gender and marital status with symptomatology in psychotic patients. *Journal of Abnormal Psychology, 94*, 42-50.

Weissman, M. M. (1979). The psychological treatment of depression. *Archives of General Psychiatry, 36*, 1261-1269.

Weissman, M. M., & Klerman, G. L. (1973). Psychotherapy with depressed women:

An empirical study of content themes and reflection. *British Journal of Psychiatry, 123,* 55-61.

Weissman, M. M., & Klerman, G. L. (1977). Sex differences in the epidemiology of depression. *Archives of General Psychiatry, 34,* 98-111.

Weissman, M. M., Klerman, G. L., Prusoff, B. A., Sholomskas, D., & Padian, N. (1981). Depressed outpatients: Results one year after treatment with drugs and/or interpersonal psychotherapy. *Archives of General Psychiatry, 38,* 51-55.

Weissman, M. M., & Paykel, E. S. (1974). *The depressed woman: A study of social relationships.* Chicago: University of Chicago Press.

Weissman, M. M., Pincus, C., Radding, C., Lawrence, R., & Siegel, R. (1973). The educated housewife: Mild depression and the search for work. *American Journal of Orthopsychiatry, 43,* 565-573.

Weissman, M. M., Prusoff, B. A., DiMascio, A., Neu, C., Goklaney, M., & Klerman, G. L. (1979). The efficacy of drugs and psychotherapy in the treatment of acute depressive episodes. *American Journal of Psychiatry, 136,* 555-558.

Wiseman, J. (1981). Sober comportment: Patterns and perspectives on alcohol addiction. *Journal of Studies on Alcohol, 42,* 106-126.

# Contributions from Psychology to an Understanding of Marriage

Neil S. Jacobson

Psychologists studying marriage begin with multiple handicaps. For one thing, the subject matter is not central to any area of psychology: Marriage is considered too far removed from psychopathology to be mainstream clinical psychology; too applied for mainstream experimental social psychology; and insufficiently child-focused for mainstream developmental psychology. With no real home in psychology, the study of marriage has been on the periphery of many subdisciplines. This has meant that the field has been quite interdisciplinary, even more so when one considers the contributions from family sociology, social work, and communication research. Although the interdisciplinary nature of marital studies could be thought of as a strength, the literature remains scattered, and cross-fertilization has been relatively uncommon. Scientists from the various disciplines publish in different journals, use distinct methodologies (see Robins, Chapter 2, this volume), and often attend different meetings.

Another factor that handicaps psychologists who study marriage is the accessibility of their subject matter to the general public. Despite the fact that we know little about marriage in the scientific sense, lay intuitions about love and marriage run rampant. Since the quest for marital satisfaction is ubiquitous in our culture, and its mysteries are on everyone's mind, theories about the nature of marriage are everywhere: in the popular media, in everyday conversation, and in endless introspection

258

on the part of millions. The upshot of all the attention devoted to marriage is that the intuitions of the lay public offer stiff competition to marriage researchers, since the folklore created by these intuitions extends much further in many cases than the research questions asked by scientists studying marriage. It is easy to be impatient with scientific progress in the field of marriage when it moves so slowly in comparison to the popular imagination.

Much of the research in which we engage seems bland and nondescript, compared to the folklore that appears in the popular media. I do not mean to be disparaging by using the term "folklore." Much of this folklore is undoubtedly true, and even the parts of it that are not true are compelling. The folklore includes work by clinicians who write books based on their clinical experience. The assertions may or may not be true, but the influence of these books and the extent to which people believe what is in them are independent of the degree of scientific rigor that led to the conclusions. Furthermore, it is not just laypeople who are influenced by these books. Clinicians and other mental health professionals often seem surprisingly unconcerned with the scientific or research base from which clinical material springs.

Consider, for example, Frank Pittman's recent book on adultery (Pittman, 1989). Pittman is a well-respected family therapist who has written an engaging book on the dynamics of extramarital affairs. The book is based largely on his clinical and personal observations. Unencumbered by research requirements, Pittman waxes eloquent about adultery, and even proposes a typology of different types of adulterers. It makes for fascinating reading. The book has been enormously successful, and is having a major impact on practitioners. Try to imagine how long it would take for a researcher to empirically derive a typology of adulterers, and then imagine how dry and sterile that typology would be compared to Pittman's. Yes, we would have greater confidence in the research-based typology, but would it play in the clinical community?

This is part of what psychologists who study marriage are up against. Relatively little is fascinating and captivating about the findings that have emerged, and the overriding impression one gets from the literature is that the psychology of marriage is a field in its infancy. A great many interesting data have been collected; ingenious methodological innovations have greatly enhanced our capacity for studying couples; and it seems as if the field is ready for substantive contributions of an explanatory nature. There are few such contributions at present.


## DEVELOPMENTS IN OBSERVATIONAL RESEARCH

A case in point is the literature involving direct observation of marital interaction, so competently summarized by Weiss and Heyman (Chapter 3, this volume). In many ways, there has been an amazing amount of progress over the last 20 years. Methodological breakthroughs have been plentiful. To begin with, reliable and valid coding systems have been developed to measure ongoing marital interaction—for example, the Marital Interaction Coding System (MICS; Weiss & Sommers, 1983); the Couples Interaction Scoring System (CISS; Gottman, Markman, & Notarius, 1977); and the Kategoriensystem für Partnerschaftliche Interaktion (KPI; Hahlweg, Revenstorf, & Schindler, 1984). Complex statistical techniques such as sequential analysis have been adapted to the analysis of observational data (Gottman, 1979). Most recently, psychophysiological techniques have been used to look at autonomic indicators of affect (Gottman & Levenson, 1985, 1986; Levenson & Gottman, 1983). Studies conducted using observational data have accumulated.

Until recently, however, the methodological wizardry greatly outstripped the substantive contributions of these findings. Until sequential data were collected routinely, the comparisons between distressed and nondistressed couples basically showed that when unhappy couples were placed in a high-conflict task, they were not as nice to each other as happy couples in a similar task. The ability to measure aggressive and friendly behavior was indeed important, but the findings themselves were not particularly interesting. Complex statistical techniques did begin to yield some counterintuitive findings that seemed to tell us something nontrivial about how distressed and nondistressed couples differ. Two examples are "negative reciprocity" (Gottman, 1979; Margolin & Wampold, 1981), the notion that a spouse in a distressed couple is particularly likely to reciprocate negative behavior from the partner, over and above base rate differences; and "reactivity" (Jacobson, Follette, & McDonald, 1982; Jacobson, Waldron, & Moore, 1980; Margolin, 1981; Wills, Weiss, & Patterson, 1974), the notion that distressed couples are particularly responsive to immediate or recently occurring relationship events, in contrast to the more long-term orientation of

happily married couples. Still, it is not clear whether findings such
as these have brought us much closer to a basic understanding of the
dynamics of marital satisfaction and distress.

It is tempting but wholly unjustified to conclude from the
aggregate findings of observational research that communication
deficiencies of various kinds are the essence of marital discord.
Such conclusions are unjustified because all of these studies have
focused on communication exclusively, so it is quite natural that
their results will implicate communication variables as important. But these findings are inconclusive. Furthermore, they do
not in any way speak to the issue of causality. What causes marital
distress? Surely not negative reciprocity. Most of the findings
from observational research have uncovered phenomena that
characterize the interaction of certain types of couples. These
phenomena help discriminate between groups, but they do not
speak to explanatory or causal questions.

We are starting to see some developments in observational research that seem to have true substantive importance. As noted by
Weiss and Heyman (Chapter 3), the longitudinal findings by Gottman, Levenson, and associates are quite interesting, especially the
discovery that various indices of autonomic nervous system arousal
predict subsequent marital satisfaction. Moreover, findings by Gottman and Krokoff (1989) that conflict engagement is associated with
marital distress in the short run but with increases in marital
satisfaction in the long run are quite provocative.

As Baucom, Notarius, Burnett, and Haefner (Chapter 5, this
volume) have noted, there are some interpretive ambiguities in
these data. Gottman and colleagues were attempting to predict
*changes* in marital satisfaction from Time 1 to Time 2, which is
very different from trying to predict *subsequent* marital satisfaction at Time 2. The former involves predicting a difference score
(marital satisfaction at Time 2 minus marital satisfaction at
Time 1), whereas the latter entails predicting marital satisfaction
at Time 2. It is probably the case that the same variables that
predict marital satisfaction at Time 1 predict marital satisfaction
at Time 2, since marital satisfaction scores typically show high
correlations over time. Thus, my guess would be that conflict
engagement is negatively associated with marital satisfaction at
Time 2 as well as at Time 1. If this is true, then it is not the case
that conflict engagement is good for couples in the long run. The
issue is whether or not the changes in marital satisfaction from
Time 1 to Time 2 are clinically significant: That is, are distressed
couples at Time 1 still distressed at Time 2 (although less dis-

tressed), or is their status changing from distressed to happily married? In the former case, Time 1 marital satisfaction will be highly correlated with Time 2 satisfaction, and what is good for couples in the short run is probably the same as what is good for them in the long run. Only in the latter case is the inference warranted that a variable predicting an increase in marital satisfaction is "good" for the couple.

Despite this caveat, the longitudinal work reported by Gottman and Levenson is the most important interactional research yet conducted, and much of it is grist for the theoretical mill. In fact, Gottman (1989) has already begun to attempt to put it all together, and his theory is a major contribution. We may hope that marital interaction research will move from the descriptive to the explanatory level over the next few decades. If it is indeed to move in this direction, Weiss and Heyman correctly note that longitudinal research will be required; this research will also have to incorporate both physiological measures and sequential data-analytic techniques.

## RESEARCH ON GENDER ISSUES

The literature on gender issues further illustrates the gap between what is "scientifically known" and the intuitions of the lay public. Book stores are replete with folklore about "women who love too much," "women who love men who hate them," "men with narcissistic personality disorders, and the borderline women who love them," and the like. Speculation abounds about the battle of the sexes, and much of this speculation has to do with gender issues. To judge by the summary provided in Chapter 5 by Baucom and colleagues, the research literature has produced a great deal of descriptive information but little in the way of theoretical integration, and most of the findings seem quite tame compared to the speculations on bookstore shelves. However, one interesting finding to emerge from this literature is that women in unhappy marriages are more negative in their interactions with partners than are either their husbands or happily married husbands and wives. As Floyd and Markman (1983) put it, women are the "barometers" of marital discord.

This increased negativity in maritally distressed women is more easily understood if one takes into account findings from fields such as sociology and epidemiology; this illustrates the desirability of cross-fertilization, which is so often lacking in the psychological literature. Baucom and colleagues have carefully documented the tendency for women to be more willing to engage in conflict in relationships, and for men to be relatively conflict-avoidant. Indeed, it may be true that the finding of greater negativity in women is a logical outgrowth of this gender difference. However, it should also be noted that women clearly complain more about their marriages than men do, and that they may be more negative because they are more unhappy with their marriages than men are (see Jacobson, 1983 and 1989, for fuller discussion of this issue). Margolin, Talovic, and Weinstein (1983) found that wives were less satisfied than were their husbands with all areas of their relationships except for sex. The pattern of complaints also suggests gender differences: Women are more inclined to be asking for *more* involvement and engagement from their partners, whereas men are more likely to be either satisfied with the status quo or desirous of changes that would enhance the traditional role structure of the marriage (Jacobson, 1983, 1989). In short, women are typically asking for more sharing of roles and more equality from marriage, whereas men are typically holding out for traditionality. Given the findings reported by Baucom et al. (Chapter 5, this volume) that androgyny seems to be the optimal path for marital satisfaction, it seems that the women may be seeking the right things.

In addition to women complaining more and about different kinds of things than men, it may be that women have more to complain *about*. A variety of studies, mostly from sociology and epidemiology (Jacobson, 1983, 1989), support the notion that the institution of marriage has worked better for men than it has for women. As Gotlib and McCabe (Chapter 8, this volume) note, marriage protects men from psychopathology, but does not do so for women. In some studies, marriage—especially traditional marital roles—places women at greater risk for psychopathology, especially depression.

Thus, many of these findings may help explain the gender-based differences in negativity. Women may seem more negative during marital interaction simply because they are less satisfied with the status quo than their husbands are. The negativity may be the outcome of a long history of discontent, and the frustration associated with the inability to change the relationship in a desirable direction.

## THE RELATIONSHIP BETWEEN MARRIAGE
## AND PSYCHOPATHOLOGY

To turn to the relationship between marriage and psychopathology, Gotlib and McCabe (Chapter 8) have provided a thorough and insightful review of the literature. Here is another area where speculation has outstripped substantive findings, and the field has shown a penchant for premature closure even when the findings are inconsistent. It is true that there is a tendency for people with some sort of behavior disorder to have marital problems. However, dysfunctional marital interaction appears to be prevalent in association with any type of disorder; specific types of interactional anomalies do not seem to be associated with particular disorders. Virtually all of the studies using psychiatric or medical patient control groups have found that the aspects of marital interaction differentiating between the psychopathological and control groups fail to discriminate between the depression and psychiatric (or medical patient) control groups.

The causal relationship between psychopathology and marital dysfunction remains obscure. It is possible, given the pervasiveness of dysfunctional marital interaction across disorders, that marital distress is causally related to various individual disorders, but that the nature of the marital dysfunction determines the specific disorder that results. For example, the symbiotic dependency hypothesized by Chambless and her colleagues to characterize agoraphobic women and their husbands may bear an etiological relationship to agoraphobia. Or it could be that marital dysfunction, of whatever variety, interacts with specific diatheses toward depression, anxiety, or alcoholism, and the resultant disorder will depend on the individual vulnerability. Finally, a causal role for marital distress may be reflected in a complex interaction between types of marital distress and individual vulnerabilities. Depression, for example, may emerge when certain types of dysfunctional marital interaction patterns interact with one or more diatheses for depression. To unravel these various relationships, designs will have to be considerably more sophisticated than the ones chosen thus far. Sample sizes will also have to be considerably larger.

The weight of the evidence suggests that the association between dysfunctional marital interaction and psychopathology is accounted for by marital distress rather than by the disorder itself (see Biglan et al., 1985; Jacobson, Holtzworth-Munroe, & Schmaling, 1989; Ruscher & Gotlib, 1988; Schmaling & Jacobson, in press). In previous studies marital distress was often confounded with the existence of a behavior disorder, so that it was impossible to separate the effects of marital distress from those of the disorder itself. When proper control groups (e.g., a group with marital distress but no behavior disorder, *and* a group with the behavior disorder but no marital distress) are incorporated into the design, the effects can be separated. For example, we (Schmaling & Jacobson, in press) studied couples with a depressed spouse, using a factorial design where depression status (yes or no) was crossed with marital distress level (distressed or nondistressed). The predominant findings were significant main effects for marital distress level, few if any main effects for depression status, and some interesting interactions between the two. But there was little indication that depression without coexisting marital distress was associated with dysfunctional marital interaction.

The most fundamental question underlying this area of research has to do with the extent of overlap between marital problems and individual psychopathology. If we were to discover that the rate of marital distress in the psychopathological subgroup fails to exceed the base rate of marital distress in the general population, the finding that marital interactions in this subgroup are dysfunctional become less interesting. Among women with diagnosed major depression, we find that about 50% have distressed marriages (Jacobson, Dobson, Fruzzetti, Schmaling, & Salusky, 1990). This rate is somewhat greater than the rate of marital distress in the general population. However, there remains a large proportion of the depressed married population whose marriages are satisfying. This fact complicates interpersonal theories of depression, and suggests that the first place to look for explanations of depression is not dysfunction in the close relationship. In the area of anxiety disorders, it is not even clear from the existing literature that the incidence of marital distress exceeds base rates in the general population (Jacobson et al., 1989).

In short, it appears that research on the association between psychopathology and marital interaction needs to be much more refined and differentiated before the true nature of the association can be determined. As the foregoing discussion implies, the association is open to multiple interpretations, including the possibility that the two types of dysfunction are independent, even when they coexist. As for the efficacy of marital therapy as a treatment for psychopathology, we can conclude little at present. In the alcoholism area, there are only two completed studies, which yield somewhat conflicting results (see Jacobson et al., 1989). In the anxiety disorders area, there has been only one study examining marital therapy, although plenty have evaluated the effects of involving the spouse in treatment. In the depression area, it appears that marital therapy can be a highly effective treatment for depression and can greatly improve the quality of the marriage, provided that the couples present with both depression and marital problems (O'Leary & Beach, in press). However, with a broader sample of married depressives, the power of maritally focused treatments may be quite limited (Jacobson et al., 1990). Given the ambiguities regarding the relationship between marriage and psychopathology, mixed results in treatment studies are not surprising.

## COGNITIVE RESEARCH ON MARRIAGE

The discussion of cognition and marriage by Fincham, Bradbury, and Scott (Chapter 4, this volume) manages to accomplish something that no other chapter in this section even attempts: It represents the state-of-the-art findings, and at the same time steps outside of the prevailing paradigms to suggest ways in which the field could move forward. Fincham and colleagues view the existing contributions of cognitive research as important but limited. In their analysis of the field, they point to some of the problems inherent in trying to make inferences about cognitive processes from responses on paper-and-pencil questionnaires. They also underscore some of the interpretive ambiguities inherent in the paradigms commonly used to study marital cognition.

My concern about the entire field is supported by the Fincham et al. commentary on cognitive research. Expanding the range of this research, as Fincham et al. suggest, will make it more likely that findings presently languishing in the archives of descriptive data will find their way into integrative theories.

In the typical paradigm used by marital cognition researchers, subjects are asked to report on their cognitions—a strategy that at its best will yield an indirect measure of cognition. However, to make matters worse, subjects are usually asked hypothetical questions: What would they think if event X were to occur? What do they think when their partner does X? Responses to such probes may bear little relationship to how spouses think during important relationship encounters. Marital researchers

who study cognition are ultimately interested in how thinking influences behavior during as well as between sequences of
marital interaction. The probes used in marital cognition research
are far removed from the ongoing interaction sequences of primary interest. Fincham et al. do an admirable job of arguing this
point.

The authors are also to be commended for going beyond the
"normal science" of current marital cognition research and providing a more differentiated version of cognitive functioning than
has been found in research paradigms until now. As they point
out, Baucom, Epstein, Sayers, and Goldman Sher (1989) have
recently distinguished among different categories of cognitive
content, such as attention, beliefs, attributions, and the like. These
distinctions are important, but Fincham et al. have gone further
and distinguished among cognitive products, processes, and structures. These distinctions have already contributed to a more refined cognitive conceptualization of depression (e.g., Hollon &
Kris, 1984), and serve to bring marital cognition research in line
with the distinctions that preoccupy cognitive psychologists. But
perhaps the most important distinction noted by Fincham and
colleagues is the one between automatic and deliberate information processing. Automatic processing is of primary interest to
marital cognition researchers. Deliberate processing is probably
quite rare in intimate relationships, and although it is of interest
when it occurs, it has little to do with the causal chains of events
that occupy the attention of marital researchers.

Thus, Fincham and colleagues remind us that information
about cognitive processes will require different methodologies
than those utilized thus far, and they offer mental chronometry as
an example of a better way to study marital cognition.

The authors are appropriately cautious in asserting what we
have learned thus far from the study of marital cognition. They
argue implicitly, and in certain places explicitly, that one test of
the value of these approaches will be their ability to account for
variance in important marital phenomena. Thus, for example, if
models that include on-line measures of cognitive process account
for more variance in marital satisfaction than models that do not
include such measures, then in some sense we understand marriage better if we include these cognitive variables in our account.

However, another type of question is, in my view, equally
important to answer when one is attempting to evaluate the role of
cognitive variables in understanding marriage. This has to do

with the extent to which the measures used to "get inside the head" actually succeed in doing so. Fincham et al. make this point in passing when they point out that response patterns consistent with a set of cognitive processes "do not speak directly to the existence of such processes." It may seem self-evident to a cognitive psychologist that reaction time is a window to cognitive schemata, but unless one is preaching to the already converted, the correspondence between an experimental procedure and the underlying cognitive construct may be obscure.

Consider the hypothetical examples chosen by Fincham et al. to illustrate the potential utility of mental chronometry. In one study, distressed spouses would be expected to recall more negative than positive material about the marriage than nondistressed couples in equivalent time periods. The converse would be expected for positive material. Results in accord with these predictions would be taken as evidence of differential construct accessibility in distressed and nondistressed couples. Is differential construct accessibility a helpful mediating construct, or is it at best a metaphor that distracts us from the more meaningful flow of interaction between marital behavior and the environment? For example, perhaps distressed spouses seem to recall more negative than positive material because there is more negative material to recall. Thus the differences between distressed and nondistressed couples may be due to differential histories and not to differential construct accessibility. Of course, it is possible that couples also differ in construct accessibility. But if construct accessibility can be inferred only from findings that can be accounted for equally well by differential histories, construct accessibility theories are in a bit of trouble.

Virtually all of the studies described by Fincham and colleagues would face similar interpretive ambiguities. Thus, not only must cognitive researchers in the marriage area put forth models that account for variance, but the variables put forth in their models as measures of cognition must be compelling to those who lack the faith of mainstream cognitive psychologists. A methodological behaviorist might argue that cognitions should not be studied because they cannot be directly measured. I would not put forth such an argument. But I would assert that cognitive theorists assume a certain burden of proof by virtue of their decision to examine variables to which we will never have direct access. Not only must their variables be useful, but they must convince skeptics that they are what they say they are.

## THE IMPACT OF CHILDREN ON MARRIAGE

Belsky (Chapter 6, this volume) provides an incisive review of the literature analyzing the impact of children on marriage. An overriding theme of this section is that the existing correlations between presence–absence of children and marital distress are not very informative in and of themselves. For one thing, the relationship accounts for precious little variance (somewhere between 3% and 8%, depending on the study), even though the effect is quite robust and pervasive. It is, in short, a real phenomenon, but one with little explanatory value. Many, many marriages include children without declines in marital satisfaction; many childless marriages deteriorate over time. The impact of this phenomenon on our understanding of marriage will depend on the uncovering of variables that moderate this relationship, and on the discovery of the processes that mediate this relationship. For example, Belsky's review indicates that child temperament may be an important moderator variable, as may gender. With gender, however, it is not clear whether sons or daughters are more "distressogenic" for couples. It seems to depend on the ages of the children and the differences in age between them, along with other factors.

We are just beginning to understand the processes and mechanisms underlying the relationship. At this stage, prime candidates for these mediating processes are reduced opportunities for high-quality relationship experiences; conflict between parents over childrearing; changes in division of labor that traditionalize the marriage (women seem to be more negatively affected than men by the presence of children); and declines in one's general sense of happiness or life satisfaction (which may lead to marital distress and/or be adversely affected *by* marital distress).

At any rate, it is undeniable that something about the process of introducing children into a family is associated with declines in marital satisfaction. What is not clear is whether or not this information obfuscates at least as much as it enlightens. It has already been stated that the effect is small; by definition, this smallness means that there will be almost as many exceptions to this association as there will be families who show the "normal" pattern. But, perhaps more importantly, how clinically significant are these changes in marital satisfaction? How much more likely is it that happily married couples will become clinically distressed following the birth of children than at other times? Probably not much more likely. Small effects of the magnitude reported in this literature are virtually always negligible in terms of clinical import (Jacobson & Christensen, 1990; Jacobson & Revenstorf, 1988).

Finally, it is important that future research focus not just on moderators and mediators of this effect, but also on the factors that reverse it. For we can be quite certain that there are conditions under which having children leads to increased marital satisfaction. It is also probably the case that certain types of marital constellations prior to childbirth are associated with such an increase. From other areas of marriage research, a number of factors might be expected to predict enhanced postpartum marital satisfaction: nontraditional or egalitarian relationship structures; conflict-engaging (as opposed to conflict-avoiding) couples; couples who solve problems efficiently and communicate effectively; and couples who are explicit about their expectations and plans for the postpartum period.

## THE RELATIONSHIP BETWEEN EMPLOYMENT AND MARRIAGE

The literature on the relationship between employment and marriage (Barling, Chapter 7, this volume) faces problems similar to those of the literature focusing on children and marriage. After reviewing a large volume of literature, Barling concludes that little is known about these interrelationships. Moreover, he acknowledges that the associations between employment problems and marital phenomena are often too modest to be considered meaningful. Finally, as in other areas of marital research, mechanisms moderating and underlying this relationship can only be speculated about. Barling seems to be suggesting that the field move in a direction that would lead to the uncovering of both moderator and mediator variables. Such suggestions should be applauded.

## THE SOCIAL PSYCHOLOGY OF MARRIAGE: A LEWINIAN APPROACH

Levinger and Huston, in their discussion of the social psychology of marriage (Chapter 1, this volume), take a different approach than do other authors in this section. Rather than reviewing and providing a critique of the methods and body of knowledge that have accumulated thus far, these authors have focused on developing a particular framework for studying marriage, and illustrating the use of this framework with a hypothetical couple. Thus, it is impossible to comment on the social-psychological approaches to marriage based on this chapter, since only one is represented.

However, the authors do make some general comments about social-psychological approaches to marriage, and contrast them with sociological and clinical-psychological approaches. Surely these contrasts exist because of tradition, rather than inherent differences in the disciplines. There is no obvious reason why social psychology, which is the psychological study of social behavior, should not have a great interest in the study of marriage per se, since it is the prototype for a close relationship, as well as a type of relationship that is extremely important in the culture. Yet Levinger and Huston accurately remind us that "social psychologists have been more interested in underlying psychological and interpersonal phenomena than in the marriage relationship itself." This focus may explain in part why both the theories and the resultant data base on marriage seem so rudimentary. Much of the research literature on relationships and social interaction—including many of the articles cited by Levinger and Huston—was based on college student strangers interacting for the first time, or at times not interacting at all but rather filling out questionnaires speculating on how they *would* interact as a function of some analogue experimental manipulation. To their credit, Levinger and Huston, both in their chapter and in their previous work, are well grounded in the study of married couples *per se*.

The framework presented by Levinger and Huston is impressive in scope and quite comprehensive. They are attempting to provide an integrative theoretical framework to organize the social-psychological study of marriage. The need for such frameworks is the major theme of this commentary. In this important sense, the work of Levinger and Huston is on the cutting edge, and is, I hope, the beginning of a trend. The framework is based on the pioneering work of Kurt Lewin. In addition to adopting Lewin's basic assumptions about causality and social-psychological phenomena, Levinger and Huston have incorporated other Lewinian notions such as "life-space" and "barrier." They use the Lewinian framework to discuss the factors that they feel influence marriages at both the micro and the macro levels. Central to their analysis is the concept of interdependence, and ways in which the "relatedness" of couples waxes and wanes according to exogenous and endogenous factors. The framework is a broad one and incorporates both contextual and motivational constructs.

The chapter places much more emphasis on the illustration of how a particular framework *could be* used than it does on validating the utility of the Lewinian approach. As such, the jury is still out on the value of the framework. I must confess that I have never understood why Lewin was as influential as he was; thus, I have some skepticism about anything that is derived from Lewin's work. According to the authors, the Lewinian framework (and, presumably, the basis for their framework) begins with his notion that "behavior is a function of person and environment." Lewin may have been the first social psychologist to say this, but it is a principle that is so self-evident that it does not seem to be a promising way to begin a conceptual framework designed to take us to places where we have not already been.

Levinger and Huston then incorporate a number of additional Lewinian concepts such as "life-space," which emphasize that human action (in this case, in a marital relationship) is a function of what the authors call the actor's "psychological world"; this in turn is affected by past experience, anticipated consequences, and changes following continued action with the environment. Concepts such as "valence" and "barrier" are used to explain how people approach and avoid aspects of their social field, and then these concepts are applied to a variety of marital phenomena. Although these concepts seem like valid metaphors, most of the applications to marriage read like truisms that can hardly be expected to take us far beyond our own lay intuitions. Examples such as the following fueled my skepticism:

> Actors are presumed to act either because they are drawn toward some activity more than to others or because barriers impede them from carrying out activities they might otherwise pursue. . . . The husband who leaves for work immediately after eating breakfast chooses this line of action over others—such as doing the dishes or talking to his son about his son's plans for the day.

Levinger and Huston's illustration of how the framework can aid in one's understanding of a marital relationship does little to assuage my concerns. Most of the discussion of the Shaw couple seems superficial and fails to approximate the in-depth understanding of marriage toward which the framework aspires. Most of the information given about the Shaws could be obtained in a relatively brief clinical interview, combined with some systematic self-monitoring or direct observation. It is unclear how the model leads to more, different kinds of, or better information than other state-of-the-art methods or frameworks do, or even whether the information obtained from this framework is reliable relative to other means of obtaining similar information.

Finally, although not many data are presented to support the utility of the framework, the authors do present some data on the relationship between gender-related attitudes and identities on the one hand, and self-reported marital behavior on the other hand. They found, presumably to no one's surprise, that gender attitudes are related to parallel reports of marital behavior, such that spouses with traditional views of marriage report that they engage in traditional marital patterns. They also produced a typology revealing that some couples have traditional patterns, some couples do not, some couples are somewhere in between, and some couples have the sex-role-reversed pattern. The relationship between attitudes and behavior found in their study may be an artifact of shared method variance, and is less impressive than already completed work relating sex-role attitudes to interactional behavior (summarized by Baucom et al., Chapter 5, this volume).

Thus, although I applaud Levinger and Huston's attempt to integrate and provide a comprehensive framework, the framework itself seems less than promising. Of course, its ultimate heuristic value remains to be determined. Since the field is in need of major substantive theoretical contributions to understanding marriage, I can only hope that my skepticism about the potential of the Lewinian framework is misguided.

I enjoyed reading and thinking about these chapters. There was immense food for thought in all of them. It made me aware of how far we have come, and of how much there is left to find out. Yes, I am impatient, and I found myself repeating the refrain, "Okay, let's get on with it." I believe that the impatience is not only warranted but constructive, lest we indulge in the tendency to pat ourselves on the back and become complacent. Complacency does not seem in order. Marriage remains a profound mystery—only slightly less of a mystery than it did before psychologists began to study it.

# R E F E R E N C E S

Baucom, D. H., Epstein, N., Sayers, S., & Goldman Sher, T. (1989). The role of cognitions in marital relationships: Definitional, methodological, and conceptual issues. *Journal of Consulting and Clinical Psychology, 57,* 31–38.

Biglan, A., Hops, H., Sherman, L., Friedman, L. S., Arthur, J., & Osteen, V. (1985). Problem solving interactions of depressed women and their spouses. *Behavior Therapy, 16*, 431–451.

Floyd, F. J., & Markman, H. J. (1983). Observational biases in spouse observation: Toward a cognitive/behavioral model of marriage. *Journal of Consulting and Clinical Psychology, 51*, 450–457.

Gottman, J. M. (1979). *Marital interaction: Experimental investigations*. New York: Academic Press.

Gottman, J. M. (1989). How marriages change. In G. R. Patterson (Ed.), *Depression and aggression in family interaction* (pp. 75–102). Hillsdale, NJ: Erlbaum.

Gottman, J. M., & Krokoff, L. (1989). Marital interaction and marital satisfaction: A longitudinal view. *Journal of Consulting and Clinical Psychology, 57*, 47–52.

Gottman, J. M., & Levenson, R. W. (1985). A valid procedure for obtaining self-report of affect in marital interaction. *Journal of Consulting and Clinical Psychology, 53*, 151–160.

Gottman, J. M., & Levenson, R. W. (1986). Assessing the role of emotion in marriage. *Behavioral Assessment, 8*, 31–48.

Gottman, J. M., Markman, H., & Notarius, C. (1977). The topography of marital conflict: A sequential analysis of verbal and nonverbal behavior. *Journal of Marriage and the Family, 39*, 461–477.

Hahlweg, K., Revenstorf, D., & Schindler, L. (1984). Effects of behavioral marital therapy on couples, communication and problem-solving skills. *Journal of Consulting and Clinical Psychology, 52*, 553–566.

Hollon, S. D., & Kris, M. R. (1984). Cognitive factors in clinical research and practice. *Clinical Psychology Review, 4*, 35–76.

Jacobson, N. S. (1983). Beyond empiricism: The politics of marital therapy. *American Journal of Family Therapy, 11*, 11–24.

Jacobson, N. S. (1989). The politics of intimacy. *The Behavior Therapist, 12*, 29–32.

Jacobson, N. S., & Christensen, A. (1990). *The outcome of psychotherapy: Efficacy of therapists and therapies*. Manuscript submitted for publication.

Jacobson, N. S., Dobson, K., Fruzzetti, A., Schmaling, K. B., & Salusky, S. (1990). *Marital therapy as a treatment for depression*. Manuscript submitted for publication.

Jacobson, N. S., Follette, W. C., & McDonald, D. W. (1982). Reactivity to positive and negative behavior in distressed and nondistressed married couples. *Journal of Consulting and Clinical Psychology, 50*, 706–714.

Jacobson, N. S., Holtzworth-Munroe, A., & Schmaling, K. B. (1989). Marital therapy and spouse involvement in the treatment of depression, agoraphobia, and alcoholism. *Journal of Consulting and Clinical Psychology, 57*, 5–10.

Jacobson, N. S., & Revenstorf, D. (1988). Statistics for assessing the clinical significance of psychotherapy techniques: Issues, problems and new developments. *Behavioral Assessment, 10*, 133–145.

Jacobson, N. S., Waldron, H., & Moore, D. (1980). A behavioral profile of marital distress. *Journal of Consulting and Clinical Psychology, 48*, 696–703.

Levenson, R. W., & Gottman, J. M. (1983). Marital interaction: Physiological linkage and affective exchange. *Journal of Personality and Social Psychology, 45*, 587–597.

Margolin, G. (1981). Behavior exchange in happy and unhappy marriages: A family cycle perspective. *Behavior Therapy, 12*, 329–343.

Margolin, G., Talovic, S., & Weinstein, C. D. (1983). Areas of Change Questionnaire: A practical approach to marital assessment. *Journal of Consulting and Clinical Psychology, 57*, 920–931.

Margolin, G., & Wampold, B. E. (1981). Sequential analysis of conflict and accord in distressed and nondistressed marital partners. *Journal of Consulting and Clinical Psychology, 49*, 554–567.

O'Leary, K. D., & Beach, S. R. H. (in press). Marital therapy: A viable treatment for depression and marital discord. *American Journal of Psychiatry.*

Pittman, F. (1989). *Private lies: Infidelity and the betrayal of intimacy.* New York: Norton.

Ruscher, S. M., & Gotlib, I. H. (1988). Marital interaction patterns of couples with and without a depressed partner. *Behavior Therapy, 19*, 445–470.

Schmaling, K. B., & Jacobson, N. S. (in press). Marital interaction and depression. *Journal of Abnormal Psychology.*

Weiss, R. L., & Sommers, A. (1983). Marital Interaction Coding System—III. In E. E. Filsinger (Ed.), *Marriage and family assessment: A sourcebook for family therapy* (pp. 85–116). Beverly Hills, CA: Sage.

Wills, T. A., Weiss, R. L., & Patterson, G. R. (1974). A behavioral analysis of the determinants of marital satisfaction. *Journal of Consulting and Clinical Psychology, 42*, 802–811.

# PART TWO
# APPLICATIONS

# Introduction

This section contains chapters that focus on several applied issues. In Chapter 9, Segraves evaluates the three major theoretical orientations that have guided marital therapy—the psychodynamic framework, general systems theory, and the behavioral approach. Although each orientation has spawned a variety of therapies that often differ markedly, Segraves identifies and evaluates critically the common elements of each orientation. He goes on to argue that recent contributions to marital therapy emphasize cognitive variables and offer an approach to treatment that integrates these contributions.

The next two chapters deal with specific problems in marriage. Heiman and Verhulst (Chapter 10) examine the conceptual and empirical foundations for the treatment of sexual dysfunction in marriage. They show how psychodynamic, systems, and cognitive–behavioral perspectives have informed our understanding of sexual dysfunction; they go on to review outcome studies on the treatment of specific disorders as well as research on arousal that might enhance sex therapy. Building on this foundation, these authors outline practical approaches to treating a variety of dysfunctions. In the final section, they reconsider the theoretical orientations discussed earlier and identify methodological issues that need to be addressed in sex therapy research. Heiman and Verhulst argue that feminist theory has considerable potential to advance our understanding and treatment of sexual problems. They call for research that reflects more closely social constructionist, feminist, and systems theory orientations.

In Chapter 11, O'Leary and Vivian note that the scientific study of physical aggression in marriage is a relatively new endeavor and offer a comprehensive overview of this field. After outlining its emergence, they summarize what is known about the prevalence of marital violence, the characteristics of abusive relationships, and the etiology of physical aggression in marriage. In the course of reviewing etiological models, they offer a new model of aggression that draws from emerging research on cognition in marriage. Their review of the treatment of marital violence underscores the difficulty of dealing with this problem and identifies several critical needs for treatment outcome research on marital violence.

Beach and Bauserman (Chapter 12) address directly an important question raised in earlier chapters: how to enhance the effectiveness of interventions with married couples. Their review of marital therapy outcome research shows that while the range of treatments investigated in well-controlled outcome studies has increased in recent years, the percentage of couples who are nondistressed following marital therapy remains far from optimal. They argue that, in the absence of attention to the mediating goals of therapy, the continuing search for new therapeutic techniques and attempts to match therapy and couple types will not enhance the effectiveness of marital interventions appreciably. Drawing on two models from basic research, they illustrate how each can be used to deal with noncompliance, a common obstacle to the attainment of mediating goals of therapy.

In Chapter 13, Bradbury and Fincham discuss the prevention of marital dysfunction, an approach that departs radically from traditional clinical intervention. After distinguishing different types of prevention, they outline the arguments for and against prevention and evaluate research on the efficacy of prevention programs. The gap between the considerable potential of preventive efforts and data demonstrating their efficacy leads these authors to consider how the empirical foundations for prevention programs can be improved. They offer a framework for future research that emphasizes an important theme in the chapter: the need to consider marriage from the perspective of the individual, the couple, the couple's interaction, the mental health profession, and the government.

CHAPTER 9

# Theoretical Orientations in the Treatment of Marital Discord

## R. Taylor Segraves

Marital therapists are faced with a baffling complexity of data and therefore need a coherent theoretical system to organize their perceptions and therapeutic interventions. Despite this need, the absence of a comprehensive theory of marital therapy has been noted by many clinicians (e.g., Manus, 1966; Olson, 1975; Segraves, 1982), and the field has been described as consisting of several "partial theories that focus either on individual psychopathology or on the properties of marital interaction systems" (Segraves, 1978, p. 450).

Marital therapists have reacted to the theoretical confusion in various ways. Whereas some clinicians have persisted in theoretical orthodoxy (e.g., Nadelson, 1978), others have made efforts to form integrated models (Feldman, 1985; Pinsof, 1983; Greenberg & Johnson, 1986), and some have combined procedures and concepts from different schools in a form of technical eclecticism (Fitzgerald, 1973; Sager, 1976).

A basic premise of this chapter is that it is necessary to have a clear theory guiding clinical interventions, insofar as theory provides the clinician with a clarity of vision and coherence of action in perplexing clinical contexts and allows the easy transmission of concepts and procedures to other clinicians. Most importantly, the limitations of a precisely formulated theory can be identified and corrected as knowledge accumulates.

In view of this premise, the purpose of this chapter is twofold. First, the major theories pertaining to marital therapy are reviewed and evaluated. Although it is doubtful that there are many pure practitioners in any given theoretical camp, the major theoretical schools are identified as psychodynamic, general systems, and behavioral in orientation for the purposes of this chapter. The second purpose of this chapter is to review recent contributions to marital therapy that emphasize cognitive variables.


## PSYCHOANALYSIS AND MARRIAGE

Psychoanalysis has been concerned mainly with the study and treatment of individual psychopathology, and psychoanalysts have shown little direct interest in marriage. Indeed, certain analytic clinicians consider marital discord a symptom of individual psychopathology in one or both spouses (e.g., Lussheimer, 1966). Other classical analysts are concerned with current interpersonal forces such as marital discord only to the extent that such forces hinder treatment of individual patients (e.g., Giovacchini, 1965). Despite the relative lack of interest that psychoanalytic theorists have in marriage, this perspective has had a major impact on the treatment of marital discord, largely as a result of the pervasiveness of psychoanalytic concepts among mental health professionals.

A major difficulty in discussing psychoanalytic theory in relationship to marriage is that a unified psychoanalytic theory does not exist. Various schools of analytic thought such as self-psychology (Kohut, 1971), object-relations theory (Guntrip, 1974), ego psychology (Hartmann, 1939), and classical object-libidinal schools emphasize different aspects of psychological function. Although the differences between these schools of thought may appear minor to other therapists, they are very important to those therapists who are psychoanalytically oriented. A second problem in evaluating psychoanalytic theory is the concept of theoretical complementarity (Gedo & Goldberg, 1973) whereby new and apparently contradictory concepts are incorporated into analytic thought without displacing extant concepts. Each concept is viewed as an equally valid although different way of viewing the same data. A third problem is that many psychodynamically oriented clinicians have gradually altered basic psychoanalytic theory as they have ventured into the arena of marital and family therapy. Psychoanalytic treatment of marital discord has evolved from individual psychoanalysis of the symptomatic spouse with no therapeutic contact with the partner (Menninger, 1958) to concurrent separate analytic treatment of each spouse by different therapists (Martin & Bird, 1953) to concurrent separate analysis of each spouse by the same therapist (Greene, 1960) and finally to conjoint therapy by the same therapist (Nadelson, 1978). With these shifts in technique, barely perceptible changes in theoretical orientation have occurred. Thus, some psychoanalytically oriented marital therapists emphasize current interpersonal forces as well as historical factors (Martin, 1976), and others seek to achieve behavioral change as well as insight (Ackerman, 1966).

Although they differ markedly, the various schools of psychoanalytic psychotherapy have certain common elements, including (1) the belief that psychopathology resides within the individual, (2) the belief in past determinants of current behavior, and (3) the assumption of unconscious determinants of behavior, and (4) the belief that accurate self-knowledge (i.e., insight) can reduce neurotic suffering. Object-libidinal theory, one of the major psychoanalytic schools, stresses the role of unconscious conflict in the etiology of psychopathology and interpersonal discord. Maladaptive behavior is thought to involve unconscious conflict, experiencing certain emotions, especially sexuality or anger, in intimate interpersonal relationships. The goal of individual psychodynamic psychotherapy is to help the patient become aware of the unconscious elements of his conflicts that interfere with healthy adult relationships.

A major curative mechanism of psychoanalytic psythotherapy involves analysis of transference, which is understood as the misperception of the analyst by the patient (Sandler, Dare, & Holden, 1970). This misperception is thought to have been learned in previous relationships (usually with the parents) and is manifest in current relationships outside of therapy, and thus it is hypothesized to play an etiological role in interpersonal conflict (Malan, 1976). Within the relative safety of the analytic situation, the patient can become aware of his or her habitual emotional–perceptual distortions of intimate others. This knowledge can help the patient to modulate the intensity of conflictful feelings and alter perception of and behavior toward intimate others outside the therapeutic context.

The psychoanalytically oriented marital therapist differs from the individual analytically oriented therapist in that the marital therapist places greater emphasis on the transference distortions regarding the mate (Meissner, 1978). Much of the work of the analytically oriented marital therapist entails helping spouses realize the extent to which their unconscious past experiences are distorting their experience of one another (Nadelson,

1978). The goal of analyzing transference in marriage is to help spouses experience the partner as a real person rather than as a transference distortion (Fitzgerald, 1973).

The other school of psychoanalytic thought that exerts an influence on the treatment of marital discord is object-relations theory. This school, which is often referred to as the British psychoanalytic school and consists of such theorists as Melanie Klein, Guntrip, and Fairbairn (Guntrip, 1974), emphasizes the intrapsychic representations of self and other and differs from object-instinctual psychoanalytic theory by emphasizing the development of personality in interpersonal contexts (Kernberg, 1976). Within the field of marital therapy, such therapists have emphasized how distressed couples project disowned parts of the self on the partner. These therapists use interpretation to disrupt such projection systems, to have each spouse reexperience good and bad parts of the self, and to allow a spouse to experience the partner as he or she is (Greenspan & Mannino, 1979).

Psychoanalytic theory violates most of the rules concerning good theory construction (Ford & Urban, 1967). It abounds with poorly defined concepts, observations and assumptions are seldom kept separate, and the nature of the theory itself precludes refutation. However, psychoanalytic theory is the only major theoretical system that attempts to address the contribution of individual psychopathology to marital discord, an issue essentially ignored by behavioral marital therapy and general system theory. Many psychoanalytically oriented psychotherapists are astute observers of human behavior and possess a wealth of clinical wisdom concerning human motivation. Unfortunately, much of this wisdom is expressed in a language that is alien to most social scientists.

Certain of the lower-order explanatory concepts of psychoanalytically oriented psychotherapists (e.g., transference) can be restated in the language of social learning without unduly distorting their original meaning (e.g. learned expectations). This retranslation may encourage clinicians of differing orientations to appreciate the possible contribution of this theoretical school to an integrated theory of marital therapy. Most personality disorders can be understood as repetitive sequences of maladaptive interpersonal behavior elicited by intimate interpersonal relationships. These interpersonal sequences were learned in previous intimate relationships (usually with parents), in which they may have been adaptive. Part of the failure of adaptation of individuals with personality disorders is their inability to learn new sequences of behavior in intimate adult relationships. Thus, the purpose of psychotherapy is to help patients to unlearn former maladaptive manners of relating, to recognize the differences between current and past relationship demands, and to learn new patterns of relating. A major factor in the unhappy relationships of patients with personality disorders is their tendency to distort the personality and motivations of intimate associates. Psychoanalytic theory differs from other theories in its assumption that knowledge of one's tendency to distort perceptions and of the origins of that distortion serves a major curative function. It bears noting that many analytic theorists emphasize the importance of experiential as well as cognitive "insight" and that the pretermination phase of analysis typically includes a brief period in which the analyst and patient (with transference distortions interpreted) experience a real relationship.

## GENERAL SYSTEM THEORY

Although general system theory has had a significant influence on the social sciences (Grinker, 1969, 1975), it was originally elaborated in the biological sciences as an alternative to the prevailing scientific model of linear reductionism by which complex systems were explained by fragmentation into smaller and smaller units of study (von Bertalanffy, 1962; also see Steinglass, 1978). General system theory is a set of assumptions that describes the formal properties of organizational systems. A major assumption of this orientation is that certain properties of organizational systems are universal and independent of the system being studied or even of the units comprising that system.

The system viewpoint was introduced into the marital and family therapy field by a relatively small group of therapists known as the Palo Alto group (Foley, 1974). The Palo Alto group actually consisted of two separate groups under the direction of either Don Jackson or Gregory Bateson (Watzlawick, 1977). Other well-known therapists and theorists associated with this group include Haley, Satir, Watzlawick, Weakland, and Sluzki. This relatively small group of individuals has had a dramatic and lasting influence on the conduct of marital and family therapy. Although there is no therapeutic school known as the Palo Alto group or the general system group, concepts from general system theory, cybernetics, and communication theory have influenced contemporary therapists in many therapeutic camps.

At the time of their original publications psychoanalytic theory dominated American psychiatry, and the theoretical orientation of the Palo Alto group represented an attempted shift in paradigms (Bateson, 1972). Specifically, in contrast to the focus on metapsychological theory of intrapsychic processes within psychoanalytic theory, these therapists emphasized the observable interactions between individuals in distress (Jackson, 1970; Satir, 1967). Whereas psychoanalytic theorists maintained that marital discord could be understood by knowing the psychodynamics of the participants, these theorists emphasized that the personalities of marital partners might be better understood via their interaction patterns. In other words, the proper level of explanation was thought to exist at the level of the system rather than at the level of the units (i.e., people) comprising the system. Accordingly, the focus of therapy was on changing the structure of rules of interaction between individuals in disturbed marriages or families.

A number of concepts introduced by this group have been adopted by marital therapists of varying disciplines. In his work with families containing a severely disturbed member, Jackson (1960) repeatedly observed the resistance of family members to change in the disturbed member. The biological concept of homeostasis was invoked to describe this phenomenon in family systems. Marital and family interactional systems were viewed as rule-governed, and the term "marital *quid pro quo*" was introduced to capture the interactional rules governing a given relationship (see Lederer & Jackson, 1968). If a member deviates too far from the established pattern of interaction, various forces tend to restore the interaction back to its previous equilibrium. The term negative feedback is used as a description of these homeostatic forces. Another term introduced by this group of therapists is positive feedback, also referred to as runaways or games without end (Lederer & Jackson, 1968; Watzlawick, Weakland, & Fisch, 1974). For example, positive feedback is said to exist when one spouse's anger or defensiveness engenders a similar reaction from the partner, and the situation continues to escalate. Such situations are common in interpersonal contexts, appear to have a life of their own independent of the initial behavior, and can be understood and modified without the therapist having an intimate knowledge of the content of the disagreement or even of the personality dynamics of the combatants.

Other major contributions of the Palo Alto group include their highlighting the subtle nuances of power struggles in interpersonal relationships, their discussion of the multiple levels of communication in relationships and how communication helps to define relationship rules as well as to transmit information, and their assumption of circular causality in interaction sequences. Of course, this group also introduced a different approach to marital and family psychotherapy. With an emphasis on changing the rules of interaction, this group popularized such novel interventions as labeling of behavior patterns to prevent their recurrence, relabeling of behavior to change its effect, and the use of strategic interventions such as paradoxical intent.

## Critique

There is no school of thought or body of knowledge or procedures that can be labeled general system theory in the field of marital therapy (Steinglass, 1978). Instead, a group of innovative clinicians introduced a new orientation toward data. Many of these new concepts have survived the test of time and have been incorporated by contemporary clinicians. In many ways, this group of clinicians helped lay the groundwork for behavioral marital therapy by emphasizing the study of observable behavior and by legitimizing the use of behavioral change *per se* in marital and family therapy.

Rather than be viewed as a theory, general system theory is regarded most appropriately as a style of thinking or, at best, a loosely connected group of concepts. The weakness of this orientation, similar to that of psychoanalysis, appears to be its ability to incorporate new concepts rather than its ability to reject false concepts. Its major contribution appears to be the emphasis on pattern recognition in complex interactive systems. This is a useful addition to the prevailing scientific method of deductive reasoning.

## BEHAVIORISM AND MARRIAGE

One of the most recent entries into the field of marital therapy is behavioral marital therapy (BMT). Its origins can be traced to an article in which Goldiamond (1965) noted that a husband complaining about his wife's behavior was providing the stimuli that controlled her behavior. The appropriate marital intervention was to reinforce the husband for behaving differently or providing different stimuli for his wife. Goldiamond's pioneering work was followed shortly by other case reports (Lazarus, 1968; Stuart, 1969). The behavioral approach grew rapidly in popularity, and an extensive literature soon developed (Weiss, Hops, & Patterson, 1973; Jacobson & Margolin, 1979).

Behavioral marital therapy represents a unique approach to the treatment of marital discord, as it is concerned solely with the modification of observable behavior. In practice, the essence of BMT is somewhat blurred, as many clinicians using this approach have chosen approaches that also address nonbehavioral aspects of therapy. Since there is some confusion in the literature as to how the term behaviorism is defined, a brief diversion to define behaviorism and BMT is warranted.

Behaviorism is a philosophical orientation that holds that the objective study of publicly observable data is the exclusive basis for scientific investigation (Chaplin & Krawiec, 1962). Behaviorism is concerned with stimulus–response or environmental–organism relationships, and covert processes are considered to be beyond the scope of scientific investigation. Behavior therapy is unique in that it emphasizes the modification of symptomatic behavior via intervention in the person–environment interaction without consideration of hypothetical intervening cognitive emotional events within the organism.

Behavioral marital therapy has been influenced by social exchange theorists (Thibaut & Kelley, 1959) who emphasize the interdependence of reinforcement in social relationships and the importance of the reward/cost ratio in dyadic relationships. Behavioral marital therapists have been concerned with increasing the ratio of rewards to costs in distressed couples (Jacobson & Holtzworth-Munroe, 1986), and behavioral marital therapists tend to be directive, structured, and educational in their approach and to focus on skill acquisition (O'Leary & Turkewitz, 1978). These therapists have focused on increasing the bilateral use of positive reinforcement as a behavior-change mechanism and decreasing the use of coercion (i.e., negative reinforcement and punishment) as a behavior-change technique (Patterson, Weiss, & Hops, 1976). Patients are taught how to define in precise terms the behaviors desired from the spouse, how to shape such behavior by positive reinforcement (Liberman, 1970), how to interrupt negative interactional chains, how to analyze the consequences of their own behavior (Friedman, 1972), and how to track desired spouse behavior (Weiss, Birchler, & Vincent, 1974).

A variety of techniques have been developed to achieve these goals including exchange of tokens (Stuart, 1969), formalized behavior-exchange contracts (Weiss, 1978), good faith contracts (Weiss et al., 1973), and caring days (Stuart, 1976). Many behavior therapists regard marital discord as the result of interpersonal skills deficits (e.g., Baucom, 1984) and have developed programs and modules designed to teach conflict-resolution skills, negotiation skills, and communication skills (Jacobson & Holtzworth-Munroe, 1986).

## Critique

With its emphasis on specifying procedures, operationalizing concepts, and evaluating the effectiveness of interventions, BMT brought a breath of fresh air to the field of marital therapy. For the first time, therapists were concerned with the precise description of problem behaviors and with the delineation of interventions in such a way that they could be adopted by other clinicians. Another major contribution of this approach was the use of concepts at a lower level of abstraction such that the data referents for these concepts was clear.

Unfortunately, some of the early advocates of behavior therapy were overly zealous, and behaviorism became an ideology or political movement in ways not totally dissimilar from psychoanalysis (London, 1972). Similarly, the wholesale extension of the behavioral approach to marital therapy appeared to predate the publication of systematic research mandating such a shift (Gurman & Knudson, 1978). The political aspect of the early behavioral movement may explain why many of the early behavioral marital therapists reported their treatment approaches in a mechanistic, procedure-based manner, whereas in reality many of these therapists were addressing cognitive–emotional events within their patients (Segraves, 1982).

One of the unique features of behaviorism as a philosophy of science is the specificity of its basic tenets. Thus, it is clear when procedures and concepts deviate from the behavioral model. This strength of the behavioral model appears to have led to its modification, and clinicians previously associated with BMT are now seeking to change cognitive events and are thus modifying the original treatment paradigm (e.g., Baucom, 1989; Weiss, 1984).

## COGNITIVE MARITAL THERAPY

The work by Albert Bandura (1977) and others within the field of social learning theory suggests that an understanding of human behavior requires consideration of events that occur within the organism. The acceptance of social learning theory has legitimized the study of cognitive variables and has contributed to the development of therapeutic approaches labeled cognitive-behaviorism or mediational-behaviorism (Meichenbaum, 1977; Mahoney, 1974). A group of clinicians and clinical theorists have evolved who are primarily data based in orientation but who also address the description and modification of cognitive events. In the field of marital therapy, clinical investigators are now free to investigate the role of cognitive factors in the genesis and maintenance of marital discord (Arias & Beach, 1987; Epstein, 1982; Fincham & Bradbury, 1988), to discuss the role of prior social learning as a contributor to current discord (Segraves, 1982), and to address cognitive factors in the treatment of marital discord (Bennun, 1986; Baucom & Lester, 1986; Jacobson & Holtzworth-Munroe, 1986).

A considerable literature in cognitive social psychology is compatible with the social learning orientation and supplies some of the necessary pieces for a beginning school of cognitive marital therapy. One of the theoretical forerunners to cognitive-behaviorism is George Kelly (1955), who hypothesized that most problems in living are the result of the idiosyncratic ways that people construe their experiences. He advocated a form of treatment called fixed-role therapy in which people could have life experiences that were discordant with their way of construing the world. Other cognitive social psychologists have stressed the relationship of inner cognitive events and events in the interpersonal environment (Carson, 1969), how people evolve interpersonal schemas to organize and predict interpersonal stimuli (Stotland & Cannon, 1972), and how certain interpersonal schemas tend to be self-confirming (Leary, 1957).

Many clinicians who are identified with social learning theory have noted the limited efficacy and explanatory power of behavioral models of therapy and have stressed the need to address cognitive variables in the treatment of marital discord (e.g., Bennun, 1986; Jacobson, 1984; Schindler & Vollmer, 1984; Weiss, 1984). These therapists have stressed that the perceptions of the marital partner's motivations may be as important as the partner's actions. Several ways in which the efficacy of behavioral exchange therapy might be affected adversely by cognitive variables include the following: (1) a spouse may not notice or may dismiss positive partner behavior as being inconsequential; (2) the importance of a partner's negative behavior may be exaggerated; (3) cognitive variables may interfere with compliance to the therapist's recommendations; and (4) faulty cognitions may become functionally autonomous such that they are minimally influenced by the spouse's actual behavior.

Consideration of cognitive variables in distressed couples has led to specific recommendations for modifying BMT. Although the focus is still on increasing the ratio of positive to negative behaviors for both spouses, each spouse is required to focus first on changing his or her own behavior to counter the sense of blaming and victimization. Because spouses in distressed marriages tend to interpret positive behaviors from the mate as being selfishly motivated, the emphasis on reciprocity of behavior exchange has been deemphasized by some therapists. To counter their frequent tendency to discount positive behaviors, spouses are requested to generate a list of potential reinforcers for the spouse and to choose which reinforcers to use. In theory, this tactic should maximize the "giver's" sense of choice (thus decreasing resistance to the directive) and increase the probability that the partner will perceive the reinforcement as internally motivated and genuine.

Additional cognitive techniques have been employed by various therapists operating under the rubric of cognitive social learning theory. This includes attributional relabeling, whereby the therapist relabels aversive behavior by a spouse as the result of skill deficit rather than of malevolent intent (Jacobson, 1984). Another example of cognitive restructuring arises when the therapist suggests that a spouse's negative behavior is situationally determined rather than the result of enduring and pejorative personality traits (Weiss, 1984). Distressed spouses have also been instructed to modify their self-referent speech on the assumption that this may decrease extreme reactivity to negative events (Schindler & Vollmer, 1984). In certain instances, maneuvers suggested by these therapists resemble those of psychoanalytic marital therapists. For example, Jacobson (1984) suggests that therapists help the couple to identify their molar conflicts (e.g., intimacy–distance) and continue to insist that the couple return to these molar problems and resolve them. Revenstorf (1984) recommends that therapists focus on the learning history of each spouse and pinpoint the idiosyncratic relationship of each spouse to his individual learning history. The goal of this intervention is to change the attribution of causality for marital discord. Although a different language is used to describe and justify the interventions, the tactics suggested by Jacobson (1984) and Revenstorf (1984) and others bear an obvious resemblance to therapeutic interventions by psychodynamically oriented marital therapists.

I (Segraves, 1978, 1982, 1986) have developed a cognitive model for treatment of marital discord on the assumption that marital therapists of varying theoretical camps have struggled with the necessity of making assumptions about the interplay of inner cognitive–emotional events and observable interaction patterns. This model is based on three major assumptions. The first assumption is that one or both spouses in a chronically disturbed relationship will tend to misperceive the partner's motivations and personality characteristics. Because of the complexity of interpersonal stimuli, people evolve templates or schemas to organize interpersonal perceptions and predict the actions of social intimates. It is assumed further that such templates are formed during previous learning experiences. This assumption is analogous to the concept of transference that is used by psychoanalytically oriented therapists (Gurman, 1978; Meissner, 1978) and to concepts used by cognitive social psychologists such as Kelly (1955), Carson (1969), and Stotland and Canon (1972).

The second major assumption of this model is that people tend to recreate their interpersonal world by eliciting behavior from others that confirms their inner representational world and by discouraging or selectively ignoring disconfirmatory behavior. Again, similar concepts have been employed by cognitive psychologists (Leary, 1957; Bandura, 1977) and by psychoanalytically oriented therapists (Offenkrantz & Tobin, 1975).

The third major assumption is that repetitive observation of spouse behavior that is discrepant with the schema for the perception of the spouse will result in a change in the schema. In other words, if each spouse can have novel and disconfirmatory experiences of the other, their habitual tendencies to distort the motivations of the other will be reduced. This assumption is an extrapolation of fixed-role therapy (Kelly, 1955) to the marital context. It is also similar to the assumption of many integrative theorists that the development of new patterns of behavior that are incongruent with the usual defensive structure will lead to intrapsychic change (Wachtel, 1977). These theoretical assumptions are represented schematically in Figure 9.1.

Based on these assumptions, a cognitive approach to marital therapy was developed. The goal of this approach is to provide

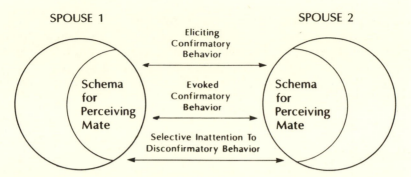

**FIGURE 9.1.** Schematic of theoretical assumptions. As illustrated, psychotherapeutic interventions in marital therapy can be focused at different levels. Classical psychoanalysis focuses on modifying the schema for perceiving the mate. Fixed-role therapy and certain forms of behavioral therapy emphasize modifying eliciting behavior. General system therapists usually focus on modifying both elicited and evoked behavior.

bilateral disproof of maladaptive schemata for perceptions of the spouse. The initial stages of therapy are nonspecific and involve the therapist gaining control over the interactional process and emotional climate so that learning can take place. Once a phase of relative calm is achieved, the therapist begins to search for the spouse's recurring negative characterological descriptions of the partner. These descriptions may be partially accurate but not truly reflective of the multidimensional complexity of the partner's personality. The next step for the therapist is to search for the eliciting behaviors from each spouse that tend to elicit confirmatory behaviors from the partner. The therapist then labels the eliciting behavior and its probable consequences and purposely undermines the spouse's manner of eliciting confirmatory behavior. At the same time, the therapist labels the confirmatory behavior and its probable consequences and coaches the partner to engage in alternative, disconfirmatory patterns of responding. In addition to disrupting the sequences of eliciting and confirmatory experiences, the therapist searches for the disconfirmatory experiences that are dismissed. These are emphasized so that they cannot be dismissed as easily. The therapist repeatedly attacks the rigid perception of the spouse, pointing out exceptions to the schemas, emphasizing the minimally perceived parts of the spouse's character, and stressing the complexity of each spouse's character and motivations. In certain instances, for example, one spouse may make a statement that the partner paraphrases in a distorted manner. The therapist will request that the spouse repeat verbatim what the partner has said and then confront the spouse repeatedly with the discrepancy between the stated message and his or her paraphrasing of it. The therapist utilizes a variety of techniques in order to disprove or refute cognitive distortions of the mate's character.

## Comment

A cognitive approach to marital therapy has the advantages of addressing both the learning histories of spouses and their current interactional difficulties. An added advantage of this approach is that it gives the clinician freedom to use a variety of techniques within a clear conceptual framework. This approach thus addresses some of the same issues as the psychoanalytic approach but phrases them in a data-based language; it therefore has the potential to address the complexity of interactional problems while remaining empirically anchored. A possible pitfall of cognitive marital therapy is that clinicians may unwittingly drift back into mentalism as they employ terminology that sounds empirical.

## SUMMARY

Theoretical perspectives on the origin and treatment of marital discord have undergone dramatic shifts in the last several decades. The situation is quite different from 1956, when Manus described marital therapy as "a therapy without a theory." Psychoanalytic theorists contributed to our study of marriage by their emphasis on the role of historical factors in personality development and marital discord. General system theorists attempted a paradigm shift by their historical approach to marriage combined with their view of marital interaction as an entity to be studied independent of the participants. Behavioral marital therapy introduced the notion of scientific accountability for clinical endeavors. Pure behavioral marital therapy enjoyed a relatively brief life span as clinicians began using inferences about their patients' cognitions in both their conceptualization and implementation of treatment. Social learning theory then opened the pathway for a more complete appreciation of cognitive variables in marriage. Cognitive marital therapy has completed the circle by addressing how past learning affects expectations in marriage and contributes to marital discord.

It appears that theoreticians from various schools of therapy have grappled with similar problems, including how to encompass in the same model individual subjective data and observable interactional data and how to be clinically relevant while remaining empirically based. Theorists associated with psychoanalysis and general system theory used molar explanatory concepts that often were tied loosely to data referents. The advantage of such approaches is their appearance of comprehensiveness, yet the vagueness of the concepts renders them nearly impossible to disprove. Behaviorism, on the other hand, offered a very restricted model with clearly defined concepts. The shift to social learning theory and cognitive therapy appears to be a natural consequence of the limitations of this model. It is my hope that the next decade will see further development of our understanding of the cognitive factors involved in marital discord and that clinical models of cognitive marital therapy will remain closely allied with an empirical data base.

# R E F E R E N C E S

Ackerman, N. W. (1966). *Treating the troubled family*. New York: Basic Books.
Arias, I., & Beach, S. R. H. (1987). The assessment of social cognition in the context of marriage. In K. D. O'Leary (Ed.), *Assessment of marital discord* (pp. 109–137). Hillsdale, NJ: Erlbaum.
Bandura, A. (1977). *Social learning theory*. Englewood Cliffs, NJ: Prentice-Hall.
Bateson, G. (1972). *Steps to an ecology of mind*. New York: Ballantine.
Baucom, D. H. (1984). The active ingredients of behavioral marital therapy: The effectiveness of problem-solving/communication training, contingency contracting, and their combination. In K. Hahlweg & N. S. Jacobson (Eds.), *Marital interaction: Analysis and modification* (pp. 73–88). New York: Guilford Press.
Baucom, D. H. (1989). The role of cognitions in behavioral marital therapy: Current status and future directions. *The Behavior Therapist, 12*, 3–6.
Baucom, D. H., & Lester, G. W. (1986). The usefulness of cognitive restructuring as an adjunct to behavioral marital therapy. *Behavior Therapy, 17*, 385–403.
Bennun, I. (1986). Cognitive components of marital conflict. *Behavioral Psychotherapy, 14*, 302–309.
Carson, R. C. (1969). *Interaction concepts of personality*. Chicago: Aldine.
Chaplin, J. P., & Krawiec, T. S. (1962). *Systems and theories of psychology*. New York: Holt, Rinehart & Winston.
Epstein, N. (1982). Cognitive therapy with couples. *American Journal of Family Therapy, 10*, 5–16.

Feldman, L. B. (1985). Integrative multilevel family therapy. *Journal of Marital and Family Therapy, 11*, 357–372.

Fincham, F. D., & Bradbury, T. N. (1988). The impact of attribution in marriage: Empirical and conceptual foundations. *British Journal of Clinical Psychology, 27*, 77–90.

Fitzgerald, R. V. (1973). *Conjoint marital therapy.* New York: Jason Aronson.

Foley, V. D. (1974). *An introduction to family therapy.* New York: Grune & Stratton.

Ford, D. H., & Urban, H. B. (1967). *Systems of psychotherapy—a comparative study.* New York: Wiley.

Friedman, P. H. (1972). Personalistic family and marital therapy. In A. A. Lazurus (Ed.), *Clinical behavior therapy* (pp. 116–154). New York: Brunner/Mazel.

Gedo, J. E., & Goldberg, A. (1973). *Models of the mind.* Chicago: University of Chicago.

Giovacchini, P. L. (1965). Treatment of marital disharmonies: The classical approach. In B. Greene (Ed.), *The psychotherapies of marital disharmony* (pp. 39–82). New York: Free Press.

Goldiamond, I. (1965). Self-control procedures in personal behavior problems. *Psychological Reports, 17*, 851–888.

Greenberg, L. S., & Johnson, S. M. (1986). Emotionally focused couples therapy. In N. S. Jacobson & A. S. Gurman (Eds.), *Clinical handbook of marital therapy* (pp. 253–276). New York: Guilford Press.

Greene, B. L. (1960). Marital disharmony: Concurrent analysis of husband and wife. *Diseases of the Nervous System, 21*, 1–6.

Greenspan, S. I., & Mannino, F. V. (1979). A model for brief interventions with couples based on projective identification. *American Journal of Psychiatry, 131*, 1103–1106.

Grinker, R. R. (1969). Symbolism and general systems theory. In W. Gray, F. Dahl, & N. Rizzo (Eds.), *General systems theory and psychiatry* (pp. 135–140). Boston: Little, Brown.

Grinker, R. R. (1975). The relevance of general systems theory to psychiatry. In D. A. Hamburg & H. K. M. Brodie (Eds.), *American handbook of psychiatry* (vol. 6, 2nd ed., pp. 251–274). New York: Basic Books.

Guntrip, H. J. S. (1974). Psychoanalytic object relations theory: The Fairburn-Guntrip approach. In S. Arieti (Ed.), *American handbook of psychiatry* (vol. 1, pp. 828–842). New York: Basic Books.

Gurman, A. S. (1978). Contemporary marital therapies: A critique and comparative analysis of psychoanalytic, behavioral and system theory approaches. In T. J. Paolino & B. S. McCrady (Eds.), *Marriage and marital therapy* (pp. 445–566). New York: Brunner/Mazel.

Gurman, A. S., & Knudson, R. M. (1978). Behavioral marriage therapy. I. A psychodynamic systems analysis and critique. *Family Process, 17*, 121–138.

Hartmann, H. (1939). *Ego psychology and the problem of adaptation.* New York: International Universities Press.

Jackson, D. D. (1960). *The etiology of schizophrenia.* New York: Basic Books.

Jackson, D. D. (1970). The study of the family. In N. W. Ackerman (Ed.), *Family process* (pp. 111–130). New York: Basic Books.

Jacobson, N. S. (1984). The modification of cognitive processes in behavioral marital therapy: Integrating cognitive and behavioral intervention strategies. In K. Hahlweg & N. S. Jacobson (Eds.), *Marital interaction: Analysis and modification* (pp. 285–308). New York: Guilford Press.

Jacobson, N. S., & Holtzworth-Munroe, A. (1986). Marital therapy: A social learning–cognitive perspective. In N. S. Jacobson & A. S. Gurman (Eds.), *Clinical handbook of marital therapy* (pp. 29–70). New York: Guilford Press.

Jacobson, N. S., & Margolin, G. (1979). *Marital therapy.* New York: Brunner/Mazel.

Kelly, G. A. (1955). *The psychology of personal constructs.* New York: Norton.

Kernberg, O. F. (1976). *Object-relations theory and clinical psychoanalysis.* New York: Jason Aronson.

Kohut, H. (1971). *The analysis of the self.* New York: International Universities Press.

Lazarus, A. A. (1968). Behavior therapy and marriage counseling. *Journal of the American Society of Psychosomatic Dental Medicine, 15,* 49–56.

Leary, T. (1957). *Interpersonal dimensions of personality.* New York: Ronald Press.

Lederer, W. F., & Jackson, D. D. (1968). *The mirages of marriage.* New York: Norton.

Liberman, R. (1970). Behavioral approaches to family and couple therapy. *American Journal of Orthopsychiatry, 40,* 106–118.

London, P. (1972). The end of ideology in behavior modification. *American Psychologist, 27,* 913–920.

Lussheimer, P. (1966). The diagnosis of marital conflicts. *American Journal of Psychoanalysis, 26,* 127–146.

Mahoney, M. J. (1974). *Cognition and behavior modification.* Cambridge, MA: Ballinger.

Malan, D. H. (1976). *The frontier of brief psychotherapy.* New York: Plenum.

Manus, G. L. (1966). Marriage counseling: A technique in search of a theory. *Journal of Marriage and the Family, 28,* 449–453.

Martin, P. A. (1976). *A marital therapy manual.* New York: Brunner/Mazel.

Martin, P. A., & Bird, H. W. (1953). An approach to the psychotherapy of marriage partners—the stereoscopic technique. *Psychiatry, 16,* 123–127.

Meichenbaum, D. (1977). *Cognitive-behavior modification.* New York: Plenum.

Meissner, W. W. (1978). The conceptualization of marriage and family dynamics from a psychoanalytic perspective. In T. J. Paolino & B. S. McCrady (Eds.), *Marriage and marital therapy* (pp. 25–88). New York: Brunner/Mazel.

Menninger, K. (1958). *Theory of psychoanalytic technique.* New York: Basic Books.

Nadelson, C. C. (1978). Marital therapy from a psychoanalytic perspective. In T. J. Paolino & B. S. McCrady (Eds.), *Marriage and marital therapy* (pp. 89–164). New York: Brunner/Mazel.

Offenkrantz, W., & Tobin, A. (1975). Psychoanalytic psychotherapy. In D. X. Freedman & J. E. Dyrud (Eds.), *American handbook of psychiatry* (vol. 5, pp. 183–205). New York: Basic Books.

O'Leary, K. D., & Turkewitz, H. (1978). Marital therapy from a behavioral perspective. In T. J. Paolino & B. S. McCrady (Eds.), *Marriage and marital therapy* (pp. 240–297). New York: Brunner/Mazel.

Olson, D. H. (1975). A critical overview. In A. S. Gurman & D. G. Rice (Eds.), *Couples in conflict* (pp. 7–62). New York: Jason Aronson.

Patterson, G. R., Weiss, R. L., & Hops, H. (1976). Training of marital skills: Some problems and concepts. In H. Leitenberg (Ed.), *Handbook of behavior modification and behavior therapy* (pp. 242–254). Englewood Cliffs, NJ: Prentice-Hall.

Pinsof, W. M. (1983). Integrative problem-centered therapy: Toward the synthesis of family and individual psychotherapies. *Journal of Marital and Family Therapy, 9,* 19–36.

Revenstorf, D. (1984). The role of attribution of marital distress in therapy. In K. Hahlweg & N. S. Jacobson (Eds.), *Marital interaction: Analysis and modification* (pp. 325–336). New York: Guilford Press.

Sager, C. J. (1976). *Marriage contracts and couple therapy.* New York: Brunner/Mazel.

Sandler, J., Dare, C., & Holden, A. (1970). Basic psychoanalytic concepts: III. Transference. *British Journal of Psychiatry, 116,* 667–672.

Satir, V. (1967). *Conjoint family therapy.* Palo Alto: Science and Behavior Books.

Schindler, L., & Vollmer, M. (1984). Cognitive perspectives in behavioral marital therapy: Some proposals for bridging theory, research, and practice. In K. Hahlweg & N. S. Jacobson (Eds.), *Marital interaction: Analysis and modification* (pp. 309–324). New York: Guilford Press.

Segraves, R. T. (1978). Conjoint marital therapy: A cognitive behavioral model. *Archives of General Psychiatry, 35,* 450–455.

Segraves, R. T. (1982). *Marital therapy: A combined psychodynamic–behavioral approach.* New York: Plenum.

Segraves, R. T. (1986). Cognitive therapy of marital discord. *International Journal of Family Psychiatry, 7,* 277–287.

Steinglass, P. (1978). The conceptualization of marriage from a systems theory perspective. In T. J. Paolino & B. S. McGrady (Eds.), *Marriage and marital therapy* (pp. 298–365). New York: Brunner/Mazel.

Stotland, E., & Cannon, L. K. (1972). *Social psychology: A cognitive approach.* Philadelphia: Saunders.

Stuart, R. B. (1969). Operant-interpersonal treatment for marital discord. *Journal of Consulting and Clinical Psychology, 33,* 657–682.

Stuart, R. B. (1976). An operant interpersonal program for couples. In D. H. L. Olson (Ed.), *Treating relationships* (pp. 119–132). Lake Mills, IA: Graphic Publishing.

Thibaut, J., & Kelley, H. H. (1959). *The social psychology of groups.* New York: Wiley.

von Bertalanffy, L. (1962). General systems theory—a critical review. *General Systems Yearbook, 8,* 1–20.

Wachtel, L. (1977). *Psychoanalysis and behavior therapy.* New York: Basic Books.

Watzlawick, P. (1977). Introduction. In P. Watzlawick & J. H. Weakland (Eds.), *The interactional view* (pp. xi–xv). New York: Norton.

Watzlawick, P., Weakland, J., & Fisch, R. (1974). *Change: Principles of problem formation and problem resolution.* New York: Norton.

Weiss, R. L. (1978). The conceptualization of marriage from a behavioral perspective. In T. J. Paolino & B. S. McCrady (Eds.), *Marriage and marital therapy* (pp. 165–239). New York: Brunner/Mazel.

Weiss, R. L. (1984). Cognitive and strategic interventions in behavioral marital therapy. In K. Hahlweg & N. S. Jacobson (Eds.), *Marital interaction: Analysis and modification* (pp. 337–355). New York: Guilford Press.

Weiss, R. L., Birchler, G. L., & Vincent, J. P. (1974). Contractual models for negotiation training in marital dyads. *Journal of Marriage and the Family, 36,* 321–330.

Weiss, R. L., Hops, H., & Patterson, G. R. (1973). A framework for conceptualizing marital conflicts: A technology for altering it, some data for evaluating it. In L. A. Hamerlynck, L. C. Handy, & E. J. Mash (Eds.), *Behavior change, methodology, concepts and practice* (pp. 309–342). Champaign, IL: Research Press.

# CHAPTER 10

# Sexual Dysfunction and Marriage

## Julia R. Heiman
## Johan Verhulst

Most marriages will at some time encounter sexual problems (Frank, Anderson, & Rubinstein, 1978). The purpose of this chapter is to review the conceptual and empirical foundations of the current treatment of sexual disorders in married couples. Treatment strategies and future pathways are also discussed.

## CONCEPTUAL FOUNDATIONS

Prior to 1900, little was known about sexual functioning, and conceptualization was limited to religious, moral, or medical opinions. Sexual problems in marriage have since been subjected to a variety of interpretations. Current approaches to understanding sexual dysfunction are reviewed in this section.

### Psychoanalytic Contributions

Although sexual problems were treated prior to the introduction of psychoanalysis, it was Freud's work that placed sexuality at the center of personality development. The most original of Freud's observations include the discovery of laws of consciousness and the demonstration that infants were not only sexual but that infantile sexual development had profound consequences for the erotic life and character of adults (e.g., Freud, 1900/1957, 1905/1957). Normal sexuality and gratifying genital intercourse were seen as difficult to achieve because of psychic hurdles, the inherent bisexuality of children, and the repressiveness required to direct and form sexuality.

From a classical Freudian perspective, unresolved oedipal conflicts were viewed as the sole etiological factor in sexual pathology, and it followed that the cure of sexual problems required resolution of unconscious conflict. Psychoanalysis was the vehicle proposed for such cures, which were accomplished by exploring unconscious elements while using the transferential aspects of the therapeutic relationship.

The contributions of object-relations theory are among the most visible extensions of analytic approaches to sexual and marital problems (e.g., Fairbairn, 1954). According to this perspective, the need for attachment in a relationship, rather than the unfolding of drives, is central to development. The infant incorporates the relationship with the mother and makes an "introject" of this relationship that has good and bad parts. The good, dependable parts remain conscious and represented as an "ideal object," whereas the bad parts, real and fantasized, are repressed into unconsciousness along with parts of the ego invested in them and accompanying affects. Fairbairn and others propose that these introjects are likely to be manifested in interactions with intimate family members and with a therapist.

Melanie Klein (1975), an influential figure for object-relations theorists, defines ideal and persecuting objects differently from Fairbairn, but the essence is similar: infants actively "split" the ideal objects from bad ones. Managing bad parts of oneself via unconscious processes such as splitting and projection can become apparent in marital situations. For example, *projective identification* involves the projection of the unacceptable parts of self (e.g., selfishness) onto an object (i.e., the spouse). This process has many functions including avoidance of separation from the ideal object, removing bad parts of self, and gaining control over bad objects.

Object-relations theory has been applied to marital interaction (e.g., Dicks, 1967), and Scharff (1982) has extended this view to sexual interaction. Following Fairbairn, Scharff posits that the sex life of the individual contains three structures of self—the central ego, the "antilibidinal" ego, and the libidinal ego—that correspond to three inner objects—the ideal or need-satisfying object, the antilibidinal or need-frustrating object, and the need-exciting or libidinal object. These structures are active in the sex life of individuals and couples, such that sexuality renews the early bonds between symbolic and physical levels of gratification and revives developmental conflicts. Given the deep and varied meanings of the physical contact between mother and infant (especially involving issues of nurturance and attachment), later adult efforts to connect physically are infused with older family issues. Thus, sex is physical as well as symbolic, and it requires partners to align internal objects developed over time. In particular, sex symbolizes the struggle to hold onto the image of the caring parent, to overcome the image of the withholding parent, and to reconcile and synthesize the two images in order to construct a flexible degree of intimacy. As a consequence, treatment of sexual problems requires examination of disjunctions in object-relations (see Scharff, 1988).

## Cognitive-Behavioral Contributions

In contrast to psychoanalysis, the focus of cognitive-behavioral thinking is on conscious processes. From this perspective, sexual problems are thought to result from a person's experience in various contexts, and principles of learning have been proposed to explain the causes of sex problems. Etiology is less of a concern than treatment to cognitive-behaviorists, however, and resolving past conflicts is less important than changing existing symptoms. Cognitive-behavioral treatment of sexual problems often involves behavioral prescriptions beyond verbal and symbolic processing, and individuals are challenged directly to think and act in different ways.

The most significant impact on the treatment of sexual problems to date was made not by psychologists but by the medical team of Masters and Johnson.[1] They took two bold steps that were crucial to the field of sexual dysfunction: first, they studied the body during sexual arousal and orgasm, thus giving physical variables greater status in relationship to prevailing psychodynamic formulations; second, using a very practical and symptom-oriented framework, they treated sexual problems in couples (Masters & Johnson, 1966, 1970). In treatment, the body's lack of sexual response was thought to result from states of mind that shut out sensual stimuli. To overcome performance anxiety, the most important of these states of mind, treatment focused on a graded series of sensual exercises (sensate focus) that elicited higher levels of arousal. In essence, the body was used to help heal the mind, which in turn healed the body.

[1]Although they have never called themselves cognitive-behaviorists, Masters and Johnson's therapeutic ingredients of education, communication, behavioral exercises, and focus on symptom remission fit very comfortably with cognitive-behavioral principles and therapeutic approach. Hence their work is discussed in this section.

Cognitive-behavioral treatments had been attempted success-fully prior to Masters and Johnson, using such techniques as edu-cation, assertiveness training, desensitization, and even graded sexual assignments (e.g., Ellis, 1961; Lazarus, 1963; Wolpe, 1958). However, Masters and Johnson's (1970) treatment book triggered a deluge of cognitive-behavioral work on sexual dysfunctions (e.g., Leiblum & Pervin, 1980; LoPiccolo & Stock, 1986), which has resulted in two major contributions. First Masters and Johnson's interventions have been reconceptualized in cognitive-behavioral terms. For those desiring to identify principles that may account for the mechanisms of symptom removal in Masters and Johnson's therapy, the concepts of *in vivo* desensitization and reciprocal inhibition fit aspects of the sensate focus procedures extremely well. Second, outcome research and studies of theoretical assump-tions have been undertaken with Masters and Johnson's version of sex therapy as well as with various alternatives. We discuss these contributions later in this chapter.

### Systems Theory Contributions

Systems theory is the most recent entry in the conceptualization and treatment of sexual problems. General systems theory claims to offer a new paradigm to account for multifactoral phenomena and has been applied to those areas of medical illness for which a traditional linear-causal model of disease is inadequate (Miller, 1978; von Bertalanffy, 1968). In psychotherapy, marital and fam-ily therapists have been the most attentive to systems approaches.

Several basic principles of systems theory are important to a discussion of couples' sexual problems. One is the principle of *emergent qualities*: a system, in this case a couple, is more than the sum of its parts. Most qualities of a relationship, such as trust or conflict management, are generated by the process of interaction and cannot be understood as a simple addition of individual char-acteristics. Furthermore, these relationship qualities influence and change the individuals. *Homeostasis*, the system's self-regula-tion process that maintains its stability, is another important prin-ciple. Without homeostasis, a system (in this case a relationship) would be in constant upheaval, and the system would lose its structure and identity. Nevertheless, change or *morphogenesis* must also be possible. *Circularity*, or circular causality, is at the heart of systems theory, describing the fact that a change in one element both influences and depends on the other elements.

In contrast to the two aforementioned theoretical perspectives, the emphasis in systems theory is on the relationship's character, power, and equilibrium rather than on each individual's strengths and weaknesses. Thus, a lack of change goes beyond being the partners' resistance (as in psychoanalysis) but may result from the protective tendency of the system's homeostatic mechanism. Learning assignments therefore focus on interactional change rather than on one individual's thoughts or behaviors (as in cognitive-behavioral theory).

Although little has been written about systems approaches to sexual dysfunction, a systemic perspective has been applied to low sexual desire (Verhulst & Heiman, 1988; Weeks, 1987) and complex cases of secondary orgasmic dysfunction (Heiman & Grafton-Becker, 1989); both disorders are less amenable to standard sex therapy interventions. The systems perspective has tried either to incorporate family therapy approaches (e.g., Regas & Sprenkle, 1984) or to explain levels of interactional patterns as an entree to treatment. Verhulst and Heiman (1988) identifed symbolic interactions (symbolic gestures and other representational cognitive features), affect-regulated interactions (proposed as territorial, ranking order, exploratory, and attachment), and sensate exchanges (including elicited sensory, neurophysiological, and motor reflexes). An interactional fit and coordination between the partners is required at each level for the sexual interaction to develop.

Although these three theoretical systems provide valuable frameworks for conceptualizing and treating sexual problems, they have very unequal support from empirical research, as we demonstrate next.

## EMPIRICAL FOUNDATIONS

Several factors hinder research on marital sexual dysfunction. Self-report methods must be relied on to examine behaviors that our culture labels as private. In cases where physiological processes are examined, the act of measurement itself may interfere with the phenomena studied. Finally, broad generalizations about normal, even statistically normal, sexual behavior are not based on data obtained from random representative samples because a certain percentage of people will always refuse to be involved with studies of sexuality. With these limitations in mind, we can examine research on sexual dysfunction.

Kinsey's works were of major importance in describing the sexual experiences of thousands of men and women (Kinsey, Pomeroy, & Martin, 1948; Kinsey, Pomeroy, Martin, & Gebhard, 1953). Topics such as orgasm, masturbation, and frequency of intercourse were assessed via structured interviews and cross-classified by such variables as age, education, and decade born. Though few detailed data were gathered on the prevalence of specific sexual disorders, data on orgasmic frequency, erectile dysfunction, and ejaculation latency were summarized.

Masters and Johnson (1966) were the pioneers in the study of the physiological sexual response patterns of nearly 700 individuals. Because of their work, we now have a greater understanding of such processes as sex flush, total body response to sexual arousal, orgasmic contractions throughout the pelvis, and the effects of pregnancy on sexual response. Learning that women and men have orgasms within a similar time frame in masturbation but not coitus helped to normalize the reports that many women took longer and sometimes "gave up" during intercourse. Although critically important, this early work is limited because it is primarily descriptive rather than quantitative (e.g., means and standards deviations are not provided for physiological measures).

Research on the outcome of clinical intervention has been the accomplishment primarily of the cognitive-behaviorists. Although Masters and Johnson's (1970) outcome figures were impressive (e.g., 80% success rate across all dysfunctions; 98% success rate for treatment of premature ejaculation), their figures have been criticized because their criteria for success are difficult to identify clearly (Zilbergeld & Kilmann, 1984). Cognitive-behaviorial research since Masters and Johnson has yielded data across a wide range of outcome variables. This literature is summarized here only briefly, and the reader is referred to other sources for further discussion (e.g., Heiman & LoPiccolo, 1983; LoPiccolo & Stock, 1986; Milan, Kilmann, & Boland, 1988).

## Specific Dysfunctions: Outcome Studies

For the primary anorgasmic (i.e., totally lacking orgasm) woman, a directed masturbation program, which includes education and cognitive and kinesthetic self-exploration, has been shown to be very effective in individual (e.g., Heiman & LoPiccolo, 1988) and group formats (e.g., Mills & Kilmann, 1982). Limited therapist intervention (four sessions), a film, and reading can be another effective modality (Morokoff & LoPiccolo, 1986). Most studies report success rates in the range of 80% to 90% of women being able to experience masturbatory orgasm, 20% to 60% being able to experience orgasm with a partner, and fewer women, often 15% to 20%, becoming coitally orgasmic.

In women with secondary orgasmic disorders (i.e., those who experience orgasm infrequently or conditionally), a variety of interventions seem to increase orgasmicity, including systematic desensitization, communication training, and sex skill training (e.g., Everaerd & Dekker, 1982). In general, women in this group have lower success rates than women with primary orgasmic dysfunction. However, given the figures in the preceding paragraph, one could say that a subset of women treated for primary orgasmic dysfunction become situationally anorgasmic, and in that case the success rates are more comparable (between 40% and 70%).

Erectile dysfunction is the major area where current success rates are most discrepant from the rates reported by Masters and Johnson. Whereas Masters and Johnson (1970) claimed that 95% of such cases were psychogenic, other reports have claimed rates of vascular, neurological, or hormonal impairment well above 60% (e.g., Spark, White, & Connolly, 1980). This reported difference may result from the increased use in the last 10 years of urological evaluation for penile blood flow, neurological and endocrine work-ups, as well as nocturnal penile tumescence studies.

Overall, the long-term follow-up rates of several studies indicate clearly that Masters and Johnson's 5-year follow-up figures are unusually optimistic. Masters and Johnson's initial failure rate was only increased by 7% when the first 24% of their 5-year follow-ups were completed. In one of the better designed studies from the United Kingdom (Hawton, Catalan, Martin, & Fagg, 1986), at least one partner in 75% of the couples was located 1 to 6 years after having been in sex therapy. Success rates were excellent for vaginismus and good for erectile failure, but they were lower for premature ejaculation and for women with low sexual desire. These data are comparable to follow-up studies with other samples in Holland and the United States (e.g., DeAmicis, Goldberg, LoPiccolo, Friedman, & Davies, 1985; Dekker & Everaerd, 1983).

Emerging from several outcome studies is the general finding that satisfaction with one's sexual relationship often increases, in spite of minimal improvement of sexual symptoms, in part because the overall relationship improves (Hawton et al., 1986; Heiman & LoPiccolo, 1983; LoPiccolo, Heiman, Hogan, & Roberts,

1985). Frank et al. (1978) found that although 40% of men and 60% of women reported a sexual dysfunction, 85% of the couples reported a satisfactory sex life. Thus, it may be important to view symptom remission as only one criterion for a couple's success.

## Psychophysiological Studies of Arousal

Psychophysiological methods have proven to be both promising and vexing in the understanding of sexual dysfunctions—promising because of the opportunity to study the interplay of cognitive and physiological responses and vexing because of limitations in genital measurement and concerns about generalizing from laboratory to nonlaboratory contexts. Nevertheless, the advantages still outweigh the disadvantages, and psychophysiology remains uniquely suited to the study of sexual arousal patterns (Rosen & Beck, 1988).

Barlow (1986) has reviewed the psychophysiological work on anxiety and sexual dysfunction and concluded that, for men, (1) arousal requires attending to erotic cues; (2) attention is an inverted-U function of anxiety, in that increasing anxiety improves concentration up to a certain point and then deteriorates concentration, conforming to the Yerkes–Dodson law; (3) dysfunctional subjects have negative affect and expectancies, focus on low erotic cues such as fear and failure, and experience increased autonomic arousal that stimulates increasingly efficient attentional focus on not responding, leading to a dysfunctional experience and a tendency afterward to avoid (i.e., not attend to) erotic stimuli; (4) functional men, on the other hand, approach a sexual situation with positive affect, attend to erotic cues, and experience increased autonomic arousal that leads to increased focus on erotic cues and a functional sexual experience.

Barlow's model is supported almost exclusively by research on men. Some support for the model in relation to women comes from Morokoff and Heiman (1980). They found that dysfunctional (i.e., low arousal and nonorgasmic) women experienced greater self-reported anxiety during vaginal vasocongestion to an erotic film, whereas nondysfunctional women reported greater sexual arousal under the same conditions. Both groups showed a similar level of genital response to erotica and fantasy, although dysfunctional women reported significantly less subjective sexual arousal.

An important aspect of Barlow's model is its delineation of specific processes that maintain the dysfunctional condition rather than a global, undifferentiated concept of distal or proximal anxiety (Kaplan, 1974). Nevertheless, not all dysfunctions will fit this model, because some dysfunctions may be driven more by interpersonal than intrapersonal factors.

Psychophysiological studies have also helped to confirm the effects of alcohol on sexual response. Increasing doses of alcohol have produced correspondingly decreasing genital vasocongestion in men (Malatesta, Pollack, Wilbanks, & Adams, 1979) and women (Malatesta, Pollack, Crotty, & Peacock, 1982). Although men also show decreasing subjective arousal with increasing alcohol dosage, women consistently show the opposite pattern, increasing subjective arousal and sexual pleasure with increasing alcohol dosage (Malatesta et al., 1982; Wilson & Lawson, 1978). Studies of arousal to orgasm (via masturbation) in the laboratory confirm the above patterns (Malatesta et al., 1982). All of the above studies refer to acute alcohol ingestion. For chronic high alcohol use, physiological and behavioral effects are more pronounced and, in the case of neural and vascular damage, may be irreversible (Snyder & Karacan, 1981).

Psychophysiology has contributed to the assessment of the relative physiological impairment in men with erectile dysfunction. The measurement of nocturnal penile tumescence (NPT), the occurrence of periodic penile tumescence associated with REM sleep, is a major assessment tool for men with erection disorder. This measurement is desirable because it circumvents any confounds that operate during waking states (e.g., reactivity effects). The hit rate for diagnosing the degree of psychological impairment with this procedure is approximately 80% (Wasserman, Pollack, Spielman, & Wertzman, 1980). Some attempts have been made to validate NPT measures using decision rules regarding penile circumference and number of nightly NPT episodes (Marshall, Surridge, & Delva, 1981). A measure of penile buckling, to determine firmness of erection, has also been recommended (Karacan, 1978).

Nocturnal penile tumescence is known to be diminished by diabetes (Schiavi, Fisher, Quadland, & Glover, 1985), major depression (Thase et al., 1988), and various pharmacological agents (Rosen & Beck, 1988). Beta-blocking antihypertensive agents appear to reduce NPT in some men (Rosen, Kostis, & Jekelis, 1988). In addition to NPT, one needs at minimum a health history, a sexual and psychological history, a physical exam, and an endocrine evaluation in order to establish valid diagnoses.

Comparing arousal measured during waking states to NPT has produced some interesting results. Wincze et al. (1988) found that most vasculogenic dysfunction patients experienced greater erections during exposure to erotic stimulation than during NPT. These results support concerns by others that NPT may be measuring an independent hypothalamic–limbic mechanism that is minimally related to erotic response at the cortical level (Fisher et al., 1979; Nath et al., 1981).

In spite of the presence of vaginal vasocongestion during REM sleep, there are no known REM studies among women. One can presume that this is related to the fact that loss of erection prevents intercourse for men, whereas loss of arousal and orgasm does not necessarily have the same effect for women. Nevertheless, there are numerous clinical complaints from women who have diabetes, use alcohol chronically, or take various medications. As women's sexual desire problems get more attention (insofar as this complaint can inhibit intercourse), perhaps increasing attention will be devoted to the interaction of physiological and psychological factors in women's sexual response.

We have just reviewed the empirical foundations for treating sexual problems. The relative effectiveness of treatment and the usefulness of assessment techniques help to determine the choice of one of the following current intervention strategies.

## INTERVENTION STRATEGIES: CURRENT STATUS

Treating sexual problems in couples requires familiarity with possible etiological factors, awareness of the context of treatment, familiarity with techniques, and a conceptual framework with which to understand and explore therapeutic material.

### Assessment and Diagnosis

Because detailed descriptions of history taking and assessment are available elsewhere (Arentewicz & Schmidt, 1983; LoPiccolo & Heiman, 1978), we review only the essential ingredients. To begin, both members of the couple need to describe in detail what they see as the sexual problem, its origins, and its development over time. Description is the initial goal, for which the Schover, Freidman, Weiler, Heiman, and LoPiccolo (1982) categorization is very useful. It divides sexual function into six axes: desire, arousal, orgasm, pain, frequency dissatisfaction, and qualifying information (e.g., homosexuality, alcohol use, medical conditions).

For each partner the presence or absence of each axis is noted, as are its duration (lifelong versus not lifelong) and pervasiveness (global versus situational). A detailed description is important for its content (for what people do and do not say) as well as for its context (what it seems to mean to the person). For example, in a couple we have seen, the woman began her first session by saying, "Sex is humiliating." Further description of her problem indicated that she had been desirous and aroused but never orgasmic, although she had pretended to experience orgasm. The sense of humiliation provided the affective color of the problem description but did not dismiss the importance of the behavioral symptom.

Heiman (1986) proposed a framework for the initial interview, history taking, and treatment planning that requires a combination of *individual, interactional,* and *sociocultural* levels. All levels are somewhat independent and yet necessarily interact, and all levels have current and past layers. Therapists bring to treatment assumptions about each level that influence their ability and flexibility to conceptualize a couple's problems.

Individual *physical and psychological health* is important because any disorder, disease, or drug that affects the neural–vascular or endocrine pathways can influence sexual desire, arousal, and orgasm. It is important to note signs of depression, phobias, anxiety or panic disorder, diabetes, alcoholism, or other serious physical conditions. Sexual pain and erectile failure also require careful medical evaluations (Rosen & Beck, 1988; Schover & Jensen, 1988).

On the *interpersonal level,* current interaction patterns may be related to those in each partner's family of origin. Positive and negative aspects of prior romantic and sexual relationships may also be influential. Identification of the structure and rules that surround a couple's interactional patterns (e.g., conflict, affection) are also essential.

The *sociocultural level* gives attention to past and current religious beliefs, social class, sex roles, ethnic and racial standards, and other cultural features. Since therapists and patients are all part of a given culture, it is often difficult to see the implicit rules, requirements, and biases placed on sexuality and marriage.

### Techniques and Strategies

The central purpose of techniques or strategies is to give the couple an opportunity to experience themselves and their relationship differently. This is an uneasy, unsettling phase because no one, therapist included, can predict accurately where the first changes will lead. Couples can, for example, solve their sex problem and then divorce; this may be a good outcome but was not the initial goal of therapy. In a couple with a sexual problem, especially a longstanding one, an equilibrium has formed around the problem, often keeping intimacy, dominance, and commitment issues in a delicate balance. Sexual problems usually have positive and negative functions for each person, and although the couple may not develop symptoms *intentionally* to solve other relationship problems, an appreciation of the positive value of the symptom can help smooth the way and decrease resistance for further therapeutic efforts (Heiman, 1986).

A number of general techniques are common to most successful sex therapy interventions (for more information see Arentewicz & Schmidt, 1983; Leiblum & Rosen, 1988; Masters & Johnson, 1970). An important and extremely robust technique is Masters and Johnson's (1970) *sensate focus*, practiced outside of the therapy session. In the early stages of sensate focus, intercourse and sexual arousal are banned, and only gradually increasing levels of arousal are permitted. Couples focus on pleasure and comfort as they touch each other, stopping when either feeling is replaced by anxiety or discomfort. By directly trying to replace anxiety with pleasure, sensate focus initially builds on the parasympathetic phase of the sexual response cycle while removing any demand for sexual arousal and orgasm.

*Systematic desensitization*, using both imagery and *in vivo* experiences, is also used, though more frequently for individuals without partners or for people with higher levels of anxiety or phobias. Similar to sensate focus, a hierarchy of relaxing/sensual to arousing/sexual images and situations are presented, helping the client to cope mentally and physically with each increasingly sexual step.

Finally in *communication training* partners are taught how to initiate and refuse sexual invitations as well as to communicate during sexual exchanges. Each couple needs to work out verbal and nonverbal media for getting their messages across, and a common challenge is to help the one who is being guided in the sexual interaction not to feel controlled and demeaned. Conflict resolution techniques are also used frequently with couples, as general marital distress is not uncommon.

These techniques can be used as components of various treatment approaches regardless of theory. However in terms of strategy and understanding, the congitive-behaviorist is more likely to look for specific exercises that each person can do to overcome negative, self-defeating feelings and images. The psychoanalytically oriented therapist may explore intrapsychic conflicts, especially object-relations themes, when one of the patients becomes stuck or upset. And the systemic therapist will look for ongoing interactional patterns that both impair and improve the couple's interactions involving sex. What follows, by dysfunction, are some examples of further techniques.

## Desire Disorders

Inhibited sexual desire (ISD) has been defined as infrequent sexual desire that causes distress to the person reporting it. In the DSM-III-R, ISD is reserved for desire problems with no known physical etiology (drugs, hormones, medical illness) that are not secondary to another psychiatric disorder such as depression. Inhibited sexual desire may be the most prevalent sexual dysfunction (see Leiblum & Rosen, 1988). The immediate and historical factors contributing to ISD are not well understood, and consequently its treatment consists more of general strategies than of specific techniques.

For ISD patients whose condition is situational or transient, typical suspected factors include interpersonal problems (including intimacy and communication issues) and intrapersonal factors (anxiety, anger, change in self-perception). The interventions proposed thus cross theoretical boundaries. Kaplan (1979) and others often include Masters and Johnson's sensate focus exercises in the treatment of ISD patients. As in other dysfunctions, the marital and individual issues are revealed in each person's difficulties in completing the assignments. For example, it is common for an ISD patient to "shut down" during the sensate focus exercises, reporting a lack of pleasure, numbness, or tension. The block against feeling pleasure or feeling sexual is explored, and the therapist may discover that anxiety or anger is the emotion replacing sensual or sexual pleasure.

After trying to understand how that emotional replacement has developed, the therapist may adopt a paradoxical stance: that the patient has a choice about what to feel (Kaplan, 1979) and that anxiety or anger is absolutely correct for the moment. An alternative to this position is cognitive restructuring, which entails identifying the specific negative emotional states that interfere with sex, exploring the basis of the negative reactions in the person's experience, identifying coping statements to overcome "irrational" negative feelings, and developing mastery imagery about being sexual. If insight, confrontation, or cognitive exercises do not affect the desire problem, more intense individual work may be warranted. Hypnotic techniques can also be useful (Araoz, 1982).

Alternatives to individually oriented treatment approaches are attempts to use the power of interactional patterns to permit a change in desire. For example, if a woman with low sexual interest experiences anger when becoming sexually aroused, the therapist may find that the woman senses that her partner is claiming ownership over her sexual response. After exploring past experiences, the sensate focus exercises are enhanced by working on territorial issues between the partners by proposing an interactional antidote such as attachment interactions (e.g., Verhulst & Heiman, 1979). Attachment interactions, which signal acknowledgment of the bond between partners, can be introduced by tender, tentative touching designed to signal respect for the other and the other's body.

### Sexual Aversion and Phobia
Sexual aversion and phobic disorders have been treated quite successfully with various cognitive-behavioral therapy techniques, including desensitization, relaxation, and cognitive restructuring (Masters & Johnson, 1970). Patients who have extreme reactions to sexual stimulation may fit the diagnosis of panic disorder, and in these cases medication may be useful to get the panic symptoms under control so that psychological treatment can continue. Appropriate medication for these conditions (e.g., tricyclic antidepressants) can have undesirable side effects (e.g., diminished libido, erectile dysfunction) and hence must be administered carefully.

### Arousal Disorders
Although women have arousal disorders, they are treated almost always in the context of orgasmic dysfunction. For men, the most common arousal disorder is erectile dysfunction, defined as an inability to attain or maintain an erection sufficient for sexual intercourse. Masters and Johnson's techniques include sensate focus and graded sexual exercises beginning with vaginal containment without orgasm with the female above, to manual orgasm and coital orgasm with the female above, and finally coital orgasm with the male above. In addition, the "tease technique," in which the woman stimulates the penis and lets the erection subside

several times before her partner has an orgasm, teaches both partners to be comfortable in the presence of an erect, a flaccid, and a becoming flaccid penis.

Since the erection process is rather paradoxical (trying harder can make it more elusive), therapy usually benefits from such paradoxical messages as, "You should not get an erection," "Do not get aroused, just let youself enjoy the stimulation," and even, "You probably will not find yourself becoming erect yet."

## Orgasmic Disorders

Treatment for orgasmic problems focuses on the preorgasmic patterns that can include excessive tension, obsessive self-monitoring, cognitive distraction, negative expectations, and interpersonal factors.

For complete anorgasmia, the woman is encouraged initially to experience her first orgasm alone and then transfer her learning to the context of her sexual relationship (see Heiman & LoPiccolo, 1988). The program for this disorder also suggests cognitive restructuring exercises, role play of orgasm, fantasy use, relaxation and focusing exercises, and ways to involve the partner.

For women who are orgasmic except with a partner, the treatment strategy depends on both interactional and individual factors. Common issues are the sense that a woman's orgasm belongs to the male partner, inhibition caused by the woman's withdrawal from the partner, and discomfort in sharing sexual responses. History taking and sensate focus exercises help clarify what is preventing responses from going beyond arousal. If the meaning of orgasm can be articulated, the therapist may prescribe preparatory self-statements such as: "I can be orgasmic and remain in control," "I can be orgasmic with my partner and be free." It is equally important early in treatment to give the woman the power and choice to be orgasmic. If she or her husband will be indirectly (but clearly) demanding orgasm each time, performance anxiety will haunt their interactions and spoil their sex.

If the woman complains of an inability to reach orgasm only during intercourse, a somewhat different approach is required. Occasionally the problem is solved by giving permission to use additional manual stimulation during intercourse, insofar as most sexually functional women need some type of additional stimulation to orgasm coitally. A systematic desensitization approach can work for women with inhibitions around loss of control. A fading procedure—intromission beginning at the woman's orgasm and gradually moving earlier in the sexual arousal progression—can be helpful to increase the frequency of coital orgasm where the woman is rarely orgasmic in coitus.

Anorgasmia is less frequent in males, though a small percentage do suffer from ejaculatory incompetence or from retarded ejaculation (i.e., the inability to ejaculate intravaginally). These men are able to maintain erections for long periods of time without ejaculating. Two useful strategies for this disorder are progressive *in vivo* desensitization and counterbypassing. Desensitization is the more common and begins with orgasm by self-stimulation in the partner's presence until orgasm can occur near the vaginal opening, followed by the same process involving instead manual stimulation by the partner. Stimulation close to orgasm is followed by vaginal insertion, and over time, vaginal stimulation decreases the need for concomitant manual stimulation.

Counterbypassing refers to a pattern of recognizing negative reactions and expressing them to one's partner (see Apfelbaum, 1980). The theory is that these men have a pattern of "bypassing" or holding back all negative feelings toward their partner, which discourages "letting go" during intercourse. With sexual surrogates, the man expresses negative feelings as they arise during sex; with his wife the feelings usually need to be dealt with differently, initially outside of the sexual activity in the relative safety of the therapy session.

A common orgasmic complaint is premature ejaculation. Straightforward behavioral techniques, including the squeeze (Masters & Johnson, 1970) or the pause technique (Kaplan, 1974; Semans, 1956), have been successful. Both involve genital stimulation to just before the point of inevitability of orgasm, and then either stopping or squeezing the penis on either side of the coronal ridge until the sense of ejaculatory inevitability recedes. Stimulation is attempted two more times before ejaculation can occur. This technique is sometimes practiced initially by the man in masturbation and eventually with a partner, manually then intravaginally. The goal is fewer squeezes or pauses over a given time period.

### Pain and Sex

The most common sexual dysfunctions involving pain are dyspareunia and vaginismus. Careful physical exams are necessary to rule out physical abnormalities before beginning treatment. A careful sexual and psychological history is especially pertinent, as the pain may be a learned response to earlier events. Treatment for dyspareunia involves methods of mental and physical relaxation, desensitization, and giving the symptomatic person temporary control over the type, intensity, and speed of the sexual interaction.

These same therapeutic features apply to vaginismus, though an additional specific behavioral program is very effective with this disorder. Vaginismus, defined as involuntary contractions of the vaginal musculature that make intercourse painful, is usually treated by gradual vaginal dilation, initially using Hegar dilators or the woman's own fingers and later followed by penile insertion. Gentle and then more vigorous thrusting is advised under the woman's direction.

## PATHWAYS TO MORE EFFECTIVE INTERVENTIONS

Because treatment of most sexual problems has far less than a 90% success rate, and problems often reappear within 2 years, it is important to consider how existing approaches can be enhanced. Theoretical and methodological factors pertinent to future progress in this domain are discussed below.

### Theoretical Issues

Although each of the theoretical positions discussed here has important and useful features, each falls short in some respect. The kind of theory needed when a distressed couple is sitting in front of a therapist is one that will direct the therapist's actions and reactions and address sexuality in a way that fits both client and therapist expectations.

Certainly the available theories partially accomplish the task of informing the therapeutic situation. But what key elements are missing from each theory? Psychoanalytic theory, particularly in its newer forms, has remained an intriguing approach to sexual problems, even though few data uphold its effectiveness. Psychoanalysis by itself does an excellent job of recognizing and valuing the unpredictable, the unexplainable, and the improper in people's experiences. This is very important in attempts to understand and influence sexual patterns. A theory about sex may need to preserve some of the *mystery* of sexuality, with its dark *and* enlightened aspects. Part of the power of human sexuality is derived from centuries of belief that it is both pleasurable and dangerous. Analytic thinking accepts the ongoing, historical, cultural role that sexuality must play, at least in Western cultures.

Cognitive-behavioral theory fills the rational–empirical vacuum left by psychoanalytic thinking and provides symptoms (as well as genitals) with a status beyond the purely symbolic. Its efficacy as an approach has been demonstrated. However, cognitive-behavioral theories have excluded the irrational from their theoretical structure. Thoughts and feelings that are connected to self-defeating, symptom-supporting beliefs or myths are driven away with cognitive restructuring, rational-emotive training, and education. This has been practical on the one hand but is theoretically insufficient on the other. The irrational, after all, is real and may reveal much about the essence of sexuality.

Systems theory promises to be a grand integrator, but this has not yet happened in the area of sexual dysfunction. Perhaps it is too new a paradigm, and few of us can accept that interactions, not ego, create our identities and our responses. The possession of one's *own* sexuality as a self-identity is still apparently culturally ingrained. Systems theory does preserve the mystery of sex, but for the moment, it places that mystery rather abstractly outside of the person.

Other theoretical positions also hold great promise for a better understanding of sexuality and its problems. A social constructionist perspective is one that deserves attention. Although it is rather impervious to current methods of empirical research, it conceptualizes sexuality as something that emerges in relationships and situations rather than as an inborn quality (see Tiefer, 1987, for a summary). Plummer (1982), for example, concludes that sexuality, rather than being a powerful universal drive shaped by culture and learning, is more like a script that is *created by* the sociocultural movement. This position is vastly different from a psychoanalytic one whereby sexuality is created early in life in an indelible, irreversible way. As elaborated by Gagnon and Simon (Simon & Gagnon, 1987), the sexual script can be altered continually for new meanings. Sexuality is in constant revision in the culture and in a person's experience. One does not have to push the metaphor of a script far to see its value for conceptualizing sexual problems: simply experiencing a sexual situation as problematic is an interpretive, socially constructed response.

The dangers of not seeing therapy and sexuality as culturally embedded are stated with riveting clarity in feminist approaches. One of the first tasks of feminist theory, not unlike social constructionism, has been to identify and criticize the construct of "sexuality" as it defines experience. In feminist theory:

> . . . the fact that the male power *has power* means that the interests of male sexuality construct what sexuality as such means, including the standard way it is allowed to be felt and expressed and experienced, in a way that determines women's biographies, including our sexual ones. Existing theories, until they grasp this, will only misattribute what they call female sexuality to women as such, as if it is not enforced on us daily. (MacKinnon, 1987, pp. 68-69)

The essential feminist theoretical ingredient here is that the definition of sexuality is socially constructed by the predominant forces—in this case males. Sexuality is not a discrete sphere of interaction but a pervasive dimension of social life. Thus, the features defining a woman as inferior—including her personality, her restraint, her struggle to present herself as attractive—become part of her sexuality.[2] Most scientists and many therapists worry about theories that implicate culture and politics, as if human activity needs to be seen "purely." Pure may mean descriptive above and beyond the culture and politics of the moment (developing, for example, laws of sexual desire), but pure often means description reduced to the individual and his or her experience. The problem remains that individual patients (as well as therapists) are people with cultural and political values. By focusing on the individual, one can be fooled into believing that the patient is the sole author of meanings ascribed to a neutral set of experiences. By diminishing the power of the culture to be part of identity, therapists diminish their capacity to treat and understand sexual problems.

The specific effects of a social constructionist or feminist position for treatment of sexual problems cannot be covered here. However, it is clear that clients and therapists need to recognize cultural demands. For example, it is not uncommon for men to request a penile implant in the absence of any physical basis to their erectile problem. Even after a careful therapeutic confrontation, a patient may still be determined to have a prosthesis. This

---

[2]A major source of data for feminist theory of sexuality is the prevalence of physical and especially sexual abuse delivered by men toward girls and women (e.g., Russell, 1982, 1986). The likelihood that violence toward women has been overlooked, trivialized, or eroticized fairly consistently in Western cultures has interacted with theories of sexual behavior. For example, Freud, whose general theory supported an essential sexual inequality, decided to disbelieve his female patients' accounts of being sexually abused as children, thus allowing this material to be theoretically viewed as unconscious fantasy (Masson, 1983).

presents a cultural and ethical dilemma. A more common problem is women who do not really enjoy intercourse and are not orgasmic during coitus. Is something wrong with them, with their partners, or with a culture that values this act well beyond its reproductive viability? These are among the important culturally imbued issues that need to be integrated in theory and practice.

## Methodological Issues

There tends to be a glibness and condescension about methodological critiques. Most disturbing is the tendency for us to believe that there is a perfect methodology to reveal a single truth. Methodologies themselves are not value-free, and data on humans are open to multiple interpretations. However, several basic changes might make our knowledge base more interesting and informative. First there is a need for large-sample, long-term longitudinal studies of the many factors that relate to sexuality in marriage. Second, there is a need for intensive case studies that permit hypothesis generation and exploration of patterns among variables, an element that is missing from most research. Third, there is a need for greater understanding of the impact of health, drugs, and medical procedures on sexual functioning. Finally, there is a need to draw stronger ties between research designs and the theoretical propositions that guide them, particularly those from social constructionism, feminism, and systems theory.

## CONCLUSION

If anything is clear from the past century of work in treating sexual problems in marriage, it is that we need to include both the physical and symbols of the physical. It is therefore not surprising that therapists who treat sexual dysfunction have evolved so many common elements: the analytically oriented include behavioral techniques, the cognitive-behaviorists deal with symbols and symptoms, and systems therapists use interactionally focused behavioral assignments to provide alternative experiences to patients. Indeed, the approaches have more similarities in how they are practiced than their formal theoretical structures would suggest.

Science continues to play a role in discovering the intricacies of the body and in providing some clues about how the mind experiences the body in a sexual context. This has afforded more control over some aspects of sexual dysfunction but has yielded very little understanding of how desire and arousal are created or diminished. These mysteries will remain while we attempt to ensure that our theories do not interfere with our ability to hear patients and see new connections.

# REFERENCES

Apfelbaum, B. (1980). The diagnosis and treatment of retarded ejaculation. In S. R. Leiblum & L. A. Pervin (Eds.), *Principles and practice of sex therapy* (pp. 263–296). New York: Guilford Press.

Araoz, D. L. (1982). *Hypnosis and sex therapy*. New York: Brunner/Mazel.

Arentewicz, G., & Schmidt, G. (1983). *The treatment of sexual disorders*. New York: Basic Books.

Barlow, D. H. (1986). Causes of sexual dysfunction: The role of anxiety and cognitive interference. *Journal of Consulting and Clinical Psychology, 54*, 140–148.

DeAmicis, L. A., Goldberg, D. C., LoPiccolo, J., Friedman, J., & Davies, L. (1985). Three-year follow-up of couples evaluated for sexual dysfunction. *Journal of Sexual and Marital Therapy, 12*, 215–228.

Dekker, J., & Everaerd, W. (1983). A long-term follow-up study of couples treated for sexual dysfunctions. *Journal of Sex and Marital Therapy, 9*, 99–113.

Dicks, H. V. (1967). *Marital tensions: Clinical studies toward a psychological theory of interaction*. London: Routledge & Kegan Paul.

Ellis, A. (1961). *The encyclopedia of sexual behavior*. New York: Hawthorn Books.

Everaerd, W., & Dekker, J. (1982). Treatment of secondary orgasmic dysfunction: A comparison of systematic desensitization and sex therapy. *Behaviour Research and Therapy, 23*, 13–25.

Fairbairn, W. R. D. (1954). *An object-relations theory of personality*. New York: Basic Books.

Fisher, C., Schiavi, R., Edwards, A., Davis, D., Reitman, M., & Fine, J. (1979). Evaluation of nocturnal penile tumescence in the differential diagnosis of sexual impotence: A quantitative study. *Archives of General Psychiatry, 36*, 431–437.

Frank, E., Anderson, A., & Rubinstein, D. (1978). Frequency of sexual dysfunction in "normal" couples. *New England Journal of Medicine, 299*, 111–115.

Freud, S. (1957). The interpretation of dreams. In J. Strachey (Ed. and Trans.), *The standard edition of the complete psychological works of Sigmund Freud* (vol. 4, pp. 1–338). London: Hogarth Press. (Original work published 1900)

Freud, S. (1957). Three essays on sexuality. In J. Strachey (Ed. and Trans.), *The standard edition of the complete psychological works of Sigmund Freud* (vol. 9, pp. 207–226). London: Hogarth Press. (Original work published 1905)

Hawton, K., Catalan, J., Martin, P., & Fagg, J. (1986). Long-term outcome of sex therapy. *Behaviour Research and Therapy, 24*, 665–675.

Heiman, J. R. (1986). Treating sexually distressed marital relationships. In N. S. Jacobson & A. S. Gurman (Eds.), *Clinical handbook of marital therapy* (pp. 361–384). New York: Guilford Press.

Heiman, J., & Grafton-Becker, V. (1989). Orgasmic disorders in women. In S. R. Leiblum & R. C. Rosen (Eds.), *Principles and practice of sex therapy* (2nd ed.): *Update for the 1990s* (pp. 53–88). New York: Guilford Press.

Heiman, J. R., & LoPiccolo, J. (1983). Clinical outcome of sex therapy: Effects of daily v. weekly treatment. *Archives of General Psychiatry, 40,* 443–449.

Heiman, J., & LoPiccolo, J. (1988). *Becoming orgasmic: A sexual and personal growth program for women.* New York: Prentice-Hall.

Kaplan, H. S. (1974). *The new sex therapy.* New York: Brunner/Mazel.

Kaplan, H. S. (1979). *Disorders of sexual desire.* New York: Brunner/Mazel.

Karacan, I. (1978). Advances in the psychophysiological evaluation of male erectile impotence. In J. LoPiccolo & L. LoPiccolo (Eds.), *Handbook of sex therapy* (pp. 137–146). New York: Plenum.

Kinsey, A. C., Pomeroy, W. B., & Martin, C. E. (1948). *Sexual behavior in the human male.* Philadelphia: Saunders.

Kinsey, A. C., Pomeroy, W. B., Martin, C. E., & Gebhard, P. H. (1953). *Sexual behavior in the human female.* Philadelphia: Saunders.

Klein, M. (1975). *Love, guilt and reparation and other works 1921–1945.* London: Hogarth.

Lazarus, A. A. (1963). The treatment of chronic frigidity by systematic desensitization. *Journal of Nervous and Mental Disease, 136,* 272–278.

Leiblum, S. R., & Pervin, L. A. (Eds.). (1980). *Principles and practice of sex therapy.* New York: Guilford Press.

Leiblum, S. R., & Rosen, R. C. (Eds.). (1988). *Sexual desire disorders.* New York: Guilford Press.

LoPiccolo, L., & Heiman, J. (1978). Sexual assessment and history interview. In J. LoPiccolo & L. LoPiccolo (Eds.), *Handbook of sex therapy* (pp. 103–112). New York: Plenum.

LoPiccolo, J., Heiman, J., Hogan, D., & Roberts, C. (1985). Effectiveness of single therapists versus co-therapy teams in sex therapy. *Journal of Consulting and Clinical Psychology, 53,* 287–294.

LoPiccolo, J., & Stock, W. E. (1986). Treatment of sexual dysfunction. *Journal of Consulting and Clinical Psychology, 54,* 158–167.

MacKinnon, C. A. (1987). A feminist/political approach: Pleasure under patriarchy. In J. H. Geer & W. T. O'Donohue (Eds.), *Theories of human sexuality* (pp. 65–90). New York: Plenum.

Malatesta, V. J., Pollack, R. H., Crotty, T. D., & Peacock, L. J. (1982). Acute alcohol intoxication and the female orgasmic response. *Journal of Sex Research, 18,* 1–17.

Malatesta, V. J., Pollack, R. H., Wilbanks, W. A., & Adams, H. E. (1979). Alcohol effects on the orgasmic–ejaculatory response in human males. *Journal of Sex Research, 15,* 101–107.

Marshall, P. G., Surridge, D., & Delva, N. (1981). The role of nocturnal penile tumescence in differentiating between organic and psychogenic impotence: The first stage of validation. *Archives of Sexual Behavior, 10,* 1–10.

Masson, J. M. (1983). *The assault on truth: Freud's suppression of the seduction theory.* New York: Farrar, Straus & Giroux.

Masters, W., & Johnson, V. (1966). *Human sexual response.* Boston: Little, Brown.

Masters, W., & Johnson, V. (1970). *Human sexual inadequacy.* Boston: Little, Brown.

Milan, R. J., Kilmann, P. R., & Boland, J. P. (1988). Treatment outcome of secondary orgasmic dysfunction: A two- to six-year follow-up. *Archives of Sexual Behavior, 17,* 436–486.

Miller, J. G. (1978). *Living systems*. New York: McGraw-Hill.

Mills, K. H., & Kilmann, P. R. (1982). Group treatment of sexual dysfunctions: A methodological review of the outcome literature. *Journal of Sex and Marital Therapy, 8*, 259–296.

Morokoff, P., & Heiman, J. R. (1980). Effects of erotic stimuli on sexually functional and dysfunctional women: Multiple measures before and after sex therapy. *Behaviour Research and Therapy, 18*, 127–137.

Morokoff, P. J., & LoPiccolo, J. L. (1986). A comparative evaluation of minimal therapist contact and 15 session treatment for female orgasmic dysfunction. *Journal of Consulting and Clinical Psychology, 54*, 294–300.

Nath, R., Menzoian, J., Kaplan, K., Millian, M., Siroky, T., & Krane, R. (1981). The multidisciplinary approach to vasculogenic impotence. *Surgery, 89*, 124–133.

Plummer, K. (1982). Symbolic interactionism and sexual conduct: An emergent perspective. In M. Brake (Ed.), *Human sexual relations: Toward a redefinition of sexual politics* (pp. 223–241). New York: Pantheon.

Regas, S., & Sprenkle, D. (1984). Functional family therapy and treatment of inhibited sexual desire. *Journal of Marital and Family Therapy, 10*, 63–72.

Rosen, R. C., & Beck, J. G. (1988). *Patterns of sexual arousal: Psychophysiological processes and clinical applications*. New York: Guilford Press.

Rosen, R. C., Kostis, J. B., & Jekelis, A. (1988). Beta blocker effects on sexual function in normal males. *Archives of Sexual Behavior, 17*, 241–256.

Russell, D. E. H. (1982). *Rape in marriage*. New York: Macmillan.

Russell, D. (1986). *The secret trauma: Incest in the lives of girls and women*. New York: Basic Books.

Scharff, D. E. (1982). *The sexual relationship: An object relations view of sex and the family*. New York: Routledge.

Scharff, D. E. (1988). An object relating approach to inhibited sexual desire. In S. R. Leiblum & R. C. Rosen (Eds.), *Sexual desire disorders* (pp. 45–74). New York: Guilford Press.

Schiavi, R. C., Fisher, C., Quadland, M., & Glover, A. (1985). Nocturnal penile tumescent evaluation of penile function in insulin-dependent diabetic men. *Diabetologia, 28*, 90–94.

Schover, L. R., Friedman, J. M., Weiler, S. J., Heiman, J. R., & LoPiccolo, J. (1982). Multiaxial problem-oriented system for sexual dysfunction: An alternative to DSM-III. *Archives of General Psychiatry, 39*, 614–619.

Schover, L. R., & Jensen, S. B. (1988). *Sexuality and chronic illness: A comprehensive approach*. New York: Guilford Press.

Semans, J. H. (1956). Premature ejaculation: A new approach. *Southern Medical Journal, 49*, 353–357.

Simon, W., & Gagnon, J. H. (1987). A sexual scripts approach. In J. H. Geer & W. T. O'Donohue (Eds.), *Theories of human sexuality* (pp. 363–384). New York: Plenum.

Snyder, S., & Karacan, I. (1981). Effects of chronic alcoholism on nocturnal penile tumescence. *Psychosomatic Medicine, 43*, 423–429.

Spark, R. F., White, R. A., & Connolly, P. B. (1980). Impotence is not always psychogenic: Newer insights into hypothalamic–pituitary–gonadal dysfunction. *Journal of the American Medical Association, 243*, 750–755.

Thase, M. E., Reynolds, C. F., Jennings, J. R., Frank, E., Howell, J. R., Houck, P. R., Berman, S., & Kupfer, D. J. (1988). Nocturnal penile tumescence is diminished in depressed men. *Biological Psychiatry, 24*, 33–46.

Tiefer, L. (1987). Social constructionism and the study of human sexuality. In

P. Shaver & C. Hendrick (Eds.), *Sex and gender* (pp. 70–94). Newbury Park, CA: Sage.

Verhulst, J., & Heiman, J. (1979). An interactional approach to sexual dysfunction. *American Journal of Family Therapy, 7,* 19–36.

Verhulst, J., & Heiman, J. (1988). A systems perspective on sexual desire. In S. R. Leiblum & R. C. Rosen (Eds.), *Sexual desire disorders* (pp. 243–267). New York: Guilford Press.

von Bertalanffy, L. (1968). *General systems theory.* New York: Brazillier.

Wasserman, M. D., Pollack, C. P., Spielman, A. J., & Wertzman, E. D. (1980). The differential diagnosis of impotence: The measurement of nocturnal penile tumescence. *Journal of the American Medical Association, 243,* 2038–2042.

Weeks, G. R. (1987). Systematic treatment of inhibited sexual desire. In G. R. Weeks & L. Hof (Eds.), *Integrating sex and marital therapy* (pp. 183–201). New York: Brunner/Mazel.

Wilson, G. T., & Lawson, D. M. (1978). Expectancies, alcohol and sexual arousal in women. *Journal of Abnormal Psychology, 87,* 358–367.

Wincze, J. P., Bansal, S., Malhorta, C., Balko, A., Sosset, J. G., & Malamud, M. (1988). A comparison of nocturnal penile response during waking states in comprehensively diagnosed groups of males experiencing erectile difficulties. *Archives of Sexual Behavior, 17,* 333–348.

Wolpe, J. (1958). *Psychotherapy by reciprocal inhibition.* Stanford: Stanford University Press.

Zilbergeld, B., & Kilmann, P. R. (1984). The scope and effectiveness of sex therapy. *Psychotherapy, 21,* 319–326.

# CHAPTER 11

# Physical Aggression in Marriage

### K. Daniel O'Leary
### Dina Vivian

The field of spouse abuse emerged in the 1970s from efforts of women with a cause that had little relationship to the priorities of established mental health professions. Until this development, mental health professionals did relatively little to address the problem of spouse abuse and even failed to alert the public and other professionals to the problem. Pagelow (1984) summarizes the issue succinctly: "Wife beating turned out to be one of the 'best kept secrets' of family life, only exposed after feminist groups around the world demanded safe houses and assistance for battered women and their children" (p. 261).

The English first provided shelters for battered women following protests about the economic and legal problems faced by the abused. A woman, Erin Pizzey, helped center publicity on spouse abuse, and she helped establish Cheswick's Women's Aid in 1971, the first English refuge for battered women. The home was quickly overcrowded and, according to Pagelow (1984), has remained so ever since. One of the first studies of battered women was completed at Cheswick (Gayford, 1975), and women's groups across Europe sent people to Cheswick to learn of their methods. By the late 1970s, there were nearly 200 shelters in Great Britain (Dobash & Dobash, 1979).

In the United States, the movement to provide safety for women began in 1974 with the opening of a shelter in St. Paul, Minnesota. In the mid-1970s, existing shelters for women beaten by alcoholic husbands opened their doors to spouse-abuse victims whether or not they had alcoholic partners (Tierney, 1982). The National Organization for Women in 1985 provided evidence that the prevalence of spouse abuse was much higher than people had thought and called for systematic research and the establishment of shelters for battered women. However, attempts to make spouse abuse a social issue met with strong resistance by politicians and community boards. Their reaction was that physical aggression against spouses was an individual problem, a problem of sick individuals. Further, it was felt that the problem came mostly from lower socioeconomic classes. Indeed, some of the early evidence of spouse abuse came from police reports filed by women primarily from lower socioeconomic groups—women who did not have a power base to represent their problems. In contrast, if well-to-do abused women sought help, they obtained it from clergy, family physicians, and mental health professionals. Regrettably, because of the stigma associated with spouse abuse, even today, the most economically and politically advantaged often spurn professional help (Fedders & Elliot, 1987).

Despite resistance, progress has been made to help abused women. All states now have laws to protect battered women, and in most states restraining or protection orders can be obtained to help prevent violence by one family member against another. Unfortunately, the restraining orders do not always prevent violence. For example, in three such cases within a year in Suffolk County, New York, men went to the homes of their wives, killed them, and later shot themselves (*New York Times*, February 26, 1989).

Grass roots organizations and women's activist groups deserve tremendous credit for founding women's shelters and for bringing the issue of spouse abuse to the attention of the public. In contrast, mental health professionals, swayed by conceptions of individual psychopathology, were slow to recognize spouse abuse as a social issue. Psychologists and psychiatrists who conducted research on marital problems had to work outside of the traditional diagnostic framework. Even today, research on spouse abuse or child abuse must be tied to individually oriented diagnostic categories of the American Psychiatric Association's *Diagnostic and Statistical Manual* or precursors of the diagnostic categories to receive funding by federal government agencies or to be published in certain journals.

A recent government initiative to focus attention of health professionals on domestic violence may ultimately lead to a change in the status of spouse abuse within the mental health profession. In 1985, Surgeon General C. Everett Koop convened a symposium on violence and public health to help focus national attention on problems such as spouse abuse, child abuse, and homicide. He noted that health problems are given priority because of the frequency with which they lead to death. Although homicide ranks 11th among the leading causes of death, Koop noted that when one considers "years of life lost prematurely," homicide ranks fourth, and violence within intimate relationships is a major contributor to that homicide statistic (Koop, 1985).

The Surgeon General's conference led to recommendations that have already begun to be implemented. Concrete examples include teaching health personnel in federal installations to detect spouse abuse and asking gynecologists to assess their patients for the presence of spouse abuse. These are significant steps because only 7% of 107 domestic violence cases in an emergency room of a metropolitan hospital were identified as such (Goldberg & Tomlanovich, 1984). Most importantly, Koop brought the issue of violence into the purview of the health professionals. As the then Surgeon General noted,

> Over the years we've tacitly and, I believe, mistakenly agreed that violence was the exclusive province of the police, the courts, and the penal system. . . . The professions of medicine, nursing, and the health-related social services must come forward and recognize violence as their issue, also, one which profoundly affects the public health. (Koop, 1985)

In sum, spouse abuse is a relatively new field. Women's groups gave it needed attention, and mental health professionals have begun to break away from conceptualizations of spouse abuse that focus on individual psychopathology. Moreover, it is clear that spouse abuse is a very important social/psychological problem, and the federal government has begun to recognize the need for systematic assessment and treatment of this problem.

## PREVALENCE OF MARITAL VIOLENCE AND CHARACTERISTICS OF ABUSIVE RELATIONSHIPS

In order to provide an overview of what is known about the characteristics of individuals involved in interspousal aggression, we review the prevalence of this phenomenon in three different populations: (1) representative population surveys, (2) a longitudinal survey of newly married individuals, and (3) a marital clinic population. We then review studies investigating the characteristics of individuals in physically abusive relationships.

## Representative Population Surveys

Straus, Gelles, and Steinmetz (1980) conducted the first representative population survey designed to assess the frequency of family violence. That survey included 2,143 households assessed in 1975. Structured interviews were conducted, and the completion rate for the sample was 65%. Specific acts of aggression against a partner were assessed with a self-report measure, the Conflict Tactics Scale (Straus, 1979). It indicated that approximately 12% of women and 12% of men had been targets of physical aggression from their partners within the year. Moreover, 28% of men and women reported that they had been the targets or victims of physical aggression at some point in their marriage. Finally, 3.8% of the wives had been victims of severe violence ("wife-beating") in the past year prior to the interview.

In 1985, Straus and Gelles again assessed the frequency of spousal aggression. This survey used a national probability sample of 6,014 households and was conducted by phone interview rather than in person (Straus & Gelles, 1986). The response rate was 84% of the eligible households. Most important for our purposes was that aggression against one's partner remained remarkably high; at least 10% of women reported that they had been the recipients of physical aggression from their partners in the past year. Straus and Gelles (1986) reported some statistically significant differences across the decade, and these differences have been the subject of intense debate. The debate appears to be both methodological and political, but details about that debate detract from our main purpose, namely, to illustrate that physical aggression in marriage is a common phenomenon in the United States. Although the overall rates of physical aggression for men and women are approximately equal for representative population samples, there may be important gender differences in the rates of *severe* aggression for groups who will not participate in population surveys by sociologists and who will not seek help from mental health practitioners. Moreover, it is generally agreed that the consequences of physical aggression by men is greater than that by women, and the development and maintenance of the physical aggression may be gender specific (cf. Straus et al., 1980; Neidig & Friedman, 1984). A review of FBI reports, for example, shows that over the past decade men have killed their partners twice as frequently as women (O'Leary & Cascardi, 1989).

## Engaged and Newly Married Individuals

Our own research has concentrated on the etiology of spouse abuse, and toward that goal, we assessed 272 couples 6 weeks prior to their marriages and at 6, 18, and 30 months into their marriages. The couples were similar to the general population in the areas sampled in terms of age at first marriage and religious affiliation, but they had somewhat higher levels of education (O'Leary, Barling, et al., 1989). To our surprise, when assessed 4 to 6 weeks prior to marriage, 31% of the men and 44% of the women reported that they had physically aggressed against their partners in the past year. Couples who participated in all phases of the study showed a decrease in the frequency of physical aggression from premarriage to 30 months for both men and women. However, even at 30 months, the self-reported rates of aggression against the partner were 24% and 32% for men and women, respectively (O'Leary, Barling, et al., 1989).

The rates of physical aggression reported by men and women were strikingly high. Nonetheless, they are consistent with those obtained in a national probability sample of young couples. Elliot, Huizinga, and Morse (1986) found nearly identical self-reported rates of physical aggression against a partner in a national probability sample of individuals originally assessed to obtain estimates of delinquent behavior and drug and alcohol abuse in the United States population. Forty-three percent of women and 37% of men reported that they aggressed physically against their married or cohabitating partner in the year prior to the assessment. The similarity of these frequencies is remarkable, and both data sets illustrate amply that the problem of aggression against a partner is common among the newly married.

## Marital Clinic Populations

A study based on a sample of 266 couples seeking marital therapy indicated that severe husband-to-wife physical violence (items 14–18 on the Conflict Tactics Scale, CTS; Straus, 1979) was present in approximately 28% of the couples (Vivian, Malone, & O'Leary, 1989). Mild physical violence (items 11–13 on the CTS) was reported by approximately 31% of the couples, and verbal conflict without physical violence was present in approximately 39% of the couples (Vivian et al., 1989). The modal forms of physical aggression were pushing, shoving, and slapping and were said to occur three to five times per year. These three subgroups of couples differed significantly in their reported frequency of verbal abuse. Compared to nonabusive couples, verbal abuse occurred three times more frequently in couples reporting severe husband-to-wife aggression and twice as frequently in couples reporting less severe forms of husband-to-wife abuse. The three groups also differed with regard to other measures of marital functioning, such as marital adjustment, evaluation of partner communication skills, and depression. In brief, as physical aggression increased, spouses exhibited lower marital adjustment, more negative evaluation of the partner's communication, and higher levels of depression. Interestingly, men and women reported similar rates of aggression against their partner.

### Characteristics of Spouses in Abusive Relationships

Controlled studies suggest that men who physically aggress against their partners are characterized by alcohol abuse, generalized aggressive tendencies, impulsive and defendant personality styles, external locus of control, and type A personalities (Arias & O'Leary, 1988; Neidig, 1986). Individual differences related to women in abusive relationships, on the other hand, have not emerged consistently from controlled studies (Margolin, John, & Gleberman, 1988). In some studies, elevated levels of depression and anxiety, helplessness, and lower levels of assertiveness and problem-solving skills have been found to characterize battered women (Claerhout, Elder, & Janes, 1982; Lanius & Jansen, 1987). It seems quite possible, however, that such differences are related more directly to the effects of domestic violence than to preexisting characteristics of battered women.

With regard to their relationship, spouses in abusive marriages report lower levels of marital satisfaction (Rosenbaum & O'Leary, 1981; O'Leary & Curley, 1986) and significant problems in communication (Margolin et al., 1988; Vivian & O'Leary, 1987; Vivian, Mayer, Sandeen, & O'Leary, 1988; Vivian, Smith, Mayer, Sandeen, & O'Leary, 1987). Anger and reciprocation of negative affect characterize the problem-solving interaction of aggressive couples (Vivian & O'Leary, 1987; Smith & O'Leary, 1987). There is also some evidence that men and women may play different roles in the process of conflict escalation, such that physically abusive husbands tend to control the outcome of a conflictual discussion by using coercive techniques (e.g., increased negative affect and anger) more frequently than their spouses (Margolin et al., 1988).

Expressed negativity toward one's spouse during problem solving appears to be a stable characteristic of abusive couples during the first 3 years of their relationship (Rosenbaum & Golash, 1987; Vivian et al., 1988). Verbal abuse is not only a correlate of spouse abuse but predicts the onset of the first instance of interspousal physical aggression (Murphy & O'Leary, 1989). In sum, research on problem solving in physically aggressive couples suggests that dysfunctional displays of negative affect and patterns of negative reciprocity during conflict may be crucial in promoting the shift from verbal to physical aggression.

## ETIOLOGY OF SPOUSAL AGGRESSION AND MARITAL VIOLENCE

### Biological Models

There has been a resurgence of interest in biological and neurological factors that relate to aggression against women. As Elliot (1988) noted, so many social and cultural factors are related to aggression within the family that biological factors tend to be overlooked. We consider the potential role of biological factors in abuse by discussing the effects of temporal lobe tumors and head injury.

Compulsive violence is associated with temporal lobe tumors. For example, Charles Whitman of Austin, Texas reported to a psychiatrist that he felt compelled to kill people, including his wife and mother. He did so and was found later to have a temporal lobe tumor. Elliot (1988) found that 16 of 21 individuals with a compulsion to be violent had a variety of neurological abnormalities, including minimal brain dysfunction, temporal lobe pathology, and head injury. It should be emphasized, however, that neurological disorders such as temporal lobe epilepsy are not usually associated with aggression against others. Pathological aggressiveness is seen in as few as 6% to 7% of temporal lobe epilepsy cases. However, in certain neurosurgical clinics that handle intractable cases of epilepsy, the rate of paroxysmal violence can be as high as 50% (Elliot, 1988). Further, when individuals with episodic rage are evaluated, the rate of temporal lobe epilepsy is higher than in the general population.

Rosenbaum and Hoge (1989) also found disproportionate rates of head injury among men who engaged in spousal violence. Of 31 consecutive referrals for marital aggression, 19 (61%) reported a positive history of head injury that had required medical attention. Although Rosenbaum and Hoge did not have control groups, the percentage of batterers who reported significant head injuries substantially exceeded liberal estimates of population rates of head injury (6%). According to Elliot (1988), the more severe the head injury, especially when the individual has been unconscious for a week, the more likely are psychological consequences.

Even if it is demonstrated that certain acts of physical aggression against a partner are sometimes associated with physical abnormalities, we should not conclude that the cause of spouse abuse is biological. Although biological abnormalities may give rise to very severe aggression, it seems likely that social/psychological factors account for most of the variance in spouse abuse.

## Sociological Models

Although latecomers to the field of spouse abuse, sociologists have had a tremendous impact on conceptualizations of family violence. They critiqued definitions of abuse, identified its social and demographic concomitants, and questioned prevailing theories of family violence, especially the view that family violence results from psychiatric problems or personality disorders (Bersani & Chen, 1988).

Several sociological theories of spouse abuse have influenced psychologists' conceptualization of this problem. Of these, we describe three of the most influential, namely, resource theory, exchange theory, and a patriarchal perspective.

### Resource Theory

The person with the greatest number of resources has the power or ability to influence his or her partner (Blood & Wolfe, 1960). Goode (1971) conceptualized the family as any other social system, a group of individuals that is a power or force system. Laws, paternal rights, property rights, and custody rights establish family patterns, and forces supported by external social institutions help keep the family patterns stable. In fact, as Goode asserted, without force the structure of families would be lessened. Ironically, Goode believed that although those with large numbers of resources (e.g., status, money, political access, and intelligence) *could* use this force to command or control others, they would not use such forces. He felt that those with the most resources would use physical force less than those without such resources. Thus, he believed that individuals from upper social classes would use force less than those from lower social classes. Indeed, there is some, albeit inconsistent, support for this position (Straus et al., 1980; Hornung, McCullough, & Sugimoto, 1981).

An interesting twist to resource theory is the notion of status inconsistency, which refers to an individual who has high rank in one group (e.g., education) and low rank in another group (e.g., income level). Status inconsistency creates tension and frustration, and to reduce this frustration, antisocial attitudes and behavior are developed. Although this view relates clearly to aggression between members of different social classes, it can relate also to aggression within families. In fact, there is some support for the status inconsistency position. When a husband feels threatened by his wife's job or economic status, he may aggress against her (O'Brien, 1971; see also Barling, Chapter 7, this volume). Further, when there is an inconsistency between one's own educational level and one's job, aggression against a spouse is more likely (Hornung et al., 1981).

## Exchange Theory

The essence of exchange theory is that people engage in behavior to maximize rewards and avoid punishment (Homans, 1961). Gelles's (1987) position on family violence is very similar and straightforward: "People hit and abuse other family members because they can" (p. 17). If one assumes that control of others can be reinforcing and that family violence is unlikely to be punished, the link between exchange theory and spouse abuse is clear. Indeed, Gelles posits that three family factors contribute to aggression against a partner: the status of being aggressive, inequality, and privacy. Gelles (1987) believes that in certain situations men actually gain status by being perceived as violent ("the *macho* man"). Inequality is reflected in physical size, strength, and economic superiority. Privacy is seen as a unique factor that contributes to spouse abuse, particularly because the privacy or security of one's home has long been held to be sacred by legislators, police, friends, and neighbors. Consequently, men can get away with aggression against a mate in a fashion that they could not against a person outside the home.

Exchange theory has guided the research of many sociologists. For example, Straus, Gelles, and colleagues used it to delineate risk factors associated with spouse abuse such as violence in the family of origin, young age of men, stress, low income, education, lack of religious affiliation, and urban status (Straus et al., 1980). Unfortunately, there are no critical tests of the central position of exchange theory, namely, that people hit because they find it rewarding or that they can get away with it. We return to that issue when we discuss psychological theories of spouse abuse. However, corollary tenets of the exchange theory such as the status of being aggressive, privacy, and inequality are concepts that place spouse abuse in the larger social context and make partly understandable why spouse abuse is more frequent than hitting individuals outside the home.

## Patriarchal Conceptualizations

Patriarchal views of spouse abuse are based on the premise that men play an authoritarian role within the family and exercise historically rooted power in the family. According to this view, the power differential between men and women is ubiquitous in Western cultures. The flavor of these patriarchal concepts is seen in the following Biblical quotations: ". . . you wives be submissive to your own husbands . . ." (Peter, 3:1); ". . . the head of woman is her husband . . ." (I Corinthians, 11:3).

Likewise, these concepts are reflected in the following legal definitions. "Stitch rules," which were applied in many states in the 1800s–1900s, stipulated the number of stitches required in order for an offense to be considered assault and battery. The expression "rule of thumb" comes from an English tradition in which a man was allowed to hit his wife with something no thicker than his thumb (Davidson, 1977).

Under English common law, husbands had the right to chastise and control their possessions, including women and children. Evaluation of the heuristic value of the patriarchal conceptualization is difficult, but variations or derivations of this view are seen in many sociological and psychological theories. According to Dobash and Dobash (1979), wife beating is related to cultural attitudes about women. In brief, the more women are seen as property of men, and the more women are economically and psychologically dependent on men, the more likely they are to be abused. With the exception of economic factors associated with spouse abuse, the patriarchal viewpoint has received little empirical support. As a single causal explanation, it is limited. On the other hand, it describes a viewpoint that has undoubtedly played a key role in fostering and maintaining spouse abuse. The historical case-study approach presented by Dobash and Dobash is cogent, has great emotional appeal, and continues to be influential.

Sociologists opened the field of family violence to theoretical and empirical scrutiny (Straus et al., 1980), and, as we see below, they guided the content of most therapeutic approaches. Resource theory, exchange theory, and patriarchy are concepts that appear in therapies for both men and women.

## Psychological Models

Numerous psychological models of spousal aggression have also been offered. Those considered in this chapter are conceptualized as relating to different social learning mechanisms through which spousal physical aggression is adopted as a conflict resolution tactic. Most importantly, the evidence linking negative communication skills to interspousal physical aggression suggests that close attention needs to be given to the role of anger and hostility in promoting the shift from verbal aggression to physical aggression. In view of this escalation pattern, particular consideration is given to learning models that highlight the role of communication skills and anger in the genesis of aggression.

### Classical Conditioning

According to Berkowitz (1962), stimuli that are associated regularly with the instigation and display of aggression may gradually acquire the capacity to elicit anger and physically aggressive behaviors in people who have been provoked. In the context of spousal aggression, previous exposures to conflictual interaction and associated stimuli (e.g., negative emotions, aggressive thoughts, exposure to partner's provocative cues) may elicit progressively stronger negative affect.

Although anger is not a sufficient or necessary condition for physical aggression, anger arousal is a major precipitant of aggression (Rule & Nesdale, 1976). Moreover, there is evidence that "residual" physiological arousal stemming from extraneous sources paired with hostile attributes can predispose the individual to perceive his or her arousal as being related to anger rather than to other emotional states (Zillman, 1971). Research on marital communication suggests that the escalation patterns observed in the conflict discussions of maritally distressed spouses may be related to interdependent conditioned physiological arousal in the spouses (Levenson & Gottman, 1983). Conditioning and negative reinforcement processes predict that a continuation of conflict over time predisposes spouses to experience increasingly higher levels of negative affect during problem solving with their partners.

## Operant Analyses

Sebastian (1983), in conceptualizing the etiology of aggressive family interactions, described how social factors that *inhibit* interpersonal violence operate more weakly in the home than in extrafamilial contexts and how some factors that *instigate* violence may operate most strongly within the family. It has been shown, for example, that neutral and hostile behaviors displayed by a family member, compared with those of a stranger, may instigate aggressive behavior (Holmes & Berkowitz, 1961). According to Sebastian (1983), this behavioral pattern stems from the individual's expectations regarding treatment by family members compared with strangers.

It is logical to assume that the maintenance of severe physical aggression against family members is related more closely to the relative lack of negative contingencies for these behaviors in the home than to the victim's instigation of violence. However, the mechanisms linked to the maintenance of less severe forms of aggression may be different. For milder forms of aggression, the instigational notion may be especially relevant and may support the view that aggression between spouses is a mutual process of instigation and retaliation in the absence of strong social inhibitory factors. Indeed, there is some evidence that anticipation of minimal negative consequences for physical aggression may support the acquisition and maintenance of physical aggression in adult intimate relationships (Breslin, Riggs, O'Leary, & Arias, in press).

We believe that a variety of learning mechanisms are related to interspousal aggression and that the degree to which these mechanisms influence behavior varies in relation to the duration and the impact of aggression for both the aggressor and the victim. Over time, the reinforcing value of control or coercion may become progressively more important for the aggressor than other factors (e.g., cognitive processes, physiological arousal related to affective states). Likewise, the partner who experiences the most severe impact of the violence and who submits to it may progressively assume a victim's role. At times, the victim may instigate violence to deal with interspousal tension-building and, even more importantly, may provide fewer and fewer negative consequences for the violent behavior over the course of time (Walker, 1979; Deschner, 1984).

Although there is evidence that negative reinforcement patterns maintain aggression in children (Patterson & Cobb, 1973), there is no systematic evaluation of the role played by operant factors in spouse abuse. The reinforcement model has clear conceptual appeal, but nobody has collected data that support or refute this model.

## Modeling

The cycle or transmission of violence across generations is among the most widely discussed issues in the marital aggression literature. It is believed that children learn to be physically aggressive in their family of origin and later exhibit such behavior in their family of procreation. In fact, there is some evidence that those who aggress physically against their partners, compared to those who do not, are more likely to come from homes where they observed violence or were the victims of beatings themselves (e.g., Straus et al., 1980; Rosenbaum & O'Leary, 1981).

Many individuals engage in physical aggression against their mates even when they have not been exposed to such aggression. For example, Arias (1984) assessed 369 engaged partners and found that only 12% of the women and 13% of the men who aggressed physically against their partner had been exposed to violence in their family of origin. Similar results have been obtained repeatedly in the dating literature (Riggs, O'Leary, & Breslin, 1990). Moreover, with time, the impact of modeling becomes less influential compared to more immediate or proximal factors such as marital discord and psychological aggression within the marriage (Malone, Tyree, & O'Leary, 1989).

## A Cognitive–Affective Model

This model is based on the premise that physical aggression results from a deficit in anger-control skills. Theories of aggression assign anger arousal to response-energizing, response-motivating, and response-activating mechanisms, respectively (Novaco, 1979). In each case, however, anger is viewed as an emotional state that *facilitates* aggression rather than a necessary condition for aggression to occur. More importantly, arousal follows from the appraisal of provoking circumstances (Novaco, 1979). There is little direct evidence to support these views in the spouse aggression area. However, suggestive evidence comes from Averill (1982), who found that intense anger occurs most frequently within the family and that the anger is a reaction to perceived violations of self-esteem or personal values. Further, the anger and verbal aggression are compounded by longstanding negative affect toward the target of aggression.

On the basis of the evidence stemming from the different

learning mechanisms of spousal aggression reviewed thus far, and on the basis of Bradbury and Fincham's (1987, 1989) contextual model of interaction in close relationships, we propose a general cognitive-behavioral model of marital communication that includes variables likely to be particularly important in conceptualizing the etiology of spouse abuse. This model is designed to provide a theoretical framework to explore the mechanisms through which negative affect, anger, and communication deficits predict physical aggression in marriage. The level of analysis focuses on each spouse's cognitions and emotions during dyadic interactions. Four major classes of variables related to each spouse's affective, cognitive, and behavioral functioning are included: (1) partner input; (2) spouse contextual variables; (3) spouse affective–cognitive processes; and (4) spouse outcome behavior or response. We describe each component of the model in turn.

First, as shown in Figure 11.1, *partner input* is the stimulus for the spouse's processing. It consists of a particular partner behavior (e.g., global criticism accompanied by negative affect).

Second, the *contextual* component of the model includes variables that affect the processing of partner input. On the basis of their stability and duration, these variables can be classified into two broad classes, namely "distal" variables and "proximal" variables. For each spouse, *distal* variables can be divided into those that relate to the environment (e.g., stressful life events, physical aggression in the family of origin) and to intrapersonal characteristics. The latter, individual characteristics, can be grouped further into those directly related to the marriage (e.g., beliefs regarding marital conflict, affect toward the spouse) and those relatively unrelated to the marriage (e.g., personality dispositions such as aggressiveness, impulsivity, defensiveness, and self-esteem). *Proximal* contextual variables are related to the individual's affective (e.g., feeling tired and irritable) and cognitive states (e.g., negative thoughts about the spouse) before the processing of the partner's input. It is expected that environmental events have a direct impact on the spouse's longstanding (or trait-related) intrapersonal characteristics and on the spouse's affective and cognitive states.

Third, following Bradbury and Fincham (1987, 1989), the *affective–cognitive* component of the model consists of two distinct processes, namely, a process of *appraisal* accompanied by an affective response (e.g., valence of the impact of communication) and a contingent *attributional* process (e.g., causal and responsibility attributions). The spouse's affective–cognitive processing is ex-

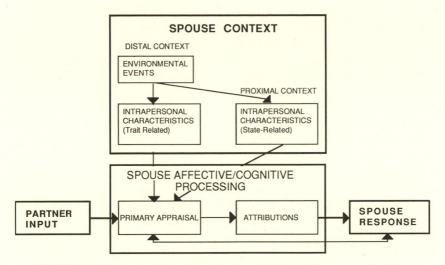

**FIGURE 11.1.** A cognitive-behavioral model of dyadic communication.

pected to be influenced by his or her affective and cognitive states and by his or her stable intrapersonal characteristics. Although it is hypothesized that the appraisal process will affect indirectly the spouse's behavior through the attributional processes, the literature suggests also that appraisal can influence the spouse's response directly (e.g., via conditioning mechanisms, when the partner's behavior has low significance for the self, and when it is highly predictable).

Fourth, the *behavioral response* or spouse output includes the spouse's attribution-dependent and appraisal-dependent responses along emotional, cognitive, behavioral, and physiological dimensions (e.g., negative contingent communication, negative affect, physiological arousal). The spouse's observable response will, in turn, serve as the input for the partner's affective–cognitive processing, and the sequence would be repeated for the partner.

On the basis of the literature, the presence of contextual factors characteristic of aggressive couples (e.g., elevated life stress, abuse in the family of origin, poor self-esteem, negative affect toward the spouse, dysfunctional attitudes regarding marital conflict) and negative mood states prior to the interaction would predispose aggressive spouses to appraise their partners' communication more negatively than nonaggressive spouses. Similarly, more negative partner-related causal and responsibility attributions are predicted in aggressive spouses than in nonaggressive spouses.

Both negative appraisal and dysfunctional attributions in aggressive spouses would in turn be highly predictive of a negative response contingent on a partner's conflictual communication. Escalation patterns and chains of negative contingent communications would be expected to ensue on the basis of this model. The shift from verbal to physical aggression is likely to occur at elevated levels of arousal, with prior exposure and/or experience with that behavioral response, and with a prior history of reinforcement for the use of that particular tactic of conflict resolution.

### A Social Learning View

We have evaluated a causal model for the etiology of spouse abuse that integrates modeling variables, personality factors, and self-report data on interactional patterns for men (see Figure 11.2). Using a longitudinal design, we attempted to predict physical aggression of men 30 months after our initial assessment from the following factors: (1) parental violence, (2) personality dispositions such as aggressive and defensive personality styles, (3) verbal aggression toward the spouse (overt and passive) as assessed at 18 months postmarriage, and (5) marital discord as assessed at 18 months postmarriage. Each of these variables was associated with use of physical aggression at 30 months. Parental violence had a direct causal path to physical aggression. On the other hand,

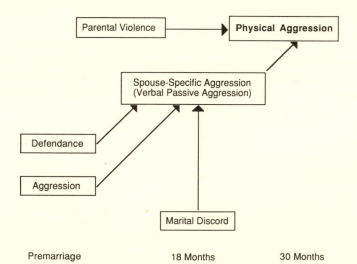

**FIGURE 11.2.** An etiological model of spouse abuse. From O'Leary, Malone, and Tyree (1989).

personality styles (defendance and aggression) and marital discord indirectly influenced physical aggression though spouse specific verbal and passive aggression (O'Leary, Malone, & Tyree, 1989). As suggested by this investigation, verbal aggression toward the spouse mediates the impact of personality factors and marital adjustment in the etiology of spouse abuse.

This model is based on a psychological conceptualization of spouse abuse, but we believe that more complete psychological accounts that include cognitive variables such as those described in Figure 11.1 will ultimately aid us in achieving greater predictability of physical aggression. Moreover, we already know that sociological variables such as demographic factors (age, lack of religious affiliation, and conservative attitudes toward women) are significant correlates of spouse abuse that could add to this model or could be used as alternative models for predicting physical aggression against spouses.

## TREATMENT OF MARITAL VIOLENCE

### Gender-Specific Models

Most psychological interventions for domestic violence focus on the treatment of men and women separately. With regard to the format of therapy, a widely held view has been that group therapy is more appropriate than individual therapy. This view is based on the notion that group dynamics will better address individual anger-control problems that stem from patriarchal attitudes and gender-specific socialization processes than one-to-one interactions in individual therapy. In men's groups, exchange theory and patriarchy are used to help men understand that they may have developed attitudes that prompted and/or condoned spouse abuse. In women's groups, resource theory serves as a guide to encourage women to become more financially and psychologically independent. Because these treatments differ greatly, we discuss the rationales for them and the treatment outcome data related to each separately.

### *Males*

Anger-containment programs for batterers that were court mandated or undertaken voluntarily became the primary method used to treat physical aggression in marriage. The rationales for treating men were manifold. First, men are stronger than women and cause more physical damage than women in domestic disputes. They engage in more physical fights outside marriage than women, and they kill their wives or partners more frequently. Second, in most states, physical abuse against one's spouse is illegal and can lead to legal sanctions, including court-mandated group therapy or reeducation. Third, the patriarchal and power views of marriage discussed earlier are key issues addressed in such interventions. Fourth, responsibility for the physical aggression is held to rest with the aggressor, and no diffusion of this responsibility or blame should occur through seeing the husband and the wife together (Adams, 1988; Edleson, 1985; Ganley & Harris, 1978). Fifth, men are seen as deficient in assertion, emotional expression, and empathy. In turn, it is felt that teaching men to express feelings should occur in men's groups, thereby minimizing blame for the physically aggressive incidents. Furthermore, resocialization of males and masculine roles are seen as an essential strategy to end domestic violence.

Individual or group programs for aggressive men have been in existence for at least a decade (Eddy & Myers, 1984). In New York State, the Rockland County program has served as a prototype for many others (Frank & Houghton, 1982). A derivative of this program was developed by Rosenbaum (1985) at Syracuse and later in Massachusetts. The essence of this program has been (1) attitude change (e.g., acceptance of responsibility for aggression), (2) reeducation (e.g., learning that anger can be controlled and that violence is a choice), and (3) cognitive-behavior modification (e.g., relaxation, self-talk, identification of discriminant stimuli for imminent violence). This program incorporates many principles discussed in the psychological models section, especially modeling and respondent and operant learning. Despite persistent attempts by Rosenbaum to collect follow-up data of court-mandated abusers, this task has proved to be extremely difficult. At best, there is only suggestive evidence for the efficacy of this treatment approach (Rosenbaum & O'Leary, 1986).

A number of other studies suggest that approximately two-thirds of the participants in treatment programs for batterers remain nonviolent at 1-year follow-up (see Shepard, 1987). Despite these encouraging results, it should be emphasized that in some instances the average period of nonviolence by men who participated in such programs is as short as 3 months (Okun, 1986). Moreover, even when physical aggression is not reported, approximately 60% of the women whose spouses participated in these programs continue to be psychologically abused via threats, intimidation, and forced compliance (Shepard, 1987; Edleson & Brygger, 1986). Given these results and our own research indicating that psychological abuse is a significant predictor of physical abuse (Murphy & O'Leary, 1989), it becomes imperative to treat both psychological and physical aspects of aggression.

Another program for men is Emerge, a Boston-based program with an emphasis on patriarchal conceptualizations of male and female roles and changing sexual stereotypes (Adams & McCormick, 1982). This program is based in part on a feminist view but was designed by men to help men understand the roots of their prejudice against women and their inclination to dominate and exploit them. We know of no treatment outcome data with this approach, but it is one type of program that has gained widespread acceptance.

Cognitive-behavioral interventions have also been used to treat male abusers (Edleson, Miller, Stone, & Chapman, 1985; Hamberger & Hastings, 1988). There is inconsistent evidence for this approach. In general, the evidence suggests that violence can be eliminated for the majority of those treated (Edleson et al., 1985; Hamberger & Hastings, 1988). In one study, however, no reduction in violence was reported (Deschner & McNeil, 1986). Rigorous controlled evaluations of treatment approaches (including long-term follow-up) are sorely needed.

### Females

Advocacy groups and supportive psychotherapy have been the dominant treatment for women in physically abusive relationships and are common in publicly supported facilities. The rationale for these programs is straightforward: abused women are victims and need to be empowered. Proponents of this approach believe that psychological problems (e.g., helplessness, depression, poor self-esteem) result from abuse (Walker, 1979). Therefore, treatment focuses on enhancing self-esteem, giving women direct social and emotional support, and providing advocacy and evaluation in coping with legal and social services. When necessary, the abused woman is assisted in finding a shelter.

Our experience indicates that these programs help many women to gain confidence, to see alternatives to marriage, and to understand why they may have stayed in a physically abusive relationship. Empirical support for such programs, however, is lacking.

## Couples Models

A number of cogent reasons support the position that couple treatment is a preferred intervention for physical aggression when both partners clearly want to remain in the relationship and when the safety of the partners can be assured. Most demographic accounts based on the topography of aggression indicate that both men and women are physically aggressive and that comparable numbers of husbands and wives are aggressive against their spouses (Straus et al., 1980; O'Leary, Barling, et al., 1989). Many women in physically abusive relationships remain in those relationships even after they have been in shelters (Gondolf, 1988). Furthermore, marital discord is one of the strongest correlates of physical abuse (O'Leary, 1988), and causal models of spousal aggression indicate that spouse-specific verbal aggression is the best predictor of physical aggression in couples 1 year later (O'Leary, Malone, et al., 1989).

Linquist, Telch, and Taylor (1983) published one of the first accounts of the treatment of couples in which physical abuse was a presenting problem. An uncontrolled clinical trial showed that this program produced significant reductions in anger and jealousy as well as increases in marital satisfaction. Research on couples treatment is subject to the same criticisms as studies of gender-specific treatments; most important, it lacks a long-term follow-up.

## Varied Treatment Formats

We believe that there is no single effective or appropriate treatment for all cases of physical aggression in a relationship. Moreover, there is only one published outcome study that compares different treatments for physical aggression in marriage. Shupe, Stacey, and Hazelwood (1987) conducted an evaluation of programs employing men-only groups, couples groups, and individual couples therapy focused on communication and sex-role problems. All groups showed reductions in aggression, but only a subsample of participants could be contacted after treatment. There were no differences across the three groups. Consistent with many other treatment programs in this area, methodological problems preclude any clear conclusions.

A recent study by Edleson and Syers (in press) compared the effects of two intensities of treatment (12 versus 32 weeks) across three treatment modalities (education, self-help, and a combination of education and self-help). The effects of these treatment variables were examined with 283 men who were randomly assigned to the group treatments. In an unprecedented manner, Edleson and Syers had an 80% treatment completion rate, and they then were able to contact 60% of the men and/or their partners at 6 months following treatment. Basically, the treatments were effective in reducing physical aggression in approximately 66% of the subjects. Interestingly, there were no significant differences with regard to the intensity of the treatment.

As discussed previously, a variety of arguments can be advanced for how to treat men, women, and couples. However, we believe that gender-specific treatments will be more likely to show relapses than treatments for couples because of the failure to address issues of communication, psychological aggression, and marital satisfaction. On the other hand, we also believe that some abusive individuals are too aggressive toward their spouses to make working with the couple feasible. In such instances, couple therapy may be counterproductive and place the couple at risk for further aggression. One option for such individuals may be individual treatment followed by couple treatment. It also must be recognized that some men are so aggressive that a combination of legal and psychological treatment efforts must be pursued concurrently. For example, psychotherapy and probation with the threat of legal sanctions (jail) may be necessary with severely aggressive individuals. Finally, individuals with serious and intractable personality disturbances associated with longstanding dysfunctional relationship patterns are likely to present the greatest challenge in achieving and maintaining treatment goals.

## SUMMARY

Spouse abuse was ignored by mental health professionals until efforts by women's groups brought the problem to the attention of community leaders and legislators in the 1970s. Nonetheless, spouse abuse remains a common phenomenon in the United States. Physical aggression against a partner also occurs very frequently in dating relationships and in couples engaged to be married.

Although a biological model of human aggressiveness has served as a conceptual guide in cases of chronic and extreme spouse abuse, sociological and psychological models of spouse abuse have been the primary theoretical guides for research in the area. Sociological concepts such as patriarchy, power differentials, and exchange theory have been influential in theoretical accounts of spouse abuse, and they have had a very strong role in shaping treatment programs for spouse abusers and victims of spouse abuse. Psychological models of primary import have been social learning models. They have featured factors such as communication deficits, anger arousal, reinforcement, and modeling. More recently, cognitive factors have also received attention. Such factors include appraisal of an event (e.g., evaluating an event as threatening to one's self-esteem) and attributions of blame and responsibility for an event. Finally, our own social learning model has provided evidence that spouse abuse can be predicted including violence in the family of origin, personality styles (aggression and impulsivity), marital discord, and spouse-specific verbal aggression.

As regards treatment, gender-specific therapies have been the modal form of treatment for spouse abuse. In men's treatment programs, the focus is on anger control, responsibility for one's actions, and changes in cognitions leading to spousal aggression. Women's treatments have focused on empowering women both to seek alternatives to the marriage and to provide support while coping with a troubled marriage. Recently, couples treatment has been presented as an alternative intervention for couples who want to remain together and where the safety of the partners can be assured. Outcome research is limited, and follow-up data are extremely rare, but there are suggestions that varied programs have some clinical utility in controlling spouse abuse. It is now important to conduct systematic research on the effectiveness and maintenance of treatment.

# R E F E R E N C E S

Adams, D. C. (1988). Stages of anti-sexist awareness and change for men who batter. In L. J. Dickstein & C. C. Nadelson (Eds.), *Family violence* (pp. 63–97). Washington, DC: AAPI Press.

Adams, D. C., & McCormick, A. J. (1982). Men unlearning violence: A group approach based on the collective model. In M. Roy (Ed.), *The abusive partner* (pp. 170–197). New York: Van Nostrand Reinhold.

Arias, I. (1984). *A social learning theory explication of the intergenerational transmission of physical aggression in intimate heterosexual relationships.* Unpublished doctoral dissertation, State University of New York at Stony Brook.

Arias, I., & O'Leary, K. D. (1988). Cognitive-behavioral treatment of physical aggression in marriage. In N. Epstein, S. E. Schlesinger, & W. Dryden (Eds.), *Cognitive-behavioral therapy with families* (pp. 118–150). New York: Brunner/Mazel.

Averill, J. (1982). *Anger and aggression: An essay on emotion.* New York: Springer-Verlag.

Berkowitz, L. (1962). *Aggression: A social psychological analysis.* New York: McGraw-Hill.

Bersani, C. A., & Chen, H. T. (1988). Sociological perspectives in family violence. In V. B. Van Haselt, R. L. Morrison, A. S. Bellack, & M. Hersen (Eds.), *Handbook of family violence* (pp. 57–86). New York: Plenum.

Blood, R. O., & Wolfe, D. W. (1960). *Husbands and wives.* New York: Free Press.

Bradbury, T. N., & Fincham, F. D. (1987). Affect and cognition in close relationships: Toward an integrative model. *Cognition and Emotion, 1,* 59–87.

Bradbury, T. N., & Fincham, F. D. (1989). Behavior and satisfaction in marriage: Prospective mediating processes. *Review of Personality and Social Psychology, 10,* 119–143.

Breslin, F. C., Riggs, D., O'Leary, K. D., & Arias, I. (in press). The impact of interparental violence on dating violence: A social learning analysis. *Journal of Interpersonal Violence.*

Claerhout, S., Elder, J., & Janes, C. (1982). Problem-solving skills of rural battered women. *American Journal of Community Psychology, 10,* 605–613.

Davidson, T. (1977). Wife beating: A recurrent phenomenon through history. In M. Roy (Ed.), *Battered women: A psychosociological study of domestic violence* (pp. 2–34). New York: Van Nostrand Reinhold.

Deschner, J. P. (1984). *The hitting habit: Anger control for battering couples.* New York: Free Press.

Deschner, J. P., & McNeil, J. S. (1986). Results of anger control training for battering couples. *Journal of Family Violence, 1,* 11–120.

Dobash, R. E., & Dobash, R. (1979). *Violence against wives.* New York: Free Press.

Eddy, M. J., & Myers, T. (1984). *Helping men who batter: A profile of programs in the U.S.* Prepared for the Texas Department of Human Resources, Austin.

Edleson, J. L. (1985). Violence is the issue: A critique to Neidig's assumption. *Victimology, 9,* 5.

Edleson, J. L., & Brygger, M. P. (1986). Gender differences in reporting of battering incidents. *Family Relations, 35,* 377–382.

Edleson, J. L., Miller, D. M., Stone, G. W., & Chapman, D. G. (1985). Group treatment for men who batter. *Social Work Research and Abstracts, 21,* 18–21.

Edleson, J. L., & Syers, M. (in press). The relative effectiveness of group treatments for men who batter. *Social Work Research and Abstracts.*

Elliot, D. S., Huizinga, D., & Morse, B. J. (1986). Self-reported violent offending: A descriptive analysis of juvenile violent offenders and their offending careers. *Journal of Interpersonal Violence, 4,* 472–514.

Elliot, F. A. (1988). Neurological Factors. In V. B. Van Hasselt, R. L. Morrison, A. S. Bellack, & M. Hersen (Eds.), *Handbook of family violence* (pp. 359–382). New York: Plenum.

Fedders, C., & Elliot, L. (1987). *Shattered dreams.* New York: Harper & Row.

Frank, P. B., & Houghton, B. D. (1982). *Confronting the batterer: A guide to creating the spouse abuse workshop.* New City, NY: Volunteer Counseling Service of Rockland County.

Ganley, A. L., & Harris, L. (1978, August). *Domestic violence: Issues in designing and implementing programs for male batterers.* Paper presented at the annual meeting of the American Psychological Association, Toronto.

Gayford, J. J. (1975). Wife beating: A preliminary survey of 100 cases. *British Medical Journal, 1,* 194–197.

Gelles, R. J. (1987). *Family violence.* Newbury Park, CA: Sage.

Goldberg, W. G., & Tomlanovich, M. C. (1984). Domestic violence victims in the emergency department: New findings. *Journal of the American Medical Association, 251,* 3259–3264.

Gondolf, E. W. (1988). The effect of batterer counseling on shelter outcome. *Journal of Interpersonal Violence, 3,* 275–289.

Goode, W. J. (1971). Force and violence in the family. *Journal of Marriage and the Family, 33,* 624–635.

Hamberger, L. K., & Hastings, J. E. (1988). Skills training for the treatment of spouse abusers: An outcome study. *Journal of Family Violence, 3,* 121–130.

Holmes, D. S., & Berkowitz, L. (1961). Some contrast effects in social perception. *Journal of Abnormal and Social Psychology, 62,* 150–152.

Homans, G. C. (1961). *Social behavior: Its elementary forms.* New York: Harcourt, Brace, Jovanovich.

Hornung, C. A., McCullough, B. C., & Sugimato, T. (1981). Status relationships in marriage: Risk factors in spouse abuse. *Journal of Marriage and the Family, 43,* 675–692.

Koop, C. E. (1985, October). *The surgeon general's workshop on violence and public health, source book* (p. i). Leesburg, Virginia.

Lanius, M. H., & Jensen, B. L. (1987). Interpersonal problem-solving skills in battered, counseling, and control women. *Journal of Family Violence, 2,* 151–163.

Levenson, R. W., & Gottman, J. M. (1983). Marital interaction: Physiological linkage and affective exchange. *Journal of Personality and Social Psychology, 45,* 587–597.

Linquist, C. U., Telch, C. F., & Taylor, J. (1983). Evaluation of a conjugal violence treatment program: A pilot study. *Behavioral Counseling and Community Interventions, 3,* 76–90.

Malone, J., Tyree, A., & O'Leary, K. D. (1989). Generalization and containment: Different effects of aggressive histories for wives and husbands. *Journal of Marriage and the Family, 51,* 687–697.

Margolin, G., John, R. S., & Gleberman, L. (1988). Affective responses to conflictual discussion in violent and nonviolent couples. *Journal of Consulting and Clinical Psychology, 56,* 1.

Murphy, C., & O'Leary, K. D. (1989). Psychological aggression predicts physical aggression in early marriage. *Journal of Clinical and Consulting Psychology, 57,* 579–582.

Neidig, P. (1986). *Spouse abuse issues and attitudes: A guide for family advocacy public information presentations in the military.* Beaufort, SC: Behavioral Sciences Associates.

Neidig, P., & Friedman, D. H. (1984). *Spouse abuse: A treatment program for couples.* Champaign, IL: Research Press.

Novaco, R. W. (1979). The cognitive regulation of anger and stress. In P. C. Kendall & S. D. Hollon (Eds.), *Cognitive-behavioral interventions* (pp. 241–285). New York: Academic Press.

O'Brien, J. E. (1971). Violence in divorce prone families. *Journal of Marriage and the Family, 33,* 692–698.

Okun, L. (1986). *Woman abuse*. Albany, NY: State University of New York Press.

O'Leary, K. D. (1988). Physical aggression between spouses: A social learning perspective. In V. B. Van Hasselt, R. L. Morrison, A. S. Bellack, & M. Hersen (Eds.), *Handbook of family violence* (pp. 31-55). New York: Plenum.

O'Leary, K. D., Barling, J., Arias, I., Rosenbaum, A., Malone, J., & Tyree, A. (1989). Prevalence and stability of physical aggression between spouses: A longitudinal analysis. *Journal of Consulting and Clinical Psychology, 57*, 263-268.

O'Leary, K. D., & Cascardi, M. (1989). *Frequency of homicide in intimate relationships: A decade of F.B.I. reporting*. Unpublished manuscript, Department of Psychology, State University of New York at Stony Brook.

O'Leary, K. D., & Curley, A. (1986). Assertion and family violence: Correlates of spouse abuse. *Journal of Marital and Family Therapy, 12*, 281-290.

O'Leary, K. D., Malone, J., & Tyree, A. (1989). *An evaluation of an etiological model of spouse abuse*. Unpublished manuscript, State University of New York at Stony Brook.

Pagelow, M. D. (1984). *Family violence*. New York: Praeger.

Patterson, G. R., & Cobb, J. A. (1973). Stimulus control for classes of noxious behaviors. In J. F. Knutson (Ed.), *The control of aggression: Implications from basic research* (pp. 144-149). Chicago: Aldine.

Riggs, D. S., O'Leary, K. D., & Breslin, F. C. (1990). Multiple correlates of physical aggression in dating couples. *Journal of Interpersonal Violence, 5*, 61-73.

Rosenbaum, A. (1985). *Marital violence workshop manual*. Unpublished manuscript, Syracuse University, Syracuse, NY.

Rosenbaum, A., & Golash, L. (1987). *Communication and aggression in beginning marriages*. Unpublished manuscript, University of Massachusetts Medical Center, Worcester, MA.

Rosenbaum, A., & Hoge, S. K. (1989). Head injury and marital aggression. *American Journal of Psychiatry, 146*, 1048-1051.

Rosenbaum, A., & O'Leary, K. D. (1981). Marital violence: Characteristics of abusive couples. *Journal of Consulting and Clinical Psychology, 49*, 63-71.

Rosenbaum, A., & O'Leary, K. D. (1986). The treatment of marital violence. In N. S. Jacobson & A. S. Gurman (Eds.), *Clinical handbook of marital therapy* (pp. 385-405). New York: Guilford Press.

Rule, B. G., & Nesdale, A. R. (1976). Emotional arousal and aggressive behavior. *Psychological Bulletin, 83*, 851-863.

Sebastian, R. J. (1983) Social psychological determinants. In D. Finkelhor, R. J. Gelles, G. T. Hotaling, & M. A. Straus (Eds.), *The dark side of families: Current family violence research* (pp. 182-192). Beverly Hills, CA: Sage.

Shepard, M. (1987, July). *Intervention with men who batter: An evaluation of a domestic abuse program*. Paper presented at the Third National Family Violence Conference, Durham, NH.

Shupe, A., Stacey, W. A., & Hazelwood, L. R. (1987). *Violent men, violent couples*. Lexington, MA: D. C. Heath.

Smith, D. A., & O'Leary, K. D. (1987, July). *Stable interspousal aggression and premarital communication of affect*. Paper presented at the Third National Family Violence Conference, University of New Hampshire, Durham, NH.

Straus, M. A. (1979). Measuring intrafamily conflict and violence: The Conflict Tactics (CT) Scales. *Journal of Marriage and the Family, 41*, 75-86.

Straus, M. A., & Gelles, R. (1986). Societal change and change in family violence from 1975 to 1985 as revealed by two national surveys. *Journal of Marriage and the Family, 48,* 465–479.

Straus, M. A., Gelles, R., & Steinmetz, S. (1980). *Behind closed doors: Violence in the American family.* New York: Doubleday.

Tierney, K. J. (1982). The battered women movement and the creation of the wife beating problem. *Social Problems, 29,* 207–220.

Vivian, D., Malone, J., & O'Leary, K. D. (1989). *Wife abuse: Impact of severity of abuse on relationship variables.* Unpublished manuscript, State University of New York at Stony Brook.

Vivian, D., Mayer, F. J., Sandeen, E., & O'Leary, K. D. (1988, September). *Longitudinal assessment of the role of communication skills in interspousal aggression.* Paper presented at the Behavior Therapy World Congress, University of Edinburgh.

Vivian, D., & O'Leary, K. D. (1987, July). *Communication patterns in physically aggressive engaged partners.* Paper presented at the Third National Family Violence Research Conference, University of New Hampshire, Durham, NH.

Vivian, D., Smith, D. A., Mayer, F., Sandeen, E., & O'Leary, K. D. (1987, November). *Problem-solving skills and emotional styles in physically aggressive couples.* Paper presented at the 21st Annual Convention of the Association for Advancement of Behavior Therapy, Boston.

Walker, L. (1979). *The battered woman.* New York: Harper Colophon.

Zillman, D. (1971). Excitation transfer in communication-mediated aggressive behavior. *Journal of Experimental and Social Psychology, 7,* 419–434.

C H A P T E R 12

# Enhancing the Effectiveness of Marital Therapy

**Steven R. H. Beach**
**Sue Ann K. Bauserman**

Approximately 20% of all married couples are experiencing marital discord at any given time (Beach, Arias, O'Leary, 1987), and about half of all newlyweds in first marriages will divorce (Glick, 1984). Further, these statistics are particularly noteworthy because the physical and mental health consequences of marital discord and marital disruption can be dramatic. Marital discord and disruption are associated with a variety of physical and mental disorders for spouses (Beach & Nelson, 1990; Somers, 1979) and with mental health problems for their children (Emery, 1988). Despite the serious consequences of marital discord and divorce, it is only within recent years that marital therapy has received appropriate scrutiny through controlled outcome research (Beach & O'Leary, 1985). It is now apparent that there is considerable variability in response to marital therapy and that the mean response to treatment is clearly less than optimal (Jacobson et al., 1984; O'Leary & Arias, 1983).

The purpose of this chapter, therefore, is to discuss ways of improving marital therapy outcome. We outline an approach for studying "process" in marital therapy that suggests several new avenues for outcome research and provides a framework for enhancing the marital therapies that have been shown to be effective. In particular, we focus on the way in which a "process" approach can help focus more basic literatures on the problems currently confronting the marital therapy area. Before doing so, however, we examine briefly research on the outcome of marital therapy. Although reviews of the outcome literature are already available (e.g., Beach & O'Leary, 1985; Baucom & Hoffman, 1986; Hahlweg & Markman, 1988; Weiss & Heyman, 1990), some discussion of the current status of outcome research in marital therapy is a prerequisite for appreciating fully our proposals for enhancing outcome.

## CURRENT STATUS OF MARITAL THERAPY

We first summarize the status of the field at the time of the Beach and O'Leary (1985) review of the outcome literature. We then discuss recent additions to the field and how these additions address earlier concerns.

### Insight-Oriented Marital Therapy

Beach and O'Leary (1985) concluded that insight-oriented marital therapy, therapy aimed at helping the couple interact in a more mature manner by resolving unconscious sources of conflict, had not been evaluated adequately. In studies by Crowe (1978) and Epstein and Jackson (1978), insight was used without any directive techniques, a form of insight therapy that differs substantially from that described by prominent writers in the area. That is, no homework assignments were used, and no attempt was made to encourage the spouses to try new patterns of relating. Accordingly, it was suggested that these studies tell us only that insight in the absence of a clearly specified direction of change is not a valuable approach to marital therapy. In contrast, Boelens, Emmelkamp, MacGillavry, and Markvoort (1980) studied an insight-oriented approach that included a clear specification of direction of desirable change. This study demonstrated an effect for insight-oriented marital therapy. It was noted, however, that maintenance of gains appeared to be poor even at 1-month follow-up. Thus, although insight-oriented approaches appeared promising and in need of further investigation, increased incorporation of directive techniques and increased attention to maintenance of gains seemed warranted.

### Behavioral Contracting

All three tests of contracting alone (Crowe, 1978; Boelens et al., 1980; Baucom, 1982) showed that the use of behavioral contracts between spouses was superior to no-treatment control conditions. In addition, the three studies complemented each other nicely in that one assessed the impact of treatment on the individual as well as the couple, and two used trained raters of marital interaction as well as self-report measures to assess the impact of treatment on marital behavior and satisfaction. Thus, it was concluded that contracting approaches or, more specifically, the directive approach to specifying and increasing positive exchange in the dyad while decreasing coercive interaction could be effective in alleviating marital discord even when used alone.

## Behavioral Contracting and Communication Training

Several studies had examined the more usual pattern of behavioral marital therapy (BMT), which involves communication training as a concomitant or precursor to contracting (Jacobson, 1977, 1978; Turkewitz & O'Leary, 1981; Hahlweg, Revenstorf, & Schindler, 1982; Baucom, 1982). Again, there was considerable consistency across studies. It was concluded that contracting in conjunction with communication training influenced a number of facets of the marital relationship and was effective whether measured from the perspective of trained observers or via self-report measures. Thus, the combination of communication and contracting approaches emerged as a very viable form of marital therapy.

## Communication Training

At the time of the earlier review, the communication approach to marital therapy had yielded the greatest number of peer-reviewed studies (Hickman & Baldwin, 1971; Ely, Guerney, & Stover, 1973; Epstein & Jackson, 1978; Hahlweg et al., 1982; Turkewitz & O'Leary, 1981; Baucom, 1982). This reflects the fact that many different schools of marital therapy view effective communication as critical for a well-functioning marriage. Despite this consensus, the outcome studies provided a somewhat inconsistent pattern of results, as some studies showed that couples' communication patterns changed (as measured by trained raters and according to spousal reports), whereas other studies failed to show these effects. Likewise, most but not all studies showed an impact of treatment on increasing marital satisfaction.

Close examination revealed that lack of effectiveness was found when the outcome measures used were unstandardized or poorly validated. More specifically, in the Ely et al. (1973) study, no effect was found on an unvalidated measure of marital satisfaction; in the Epstein and Jackson (1978) study, changes were found on only 4 of 14 disparate change measures, 11 of which were from an unvalidated observational measure; and Turkewitz and O'Leary (1981) found change on their standardized measures of marital satisfaction and communication but not on their unstandardized observational measure. Thus, it was concluded from these studies that poorly standardized or poorly validated measures are unlikely to show change as a function of marital therapy and hence should be avoided in marital therapy outcome research. When the error introduced by unreliable measurement was removed, communication training alone emerged as a well-documented treatment modality.

## Overall Conclusions

Two observations that emerged from our initial review of the literature were disturbing. The first concerned the extent to which the field of marital therapy was (and is) based on relatively few peer-reviewed studies comparing treatment to no treatment. There was a relatively small number of well-controlled, peer-reviewed studies even for categories of communication skills and behavioral contracting approaches, the two categories that were best represented. Even more striking was the paucity of outcome studies investigating the effectiveness of other potentially valuable approaches to marital intervention from systems, gestalt, or analytic traditions. Second, despite several studies that examined "combination" approaches, there was no evidence that any of them enhanced the overall outcome of marital therapy. Thus, we appeared to be approaching an asymptote with regard to effectiveness in marital therapy, with no breakthroughs being promised by the traditional approach to marital therapy outcome research.

The second observation was particularly disturbing because, as mentioned earlier, the effectiveness of marital therapy had not reached a level where the field could rest content. Although gains made following some forms of marital therapy (i.e., communication with contracting) remained relatively stable for up to 1 year following therapy (Hahlweg, Baucom, & Markman, 1988), rates of divorce for couples completing such therapy were between 10% and 15% for this same period (Hahlweg et al., 1982), and rates of relapse after 1 year could not be estimated reliably. Further, when the effects of marital therapy were considered from the standpoint of how many couples moved from the distressed range to the nondistressed range, improvement rates tended to be about 50% or less (Jacobson et al., 1984).

## Suggested Direction for Outcome Research

Beach and O'Leary (1985) argued that before outcome in marital therapy could be enhanced, the reasons for nonresponse and less than optimal response to marital therapy needed to be better understood. They suggested that greater attention needed to be paid to mediating goals of therapy, that is, those goals of therapy that are not redundant with the criterion of success but whose attainment is held to produce improvement on the criterion of success. If the large variability in response to treatment and the less than optimal average change in satisfaction produced by treatment could be ascribed to variability in attainment of mediating goals of therapy, then it could be argued that the treatment was on the right track but had not yet fulfilled its potential. In particular, it could be argued that strategies for enhancing gains on these mediating goals could be expected to result in greater average gains and a greater percentage of couples showing clinically significant change.

On the other hand, to the extent that modest average change in satisfaction and considerable variability in response to treatment could not be ascribed to variability in gains on mediating goals of therapy, this would demonstrate a likely need to incorporate new mediating goals into the approach to therapy or else to revise the set of mediating goals proposed (cf. Gottman, 1979). Thus, the first result (i.e., variability is related to nonattainment of mediating goals) would suggest that there should be a more in-depth examination of the reasons for nonattainment of the mediating goals of therapy. The second result (i.e., variability is *not* related to nonattainment of mediating goals) would suggest a need to turn to more basic work on the structure of marital relationships and to elaborate the set of mediating goals of therapy by including new constructs derived from this more basic work.

To clarify the proposal made by Beach and O'Leary (1985), we consider the logic of the proposal with regard to a particular set of mediating goals. For example, if a researcher hypothesizes that enhanced marital satisfaction results from improvement on a particular set of relationship skills, the extent to which the specified relationship skills are mastered constitutes the degree of attainment of the mediating goals of therapy. Further, it should be possible to show that the couple's attainment in level of relevant skills (the mediating goals of therapy) accounts for the posttherapy level of marital satisfaction (the criterion of successful outcome). That is, outcome variability in response to treatment should be a function of couple differences in attainment of the hypothesized mediating goals of therapy. This logic should fail only if the therapy is very successful and all couples are making relatively equivalent positive changes or if the treatment is so inert that no gains are being made by anyone on the mediating goals of therapy. Stated differently, there will be problems for this approach to the validation of mediating goals when there is little variability in either the predictor variables (the mediating goals) or the dependent variable (the criterion of success). In other situations, failure to find a strong relationship between attainment of mediating goals and the outcome of therapy suggests either problems of measurement or problems with the proposed set of mediating goals of therapy.

When a researcher is successful in formulating an integrated set of mediating goals of therapy, each of which constitutes an independent point of therapeutic intervention, the product is a clinically useful model of change. At its best a model of change helps organize clinical activity in a natural and fluid manner, allowing the clinician to focus on tailoring specific interventions to fit the client couple while keeping the clinician well grounded in the relevant research literature. It follows, then, that the mediating goals of therapy should be specified in a way that ties them back to a literature capable of providing guidance about the production of change in each goal (Beach, Sandeen, & O'Leary, 1990). In some cases this literature may be an applied literature dealing with particular marital techniques. In other cases, the literature may be more basic but provide suggestions or the broad outlines of potentially effective interventions. It is likely to be clinically unhelpful to propose as "mediating goals of therapy" facets of the relationship that are in no way tied to possible intervention strategies or that all imply the same intervention approach.

## RECENT OUTCOME WORK IN MARITAL THERAPY

Since the Beach and O'Leary (1985) review, several studies have been added to the literature that broaden the empirical base of marital therapy and address issues that were left unanswered previously.[1] In particular, newer studies examine nonbehavioral marital therapies and the issue of maintenance of treatment gains over longer periods of time.

In an important addition to the field, Baucom and Lester (1986) examined a combination treatment of cognitive-behavioral techniques and traditional BMT techniques. The cognitive techniques focused almost exclusively on causal attributions for marital events and individual and relationship standards. Twenty-four maritally distressed couples were used in the study, and the two authors served as therapists. Results showed both treatments to be superior to a wait-list control group, with neither active treatment clearly superior to the other at posttest or at 6-month follow-up. Examination of within-group change patterns, however, suggested that the cognitive interventions were exerting consistent positive effects on cognitive variables in a way that was not true of the behavioral intervention. Thus, to the extent that these cognitive variables are important in marital satisfaction or the process of therapeutic change, the Baucom and Lester (1986) study indicates a promising set of techniques to be used in effecting cognitive change. Interestingly, the study did not demonstrate that marital therapy will be enhanced by the routine addition of a cognitive intervention component. Rather, the promise of this study lies in the possibility that therapists can choose the right cognitive intervention at the right point in therapy for the right couple (cf. Baucom, 1989). The Baucom and Lester (1986) study, therefore, leaves intact the conclusion that adding new components to existing behavioral interventions leaves average outcome unchanged.

In a second important addition to the field, Johnson and Greenberg (1985a) evaluated the effectiveness of "emotionally focused" marital therapy (Greenberg & Johnson, 1988). This approach borrows techniques from gestalt and systems approaches and utilizes techniques common to cognitive and behavioral approaches. Its unique contribution lies in its focus on unexpressed and/or unacknowledged feelings and on helping couples come to a new understanding of their relationship based on the exploration

---

[1]Beach and O'Leary (1985) reviewed only outcome studies performed with initially discordant couples that included both random assignment to condition and the presence of a control group and that had gone through the peer-review process. These inclusion criteria yielded reliable judgments and provided a reasonable level of protection against individual reviewer bias. In the present review we use these same criteria.

of these feelings. In their study, 45 couples were assigned randomly to emotion-focused, problem-solving, or wait-list control groups. Moderately to severely discordant couples were excluded from the sample (Dyadic Adjustment Scale [DAS] scores below 65). Johnson served as one of the therapists in the emotion-focused condition, with therapists nested under treatment in the study design. Baucom and Hoffman (1986) and Weiss and Heyman (1990) rightly point out that this design feature poses serious problems in the interpretation of the comparison between the two active treatments, yet it does not compromise the comparison of emotion-focused therapy with the control group. Emotion-focused therapy produced an overall change in marital satisfaction, whereas the control group showed no change.

Although subsequent studies using less experienced therapists and more discordant couples have not replicated the dramatic effects found in the initial study (Johnson & Greenberg, 1985b; Goldman, 1987, as cited by Greenberg & Johnson, 1988), the Johnson and Greenberg (1985a) study highlights another source of potentially useful techniques in the treatment of mild to moderate marital discord. In light of the failure to replicate the initial strong effects in more discordant samples, however, one must conclude that a strong case has not yet been made that marital outcome can be substantially enhanced simply through the use of emotion-focused techniques in addition to, or instead of, standard behavioral marital therapy. Indeed, other outcome work in progress suggests that there is no additive effect when standard BMT and emotion-focused therapy are combined (Baucom & Sayers, 1988). However, to the extent that some couples respond particularly well to emotion-focused therapy or to emotion-focused techniques used at certain points in therapy, the potential for the enhancement of marital therapy outcome is clear (Baucom & Sayers, 1988; Margolin, 1987; Weiss & Heyman, 1990).

A third contribution to the outcome literature is reported by Snyder and Wills (1989). In this study, 79 couples seeking treatment for relationship distress were assigned to either a BMT condition, an insight-oriented marital therapy condition, or a treatment-on-demand wait-list condition. Both treatment conditions resulted in significant improvement, but they did not differ significantly from each other. Snyder and Wills (1989) note the similarity between their insight-oriented approach and the therapeutic approach used by Johnson and Greenberg (1985a). Indeed, taken together, these two studies substantially answer Beach and O'Leary's (1985) call for more work aimed at establishing the effectiveness of insight-oriented approaches. As predicted, these two effective insight-oriented approaches have strong directive components and provide clear messages about the direction of change that would be desirable. The Snyder and Wills (1989) study shows also that treatment gains were maintained at 6-month follow-up. Thus, insight-oriented therapies with strong directive components can now be said to be roughly equal to contracting approaches with regard to apparent effectiveness, although maintenance beyond 6 months remains unknown. Again, however, effectiveness is well below the level most marital therapists would hope for, despite the increased length of marital therapy in the Snyder and Wills (1989) study (19 sessions). Thus, once again, although there is evidence pointing to potentially useful new technologies, there is little reason to expect substantially enhanced average outcomes to result from their addition as a standard treatment component.

A fourth contribution to the empirical literature is reported by Jacobson (Jacobson, 1984; Jacobson et al., 1985; Jacobson, Schmaling, & Holtzworth-Munroe, 1987). This study compared the effectiveness of behavior exchange, communication problem-solving training, and the combination of these two approaches. As expected, all treated couples improved significantly more than wait-list couples. Consistent with prior research, the combined treatment was not significantly better than the component treatments. However, differences did emerge with regard to maintenance of treatment effects. Good maintenance of gains at 6 months was found for both groups receiving intervention targeted at increasing communication and problem-solving skills. However, the group receiving only the behavior exchange (i.e., contracting) intervention showed a significant decline in marital satisfaction by 6-month follow-up. At longer follow-ups, the combined treatment was nonsignificantly superior to the behavior exchange treatment. Jacobson et al. (1985) concluded that the superiority of the combined treatment, relative to the behavior exchange treatment alone, is only temporary.

## Summary

The work that has appeared since the Beach and O'Leary (1985) review has clearly expanded the field of marital therapy. New forms of marital therapy have been explicated and tested in a way that allows them to join the ranks of empirically substantiated therapies. Cognitive marital techniques and techniques focused on insight into unspoken or unrecognized feelings toward the partner have been added to the clinician's armamentarium. Indeed, some authors have already heralded the beginnings of a "cognitive-behavioral-affective" approach to marital therapy (Margolin, 1987). However, whereas technological options continue to proliferate, there is no evidence of enhancement of the overall effectiveness of marital therapy or enhancement of the percentage of couples improving in marital therapy. We conclude that greater emphasis needs to be placed on addressing the thorny issue of enhancing marital therapy outcomes. Now more than ever, it would appear that attention must be directed toward the specification and testing of clinically useful change models in marital therapy, particularly those models that specify the mediating goals of marital therapy.

## A PROCESS APPROACH TO ENHANCING MARITAL THERAPY

How can outcome researchers build on the available base of empirically validated marital therapy techniques in such a way that they *accumulate* gains rather than merely introduce new variations or new systems of therapy with similar outcomes? Several goals are clearly discernible in the literature: (1) we can continue to search for new techniques that can be added to our standard marital therapy approaches; (2) we can attempt to improve our ability to match "types of couples" to the particular marital packages most appropriate for them; and (3) we can improve our ability to target flexibly and accurately particular problem domains most relevant to particular couples. Although each of these goals seems reasonable, we would argue that they are unlikely to prove fruitful unless they are pursued in the context of rigorous process research aimed at producing empirically tested, integrated sets of mediating goals for marital therapy (i.e., models of change in marital therapy). We address each proposal in turn.

The search for new techniques is likely to continue technical diversification without increasing the effectiveness of marital therapy unless these techniques are proposed in the context of well-specified change models with new techniques clearly tied to particular mediating goals of therapy. Already the search for new techniques has led to treatment packages with broad areas of overlap. Continuing technical diversification in the absence of process work is likely to muddy further the issue of which particular techniques constitute real additions to an optimal, empirically based marital therapy, and which are simply redundant with already existing technologies. Conversely, if new techniques are tied to particular mediating goals of therapy, it becomes possible to evaluate the need for the technology based on couples' average response to the other techniques aimed at addressing each particular mediating goal. If other techniques intended to address the mediating goal are weak or inert, then the need to develop the new technology is clear. At the same time, by focusing on mediating goals rather than on "outcome," it becomes easier to isolate the effects of a particular technique and refine the technique in a cost-effective manner.

Just so, the search for couple "types" could have substantial clinical importance if this variable were shown to moderate the relationship between the mediating goals of therapy and outcome. In the context of rigorous process research, specification of couple type could lead to an assessment technology capable of identifying couples for whom different mediating goals were required (i.e., couple type would moderate the relationship of the mediators to outcome). In the absence of process work, research strategies examining couple type as a predictor of response to treatment are likely to be cumbersome and unenlightening. In particular, since most marital therapy programs are conducted over 10 or more weeks, there is ample opportunity for change to occur on a variety of potentially mediating goals. Different types of couples can change for entirely different reasons but nevertheless show similar amounts of change. Analyses examining only couple type and outcome would risk overlooking the differences between the couple types that are of greatest clinical interest, that is, the fact that different goals should be targeted by the clinician working with different "types" of couples.

Finally, flexible therapy programs tailored to the needs of particular couples would appear very reasonable. Indeed, this constitutes the ideal of marital therapy, but currently there is no empirically based guidance for the clinical decision making required by flexible therapy. However, a well-validated set of mediating goals of therapy along with a well-validated measurement technology would provide this type of clinically useful guidance. In particular, if couples could be assessed prior to therapy on those areas hypothesized to be relevant for a successful outcome (i.e., the mediating goals of therapy), it would follow naturally that only those areas found to be in need of remediation would be targeted for change. However, in the absence of a well-specified set of mediating goals of therapy and a valid assessment technology, decisions about which areas to address and which areas to ignore will be intuitive at best, and flexible therapy programs are likely to fail to perform up to their full potential. Flexible therapy programs will presumably be most effective when clinicians are able to address mediating goals that result in change in satisfaction. Thus, rigorous process research is a necessary precursor of an optimal, flexible marital therapy.

Each of the strategies for enhancing outcome currently being discussed in the marital literature may be pursued most appropriately by first adopting a "process" approach to the study of outcome in marital therapy. A process approach begins with a multiple correlational strategy to relate hypothesized mediating variables to outcome measures of interest. Of particular importance for the success of this type of investigation are the development of a better and more theoretically sound measure of marital outcome than is currently available (Fincham & Bradbury, 1987a; Weiss & Heyman, 1990) and the development of measurement technologies for assessing the attainment or nonattainment of the mediating goals of therapy. Clearly, in the absence of a good measurement technology very little information can come from a strategy aimed at accounting for variance in outcome using a multiple correlational approach. These basic prerequisites of a process approach are not yet available. Nevertheless, it is instructive to examine in more detail both what process-oriented research might look like and how researchers using this approach might proceed.

## Elaboration of the Process Approach

A process approach can lead in one of two directions, depending on the ability of the set of mediating goals proposed by the researcher to account for change. First, if the specified set of mediating goals of therapy *failed* to account for much of the variability in treatment response, it would be reasonable to conclude that some change in the mediating goals of therapy was called for. The researcher might hypothesize that *additional* mediating goals of therapy were needed, or she might hypothesize that a somewhat different formulation of the change process was necessary.

For example, if the researcher had specified previously a set of mediating goals of therapy that included only skill attainment, the failure of these variables to account for a substantial portion of the variance in outcome might prompt the researcher to add, for example, cognitive variables or ability to verbalize reasons for negative feelings as additional or alternative mediating goals of therapy. The utility of these additions could be tested directly by including measures of these constructs in the study along with the original set of hypothesized mediating goals of therapy. If the new variables accounted for additional variance in outcome, there would be a strong argument for the addition of technologies tied to each new mediating goal. In particular, it would be reasonable to add the new technologies for persons responding poorly to the standard marital therapy package and scoring low on the newly added mediator of change. Thus, in addition to support for a new technology, there would be some guidance as to when and for whom the new technologies would be likely to make the greatest difference. This direction of research should lead to technological diversification that has a high likelihood of being *additive* to existing marital therapy programs.

The second direction that might result from adopting a process approach to the enhancement of marital therapy would be the study of how to enhance the magnitude of change on particular mediating goals of therapy. The researcher pursuing a process approach may find that variability in gains in marital satisfaction *is* well accounted for by couple differences in attainment of the hypothesized set of mediating goals of therapy. In this case, the researcher is led to focus on finding methods for enhancing attainment of particular mediating goals or reasons why couples do not make sufficient progress with regard to the mediating goals of therapy.

The assessment of reasons for nonattainment of particular mediating goals of therapy may be pursued fruitfully through clinical interview or intuition in the initial stages of investigation. However, it is likely that a clearer specification of obstacles to attainment of mediating goals will be forthcoming if researchers draw explicitly on well-articulated models of social behavior. Whereas basic work in social psychology and the social–clinical interface is likely to be pertinent in all phases of process work, it is likely to be particularly pertinent as researchers attempt to elaborate the reasons for nonattainment of mediating goals by some couples.

Change models are not currently well elaborated, and the measurement technology necessary for investigating them is lacking. However, already we have seen that a directive component is present in all the effective marital therapies. Accordingly, compliance with therapist directives is likely to emerge as a variable that sets the stage for enhanced change on proposed mediating goals for almost any effective marital therapy. That is, compliance is likely to emerge as a mediator of change through its impact on attainment of the mediating goals of therapy. Process work aimed at explicating noncompliance in marital therapy should therefore prove useful in conjunction with almost any set of mediating goals of therapy. This suggests that work on understanding noncompliance in marital therapy will ultimately prove fruitful within the broad framework provided by a process approach regardless of the particular set of mediating goals of therapy ultimately uncovered through empirical work.

Since compliance seems likely to be important for most forms of effective marital therapy, we provide an analysis of noncompliance as an example of how researchers using a process approach might approach obstacles to the attainment of important mediating goals in therapy. We attempt to develop the implications of two rather different approaches to understanding noncompliance in marital therapy and show how testable implications for new marital therapy techniques might be forthcoming. The remainder of the chapter is devoted to the particular issue of noncompliance in marital therapy. However, it should be understood that the process approach is predicated on the idea that models from more basic literatures can be utilized both at the level of defining the basic model of change and at the level of better understanding of difficulty in attaining particular mediating goals. The same multiple correlational strategy suggested for the examination of mediating goals in outcome could be adopted in the examination of obstacles to attaining a particular mediating goal. Thus, elaborating and deriving therapeutic implications from models of noncompliance are no different from elaborating models of change in therapy and deriving new mediating goals from basic work on intimate relationships. Process work can proceed at multiple interlocking levels simultaneously.

## Two Examples of Models Relevant to Noncompliance

We have selected two models that help illustrate some of the likely forces at work in noncompliance. The first model is Ajzen's theory of planned behavior, and the second model is Fincham and Bradbury's attribution-efficacy model of conflict in close relationships. These models complement each other in highlighting potentially different causes of noncompliance. The theory of planned behavior helps address the rather common occurrence in therapy where one spouse does not intend to carry out the therapist's directives. Although this is not the most exciting reason for therapeutic failure, it may well be the most common. The attribution-efficacy model, on the other hand, helps explicate the commonly encountered problem of couples who are too locked into blame and retribution to listen to the therapist and to comply with treatment. It is important to note that these models are not the only ones that could be examined for relevance to compliance in marital therapy. They were chosen to illustrate the potential contribution of more basic models to therapy process research and, ultimately, to marital therapy practice. Similarly, compliance is not the only variable of potential interest in accounting for the attainment of mediating goals in directive forms of therapy. Again, the purpose is to illustrate rather than exhaust the case for this type of process research.

## The Theory of Planned Behavior

Finding a general model that might help guide clinical activity regarding the noncompliant client is particularly relevant to marital therapy. The current evidence suggests that even at the outset of therapy, spouses are not typically suffering from generalized skill deficits but, rather, from a failure to implement commonly used interpersonal skills with their spouse (Birchler, Weiss, & Vincent, 1975; Noller, 1984). Thus, many of the problems addressed most commonly in the course of marital therapy relate to behavior that is voluntary in nature.

The model proposed by Ajzen (Ajzen, 1985; Ajzen & Madden, 1986) is designed to account for the occurrence of single, voluntary actions. Ajzen's model has been designed to highlight a small set of predictor variables and specify the way in which they are expected to influence behavior. It is proposed that voluntary behavior is determined primarily by the intention to perform the behavior in conjunction with any real constraints in the environment on performing the behavior. Three variables are hypothesized to influence intention to perform an act: (1) attitudes, (2) subjective norms, and (3) perceived behavioral control. The intention to perform the behavior is, in turn, hypothesized to be a powerful and immediate antecedent of actually attempting the behavior. Although other factors are presumed to influence the success of the attempt, the stronger the intent, the more successful the outcome is expected to be on average. Indeed, to the extent that the individual has the opportunity and the necessary resources to perform a behavior, the theory of planned behavior predicts that intent to perform the behavior is the primary variable determining extent of success.

The model also provides considerable guidance with regard to each of the antecedents of intent to perform the given behavior. Behavioral beliefs are hypothesized to influence attitudes toward the behavior. Behavioral beliefs are those beliefs that link the behavior to some positive or negative outcome. That is, it is assumed that individuals will see a variety of outcomes following from a given behavior. The strength of each belief, along with the value of the expected outcome, is summed across all beliefs to result in a general attitude toward the behavior. Subjective norms are hypothesized to reflect the perceived approval or disapproval of various important referent individuals or groups. Again, it is assumed that there may be a variety of normative beliefs, and the strength of each belief along with the motivation to comply with the referent group summed across all groups will result in the valence and strength of the subjective norm. Perceived behavioral control reflects the control beliefs relevant to the behavior. It is assumed that these beliefs may reflect past experience, second-hand information, or other factors that influence perceived resources, opportunities, obstacles, and impediments.

When no obvious constraints can be determined by the marital therapist (i.e., the individual appears able to comply, is not constrained by obvious negative consequences, and has had opportunity to comply) and some lack of intention to comply with the therapist's directives can be inferred or has been directly stated, the model directs the therapist to examine each of the three areas influencing intention in turn: (1) the attitude toward the behavior, including both the connotations for the individual of engaging in the behavior and any perceived consequences of engaging in the behavior; (2) the social pressure felt by the individual, including the likely evaluations of significant others and the degree of motivation to conform to the expectations of these significant others, and (3) the individual's perception that he or she can perform the behavior, including perceptions of having the requisite skills, having the necessary opportunities, and having the required resources to comply. As can be seen, the theory of planned behavior provides a road map for the idiographic assessment of compliance-relevant cognition. Attitudes, connotation, self-perceptions, perceptions of the spouse, and predicted consequences are all germane to the compliance decision-making process.

Ajzen's model thus provides a clear set of possible points of intervention in marital work with a noncompliant spouse. Although the model does not provide particular techniques relevant to each point of intervention, a number of options can be inferred from the literature on cognitive techniques already available (Baucom & Epstein, 1990). For example, if the spouse or couple perceive themselves as not having the requisite opportunities or resources to carry out the assignment, this could be addressed in a straightforward problem-solving manner with the couple. If this approach failed to alter the perception despite what appeared to the therapist to be a workable plan, cognitive rehearsal could be used to increase the couple's perception of their own capacity to carry out the assignment.

In the case of negative subjective norms for the prescribed behavior, the model suggests two alternative approaches. First, the therapist might help the spouse dispute the belief that important referent individuals or groups would in fact disapprove of the behavior assigned. Alternatively, the therapist could help the spouse decrease his or her motivation to comply with the disapproving individual or group. In either case, the influence of the disapproving individual or group should decrease, since the strength of the normative beliefs is hypothesized to be a product of the normative beliefs and the motivation to comply.

Finally, if lack of intention to perform a given behavior is the result of negative attitudinal factors, the model suggests that the therapist investigate the spouse's perception of the outcomes that would result from complying or that might result from complying. The model suggests that the value of each possible outcome in combination with its subjective probability of occurring should determine the resulting attitude. Thus, if the therapist can help the spouse examine expected negative consequences of complying and find ways to avoid these consequences or help the spouse decrease the subjective probability that they will come to pass, the attitude should be moved in the direction of being more positive. This type of work may be particularly important in marital therapy, which focuses on helping the husband be more emotionally expressive or accepting of intimacy (cf. Markman & Kraft, 1989). In particular, husbands are likely to have appraisals of sharing personal problems or saying they are sorry that involve strong images of personal powerlessness (Guthrie & Snyder, 1988). Thus, it should not be surprising if husbands' compliance with therapist directives for increased intimacy is less on average than their compliance with other aspects of marital therapy.

To the extent that intentional noncompliance is an important factor in lowering treatment effectiveness by decreasing attainment of the mediating goals of therapy, the theory of planned behavior suggests that the marital therapist should be ready to utilize cognitive techniques, not as a discrete module in therapy but rather on an as-needed basis throughout the course of therapy (cf. Baucom, 1989). Furthermore, to the extent that intentional noncompliance can be differentiated from other types of noncompliance during the course of marital therapy, the theory of planned behavior provides a framework for tailoring therapy to the individual couple.

Should the theory of planned behavior be validated in the context of noncompliance with therapist directives in marital therapy, it can be used immediately to provide guidance for effective therapeutic response. In addition, it provides a rich set of testable hypotheses about the role of not intending to comply on actual compliance in marital therapy and the many variables influencing the decision to not comply.

## The Attribution-Efficacy Model of Conflict

Couple members may be so focused on blaming the spouse and exacting retribution for his or her perceived wrongdoing that the discussion of constructive behavior seems irrelevant. Indeed, discordant couples are quite willing to attribute blame to each other (Fincham, Beach, & Baucom, 1987) and do so with high levels of certainty (Noller & Vernardos, 1986). To the extent that this focus on blame limits the ability of one or both members of the dyad to take part effectively in therapy, one must expect that this process would be associated with poorer overall compliance. Thus, a second type of commonly occurring noncompliance in marital therapy might be the type associated with the extreme attribution of blame to the partner for marital problems and the associated high level of desire for retribution. A framework that could guide research and intervention regarding this process is the attribution-efficacy model (Fincham & Bradbury, 1987b; Fincham, Bradbury, & Grych, 1990).

The attribution-efficacy model highlights three stages in the process of attributing blame to the partner. First, an attribution that locates the cause of an event in the partner must be made before any blame can be assigned. Further, it is proposed that judgments of causal stability and globality will also ultimately influence blame. Second, inferences relating to responsibility criteria are critical. That is, consideration of the perceived motivation of the act, the apparent voluntariness of the act, and the perceived intent of the act are hypothesized to influence blame profoundly. Third, judgments about the capacities of the partner (e.g., his or her skills) can mitigate blame. By highlighting these areas, the model draws our attention to them as potential points of intervention and as variables that may account for less than optimal response to marital therapy. A thorough review of the model and its implications for process research would require a review of the very extensive literatures on causal attribution and the work on cognitive marital therapy aimed at changing problematic causal attributions (e.g., Baucom & Epstein, 1990). Discussions of techniques for addressing causal attributions are widely available elsewhere, however, so we focus only on responsibility criteria.

The application of responsibility criteria after the cause has been located within the spouse requires judgments regarding (1) motivation, (2) voluntariness, and (3) intent before any blame can be assigned. Each judgment represents an opportunity for therapeutic intervention. Of particular importance in intervening on spouses' ascriptions of the partner's motivation are the processes of "discounting" and "augmentation" (Kelley, 1972). Discounting is the process that leads a person to consider an act less significant as evidence of underlying motivation because of the presence of other factors that could also account for that behavior. For example, a wife might not ascribe her husband's behavior of spending more time at home to his unselfish motivation to show caring for her if this behavior only began after his best friend and drinking buddy moved away. "Augmentation" is the mirror image of "discounting." This is the process that leads a person to infer a strong motivational state because the behavior under consideration occurs in the face of powerful constraints that would be expected to inhibit its display. For example, if a husband is spending less time at home despite considerable nagging from his wife, this would be likely to strengthen his wife's conviction that he was deeply motivated to stay away from home.

To begin to work therapeutically on the ascription of a particular negative, destructive motive to the spouse, the therapist would first examine the extent to which the perceived strength of the motive was a reflection of augmentation and discounting processes. In the above example, it might be possible to reinterpret what was previously seen as particularly strong evidence of a negative motive caused by the operation of augmentation processes. By exploring the possibility that "nagging" actually worked to keep the husband away from the house rather than as a powerful force to get him to come home, the therapist may reverse an augmented perception of motivation and allow it to be discounted entirely. Discordant spouses who are the most blaming of each other are also often those who have used the most coercive strategies to influence their partner's behavior. Since the coercive behaviors are meant to control the partner's responses but more commonly aggravate problem behaviors, one might expect the exploration of augmentation and discounting to be applicable in many cases.

A second responsibility criterion involves the ascription of voluntariness to the problem behavior. Indeed, a freely chosen action intended to bring about the outcome that then actually occurs is the quintessential act for which one can be held responsible (Hart, 1968). However, it is relatively easy for observers to see an actor's behavior as free and voluntary, even in the face of rather obvious constraints (cf. the "fundamental attribution error"; Ross, 1977). Thus, it should not be expected that this will represent a particularly easy point of therapeutic intervention.

Interestingly, two strategies that derive from different marital therapy traditions and may appear markedly different to the practitioners within each tradition seem remarkably similar when viewed from the framework of the attribution-efficacy model. On the one hand cognitive-behavioral marital therapists have often used a strategy of identifying skill deficits or poor models as the "true" cause of a problem behavior even though we often have reason to believe this is only partially the case. However, as Fincham et al. (1990) point out, identifying limited capacities in this way is clearly one way to reduce the perceived voluntariness of the behavior. Thus, if the spouse could not foresee that the behavior would result in conflict, did not know any alternative behaviors, or simply did not have the ability to behave differently, then it should be difficult to ascribe blame (Fincham, 1983). This approach reduces the perceived voluntariness of the problem behavior by pointing to a plausible constraint (i.e., limited capacity). The conceptually parallel approach put forward by systems therapists is to ascribe the problem behavior to a need of the larger family unit. For example, a recurrent problem behavior might be interpreted as protecting the couple from too rapid change. Again, the problem behavior is not the voluntary decision of the individual performing it. Rather, the problem behavior is produced by the powerful constraint of the family system. In both approaches the "naive" view that individuals freely choose their own behavior is challenged through the presentation of a compelling alternative construction of reality. When accepted by the couple, this account of the constraints operating on the previously "blameworthy" behavior should rapidly reduce perceived blame-worthiness.

The third and perhaps most central responsibility criterion is the ascription of intent. Considerable basic research has shown that observers are more likely to attribute intent to produce a particular outcome when the actor is seen as having selected from among many alternatives the one behavior that would have produced that particular outcome (Ajzen & Holmes, 1976). Thus, to the extent that therapists can identify unique positive consequences of problem behavior or reduce the perception of many unique negative effects of problem behavior, they may have a powerful impact on the ascription of intent. Consider, for example, the case of Melissa and Jim. After dinner Melissa tells her husband, Jim, that she has not been able to balance the family checking account for the past 6 months; consequently, the check she wrote to pay the monthly mortgage payment bounced. Jim, in a fit of anger, calls her a "worthless incompetent" and then storms out of the house and does not return until morning. Melissa cries all night and reports to her therapist that Jim is simply a mean person because he wanted to punish her for making a mistake. Melissa bases her assertion on the fact that she cannot imagine being hurt by other things that Jim could have done, such as offering to help her balance the account, taking responsibility for the account himself, or getting annoyed, but without calling her names and staying out all night. Thus, it seems to her that Jim chose the one option designed to produce the greatest upset possible to her. If the therapist is able to find other outcomes that are unique to the behavior Jim displayed, this should decrease the certainty with which Melissa holds her inference of negative intent. Thus, if Melissa had been abused physically by Jim in the past and she comes to view not being abused as a second unique outcome of Jim's leaving the house, she may well change the intent she ascribes to his behavior.

Since most problem behavior is at least ambiguous with regard to its unique effects, and since discordant couples are likely to find the negative effects of a problem behavior more salient than any positive effects, it is likely that in many cases unique positive effects of problem behaviors that have been overlooked by the members of the discordant dyad can be found. Indeed, systems approaches routinely ascribe unique positive effects to problem behaviors by "positive reframing" of the problem behavior. For example, recurrent severe arguments may be ascribed to the couple's passion for each other and unwillingness to accept a less intense relationship. These interventions can be seen as explicit attempts to reduce self- and/or partner blame by altering the perception of the extent to which the intent of the problem behavior was a positive outcome as opposed to a negative outcome.

The attribution-efficacy model appears to be promising as a source of additional cognitive techniques in behavioral marital therapy. If it is found that compliance is central to improvement on important mediating goals of marital therapy, and if extreme blame in the dyad is found to reduce compliance markedly, this model provides guidance for the development of clinically useful measurement and intervention strategies. Since both propositions seem quite plausible, this represents one avenue for future "process" research. In addition, if supported empirically through "process" research, the attribution-efficacy model is capable of providing a framework that allows for the systematic exploration and appropriate integration of "systems theory" techniques with established directive approaches to marital therapy. Again, the goal of this type of process research would not be to build a new system of marital therapy but rather to help existing directive interventions reach couples who would otherwise appear as noncompliant early in therapy and as treatment failures at the end of therapy. With effective techniques to reduce noncompliance, these couples should show enhanced gains on the mediating goals of therapy and, as a result, show enhanced outcome.

## CONCLUSION

Our review of the outcome literature shows that there already exist some basic technologies that can influence discordant couples and produce reliable changes in satisfaction. However, it also appears that about 30% of couples receiving standard marital therapies do not benefit at all, and a substantial number of others do not benefit to a degree with which we can be comfortable. As noted earlier, this evidence should not lead us to reject proven technologies and continue building "new" schools of marital therapy *de novo*. New schools of marital therapy tend to show broad areas of technical overlap with existing approaches and similar outcomes. Nor should we add new approaches as modules to marital therapy packages. Combinations of modules have not shown an ability to enhance outcome significantly. Rather, what is needed at present is research aimed at illuminating the process of change in therapy and lack of response to existing marital therapies. Work both at the level of better explicating mediating goals and at the level of better explicating obstacles to the attainment of mediating goals of therapy is necessary. Process research of this type offers the promise of systematic enhancement of the effectiveness of marital therapy.

# REFERENCES

Ajzen, I. (1985). From intentions to actions: A theory of planned behavior. In J. Kuhl & J. Beckmann (Eds.), *Action control: From cognition to behavior* (pp. 11-39). Heidelberg: Springer.

Ajzen, I., & Holmes, W. H. (1976). Uniqueness of behavioral effects in causal attribution. *Journal of Personality, 44,* 98-108.

Ajzen, I., & Madden, T. (1986). Prediction of goal directed behavior: Attitudes, intentions, and perceived behavioral control. *Journal of Experimental Social Psychology, 22,* 453-474.

Baucom, D. H. (1982). A comparison of behavioral contracting and problem solving/communications training in behavioral marital therapy. *Behavior Therapy, 13,* 162-174.

Baucom, D. H. (1989). The role of cognitions in behavioral marital therapy: Current status and future directions. *The Behavior Therapist, 12,* 3-6.

Baucom, D. H., & Epstein, N. (1990). *Cognitive-behavioral marital therapy.* New York: Brunner/Mazel.

Baucom, D. H., & Hoffman, J. A. (1986). The effectiveness of marital therapy: Current status and application to the clinical setting. In N. S. Jacobson & A. S. Gurman (Eds.), *Clinical handbook of marital therapy* (pp. 597-620). New York: Guilford Press.

Baucom, D. H., & Lester, G. W. (1986). The usefulness of cognitive restructuring as an adjunct to behavioral marital therapy. *Behavior Therapy, 17,* 385-403.

Baucom, D. H., & Sayers, S. L. (1988, November). *Expanding behavioral marital therapy.* Paper presented to the 22nd Annual convention of the Association for Advancement of Behavior Therapy, New York.

Beach, S. R. H., Arias, I., & O'Leary, K. D. (1987). The relationship of social support to depressive symptomatology. *Journal of Psychopathology and Behavioral Assessment, 8,* 305-316.

Beach, S. R. H., & Nelson, G. M. (1990). Pursuing research on major psychopathology from a contextual perspective: The example of depression and marital discord. In G. Brody & I. E. Siegel (Eds.), *Family research* (vol. II, pp. 227-259). Hillsdale, NJ: Erlbaum.

Beach, S. R. H., & O'Leary, K. D. (1985). Current status of outcome research in marital therapy. In L. L'Abate (Ed.), *The handbook of family psychology and therapy* (pp. 1035-1072). Homewood, IL: Dorsey Press.

Beach, S. R. H., Sandeen, E. E., & O'Leary, K. D. (1990). *Depression in marriage: A model for etiology and treatment.* New York: Guilford Press.

Birchler, G. R., Weiss, R. L., & Vincent, J. P. (1975). Multimethod analysis of social reinforcement exchange between maritally distressed and nondistressed spouse and stranger dyads. *Journal of Personality and Social Psychology, 31*, 349–360.

Boelens, W., Emmelkamp, P., MacGillavry, D., & Markvoort, M. (1980). A clinical evaluation of marital treatment: Reciprocity counseling versus system-theoretic counseling. *Behaviour Analysis and Modification, 4*, 85–96.

Crowe, M. J. (1978). Conjoint marital therapy: A controlled outcome study. *Psychological Medicine, 8*, 623–636.

Ely, A. L., Guerney, B. G., & Stover, L. (1973). Efficacy of the training phase of conjugal therapy. *Psychotherapy: Theory, Research and Practice, 10*, 201–207.

Emery, R. E. (1988). *Marriage, divorce, and children's adjustment*. Newbury Park, CA: Sage.

Epstein, N., & Jackson, E. (1978). An outcome study of short term communication training with married couples. *Journal of Consulting and Clinical Psychology, 46*, 207–212.

Fincham, F. D. (1983). Clinical applications of attribution theory: Problems and prospects. In M. Hewstone (Ed.), *Attribution theory: Social and functional extensions* (pp. 187–203). Oxford: Basil Blackwell.

Fincham, F. D., Beach, S. R. H., & Baucom, D. H. (1987). Attribution processes in distressed and nondistressed couples: 4. Self–partner attribution differences. *Journal of Personality and Social Psychology, 52*, 739–748.

Fincham, F. D., & Bradbury, T. N. (1987a). The assessment of marital quality: A reevaluation. *Journal of Marriage and the Family, 49*, 797–809.

Fincham, F. D., & Bradbury, T. N. (1987b). Cognitive processes and conflict in close relationships: An attribution-efficacy model. *Journal of Personality and Social Psychology, 53*, 1106–1118.

Fincham, F. D., Bradbury, T. N., & Grych, J. H. (1990). Conflict in close relationships: The role of intrapersonal phenomena. In S. Graham & V. Folkes (Eds.), *Attribution theory: Applications to achievement, mental health, and interpersonal conflict* (pp. 161–184). Hillsdale, NJ: Erlbaum.

Glick, P. C. (1984). How American families are changing. *American Demographics, 6*, 20–27.

Goldman, A. (1987). *Systematically and emotionally focused marital therapies: A comparative outcome*. Unpublished doctoral dissertation, University of British Columbia, Vancouver.

Gottman, J. M. (1979). *Marital interaction: Experimental investigations*. New York: Academic Press.

Greenberg, L. S., & Johnson, S. M. (1988). *Emotionally focused therapy for couples*. New York: Guilford Press.

Guthrie, D. M., & Snyder, C. W. (1988). Spouses' self-evaluation for situations involving emotional communication. In P. Noller & M. A. Fitzpatrick (Eds.), *Perspectives on marital interaction* (pp. 153–181). Philadelphia: Multilingual Matters.

Hahlweg, K., Baucom, D. H., & Markman, H. (1988). Recent advances in therapy and prevention. In I. R. H. Falloon (Ed.), *Handbook of behavioral family therapy* (pp. 413–448). New York: Guilford Press.

Hahlweg, K., & Markman, H. J. (1988). The effectiveness of behavioral marital therapy: Empirical status of behavioral techniques in preventing and alleviating marital distress. *Journal of Consulting and Clinical Psychology, 56*, 440–447.

Hahlweg, K., Revenstorf, D., & Schindler, L. (1982). Treatment of marital distress: Comparing formats and modalities. *Advances in Behavior Research and Therapy, 4*, 57–74.

Hart, H. L. A. (1968). *Punishment and responsibility*. New York: Oxford University Press.

Hickman, M. E., & Baldwin, B. A. (1971). Use of programmed instruction to improve communication in marriage. *Family Coordinator, 20*, 121-125.

Jacobson, N. S. (1977). Problem solving and contingency contracting in the treatment of marital discord. *Journal of Consulting and Clinical Psychology, 45*, 92-100.

Jacobson, N. S. (1978). Specific and non-specific factors in the effectiveness of a behavioral approach to the treatment of marital discord. *Journal of Consulting and Clinical Psychology, 46*, 442-452.

Jacobson, N. S. (1984). A component analysis of behavioral marital therapy: The relative effectiveness of behavior exchange and communication/problem-solving training. *Journal of Consulting and Clinical Psychology, 52*, 295-305.

Jacobson, N. S., Follette, V. M., Follette, W. C., Holtzworth-Munroe, A., Katt, J. L., & Schmaling, K. B. (1985). A component analysis of behavioral marital therapy: 1-year follow-up. *Behaviour Research and Therapy, 23*, 549-555.

Jacobson, N. S., Follette, W. C., Revenstorf, D., Baucom, D. H., Hahlweg, K., & Margolin, G. (1984). Variability in outcome and clinical significance of behavioral marital therapy: A reanalysis of outcome data. *Journal of Consulting and Clinical Psychology, 52*, 497-504.

Jacobson, N. S., Schmaling, K. B., & Holtzworth-Munroe, A. (1987). Component analysis of behavioral marital therapy: 2-year follow-up and prediction of relapse. *Journal of Marital and Family Therapy, 13*, 187-195.

Johnson, S. M., & Greenberg, L. S. (1985a). The differential effects of experiential and problem-solving interventions in resolving marital conflict. *Journal of Consulting and Clinical Psychology, 53*, 175-184.

Johnson, S. M., & Greenberg, L. S. (1985b). Emotionally focused marital therapy: An outcome study. *Journal of Marital and Family Therapy, 11*, 313-317.

Kelley, H. H. (1972). Attribution in social interaction. In E. E. Jones, D. E. Kanouse, H. H. Kelley, R. E. Nisbett, S. Valins, & B. Weiner (Eds.), *Attribution: Perceiving the causes of behavior* (pp. 151-174). Morristown, NJ: General Learning Press.

Margolin, G. (1987). Marital therapy: A cognitive-behavioral-affective approach. In N. S. Jacobson (Eds.), *Psychotherapists in clinical practice* (pp. 232-285). New York: Guilford Press.

Markman, H. J., & Kraft, S. A. (1989). Men and women in marriage: Dealing with gender differences in marital therapy. *The Behavior Therapist, 12*, 51-56.

Noller, P. (1984). *Nonverbal communication and marital interaction*. Oxford: Pergamon.

Noller, P., & Venardos, C. (1986). Communication awareness in married couples. *Journal of Social and Personal Relationships, 3*, 31-42.

O'Leary, K. D., & Arias, I. (1983). The influence of marital therapy on sexual satisfaction. *Journal of Sex and Marital Therapy, 9*, 171-181.

Ross, L. (1977). The intuitive psychologist and his shortcomings: Distortions in the attribution process. In L. Berkowitz (Ed.), *Advances in experimental social psychology* (vol. 10, pp. 173-220). New York: Academic Press.

Snyder, D. K., & Wills, R. M. (1989). Behavioral versus insight oriented marital therapy: Effects on individual and interspousal functioning. *Journal of Consulting and Clinical Psychology, 57*, 39-46.

Somers, A. R. (1979). Marital status, health, and the use of health services. *Journal of Marriage and the Family, 41*, 267-285.

Turkewitz, H., & O'Leary, K. D. (1981). A comparative outcome study of behavioral marital therapy and communication therapy. *Journal of Marital and Family Therapy, 7,* 159-169.

Weiss, R. L., & Heyman, R. E. (1990). Marital distress and therapy. In A. S. Bellack, M. Hersen, & A. Kazdin (Eds.), *International handbook of behavior modification* (2nd ed.; pp. 475-501). New York: Plenum.

# CHAPTER 13

# Preventing Marital Dysfunction: Review and Analysis

**Thomas N. Bradbury**
**Frank D. Fincham**

Marital discord and divorce are associated with a variety of psychological and physical disorders among adults (Segraves, 1982) and are known to have deleterious effects on children (Grych & Fincham, in press). The alleviation of marital problems therefore could have far-reaching consequences for the well-being of spouses, their families, and society at large. Since the 1930s, the standard strategy adopted by mental health professionals to contend with marital dysfunction has been to treat couples who come to clinical settings complaining of problems in their marriage. Although some of the interventions developed for this purpose benefit distressed couples (see Beach & Bauserman, Chapter 12, this volume), there is growing realization that this strategy is inadequate to stem the rising incidence of marital dysfunction (e.g., Markman & Floyd, 1980). As a consequence, considerable energy has also been devoted to the design and implementation of programs intended to prevent marital dysfunction before it occurs. Attempting to prevent marital problems represents a radical departure from traditional clinical intervention and if successful could serve as a valuable complement to such intervention.

The purpose of this chapter is to review and evaluate the large literature on the prevention of marital dysfunction. The first section introduces the arguments in favor of prevention programs for marital dysfunction as well as some of the barriers to prevention. The second section reviews and evaluates research addressing the efficacy of prevention programs. This leads to a discussion in the third section of several issues that we believe are necessary to address if prevention is to become a viable complement to clinical intervention. In the final section we offer an overview of the chapter and draw conclusions about preventing marital dysfunction.

Before undertaking these tasks it is necessary to comment on the scope and terminology of the chapter. The chapter focuses on the marital dyad, and little attention is devoted to prevention that involves programs designed for parent–child, sibling, step-family, and intergenerational family relationships (for a review see L'Abate & Weinstein, 1987), transition to parenthood (for reviews see Belsky, Chapter 6, this volume; Duncan & Markman, in press), and postdivorce adaptation (for a review see Bloom, Hodges, Kern, & McFaddin, 1985). Exclusion of this material reflects the view that a single chapter cannot do justice to all pertinent aspects of prevention in marriages and families; however, it is probably reasonable to assume that the integrity of the marital dyad is central to the strength of the family and hence deserves particular attention. Although valuable for a thorough appreciation of work on preventing marital dysfunction, space limitations also preclude a historical analysis of work on this topic (for a review see Mace & Mace, 1976).

In regard to terminology, it is important to distinguish among various types of prevention. *Primary prevention* attempts to reduce new cases of marital dysfunction in the population at large, and it is this level of prevention to which we refer when we use the term *prevention* without qualification. This contrasts with *secondary prevention*, which is undertaken to assist marriages that are identified as vulnerable in some way to subsequent difficulties, and with *tertiary prevention*, which is undertaken in order to treat and rehabilitate marriages that have already become dysfunctional. To paraphrase L'Abate (1983), these three levels of prevention are distinguished by the point in the temporal course of dysfunction at which they are instituted: "before it happens, before it gets worse, and before it is too late." Within this framework, marital therapy is an example of tertiary prevention.

## PREVENTING MARITAL DYSFUNCTION: RATIONALE AND RESISTANCE

The concept of prevention, particularly primary prevention, enjoys widespread and often uncritical appeal. It is "a glittering, diffuse, thoroughly abstract term. Its aura is so exalted that some put it on the same plane as the Nobel prize. It holds the mysterious, exciting promise of 'breakthrough.' It offers a sharp contrast to all that mental health has done, a shadowy, but nevertheless grand, alternative" (Cowen, 1977, p. 1). One goal of this section is to articulate the major reasons why prevention is held in such high esteem and why it deserves attention as an approach to minimizing marital dysfunction. Although few disagree with it in principle, prevention is not yet a common strategy in mental health settings. This paradox, between the considerable appeal of prevention and its circumscribed application, is the focus of the second part of this section, where we outline several factors that appear to limit the expansion of prevention programs.

## Rationale for Prevention

Relationship problems are a common source of psychological distress, yet most couples experiencing marital difficulties do not seek formal assistance in dealing with them. Of those who do seek help, relatively few bring their problems to mental health professionals, preferring instead to consult the clergy and family physicians (cf. Doherty, 1986; Veroff, Kulka, & Douvan, 1981). Although a greater number of couples could be encouraged to seek treatment if more were known about the factors that account for variability in help-seeking (e.g., who seeks help, when, where, and with what expectations), such knowledge is unlikely to reduce significantly the number of distressed couples in our communities. In short, one argument in favor of prevention is that it could alleviate marital distress that would otherwise remain untreated as a consequence of the divergence between available therapeutic resources and couples' inclinations toward using them.

One response to the above argument is to ensure that available services match the demand for such services, thereby reducing prevention to a reasonable but nonessential undertaking. This probably would prove beneficial to many couples, yet such a response rests on the assumption that the services delivered would be effective in resolving marital problems. For nearly all forms of marital therapy this assumption remains untested. A notable exception is behavioral marital therapy (BMT), a treatment modality that in its present form typically emphasizes modification of communication skills, problem-solving abilities, and maladaptive expectations and attributions (see Jacobson & Holtzworth-Munroe, 1986). The efficacy of BMT has now been examined in 17 outcome studies involving over 600 couples in Europe and North America, and a recent meta-analysis of these studies by Hahlweg and Markman (1988) revealed improvement in 72% of the couples receiving BMT compared with an improvement rate of 28% among couples receiving another form of therapy or serving in waiting-list control groups. Based on the five studies reporting follow-up data, some support was also found for the maintenance of treatment gains 9 to 12 months after treatment.

Although the statistical significance of BMT relative to control conditions is now beyond doubt, the clinical significance of BMT remains a major concern. As Hahlweg and Markman (1988, p. 445) conclude, a substantial proportion of couples receiving BMT are "still describing their relationships as unsatisfying and distressful after therapy." The finding that BMT does not yet enable couples to attain reliably a nondistressed level of marital functioning suggests not only the need to refine this form of therapy and to examine forms of therapy deriving from other theoretical perspectives but also the need to develop and implement altogether different approaches to marital dysfunction, such as that afforded by prevention. Thus, a second argument in favor of prevention is that marital therapies have not been shown to produce clinically significant change in a reliable fashion.[1]

The rationale for prevention discussed thus far derives largely from the limitations of existing approaches to minimizing marital dysfunction, yet other factors suggest that prevention is a valuable undertaking in its own right. Thus, even if we could be certain that most people needing marital therapy actually sought it and were helped by it, prevention programs would be useful nevertheless because intervening early could (1) alleviate the tension and suffering that spouses and their families might experience between the onset of their relationship problems and the point at which they begin therapy; (2) enable spouses to gain mastery over any difficulties while they were relatively minor and not yet established as major problems in the relationship; (3) reach large numbers of couples, particularly if programs are targeted at groups and communities and if paraprofessionals deliver services; and (4) lead to economic gains insofar as preventing marital dys-

---

[1]This raises the issue of the ultimate efficacy of marital therapies. The prevailing assumption is that treatment of most forms of marital dysfunction can yield clinically significant change (cf. Jacobson, 1989), yet the BMT outcome data appear inconsistent with this assumption. To the extent that further improvement in BMT outcome is not found, the possibility increases that relatively immutable factors (e.g., memories of violence and abuse in the relationship, mismatch of spouses' personalities) play an important role in marital quality. Although difficult to change retroactively, some of these factors may be preventable.

function would lead to a diminished need for a variety of services (e.g., medical, psychological, legal).

## Resistance to Prevention

The above arguments provide a strong justification for preventing marital distress and its sequelae. However, the fact that remedial efforts far outweigh preventive efforts in this domain indicates that strong forces operate to counter or inhibit the development and implementation of prevention programs. Several such forces, ranging from intrapersonal to societal factors, are described below.

Whitfield (1985, p. 137), noting a decline in teaching about marriage in secondary schools, asked, "Is this at least in part the result of adults' guilt, uncertainty or acknowledgment of the fundamental instability of marriage among our social relationships? Is there a basic loss of hope about marriage for fear of the likelihood of its painful death in divorce?" We believe that this pessimism may extend well beyond school settings and result in people being less likely to request and take part in prevention services.

Any such pessimism about the institution of marriage is worsened by difficulties encountered in attempts to alleviate marital problems. These difficulties can, in turn, be ascribed to the complexity of the system that gives rise to marital dysfunction. That is, the forces that initiate and maintain marital distress in our culture are likely to be complicated, involving a combination of societal, psychological, religious, economic, and governmental factors. The multidimensional nature of this complexity is thus likely to serve as a barrier to developing effective preventive interventions and to keeping them in place (see Broskowski & Baker, 1974). A related consideration, and a further barrier to prevention, is the problem of demonstrating that an intervention is having the desired effect. Although efficacy often can be demonstrated when a prevention program takes the form of a highly controlled outcome study (e.g., when the preventive intervention is essentially a clinical treatment package administered to small groups of couples who have not yet experienced major problems), it is less readily established in situations where individuals or couples are not contacted directly and when more variables are left uncontrolled.

Regardless of whether a given program is administered directly or indirectly, couples' involvement and motivation form an important aspect of successful prevention efforts. Unfortunately, however, couples typically do not behave to decrease the likelihood of future problems, tending instead to take action only after significant difficulties occur. Though most couples would probably acknowledge that "an ounce of prevention is worth a pound of cure," the adage that "if it's not broken don't fix it" characterizes their behavior more accurately, and this tendency places limits on the potential impact of marital prevention efforts (see Olson, 1983). Moreover, a lack of motivation (or absence of problems) not only restricts what can be achieved when couples are actually participating in prevention programs, but it is also likely to suppress requests for the development and offering of such programs.

The reluctance among couples to take steps to prevent future problems is also fostered by cultural myths. Mace (1987) argues that a "myth of privatism" or an "intermarital taboo" leads most people to view marriage as a highly private matter and makes them hesitant or unwilling to admit their problems to others. This taboo not only discourages people from participating in prevention programs but can also limit the value of prevention programs insofar as it makes professionals reluctant to probe the relationship between ostensibly happy spouses, especially without their explicit permission. This issue is compounded by the "myth of naturalism" (Vincent, 1973), which asserts that a satisfying marriage should come naturally and effortlessly. To seek assistance for one's marriage, either before or after significant problems have arisen, is to admit that one is inadequate and unsuccessful and that one has failed at what is believed to be a simple task; seeking help is therefore discouraged, and steps to prevent marital dysfunction are compromised.

Values among mental health professionals also impede prevention efforts. Many professionals endorse the notion of prevention in theory but do not value it in practice. As Goldston (1977, p. 35) states, "the barrier of professional values is in my view the most important of all. So long as public health values are regarded by mental health workers as inferior to clinical values, primary prevention efforts will lag." L'Abate (1983) concluded that people in established mental health professions generally are not interested in prevention because the field does not provide clear and lucrative career options, is not glamorous enough, stifles creativity, and is too limited and structured, especially when compared to psychotherapy. Similarly, Glidewell (1983, p. 310) has commented that the nemesis of prevention is "the great power of the healer," which our society assigns to those who work in clinical capacities. Although some see the resistance of the mental health establishment as an asset because it leaves the field open to those new professionals who can import ideas from other disciplines (e.g., L'Abate, 1983), the incomplete acceptance of the ideology of prevention hinders its impact on marital dysfunction.

One specific consequence of this lack of acceptance is the relative dearth of funds that are allocated to prevention programs. Historically, far greater financial resources have been available for treating and rehabilitating people already experiencing disorder (tertiary prevention) than for preventing those disorders from occurring (primary prevention). When the pool of resources is finite, the reactive (rather than proactive) stance of many funding agencies dictates that most funds will go to treating those individuals with more pressing and immediate problems. This viewpoint is summarized by Lamb and Zusman's (1979, p. 16) statement that "there is not enough money to go around, not even to support the basic mental health direct service programs that all recognize as fundamental and essential. . . . To undertake programs that are expensive and quite likely not even preventive of mental illness out of funds allocated to mental health services seems to be a dangerously foolish gamble." Although most would acknowledge the importance of providing care for those experiencing psychological problems, a problem with this view is that it is self-perpetuating: demonstrating the efficacy of programs that prevent marital dysfunction will require money, but that money will not be forthcoming unless the programs are known to be effective. There are signs that funding priorities are beginning to change (see Price, Cowen, Lorion, & Ramos-McKay, 1988), but it seems clear that a relative lack of financial support continues to limit the development and evaluation of prevention programs.

## Summary

In this section, we hope to have shown that prevention can be viewed from many perspectives, including that of the individual, the couple, the couples' interactions, the mental health professional, and the government; this prepares us to address in a later section the question of whether these perspectives are being adequately considered in existing attempts to prevent marital dysfunction. Although the barriers identified above are formidable, even in their absence the case for prevention can be realized only if effective prevention programs are available. We turn therefore to a review of research that evaluates the efficacy of available prevention programs.

## CAN WE PREVENT MARITAL DYSFUNCTION?
## A REVIEW OF RESEARCH

A number of programs have been designed to prevent marital dysfunction. They vary widely along several dimensions, including the
phase of marriage to which they are targeted, the settings in which
they are offered, the number and duration of sessions, the level of
training of the service providers, the extent to which didactic versus
experiential forms of learning are emphasized, and the amount of
group versus dyadic interaction that occurs (for representative
overviews see Guerney, Guerney, & Cooney, 1985; Levant, 1986).

It is important to examine closely two additional dimensions
that underlie marital prevention programs because they help to
convey a sense of what these programs seek to modify in order to
prevent marital problems. The first dimension concerns the conceptual underpinnings of the programs, which appear to involve
various combinations of four perspectives (cf. Garland, 1983; Hof
& Miller, 1980): (1) behavior theory, with an emphasis on how
interaction behaviors are exchanged and reinforced by spouses;
(2) Rogerian theory, with an emphasis on empathy between
spouses, the open expression of feelings, and knowledge and acceptance of oneself; (3) general systems theory, with an emphasis on
the couple or family as a system and the responses of that system
to changes from within and without; and (4) theories of group
process, with an emphasis on how a group context can facilitate
growth and change. The second dimension, concerning the actual
content of the programs, derives in part from these conceptual
reference points and typically includes communication and problem solving, clarification of values and expectations, sexuality and
intimacy, negotiation of roles and responsibilities, developmental
changes, and awareness of relationship dynamics.

The task of reviewing research that has been conducted to
assess the effectiveness of marital prevention programs is complicated by the tremendous variety in theory and content that is
evident among these programs. This complexity, together with
the large number of outcome studies that have been conducted,
renders infeasible the usual study-by-study review that was once
possible (see reviews by Bagarozzi & Rauen, 1981; Beck, 1976;
Cooper, 1985; Gurman & Kniskern, 1977; Hof & Miller, 1980;
Wampler, 1982). We turn our attention instead to a meta-analysis
of 85 outcome studies of prevention and enrichment programs
reported between 1971 and 1982, representing data from nearly
4,000 couples and families (Giblin, 1986; Giblin, Sprenkle, & Shee-

han, 1985). Meta-analysis is a quantitative approach to reviewing research in which the results of studies are combined using a common metric. One such metric is the "effect size," which in this case is defined as the difference obtained by subtracting, for a given dependent variable, the mean score for the control group from that of the treatment group and dividing this difference by the standard deviation of the control group (for discussion of this technique see *Journal of Consulting and Clinical Psychology*, 1983, *51*[1]).[2] Although there are limitations to both this strategy (e.g., it is *post hoc* and in most applications does not permit examination of statistical interactions) and this particular data set (e.g., studies of families were included; 75% of the studies have not undergone peer review for publication; distressed couples were included in some studies that are therefore less relevant to primary prevention), Giblin's analysis does provide a panoramic view of the prevention literature and the opportunity to compare studies that use different measures.

## Review and Commentary

The 85 studies in Giblin's analysis yielded 1,691 effect sizes with an average size of 0.44. Effect sizes are $z$-scores and therefore can be understood in reference to the distribution of $z$-scores. Thus, a $z$-score of 0.44 indicates that, from pretest to posttest, the average person in a prevention program improved more than did 67% of those in the control group. This figure reflects a somewhat smaller effect for prevention programs than for individual psychotherapy (effect size = 0.85; the average treated person is better than 80% of the controls; see Smith, Glass, & Miller, 1980) and, more germane to the present topic, for behavioral marital therapy (effect size = 0.95; the average treated person is better than 83% of the controls; see Hahlweg & Markman, 1988). The positive effect size for prevention programs can be viewed as cause for some optimism and, indeed, nearly all qualitative reviews of this literature conclude with a favorable evaluation of the outcome data. A more thorough understanding of the impact of these programs, however, requires consideration of at least five additional issues.

[2]The procedure followed by Giblin et al. (1985) differed from this procedure in that (1) the numerator of effect sizes involved a difference of gain scores (i.e., pretest scores were taken into account by subtracting them from posttest scores, and the difference score for the control group was then subtracted from that of the treatment group) and that (2) the denominator of effect sizes was a pooled error term computed from the posttest standard deviations of both groups.

First, in evaluating effect sizes, it is important to recognize that an ineffective treatment has an effect size of 0.00, in which case the average treated person is better off than 50% of the controls and the average control person is better off than 50% of the treated subjects. The effect of prevention programs relative to no-treatment control groups therefore must be judged with respect to the figure of 50%. Moreover, Giblin et al. found that control conditions involving discussions only (i.e., groups controlling for placebo effects resulting from attention only) showed that the average person in this condition is better than 59% of the no-treatment controls (average effect size = 0.22). Thus, prevention programs have modest incremental effects of 17% relative to all controls (67% versus 50%) and of 8% relative to attention-placebo controls (67% versus 59%).

Second, the overall finding reported by Giblin (average effect size = 0.44) can be decomposed into that pertaining to premarital and marital programs. Twelve studies were conducted on premarital programs and showed that the average treated person is better than 70% of the controls (average effect size = 0.53). In contrast, Hahlweg and Markman's (1988) review of seven premarital prevention programs indicates that the average person is better than 79% of the controls (average effect size = 0.79); the discrepancy between analyses is probably accounted for by Hahlweg and Markman's exclusion of most dissertations and their inclusion of an unpublished manuscript. In Giblin's study, the 60 marital programs that were evaluated indicated that the average treated person is better than 66% of the untreated controls (average effect size = 0.42).[3] Thus, even though effects for premarital and marital programs are similar, there is some evidence that the outcome of prevention programs is more favorable when provided before rather than after marriage. The lack of association between age and effect size helps rule out the potentially confounding effect of age and thus lends further support to the slightly stronger premarital effects (Giblin, 1986).

Third, average effect sizes varied widely across programs. Because of the small number of studies, these figures were not available for premarital programs, but in programs for married couples average effect sizes ranged from 0.04 for a rational-

---

[3]The remaining 13 studies involved prevention programs for families and had an average effect size of 0.55; this indicates that the average person receiving treatment was better than 71% of those that did not.

emotive program to 0.96 for a Relationship Enhancement program (the latter figure indicating that the average treated person is better than 83% of the controls); the next highest effect size for a specific marital program was 0.45.[4] Further analysis is needed to determine the factors responsible for the divergent effects of the different programs.

Fourth, greater confidence can be placed in the impact of prevention programs when outcome is favorable across different classes of measurement and for measures that are less susceptible to socially desirable response sets. Seventy-six percent of the effects sizes studied by Giblin were derived from self-report measures, and the remainder were obtained via behavioral observation. Although this distribution is not unexpected in view of the difficulties involved in collecting observational data, it was surprising that prevention programs were found to have a significantly greater impact when evaluated with behavioral measures (average effect size = 0.76) than with self-report measures (average effect size = 0.35). Similar results were reported in the review of premarital programs by Hahlweg and Markman (1988), with behavioral measures (average effect size = 1.51) again being more sensitive than self-report indices (average effect size = 0.52). This difference suggests that there may be a limit to how much change occurs on self-report measures, perhaps because subjects are already functioning very well at pretest (i.e., there is a ceiling effect) or because prevention programs genuinely have a greater or more immediate effect on observable behavior than on perceptions and beliefs; perceptions and beliefs may then change as a consequence of changes in behavior.

A fifth issue, and by far the most important, is whether the programs actually *prevent* marital dysfunction. This question necessarily requires data collected over relatively long periods of time. Unfortunately, this requirement was not met in any of the

---

[4]In view of these striking results, the Relationship Enhancement (RE) program is described briefly. Developed by Guerney and his colleagues over the past 15 years (see Guerney, 1977; Guerney et al., 1985), RE is a 16- to 20-hour program in group format that involves training and practice in nine specific skills, including awareness and expression of one's own feelings, empathy, discussion and negotiation, facilitating growth in others, conflict resolution, changing one's habits, helping the partner to change his or her habits, generalization of skills to daily interactions, and maintenance of skills over time. The impressive effects obtained with RE no doubt owe to the nature of this training, yet because many other approaches to prevention share some similar content, it may be that the impact of RE is also attributable to an ongoing program of research and development.

studies reviewed by Giblin et al. (1985) Specifically, of the 85
studies reviewed, only 40% included follow-up measures at some
point after posttest (mean interval between posttest and follow-up
= 12 weeks), and the longest follow-up assessment occurred at 12
months. For those studies reporting follow-up data, the average
subject receiving treatment was better at follow-up than 63% of
the control subjects (average effect size = 0.34); comparable figures for attention-only control groups were not reported. This is a
significant drop from posttest (where the average effect size was
0.44) but remains above pretest levels. According to Hahlweg and
Markman's (1988) analysis of premarital prevention programs,
three studies reported follow-up assessments between 6 and 18
months and showed that the average subject receiving treatment
is better than 84% of the controls (average effect size = 1.01), and
one study reported a follow-up assessment at 3 years and found
that the average subject receiving treatment is better than 74% of
the controls (effect size = 0.65). Thus, even though very few studies
address the question of whether the program under consideration
actually prevents marital dysfunction, those that do suggest that
there may be long-term benefits to prevention programs and that
these benefits decline over time (cf. Markman, Floyd, Stanley, &
Storaasli, 1988).

## Conclusion

There appears to be a slight tendency for prevention programs to
improve premarital and marital relationships from immediately
before to immediately after the intervention, relative to no-treatment controls and, to a lesser degree, relative to attention-only
controls. This conclusion must be tempered, however, by the quality of the research on which it is based, and we join with several
previous reviewers in calling for research of a higher caliber that
attends to essential aspects of research design and analysis (e.g.,
appropriate control groups, random assignment of subjects to
groups, use of reliable and valid measures).

    Although it is valuable to know that programs can be devised
to aid relationships over brief intervals, the goal of prevention
programs is to produce lasting change in relationships. As we
have seen, little research is available on long-term changes; hence,
the question posed in the title of this section must be left without a
conclusive answer. We argue therefore that evaluation of prevention programs that involves only pre- and postintervention assess-

ments over short time intervals is no longer a priority and that attention must shift to a new phase of examining whether these programs are capable of producing a durable and beneficial impact on marriages.

Although the large body of existing research could be viewed as a necessary step toward addressing the issue of producing lasting change in relationships, a recent study by Markman et al. (1988) suggests that this view may not be entirely accurate. Specifically, they found that their 15-hour Premarital Relationship Enrichment Program (PREP) taught subjects how to communicate more effectively than controls immediately after training, but it did not influence relationship satisfaction, sexual satisfaction, perception of partner behavior, or ratings of problem intensity from pretest to posttest. It was only 18 and 36 months after posttest that differences between the groups became apparent, as the treated subjects maintained their level of marital quality, whereas those in the control group declined in marital quality over time. Thus, this study shows that short-term and long-term effects can differ dramatically and that long-term, preventive effects can emerge even when short-term results reveal few effects. A consequence of overlooking this possibility is that if the content and structure of programs is revised on the basis of short-term effects, then program components that might become effective with time would be excluded. Alternatively, components yielding little in the way of durable change in marriages would be included. In sum, a lack of long-term longitudinal data is incongruent with the purpose of prevention programs and is likely to impede further progress in this domain.

## FUTURE DIRECTIONS IN THE PREVENTION OF MARITAL DYSFUNCTION

The gap that is evident between the great potential of preventive efforts and the lack of data demonstrating their capacity to alleviate marital dysfunction underscores the need to outline directions for future progress in this domain. A distinction drawn by Watzlawick, Weakland, and Fisch (1974) between *first-order* and *second-order* change aids in identifying the sorts of directions that can be taken. According to Watzlawick et al. (pp. 10–11), "there are two different types of change: one that occurs within a given system which itself remains unchanged [i.e., first-order change], and one whose occurrence changes the system itself [i.e., second-order change]."[5]

*First-order change* would involve working within the domain of marital prevention as it is presently defined and conceptualized. Nearly all of the recommendations from the foregoing review and from prior analyses of the marital prevention literature can be understood in this light, and they include such changes as improving programs that already show some promise (most notably RE and PREP), making structural modifications in programs (e.g., including occasional follow-up sessions after the main program is complete), tailoring programs to the particular needs of participants, collecting long-term follow-up data, and improving the quality of measurement. Although the programmatic thrust of first-order change could pay handsome dividends, the history of the field suggests that it may be unrealistic to expect this sort of change to occur. For instance, many of the recommendations made over a decade ago by Gurman and Kniskern (1977) for enhancing research on marital prevention remain largely unaddressed (e.g., demonstration of durability of change in marriage and the generalization of change to other family relationships; elucidation of the factors that are responsible for change). In addition, Giblin (1986) reports no significant association between the magnitude of effect sizes and the dates they were reported, suggesting that later investigations have not benefited from shortcomings of earlier studies. Though the next decade of work on preventing marital dysfunction need not resemble the last, this lack of programmatic development is troublesome and highlights the need to pursue more than first-order change.

*Second-order change*, in contrast, involves a more fundamental alteration in the way that one seeks to bring about change—where first-order change can be thought of as quantitative in form (i.e., emphasizing or deemphasizing features within a defined system), second-order change is qualitative in nature and entails

[5]Watzlawick et al. (1974, p. 10–11) continue: "To exemplify this distinction in more behavioral terms: a person having a nightmare can do many things *in* his dream ... but no change from any one of these behaviors to another would ever terminate the nightmare. *We shall henceforth refer to this kind of change as first-order change.* The one way *out* of a dream involves a change from dreaming to waking. Waking, obviously, is no longer a part of the dream, but a change to an altogether different state. *This kind of change will from now on be referred to as second-order change.*"

modifying the system itself.[6] In the domain of preventing marital dysfunction, this could imply many possibilities. Two issues that seem most promising are emphasized in the remainder of this section, namely, *clarifying the causes* of marital dysfunction and *working indirectly* with couples to bring about change in their marriages.

## Clarifying the Causes of Marital Dysfunction

Efforts to treat and prevent problems in marriage have a long history in the social sciences, yet the causes of marital dysfunction are not well understood. This anomaly of trying to treat or prevent a problem without knowing its cause is understandable when it is realized that marital dysfunction often demands immediate attention and must be treated in the absence of clear causal data and that the causes of marital dysfunction are likely to be complex. Moreover, in many cases reasonably effective interventions can be undertaken without knowing the factors that give rise to marital problems, and even knowing such factors does not guarantee that application of causal data will be straightforward or that alleviation of marital dysfunction will be automatic. The loose relationship between the cause of marital dysfunction and its resolution therefore leads us to reject as too strong the view that "without knowledge of cause, primary prevention programs can only be shots in the dark" (Lamb & Zusman, 1979, p. 13), but we do maintain that establishing a solid understanding of the causes of marital dysfunction would be a valuable step toward preventing it reliably.

An important exception to the general rule that "most prevention programs for couples have been based on clinical intuition and common sense" (Hahlweg, Baucom, & Markman, 1988, p. 422) is an ongoing project by Markman and his colleagues designed to use data about the causes of marital distress to inform the development and implementation of marital prevention programs (e.g., Markman, 1984; Markman, Duncan, Storaasli, & Howes, 1987; Markman, Floyd, Stanley, & Jamieson, 1984; related approaches

---

[6]In fact, the notion of preventing marital dysfunction can itself be thought of as an instance of second-order change. Thus, whereas a first-order change in this regard would involve proposing an alternate theoretical perspective for treating couples in clinical settings (e.g., such as the behavioral perspective that gained prominence in the 1970s), a second-order change would involve seeking to help couples in a fundamentally different way (e.g., by working with them before their problems occurred).

can be found in Guerney, 1977, and in Miller, Nunally, & Wackman, 1975). The conceptual framework that guides this work is largely behavioral in orientation and derives from social exchange principles and social learning theory. Extrapolated to the context of close relationships, the model emphasizes the role of interpersonal behavior and communication as determinants of marital quality, such that later marital distress is expected to be a function of (1) lower rates of positive behaviors and reciprocation of positive behaviors and of (2) higher rates of negative behaviors and reciprocation of negative behaviors.

Initial research supported this framework, as a significant relationship was reported between how positively spouses rated their partner's communications in the course of an interaction and how satisfied they were with their marriages 5 years later (Markman, 1981). This finding served as a point of departure for subsequent efforts to prevent marital dysfunction and helped form the basis for the Premarital Relationship Enhancement Program (see Markman, Floyd, Stanley, & Lewis, 1986). The PREP consists of five 3-hour meetings of three to five couples during which couples are trained in communication skills, problem-solving skills, clarification of marital expectations, and sexual functioning. As noted earlier, outcome data from this program indicate that couples in the treatment condition maintain a high level of marital quality across a 3-year follow-up assessment, whereas control couples exhibit a clear decline in marital quality (Markman et al., 1988).

Markman's program is a significant transition point in work on marital prevention because of its basic assumption that preventive interventions must be guided by knowledge of the causes of marital distress. In view of the success of this approach, a reasonable next step is to clarify further the longitudinal relationship between aspects of spousal communication and the quality of marriage. This is indicated because more recent data show that the association between spouses' reactions to partner behavior in interaction and later satisfaction is not as reliable as was initially believed, particularly after earlier levels of relationship satisfaction are held constant (e.g., Markman et al., 1987). Similarly, the importance of spouses' reactions in interaction is called into question by the 3-year longitudinal PREP outcome study by Markman et al. (1988), which showed that the treatment and control groups diverged over time in their marital quality yet were not differentiated by spouses' ratings of partner interaction behavior.

Further questions about the adequacy of the behavioral model for understanding the causes of marital distress arise from studies in which communication is rated not by the interacting spouses but by trained observers. For example, in a 3-year longitudinal study reported by Gottman and Krokoff (1989), marital distress was related cross-sectionally to higher levels of negative behavior and lower levels of positive behavior, but marital dysfunction was predicted over time by *lower* levels of negative behavior and *higher* levels of positive behavior at Time 1—the latter findings being directly opposite to those expected from the behavioral perspective. A 5-year longitudinal study by Filsinger and Thoma (1988) uncovered only one behavioral variable that was a consistent predictor of subsequent dissatisfaction (i.e., a higher rate of interruptions by females) and determined that higher rates of Time 1 *positive* reciprocity, but not negative reciprocity, were a reliable indicator of which couples would be separated 5 years later.

This pattern of results indicates that predictions made on the basis of the behavioral conception of marriage (e.g., that higher rates of negative behaviors predict distress) are not clearly supported and, in fact, that predictions opposite to those may be more accurate in some instances (e.g., that lower rates of negative behaviors predict distress). Indeed, the possibility also remains that the opposite relationship, between earlier satisfactions and later behavior, is stronger than that between behavior and later satisfaction and that unmeasured variables are driving these associations. What are the implications of these concerns? For marital prevention, the data suggest that there is no clear empirical justification for the social learning/behavioral formulation that changing behavior will lead to lasting improvement in relationships.[7] For understanding the causes of marital dysfunction, they suggest that cross-sectional data can provide only limited information about causal agents and that additional longitudinal data are badly needed.

---

[7]The uncertain relationship between behavior and later satisfaction, coupled with the success of Markman et al.'s (1988) PREP intervention, supports the aforementioned idea that prevention can occur in the absence of causal knowledge. This raises the question of why the PREP intervention has been found to be effective. One possibility is that other components of the program are responsible for the significant improvements; presumably these factors would emerge as predictors of change in relationship quality in logitudinal research. Equally plausible is the possibility that the couples in the intervention group improved as a result of receiving attention and feedback about their marriage, a variable that distinguishes them from the no-treatment control couples.

Even assuming that marital behavior influences marital satisfaction, the strength of any such association is likely to leave unexplained a significant proportion of the variance in marital satisfaction. It follows that an understanding of marital quality, as well as any empirically based consideration of how to prevent marital distress, will require more inclusive models than have been proffered to date. Models of this sort have begun to appear (e.g., Bradbury & Fincham, 1988, 1989; Kelley et al., 1983), and they incorporate a number of constructs that, according to recent research, may play a causal role in marital distress and instability.

For example, there is evidence that declines in marital quality over time are a function of (1) expressions of specific emotions in marital interaction, including higher levels of sadness and fear by wives and higher levels of whining by husbands (Bradbury, 1989; Gottman & Krokoff, 1989); (2) cognitive variables, including the extent to which husbands and wives offer disparaging attributions for events in their relationship (Bradbury, 1989; Fincham & Bradbury, 1987, 1990); (3) physiological arousal, including higher levels of husbands' and wives' sweat gland activity and husbands' faster heart rates (Levenson & Gottman; 1985); (4) aspects of spouses' personality, including husbands' and wives' higher levels of neuroticism and husbands' low levels of impulse control (Kelly & Conley, 1987); and (5) psychopathology, including depression (Fincham & Bradbury, 1990; Ulrich-Jakubowski, Russell, & O'Hara, 1988).

If replicated and extended within the context of emerging models of marital interaction, these studies could provide valuable information about the causes of marital dysfunction that, in turn, could form the basis for a more refined appreciation of what needs to be changed in order for such dysfunction to be prevented. One important qualification of this view is that some causal factors (e.g., impulsivity, neuroticism) might prove difficult to change. This becomes less of a problem when such factors are viewed not as something to be changed (as in primary prevention) but as variables that permit identification of couples "at risk" for marital problems who might then be offered counseling that addresses their special needs (as in secondary prevention). Perhaps a more important qualification of this view, at least as it has been presented thus far, is that the causes of marital problems have been assumed to reside either within the individuals or within the couples' interactions—little allowance has been made for the possibility that external factors, either alone or as they interact with intra- and interpersonal variables, play a causal role in marital dysfunction. When this possibility is realized, greater attention becomes focused on influencing the external factors directly and working only indirectly with the couples themselves, a topic to which we now turn.

## Working Indirectly with Couples

In view of the observation that throughout its history "American psychology has been quintessentially a psychology of the individual organism" (Sarason, 1981, p. 827), it is not surprising that psychological research on the quality of marriage has focused on features of spouses, and to a lesser extent on their interactions, at the expense of understanding the situations and contexts in which marriages occur and the transitions that they undergo. To the extent that they are based on research, interventions are then designed to change individual and dyadic aspects of couples, either before their problems arise (as in the case of prevention) or after the difficulties have emerged (as in the case of therapy). Although the increasing emphasis on causal data in this domain represents an important step forward, an unfortunate shortcoming of this approach is that variance in marital stability and quality is assumed to be in large part a function of intrapersonal and interpersonal variables; sources of variance outside the person and dyad are often presumed to be incidental to this equation, and hence little effort is made to change these factors in the service of improving relationships.

Sources of variance outside individuals and couples are, however, likely to be associated in significant ways with the stability and quality of marriages. For example, it is theoretically feasible that two couples having very similar psychological profiles could, if confronted with different situations or stressors, have very different levels of marital quality. Such situations might include, for example, medical illness in a spouse or child, financial problems, conflicting work schedules, lack of affordable day care, insufficient schools for children, inadequate living conditions, conflicts with families of origin, and the transition to retirement.

Despite their importance, examination and modification of situational and environmental contributors to marital dysfunction are only rarely investigated. This contrasts sharply with the orientation within preventive or community psychology, where the approach to various problems emphasizes three targets of change. According to Gesten and Jason (1987, p. 431), these include (1) modifying the *environmental surround* in which these events occur to, for example, increase social support and reduce the effects of stress, (2) "eliminating the *agent* as, for example, reducing the incidence of abuse via legislature, religious, or psychological intervention," and (3) "strengthening the competence of the *host* to deal with specific stressors or classes of stress." Most approaches to the prevention of marital problems have focused almost exclusively on the host, seeking to prevent marital dysfunction by strengthening the individuals and couples involved.

Although there is no reason to abandon this strategy, it is important to attack the problem of marital dysfunction from alternative perspectives. Further justification for broadening the scope of marital prevention comes from data by Olson (1983), which indicate that more than half of all couples that marry do not avail themselves of marital preparation programs, and from Markman et al. (1987), which indicate that more than 60% of the couples offered the PREP program either declined the treatment or dropped out before completing it. We therefore argue that a comprehensive and effective approach to preventing marital dysfunction will involve not only the person-centered efforts that now dominate the field but also steps taken to change the context in which marriages and marital problems arise (e.g., by facilitating the development of self-help groups to enable spouses and couples to solve marital difficulties) and to identify and eliminate factors external to the couple that contribute to the decline in the quality of their marriage (e.g., by lobbying to pass legislation that would permit absence from work following the birth of a child, by developing programs that would provide lowered mortgages for first-time homeowners).

By moving from the current formulation, in which both the cause and resolution of marital dysfunction are thought to reside within individuals and couples, to one in which dysfunction is viewed as an emergent property of individuals and couples *in relation to* their social and physical environments, it is likely that a more successful battle can be waged in the prevention of marital distress. Thus, the central feature of the new formulation that would distinguish it from its predecessor is a much greater emphasis on factors outside spouses and their interactions, with an attendant increase in working indirectly with couples to improve their relationships. In the remainder of this section we illustrate briefly how such a model might be realized.

## A Blueprint for Future Research

The three-part recommendation made by Gesten and Jason (1987) for undertaking prevention in the field of mental health receives a more detailed treatment in Cowen's (1986) general structural model for the development of prevention programs. Although not specific to any one mental health problem, this model is valuable in the present context because it provides a practical five-step approach that can lead investigators from the initial realization that environmental and situational factors interact with personal and interpersonal factors to produce marital dysfunction to the actual design and implementation of programs that address this need.

The first step involves the establishment of a generative knowledge base and emphasizes the need to gather data to determine (1) the individual competencies that relate to positive outcomes and adjustment and (2) the circumstances, situations, and events that are linked to negative outcomes and poor adjustment. In view of our discussion in the previous section, we would emphasize that this first step implies the need to collect *causal* data. We are particularly struck by the paucity of systematic data on the transition to marriage and, given that most marriages end within their first several years, we view research on the newlywed phase as a high priority for improving future work on preventing marital problems. Returning to Cowen's recommendations, it also appears that this initial phase of data collection should be expanded so that the interaction of personal and situational factors is addressed. That is, although it is important to know which transitions are difficult for couples in general *or* which couples have difficulties dealing with stressful circumstances, it would be especially valuable to know which particular sorts of couples would be particularly vulnerable to having difficulties with particular transitions.

The second step in Cowen's model consists of sifting through the generative knowledge base in order to identify the competencies that are necessary for successful adjustment and the situations that make such adjustment difficult; this information is then used to define the concepts that will guide the program. Although the clinical intuition that informs most work on prevention has been valuable, this source of information must be supplemented with empirical data if guiding concepts of demonstrated utility are to be identified.

In Cowen's third step, the broad heuristic concepts are translated into specific interventions, and they are then implemented in the fourth step. This could involve working with couples indirectly (e.g., mobilizing resources to introduce legislation that will allow couples to take time off from work around the birth of their children), directly (e.g., teaching couples how to cope with the transition to parenthood), or some combination of the two. In the final step the outcome of the program is assessed to determine whether the intended effect was obtained, and, on the basis of this assessment, modifications can then be made in the preceding steps.

It would be inappropriate to conclude that this model or others like it are a panacea for marital dysfunction. Nevertheless, extrapolation of ideas from outside the current marital prevention literature, particularly those from community and preventive psychology, can have important implications for conceptualizing prevention programs. Approaching prevention of marital dysfunction from this route not only affords another perspective on the problem but also helps to relieve the responsibility that is often placed on couples seeking marital therapy. This alternative perspective may serve to decrease the need for therapy as well as to increase the likelihood that those couples needing therapy will actually seek it. To our knowledge, this route remains largely unexplored (cf. Elkin, 1977; Shonick, 1975).

## Summary

Prevention of marital dysfunction can be advanced by following a number of suggestions that emerge from an analysis of existing research as well as by pursuing qualitatively different approaches to address the problem. Although we recognize the incomplete correspondence between the causes and the remediation of marital dysfunction, we argue that prevention programs will be more effective to the extent that the factors that give rise to marital dysfunction are isolated and understood. In addition, the observation that situational and circumstantial causes of marital distress have been overlooked leads us to consider how marriages might be strengthened by working indirectly (e.g., by providing couples with needed resources; by changing policies that cause stress for marriages) rather than or in addition to working directly with couples. As Sarason (1981, p. 836) maintained, "human illness and misery have diverse sources within and without the individual. If only because of this glimpse of the obvious, we must radically reexamine how we conceptualize the individual organism. This reexamination is crucial if we are to deepen our understanding and direct more effectively our capacities to prevent and repair."

## OVERVIEW AND CONCLUSION

We began with the observation that clinical intervention with distressed couples is likely to prove inadequate as a comprehensive strategy for addressing the rising rates of divorce and distress in marriage and we then outlined the arguments that favor prevention and identified factors that inhibit its implementation. Following a review and evaluation of the large literature on the prevention of marital dysfunction, we concluded that (1) there is a slight tendency for prevention programs to improve relationships relative to no-treatment and attention-only control groups, and (2) prevention programs have not yet been shown to produce lasting changes in relationships.

In addition to emphasizing the need to address these shortcomings, we identified and discussed two directions necessary for further progress in this domain. Specifically, we discussed the value of conducting research to clarify the causes of marital dysfunction and, because factors external to marital dyads are likely to be prominent causal agents (e.g., economic factors, life transitions), we highlighted the possibility of working indirectly with couples to prevent declines in marital quality. Finally, a simple five-stage model that incorporates these two recommendations was outlined.

Although there has been a tendency to conceptualize and study marital therapy and primary prevention of marital dysfunction as distinct and separate undertakings, to continue to do so may prohibit the growth of both areas. By recognizing that marital therapy (i.e., tertiary prevention) and primary prevention represent different strategies within the spectrum of preventive interventions, greater attention might be paid to forging a common research agenda for identifying the precursors of marital dysfunction as well as establishing an integrated network of services that would be valuable to couples at all levels of marital quality and all stages of marriage. To do so would underscore the importance of providing effective services that could benefit all couples who may one day experience marital distress, not only those who seek therapy. In an era when marriage as a social institution is undergoing dramatic change, it is opportune to reassess our present strategies for contending with marital dysfunction so that its harmful effects on children, spouses, and society can be minimized.

# ACKNOWLEDGMENTS

Thomas N. Bradbury was supported in the preparation of this chapter by a National Research Service Award from the National Institute of Mental Health and by a grant from the National Science Foundation. The chapter was written while Frank D. Fincham was supported as a Faculty Scholar of the W. T. Grant Foundation and by Grant R01 MH44078-01 from the National Institute of Mental Health.

# REFERENCES

Bagarozzi, D. A., & Rauen, P. (1981). Premarital counseling: Appraisal and status. *American Journal of Family Therapy, 9,* 13–30.

Beck, D. F. (1976). Research findings on the outcomes of marital counseling. In D. H. L. Olson (Ed.), *Treating relationships* (pp. 433–473). Lake Mills, IA: Graphic Publishing.

Bloom, B. L., Hodges, W. F., Kern, M. B., & McFaddin, S. C. (1985). A preventive intervention program for the newly separated: Final evaluations. *American Journal of Orthopsychiatry, 55,* 9–26.

Bradbury, T. N. (1989). *Cognition, emotion, and interaction in distressed and nondistressed marriages.* Unpublished manuscript.

Bradbury, T. N., & Fincham, F. D. (1988). Individual difference variables in close relationships: A contextual model of marriage as an integrative framework. *Journal of Personality and Social Psychology, 54,* 713–721.

Bradbury, T. N., & Fincham, F. D. (1989). Behavior and satisfaction in marriage: Prospective mediating processes. *Review of Personality and Social Psychology, 10,* 119–143.

Broskowski, A., & Baker, F. (1974). Professional, organizational, and social barriers to primary prevention. *American Journal of Orthopsychiatry, 44,* 701–718.

Cooper, A. (1985). Sexual enhancement programs: An examination of their current status and directions for future research. *Journal of Sex Research, 21,* 387–404.

Cowen, E. L. (1977). Baby-steps toward primary prevention. *American Journal of Community Psychology, 5,* 1–22.

Cowen, E. L. (1986). Primary prevention in mental health: Ten years of retrospect and ten years of prospect. In M. Kessler & S. E. Goldston (Eds.), *A decade of progress in primary prevention* (pp. 3–45). London: University Press of New England.

Doherty, W. J. (1986). Marital therapy and family medicine. In N. S. Jacobson & A. S. Gurman (Eds.), *Clinical handbook of marital therapy* (pp. 217–236). New York: Guilford Press.

Duncan, S. W., & Markman, H. J. (in press). Intervention programs for the transition to parenthood: Current status from a prevention perspective. In G. Y. Michaels & W. A. Goldberg (Eds.), *Transition to parenthood: Current theory and research.* Cambridge: Cambridge University Press.

Elkin, M. (1977). Premarital counseling for minors: The Los Angeles Experience. *Family Coordinator, 26,* 429–443.

Filsinger, E. E., & Thoma, S. J. (1988). Behavioral antecedents of relationship stability and adjustment: A five-year longitudinal study. *Journal of Marriage and the Family, 50,* 785–795.

Fincham, F. D., & Bradbury, T. N. (1987). The impact of attributions in marriage: A longitudinal analysis. *Journal of Personality and Social Psychology, 53,* 510–517.

Fincham, F. D., & Bradbury, T. N. (1990). *Attributions, depression, and marital satisfaction: A longitudinal analysis.* Manuscript submitted for publication.

Garland, D. S. R. (1983). *Working with couples for marriage enrichment.* San Francisco: Jossey-Bass.

Gesten, E. L., & Jason, L. A. (1987). Social and community interventions. *Annual Review of Psychology, 38,* 427–460.

Giblin, P. (1986). Research and assessment in marriage and family enrichment: A meta-analysis study. *Journal of Psychotherapy and the Family, 2,* 79–96.

Giblin, P., Sprenkle, D. H., & Sheehan, R. (1985). Enrichment outcome research: A meta-analysis of premarital, marital, and family interventions. *Journal of Marital and Family Therapy, 11,* 257–271.

Glidewell, J. C. (1983). Afterword: Prevention—The threat and the promise. In R. D. Felner, L. A. Jason, J. N. Moritsugu, & S. S. Farber (Eds.), *Preventive psychology* (pp. 310–312). New York: Pergamon.

Goldston, S. E. (1977). An overview of primary prevention programming. In D. C. Klein & S. E. Goldston (Eds.), *Primary prevention: An idea whose time has come* (pp. 23–40). Rockville, MD: National Institute of Mental Health.

Gottman, J. M., & Krokoff, L. J. (1989). Marital interaction and satisfaction: A longitudinal view. *Journal of Consulting and Clinical Psychology, 57,* 47–52.

Grych, J., & Fincham, F. D. (in press). Marital conflict and children's adjustment: A cognitive–contextual framework. *Psychological Bulletin.*

Guerney, B. G. (1977). *Relationship enhancement.* San Francisco: Jossey-Bass.

Guerney, B. G., Guerney, L., & Cooney, T. (1985). Marital and family problem prevention and enrichment programs. In L. L'Abate (Ed.), *The handbook of family psychology and therapy* (vol. 2, pp. 1179–1217). Homewood, IL: Dorsey.

Gurman, A. S., & Kniskern, D. P. (1977). Enriching research on marital enrichment programs. *Journal of Marriage and Family Counseling, 3,* 3–11.

Hahlweg, K., Baucom, D. H., & Markman, H. J. (1988). Recent advances in therapy and prevention. In I. R. H. Falloon (Ed.), *Handbook of behavioral family therapy* (pp. 413–448). New York: Guilford Press.

Hahlweg, K., & Markman, H. J. (1988). Effectiveness of behavioral marital therapy: Empirical status of behavioral techniques in preventing and alleviating marital distress. *Journal of Consulting and Clinical Psychology, 56,* 440–447.

Hof, L., & Miller, W. R. (1980). Marriage enrichment. *Marriage and Family Review, 3,* 1–27.

Jacobson, N. S. (1989). The maintenance of treatment gains following social learning-based marital therapy. *Behavior Therapy, 20,* 325-336.

Jacobson, N. S., & Holtzworth-Munroe, A. (1986). Marital therapy: A social learning–cognitive perspective. In N. S. Jacobson & A. S. Gurman (Eds.), *Clinical handbook of marital therapy* (pp. 29-70). New York: Guilford Press.

Kelley, H. H., Berscheid, E., Christensen, A., Harvey, J. H., Huston, T. L., Levinger, G., McClintock, E., Peplau, L. A., & Peterson, D. R. (1983). *Close relationships.* New York: W. H. Freeman.

Kelly, E. L., & Conley, J. J. (1987). Personality and compatibility: A prospective analysis of marital stability and marital satisfaction. *Journal of Personality and Social Psychology, 52,* 27-40.

L'Abate, L. (1983). Prevention as a profession: Toward a new conceptual frame of reference. In D. R. Mace (Ed.), *Prevention in family services* (pp. 49-62). Beverly Hills: Sage.

L'Abate, L., & Weinstein, S. E. (1987). *Structured enrichment programs for couples and families.* New York: Brunner/Mazel.

Lamb, H. R., & Zusman, J. (1979). Primary prevention in perspective. *American Journal of Psychiatry, 136,* 12-17.

Levant, R. F. (1986). An overview of psychoeducational family programs. In R. F. Levant (Ed.), *Psychoeducational approaches to family therapy and counseling* (pp. 1-51). New York: Springer Publ. Co.

Levenson, R. W., & Gottman, J. M. (1985). Physiological and affective predictors of change in relationship satisfaction. *Journal of Personality and Social Psychology, 49,* 85-94.

Mace, D. (1987). Three ways of helping married couples. *Journal of Marital and Family Therapy, 13,* 179-185.

Mace, D. R., & Mace, V. C. (1976). Marriage enrichment: A preventive group approach for couples. In D. H. L. Olson (Ed.), *Treating relationships* (pp. 321-336). Lake Mills, IA: Graphic Publishing.

Markman, H. J. (1981). Prediction of marital distress: A 5-year follow-up. *Journal of Consulting and Clinical Psychology, 49,* 760-762.

Markman, H. J. (1984). The longitudinal study of couples' interactions: Implications for understanding and predicting the development of marital distress. In K. Hahlweg & N. S. Jacobson (Eds.), *Marital interaction: Analysis and modification* (pp. 253-281). New York: Guilford Press.

Markman, H. J., Duncan, S. W., Storaasli, R. D., & Howes, P. W. (1987). The prediction of marital distress: A longitudinal investigation. In K. Hahlweg & M. J. Goldstein (Eds.), *Understanding major mental disorder: The contribution of family interaction research* (pp. 266-289). New York: Family Process Press.

Markman, H. J., & Floyd, F. J. (1980). Possibilities for the prevention of marital discord: A behavioral perspective. *American Journal of Family Therapy, 8,* 29-48.

Markman, H. J., Floyd, F. J., Stanley, S. M., & Jamieson, K. (1984). A cognitive-behavioral program for the prevention of marital and family distress: Issues in program development and delivery. In K. Hahlweg & N. S. Jacobson (Eds.), *Marital interaction: Analysis and modification* (pp. 396-428). New York: Guilford Press.

Markman, H. J., Floyd, F. J., Stanley, S. M., & Lewis, H. C. (1986). Prevention. In N. S. Jacobson & A. S. Gurman (Eds.), *Clinical handbook of marital therapy* (pp. 173-195). New York: Guilford Press.

Markman, H. J., Floyd, F. J., Stanley, S. M., & Storaasli, R. D. (1988). Prevention of marital distress: A longitudinal investigation. *Journal of Consulting and Clinical Psychology, 56,* 210–217.

Miller, S., Nunally, E. W., & Wackman, D. B. (1975). *Alive and aware: Improving communication in relationships.* Minneapolis: Interpersonal Communication Programs.

Olson, D. H. (1983). How effective *is* marriage preparation? In D. R. Mace (Ed.), *Prevention in family services* (pp. 65–75). Beverly Hills: Sage.

Price, R. H., Cowen, E. L., Lorion, R. P., & Ramos-McKay, J. (1988). The search for effective prevention programs: What we learned along the way. *American Journal of Orthopsychiatry, 59,* 49–58.

Sarason, S. B. (1981). An asocial psychology and a misdirected clinical psychology. *American Psychologist, 36,* 827–836.

Segraves, R. T. (1982). *Marital therapy.* New York: Plenum.

Shonick, H. (1975). Pre-marital counseling: Three years' experience of a unique service. *Family Coordinator, 24,* 321–324.

Smith, M. L., Glass, G. V., & Miller, T. I. (1980). *The benefits of psychotherapy.* Baltimore: Johns Hopkins University Press.

Ulrich-Jakubowski, D., Russell, D. W., & O'Hara, M. W. (1988). Marital adjustment difficulties: Cause or consequence of depressive symptomatology? *Journal of Social and Clinical Psychology, 7,* 312–318.

Veroff, J., Kulka, R. A., & Douvan, E. (1981). *Mental health in America: Patterns of help-seeking from 1957–1976.* New York: Basic Books.

Vincent, C. E. (1973). *Sexual and marital health.* New York: McGraw Hill.

Wampler, K. S. (1982). The effectiveness of the Minnesota Couple Communication Program: A review of research. *Journal of Marital and Family Therapy, 8,* 345–355.

Watzlawick, P., Weakland, J., & Fisch, R. (1974). *Change: Principles of problem formation and problem resolution.* New York: Norton.

Whitfield, R. (1985). The prevention of marital distress. In W. Dryden (Ed.), *Marital therapy in Britain* (vol. 2, pp. 125–148). London: Harper & Row.

# Marriage in Perspective

## David H. Olson

The purpose of this chapter is to provide an overview of marriage in the United States and to review some of the work that has been done theoretically, empirically, and clinically to advance the field. The chapter is divided into two parts. The first part is a general commentary on salient issues in the field of marriage and some breakthroughs in understanding couple dynamics. The second part reviews the five chapters in this section of the book and comments on their contributions. The first section provides a format for the review of the second section, and also provides additional data on marriage that are not discussed in the five chapters.

## ISSUES AND BREAKTHROUGHS IN THE FIELD OF MARRIAGE

### Marriage as a High-Risk Institution

The failure rate of marriage in the United States today is about 50% (Glick, 1989a). In fact, marriage is such a risky institution that no insurance company is willing to insure it.

One of the paradoxes of marriage is that in spite of its high risk level, almost 90% of the U.S. population chooses to marry at least once (Glick, 1989a, 1989b). Although about half of these first marriages fail, about 75% of these individuals later remarry; about half of those remarriages also fail. As the late Margaret Mead once noted, our society is increasingly moving toward what can be described as "serial monogamy": People pair up, break up, and then pair up again, usually with new partners. A consequence of this marriage–remarriage cycle is that an individual could potentially have six to seven partners over his or her lifetime. (This is not unheard of among some movie stars, who are often trend setters.)

## The Paradox of Marriage

The basic paradox of marriage was aptly stated by the 16th-century French philosopher Michel de Montaigne (quoted in Beck, 1968, p. 190): "It [marriage] happens as with cages: the birds without despair to get in, and those within despair of getting out."

One of the complexities revealed by a recent Gallup Poll (1989) is the fact that when first asked, people say they are satisfied with their marriages, but more in-depth questions often reveal underlying problems. More specifically, the poll found that 84% of married people said they were "very satisfied" with their marriages. However, further questioning revealed that 40% had considered leaving their partners, 20% had bad marriages half the time, and 28% had already been divorced at least once.

Even newlywed couples have quite serious problems during their first year of marriage. In a study of several hundred couples, Arond and Parker (1987) found that 63% of the couples had problems related to money, 51% had serious doubts that their marriages would last, 49% had significant marital problems, 45% said they were not satisfied with their sexual relationship, 42% found marriage harder than they expected, and 35% said their mates were often critical of them.

These data make us aware that even though half of the marriages in our society survive, the quality of those marriages is often not good, and some of them are rather poor. Many marriages survive in spite of the fact that one or both partners are unhappy. These findings about marriage failure also clearly indicate that individuals are rarely prepared for the challenges of marriage. As Erich Fromm (1956) has noted: "There is hardly any activity, any enterprise, which has started with such tremendous hopes and expectations and which fails so regularly as love."

## High Predictability of Divorce

It is now possible to identify, before marriage, couples with a high probability of divorce. My colleagues and I collected recent evidence of this in two separate 3-year longitudinal studies.

Using self-report data obtained from engaged couples, we (Olson & Fowers, 1986) were able to predict with 80–90% accuracy which couples would be separated or divorced and which would be happily married 3 years later. Specifically, 3 months before marriage, engaged couples completed an inventory called PREPARE (for the most recent version, see Olson, Fournier, & Druckman, 1989). PREPARE consists of 125 questions, with generally 10 questions in each of 12 content areas. The questions focus on specific issues within a relationship, and each partner responds separately. A computer report (with scores for both individuals and the couple) is generated, and the information is shared with the couple by a counselor or member of the clergy.

Using discriminant analysis of PREPARE scores from the premarital couples, we were able to predict with 81% accuracy which couples would be separated or divorced and which would be happily married. The predictability was somewhat less, about 75%, when the couple scores only were used, and it increased to 91% accuracy when both individual and couple scores were used.

Because of the surprisingly high predictability of separation or divorce, this study was replicated (Olson & Larsen, 1989). This 3-year follow-up study of 179 couples found similar rates of predictability, with 84% accuracy using couple scores and 77% accuracy using individual scores.

The two studies also identified the importance of certain content areas that were consistently good predictors. Both studies clearly indicated that couples who scored high on the following scales had more successful marriages: Communication, Conflict Resolution, Realistic Expectations, Family and Friends, and Religious Orientation. The Olson and Larsen (1989) study also demonstrated the importance of the Equalitarian Roles and Leisure Activities scales. Both studies showed that the scales of Financial Management and Children and Parenting were not good predictors of marital success, mainly because most of the premarital couples had low scores on these scales.

## Significance of the Premarital Relationship

The two studies described above (Olson & Fowers, 1986; Olson & Larsen, 1989) clearly demonstrate that the core of the marriage is formed during the premarital period, and also illustrate that self-reported relationship characteristics are predictive of ultimate marital success or failure. In addition, these two studies show that the self-report instrument PREPARE has good predictive validity.

Surprisingly, love was *not* a significant predictor of marital success in our studies, possibly because all of these premarital couples were in love. What were predictive, however, were relationship characteristics as described by the couple. So, even though the couples were in love and often saw their relationships through rose-colored glasses, it was still possible to identify those couples at greater risk for divorce. This was in part due to the fact that an Idealistic Distortion scale included in PREPARE was used to revise the individual and couple scores to reflect this bias in reporting. (For more details on this correction procedure, see Olson, Fournier, & Druckman, 1989.)

Because of the negative consequences of divorce, it is important to consider premarital preparation programs (Olson, 1983). One of the earliest premarital programs was developed by Bader, Microys, Sinclair, Willett, and Conway (1980) in Canada. This innovative and successful program had two major themes: communication and conflict resolution. It was an eight-session program, involving four sessions before marriage and four sessions after marriage. A small-group discussion format was used rather than lectures, and film segments were used to generate discussion.

Based on a pretreatment assessment, a 6-month follow-up, and a 1-year follow-up with both experimental and control groups of couples, Bader et al. (1980) found that the experimental couples significantly improved their constructive conflict resolution skills between pretreatment and the 6-month follow-up, and that this improvement increased between the 6-month and 1-year follow-ups. The control group did not change over time. In a 5-year follow-up of the same two groups, Bader, Riddle, and Sinclair (1981) found that positive conflict resolution scores remained stable between years 1 and 5, and that the experimental group continued to have significantly better skills than the control group.

Another successful premarital program, the Premarital Relationship Enhancement Program (PREP), was developed by Markman (1984) and colleagues. PREP is a cognitive-behavioral program that provides couples with information, skills, and strategies to improve the quality of their marriages. The program consists of five sessions, each lasting from 2 to 2½ hours. The program focuses on communication skills, behavioral change, relationship expectations, and sexual/sensual enhancement. The outcome research on the effectiveness of this program demonstrated that treatment couples were more satisfied than control couples with their relationships 1 year later (Markman, Floyd, Stanley, & Lewis, 1986).

In a recent meta-analysis focusing on premarital intervention, Hahlweg, Baucom, and Markman (1988) summarized the effectiveness of premarital intervention across seven studies that included a total of 238 premarital couples. They found an effect size of 0.79 for the seven studies, indicating that the average couple participating in these programs was 79% better off than the average couple receiving no treatment. Effect size was also much higher (1.51) on observational measures and much lower (0.52) on the self-report measures. These findings indicate that for the premarital couples, their interaction changed more significantly than their perceptions of their relationships.

Finally, a meta-analysis by Giblin (1986; Giblin, Sprenkle, & Sheehan, 1985) revealed a larger effect size for couples in premarital programs than for any other group (i.e., couples in marital communication skills programs, couples in marital therapy, and families in therapy). Giblin's results clearly demonstrate that it is easier to make positive and constructive changes in a premarital relationship than in an existing marriage or family system.

### Significance of Marital Dynamics versus Background Characteristics

One of the issues of theoretical and clinical interest about couples is the significance of the marital system versus the background characteristics brought by a couple to the relationship. Until recently, few studies have systematically investigated the relative significance of relationship dynamics versus background dimensions in a large sample of couples.

A recent study (Olson & Fowers, 1989) found that background characteristics only accounted for about 2% of the variance in marital quality, whereas relationship characteristics, as measured by the ENRICH scales, accounted for approximately 60% of the variance. This study used the ENRICH marital inventory (for the most recent version, see Olson, Fournier, & Druckman, 1989) with a national sample of 5,039 couples. ENRICH is similar to PREPARE, in that it is a 125-item self-report scale measuring 12 dimensions with generally 10 items assesssing most of the content scales.

Using discriminant analysis of ENRICH scores for 2,629 happily married couples and 2,353 dissatisfied couples, we were able to distinguish the happily from the unhappily married couples with about 90% accuracy. Clearly, these data indicate the significance of relationship dynamics in discriminating happy from unhappy couples, as opposed to background characteristics. Regardless of the similarity or difference in background characteristics of these couples, these variables were not good predictors of marital success.

The study also identified the content areas that distinguished happily married couples from unhappily married couples; 8 of the 13 ENRICH scales were significant in discriminating the two groups. Couples with good relationships were ones with higher scores in the following categories: Communication, Conflict Resolution, Sexual Relationship, Leisure Activities, Equalitarian Roles, Religious Orientation, and Personality Compatibility.

## Typologies of Couples and Families

In the last decade, a number of typological systems have been developed for describing couple and family dynamics. These include the Circumplex Model of Marital and Family Systems (Olson, Russell, & Sprenkle, 1989), the Family System Model (Beavers & Voeller, 1983), the Family Paradigm Model (Constantine, 1986), and the McMaster Model of Family Functioning (Epstein, Bishop, & Lewis, 1978). All of these theoretical models have generally dealt with the three central dimensions of cohesion, adaptability, and communication. They have used different terminology but have defined each of these dimensions in similar ways. To illustrate the utility of a typological approach to marriage, the Circumplex Model of Marital and Family Systems is described briefly.

### Circumplex Model of Marital and Family Systems

The Circumplex Model of Marital and Family Systems has been the most extensively used model for describing both couple and family systems. There are currently 200 completed studies testing the Circumplex Model, and an additional 600 studies are in progress. These studies have focused primarily on the family system rather than the marital system, although the model is appropriate for both (Olson, McCubbin, et al., 1989).

As noted above, the Circumplex Model uses the three central dimensions that have been found to be important theoretically, empirically, and clinically in working with couples and families. These are marital and family cohesion, adaptability, and communication. Both cohesion and adaptability are built directly into the Circumplex Model and are considered curvilinear dimensions. "Cohesion" is defined as emotional closeness with an emphasis on balancing separateness and togetherness in a marital or family system. "Adaptability" refers to the flexibility of the system as it balances stability and change. Too much or too little cohesion and adaptability are seen as dysfunctional for intimate relationships over the life cycle. However, functioning in the extremes can be appropriate and even helpful for short periods of time.

The Circumplex Model (see Figure 1) describes 16 types of marital and family systems. There are four levels of cohesion: The disengaged (too much separateness) and enmeshed (too much closeness) types are seen as more dysfunctional, whereas the separated and connected types of relationships are seen as more functional. In terms of adaptability, the rigid (too little change) and chaotic (too much change) types are seen as more dysfunctional, while the structured and flexible types of systems are seen as more functional.

The 16 specific types of couple and family relationships can be grouped into three more general types: balanced, midrange, and extreme. The four balanced types of relationships are those that are separated or connected on cohesion and structured or flexible on adaptability. The four extreme types are those that are disengaged or enmeshed on cohesion and rigid or chaotic on adaptability. The remaining eight types are midrange, in that they are extreme on one dimension and balanced on the other dimension.

It is assumed that these 16 types of marital and family systems are dynamic; that is, they can change over time (unlike personality types, which are seen as more stable). In other words, it is assumed that couple and family systems change across the life cycle and that this change is both appropriate and desirable. Also, balanced systems are hypothesized to be more capable of change than extreme systems.

Communication is the third dimension in the Circumplex Model; it serves as a facilitating dimension, in that it helps couples and families change their type of system over time. One of the hypotheses that has received clear support is the hypothesis that extreme couple/family types have less positive communication, and therefore more stability, than more balanced types of couple and family systems.

One of the advantages of a typological model is that the couple or family system can be the unit employed at the conceptual level, at the level of analysis, and at the level of clinical intervention. This enables one to bridge research, theory, and practice more adequately. Another advantage of such a theoretical model is that hypotheses can be derived, tested, and validated, and new ones discovered. Six general hypotheses have been developed and

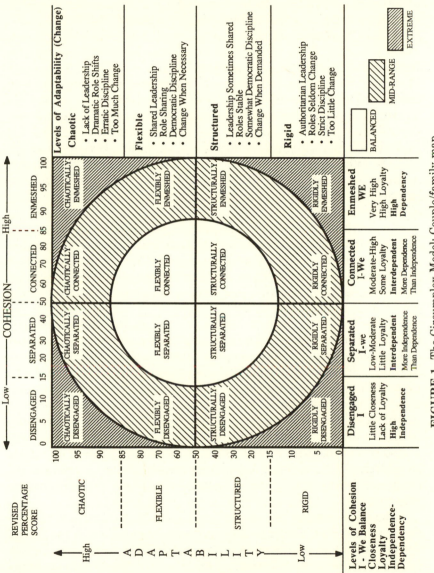

FIGURE 1. The Circumplex Model: Couple/family map.

tested regarding the Circumplex Model. Most of the work has focused on testing the hypothesis that balanced types of couple and family systems are more functional than extreme types. This hypothesis has generally received support, but most of the research has focused on family systems rather than on couples (Olson, Russell, & Sprenkle, 1989).

### Assessment with the Circumplex Model

There are two types of assessment procedures used with the Circumplex Model. One is a self-report assessment; the instrument for couples is called the Marital Adaptability and Cohesion Evaluation Scales (MACES III), and the one for families is called the Family Adaptability and Cohesion Evaluation Scales (FACES III) (Olson et al., 1982). Each of these two self-report instruments contains 20 items, 10 for cohesion and 10 for adaptability. Separate couple and family communication scales are also available (Olson et al., 1982).

In addition, the Clinical Rating Scale (CRS) was developed (Olson, 1988) to be used in a clinical assessment based on observation of a couple or family system. Figures 2, 3, and 4 provide a summary of this rating scale. The scale has been used extensively with couples and families, and has a reliability on each of the dimensions of about .85 to .90.

When the Circumplex Model is used in the treatment of a couple or family system, the first step is an assessment preferably using (1) one of the two self-report scales, which provides data on the insiders' perspective; and (2) the CRS, summarizing the therapist's or outsider's perspective. Often these two types of assessments differ, but the differing information can often be very useful in clinical intervention. The assessment should first focus on the way the couple or family system currently operates. Often it is also useful to assess how it functions under high levels of stress. In addition, a developmental history can be taken to see how the couple or family system has changed over time since the relationship began.

Based on the assessment information, the general goal of therapy is to move the couple or family system from an extreme type of system to a more balanced system on both the cohesion and adaptability dimensions. A variety of clinical intervention approaches can be used to focus on the cognitive, behavioral, and affective dimensions by using techniques relevant in each of those domains. For more details on the clinical use and development of the model, see the recent book entitled *Circumplex Model: Systemic Assess-*

| COUPLE/FAMILY SCORE | DISENGAGED 1 | SEPARATED 2 | CONNECTED 3 | ENMESHED 4 |
|---|---|---|---|---|
| **EMOTIONAL BONDING** | Extreme emotional separateness. Lack of c/f loyalty. | Emotional separateness, limited closeness. Occasional c/f loyalty. | Emotional closeness, some separateness. Loyalty to c/f expected. | Extreme emotional closeness, little separateness. Loyalty to c/f demanded. |
| **FAMILY INVOLVEMENT** | Very low involvement or interaction. Infrequent affective responsiveness. | Involvement acceptable, personal distance preferred. Some affective responsiveness. | Involvement emphasized personal distance allowed. Affective interactions encouraged and preferred. | Very high involvement. Fusion; over-dependency; High affective responsiveness and control. |
| **MARITAL RELATIONSHIP** | Extreme emotional separateness. | Emotional separateness, limited closeness. | Emotional closeness, some separateness. | Extreme closeness, fusion; limited separateness. |
| **PARENT-CHILD RELATIONSHIP** | Entrenched generational boundaries (Impermeable). | Clear generational boundaries some p/c closeness (Permeable). | Clear generational boundaries with p/c closeness (Permeable). | Lack of generational boundaries (Diffuse). |
| **INTERNAL BOUNDARIES** | *Separateness dominates* | *More separateness than togetherness* | *More togetherness than separateness* | *Togetherness dominates* |
| **TIME** (physical & emotional) | Time apart maximized Rarely time together. | Time alone important Some time together. | Time together important. Time alone permitted. | Time together maximized. Little time alone permitted. |
| **SPACE** (physical & emotional) | Separate space needed and preferred. | Separate space preferred; sharing of family space. | Sharing family space. Private space respected. | Little private space permitted. |
| **DECISION MAKING** | Individual decision making. (Oppositional) | Individual decision making but joint possible. | Joint decisions preferred. | Decisions subject to wishes of entire group. |
| **EXTERNAL BOUNDARIES** | *Mainly focused outside the family.* | *More focused outside than inside family.* | *More focused inside than outside family.* | *Mainly focused inside the family.* |
| **FRIENDS** | Individual friends seen alone. | Individual friendships seldom shared with family. | Individual friendships shared with family. | Family friends preferred limited individual friends. |
| **INTERESTS** | Disparate interests. | Separate interests. | Some joint interests. | Joint interests mandated. |
| **ACTIVITIES** | Mainly separate activities. | More separate than shared activities. | More shared than individual activities. | Separate activities seen as disloyal. |
| **GLOBAL COHESION RATING (1-4)** | Very Low | Low to Moderate | Moderate to High | Very High |

FIGURE 2. Couple/family cohesion as measured by the Clinical Rating Scale (CRS).

| COUPLE/ FAMILY SCORE | | RIGID 1 | STRUCTURED 2 | FLEXIBLE 3 | CHAOTIC 4 |
|---|---|---|---|---|---|
| **LEADERSHIP** (control) | | Authoritarian leadership. Parent(s) highly controlling. | Primarily authoritarian but some equalitarian leadership. | Equalitarian leadership with fluid changes. | Limited and/or erratic leadership. Parental control unsuccessful, rebuffed. |
| **DISCIPLINE** (for families only) | | Autocratic "law & order". Strict, rigid consequences. Not lenient. | Somewhat democratic. Predictable consequences. Seldom lenient. | Usually democratic. Negotiated consequences. Somewhat lenient. | Laissez-faire and ineffective. Inconsistent consequences. Very lenient. |
| **NEGOTIATION** | | Limited negotiations. Decisions imposed by parents. | Structured negotiations. Decisions made by parents. | Flexible negotiations. Agreed upon decisions. | Endless negotiations. Impulsive decisions. |
| **ROLES** | | Limited repertoire, strictly defined roles. | Roles stable, but may be shared. | Role sharing and making. Fluid changes of roles. | Lack of role clarity, role shifts and role reversals. |
| **RULES** | | Unchanging rules. Rules strictly enforced. | Few rule changes. Rules firmly enforced. | Some rule changes. Rules flexibly enforced. | Frequent rule changes. Rules inconsistently enforced. |
| **GLOBAL COHESION RATING (1-4)** | | **Very Low** | **Low to Moderate** | **Moderate to High** | **Very High** |

FIGURE 3. Couple/family change (adaptability) as measured by the CRS.

COUPLE/FAMILY SCORE

LOW ◄──── ──── Facilitating ──── ────► HIGH

| | 1 | 2 | 3 | 4 | 5 | 6 |
|---|---|---|---|---|---|---|
| **LISTENER'S SKILLS**<br>Empathy<br>Attentive Listening | Seldom evident<br>Seldom evident | | Sometimes evident<br>Sometimes evident | | Often evident<br>Often evident | |
| **SPEAKER'S SKILLS**<br>Speaking for Self<br>Speaking for Others*<br><br>(*Note reverse scoring) | Seldom evident<br>*Often evident* | | Sometimes evident<br>*Sometimes evident* | | Often evident<br>*Seldom evident* | |
| **SELF DISCLOSURE** | Infrequent discussion of self, feelings and relationships. | | Some discussion of self, feelings and relationships. | | Open discussion of self, feelings and relationships. | |
| **CLARITY** | Inconsistent and/or unclear verbal messages.<br><br>Frequent incongruencies between verbal and non-verbal messages. | | Some degree of clarity; but not consistent across time or across all members.<br>Some incongruent messages. | | Verbal messages very clear.<br><br>Generally congruent messages. | |
| **CONTINUITY/TRACKING** | Little continuity of content.<br><br>Irrelevant/distracting non-verbals and asides frequently occur.<br><br>Frequent/inappropriate topic changes. | | Some continuity but not consistent across time or across all members<br>Some irrelevant/distracting non-verbals and asides.<br>Topic changes not consistently appropriate. | | Members consistently tracking.<br><br>Few irrelevant/distracting non-verbals and asides; facilitative non-verbals.<br>Appropriate topic changes. | |
| **RESPECT & REGARD** | Lack of respect for feelings or message of other(s); possibly overtly disrespectful or belittling attitude. | | Somewhat respectful of others but not consistent across time or across all members.<br>Some incongruent messages. | | Consistently appears respectful of other's feelings and message. | |
| **GLOBAL FAMILY COMMUNICATION RATING (1-6)** | | | | | | |

FIGURE 4. Couple/family communication as measured by the CRS.

413

*ment and Treatment of Families* (Olson, Russell, & Sprenkle, 1989).

## COMMENTARY ON CHAPTERS

The purpose of this section is to comment on the five chapters in the section of the book entitled "Applications." This commentary builds on the information provided in the preceding discussion and reviews each of the five chapters in turn.

In the first chapter of this section (Chapter 9 of the volume), "Theoretical Orientations in the Treatment of Marital Discord," Segraves reviews five of the major theoretical orientations that can be applied to marriage: psychoanalytic, general systems, behavioral, social learning, and cognitive-behavioral. He provides a concise overview of each of these perspectives and then does a useful critique, indicating both the strengths and limitations of these theories. Although the psychoanalytic orientation provides information about pathology, it has yet to contribute any major breakthroughs in understanding interpersonal dynamics. Segraves highlights some of the key concepts in general systems theory, but does not indicate the depth of its contribution to the field of family therapy, where it has been accorded prominent status. The review of behavioral marital therapy is useful but dated. Segraves is more knowledgeable about and shows a preference for the cognitive-behavioral orientation, which is described as more inclusive and useful clinically.

On the topic of "Sexual Dysfunction and Marriage," Heiman and Verhulst (Chapter 10) review the conceptual foundations for understanding sexual functioning. They begin by describing the contributions of the psychoanalytic tradition, the cognitive-behavioral approach, and general systems theory. They also provide a brief but useful review of the empirical traditions provided by Kinsey, Masters and Johnson, and LoPiccolo and colleagues, and outline a useful integration of cognitive and physiological orientations for understanding sexual arousal (or the lack thereof). Their review then considers the current status of assessment strategies, including history taking (both individual physical and psychological health), interpersonal issues (particularly with family of origin), and social–cultural background; it then goes on to describe the effectiveness of such interventions as sensate focus, systematic desensitization, and communication training. The effectiveness of various treatments is documented, including approaches for dealing with sexual aversions and phobias, arousal disorders, orgasmic disorders, and issues related to pain and sexual dysfunction.

Heiman and Verhulst's review concludes with a useful commentary on the importance of a feminist perspective and the cultural context of sexuality. I have observed that the female and feminist perspective is conspicuously absent from most sexual theories and research. This has left a significant gap in our understanding not only of marital sexuality, but also of marital dynamics in general.

The chapter "Physical Aggression in Marriage," by O'Leary and Vivian (Chapter 11), provides an excellent overview of the major problems created by violence and spouse abuse in our society. The authors provide a useful addition to the literature by describing their own research on 272 couples, who were studied before marriage and at 6, 18, and 30 months after marriage. To their surprise, 31% of the men and 44% of the women reported having physically abused their partners in some way prior to marriage. Another surprising finding was that the self-reported rates of aggression 30 months after marriage *decreased* to 24% for men and 32% for women. Although the rates both before marriage and after marriage seem high, they are similar to those found in other national studies. O'Leary and Vivian's review is also very useful in identifying the characteristics related to abuse and the fact that it is often correlated with lower rates of marital satisfaction, poor communication, poor problem-solving skills, and higher rates of marital distress and divorce.

In order to understand the etiology of partner/spouse abuse, these authors document recent work using biological and sociological models, including resource theory, exchange theory, and role theory. The psychological models examined include classical conditioning, operant approaches, cognitive–affective theories, and approaches integrating behavioral–affective–cognitive components. They conclude by describing briefly the recent emergence of gender-specific treatment programs that have been effective in improving sexual functioning. This chapter provides a useful integration of ideas and current research with some suggestions about future directions of inquiry.

In their chapter, "Enhancing the Effectiveness of Marital Therapy," Beach and Bauserman (Chapter 12) do an excellent job of reviewing outcome research on the effectiveness of marital therapy. Their review covers insight-oriented therapy, behavioral contracting, communication training, and research that combines various approaches. Surprisingly, they find that only a relatively small number of well-controlled, peer-reviewed studies have been conducted, especially those using systems theory and psychoanalytic theory. They also note that combined approaches did not enhance the overall outcome of therapy. In particular, adding a cognitive component to behavioral techniques did not enhance the effectiveness of marital therapy; nor did adding an emotional component to marital therapy produce any greater changes in effectiveness. So, while some therapists have emphasized the importance of the cognitive–behavioral–affective integration, there is little evidence indicating that this enhances therapeutic outcome. Finally, the authors conclude that gains made in marital therapy, while statistically significant, often do not hold up over time and do not seem to reduce the overall divorce rate.

Beach and Bauserman's conclusions lead to the recommendation that future research focus more on intervening goals related to relationship skills and match "types of couples" to particular types of intervention programs. This idea of finding what types of couples are most effectively treated with what types of programs is one my colleagues and I proposed years ago (Olson, Russell, & Sprenkle, 1980), but it has not been systematically studied to date in the marital or family therapy field. Perhaps it is time for this approach to be utilized more fully; the current typological models of couple and family systems could facilitate such an integrated intervention–evaluation approach. Beach and Bauserman also recommend that future research should pay more attention to the process of change in therapy and determine why existing therapies are not successful with at least 30% of couples in treatment.

In the final chapter, "Preventing Marital Dysfunction: Review and Analysis," Bradbury and Fincham (Chapter 13) provide a very useful focus on the often neglected topic of prevention. "Prevention" is a word that is often overused, but preventive programs are rarely funded or available; thus, while people give lip service to the importance of prevention programs, little actually happens in practice. This is certainly true at the couple level. As noted at the beginning of this chapter, we have a divorce rate of 50%, yet little is being done to provide prevention programs and early intervention programs for couples. Bradbury and Fincham clearly demonstrate some of the positive consequences of prevention programs, but also clearly discuss the resistance to and lack of programming in these areas.

They also do an excellent job of describing and critiquing the various meta-analyses of premarital and marital programs that have been completed to date (Giblin, 1986; Hahlweg & Markman, 1988). In particular, they emphasize the importance of future research to document the long-term impact of interventions. This is especially necessary in evaluating prevention programs that are designed to produce more lasting changes.

Bradbury and Fincham also introduce the important distinction between first- and second-order change. Whereas first-order change is change within the current relationship, second-order change is change the system generates in itself over time. Although they provide an in-depth review of the Markman (1984) PREP program, Bradbury and Fincham do not review Bader et al.'s (1980, 1981) premarital program, which included the 5-year follow-up study described earlier in this chapter. In their chapter, Bradbury and Fincham maintain that programs with behavioral and social learning orientations have not shown long-term change, and also that behavioral and social learning variables do not account for a significant portion of the variance in describing a marital relationship. They recommend, therefore, a more comprehensive orientation that includes a cognitive component.

I disagree with these authors' view that background characteristics and other variables outside individuals and couples account for much of the variance in understanding couples. Our research with the ENRICH inventory (Olson & Fowers, 1989) clearly demonstrates that background variables account for little of the variance in understanding marital and family dynamics, compared to more relationship-oriented characteristics.

Bradbury and Fincham do, however, provide a very useful blueprint for future research involving a five-step plan. The first step includes developing more basic knowledge of causal factors. The second step involves identifying the competencies needed for a good marriage. In the third step these competencies are translated into specific interventions, which are then implemented in the fourth step through both direct programs with couples and indirect services. The final step is assessment to measure the overall effectiveness of change.

The authors conclude by emphasizing the need for prevention programs and higher-quality research to demonstrate the potential contributions of these programs, both for couples and for society in general. On the whole, this is an excellent chapter that provides a much-needed focus on the importance and value of prevention in the field of marrage.

# ACKNOWLEDGMENT

Work on this chapter was supported in part by funds from the Agricultural Experiment Station, University of Minnesota.

# REFERENCES

Arond, M. A., & Parker, S. L. (1987). *The first year of marriage.* New York: Warner Books.

Bader, E., Microys, G., Sinclair, L., Willett, E., & Conway, B. (1980). Do marriage preparations really work? A Canadian experiment. *Journal of Marital and Family Therapy, 6,* 171–179.

Bader, E., Riddle, R., & Sinclair, C. (1981). Do marriage preparation programs really help?: A five year study. *Family Therapy News, 2,* 3–4.

Beavers, W. R., & Voeller, M. N. (1983). Family models: Comparing and contrasting the Olson Circumplex Model and Beavers System Model. *Family Process, 22,* 250–260.

Beck, E. M. (Ed.). (1968). *Bartlett's familiar quotations* (14th ed.). Boston: Little, Brown.

Constantine, L. (1986). *Family paradigms.* New York: Guilford Press.

Epstein, N. B., Bishop, D. S., & Lewis, S. (1978). The McMaster model of family functioning. *Journal of Marriage and Family Counseling, 4,* 19–31.

Fromm, E. (1956). *The art of loving.* New York: Harper.

Gallup Poll. (1989). *Marriage satisfaction.* Los Angeles: Los Angeles Times Syndicate.

Giblin, P. (1986). Research and assessment in marriage and family enrichment: A meta-analysis study. *Journal of Psychotherapy and the Family, 2,* 79–86.

Giblin, P., Sprenkle, D. H., & Sheehan, R. (1985). Enrichment outcome research: A meta-analysis of premarital, marital and family interventions. *Journal of Marital and Family Therapy, 11,* 257–271.

Glick, P. C. (1989a). Remarried families, stepfamilies and stepchildren: A brief demographic profile. *Family Relations, 38,* 24–27.

Glick, P. C. (1989b). The family life cycle and social change. *Family Relations, 38,* 123–129.

Hahlweg, K., Baucom, D. H., & Markman, H. J. (1988). Recent advances in therapy and prevention. In I. R. H. Falloon (Ed.), *Handbook of behavioral family therapy* (pp. 413–448). New York: Guilford Press.

Hahlweg, K., & Markman, H. J. (1988). Effectiveness of behavioral marital therapy: Empirical status of behavioral techniques in preventing and alleviating marital distress. *Journal of Consulting and Clinical Psychology, 56,* 440–447.

Markman, H. J. (1984). The longitudinal study of couples' interactions: Implications for understanding and predicting the development of marital distress. In K. Hahlweg & N. S. Jacobson (Eds.), *Marital interaction: Analysis and modification* (pp. 253–281). New York: Guilford Press.

Markman, H. J., Floyd, F. J., Stanley, S. M., & Lewis, H. C. (1986). Prevention. In N. S. Jacobson & A. S. Gurman (Eds.), *Clinical handbook of marital therapy* (pp. 173–195). New York: Guilford Press.

Olson, D. H. (1983). How effective is marriage preparation? In D. Mace (Ed.), *Prevention in family services* (pp. 65–75). Beverly Hills, CA: Sage.

Olson, D. H. (1988). *Clinical Rating Scale*. St. Paul: Department of Family Social Science, University of Minnesota.

Olson, D. H., Fournier, D. G., & Druckman, J. M. (1989). *Counselor's manual for PREPARE, PREPARE-MC and ENRICH inventories* (rev. ed.). Minneapolis: PREPARE/ENRICH.

Olson, D. H., & Fowers, B. J. (1986). Predicting marital success with PREPARE: A predictive validity study. *Journal of Marital and Family Therapy, 12*, 403–413.

Olson, D. H., & Fowers, B. J. (1989). ENRICH marital inventory: The discriminant validity and cross validation assessment. *Journal of Marital and Family Therapy, 15*, 65–79.

Olson, D. H., & Larsen, A. S. (1989). Predicting marital satisfaction using PREPARE: A replication study. *Journal of Marital and Family Therapy, 15*, 311–322.

Olson, D. H., McCubbin, H. I., Barnes, H., Larsen, A. S., Muxen, M., & Wilson, M. (1982). *Family inventories*. St. Paul: Department of Family Social Science, University of Minnesota.

Olson, D. H., McCubbin, H. I., Barnes, H., Larsen, A. S., Muxen, M., & Wilson, M. (1989). *Families: What makes them work?* (2nd ed.). Beverly Hills, CA: Sage.

Olson, D. H., Russell, C. S., & Sprenkle, D. H. (1980). Marital and family therapy: A decade review. *Journal of Marital and Family Therapy, 6*, 973–993.

Olson, D. H., Russell, C. S., & Sprenkle, D. H. (Eds.). (1989). *Circumplex Model: Systemic assessment and treatment of families*. New York: Haworth Press.

# Index